WORLD BANK LATIN AMERICAN
AND CARIBBEAN STUDIES

CLOSING THE GAP
IN EDUCATION
AND TECHNOLOGY

by
David de Ferranti
Guillermo E. Perry
Indermit Gill
J. Luis Guasch
William F. Maloney
Carolina Sánchez-Páramo
Norbert Schady

THE WORLD BANK
Washington, D.C.

About This Book
David de Ferranti is vice president and Guillermo E. Perry is chief economist in the World Bank's Latin American and Caribbean Regional Office. J. Luis Guasch is a regional adviser on regulation and competition, and William F. Maloney and Carolina Sánchez-Páramo are economists in the Latin American and Caribbean Regional Office. Indermit Gill is an economic adviser in the Bank's Poverty Reduction and Economic Management Department, and Norbert Schady is a senior economist in the Bank's Vice Presidency for Development Economics.

For more information on publications from the World Bank's Latin America and Caribbean Regional Office, please visit us at www.worldbank.org/lacpublications (o en Español: www.bancomundial.org/publicaciones).

Cover design by Jeffrey Kibbler, The Magazine Group.
Cover photograph: *The Explosion of the Green Chairs*, by Pedro Meyer, is from the World Bank Art Program and can also be found in the book *Truths and Fictions: A Journey from Documentary to Digital Photography* by Pedro Meyer (1995. New York: Aperture).

The World Bank Art Program makes particular efforts to identify artists from developing nations and make their work available to a wider audience. The art program organizes exhibits, education and cultural partnerships, competitions, artists' projects, and site-specific installations.

ISBN 0-8213-5172-9

Library of Congress Cataloging-in-Publication Data
Closing the gap in education and technology / David de Ferranti ... [et al.] with William F. Maloney, Carolina Sanchez-Paramo.
    p. cm. — (World Bank Latin American and Caribbean studies)
Includes bibliographical references.
ISBN 0-8213-5172-9
    1. Education—Economic aspects—Latin America.   2. Education—Effect of technological innovations on—Latin America.
I. De Ferranti, David M.   II. Series.
LC67.L3 C56 2003
338.4'7378'098—dc21
                       2002034304

Contents

Tables

Acknowledgments

THIS REPORT IS THE RESULT OF A COLLECTIVE EFFORT BY A WORLD BANK TEAM coordinated by the Office of the Chief Economist for the Latin America and the Caribbean Region and led by Guillermo E. Perry. The principal authors by chapter were Guillermo E. Perry (chapter 1), Carolina Sánchez-Páramo and Norbert Schady (chapters 2, 3, and 4), Indermit S. Gill (chapter 5), J. Luis Guasch (chapter 6), and William F. Maloney (chapter 7). Manjula Luthria and Prita Subramanian coauthored preliminary versions of chapters 6 and 7.

Friends and colleagues from the World Bank made efforts that went well beyond the call of duty. We received important contributions from Harold Alderman, Ana-Maria Arriagada, Daniel Brehon, Soumya Chattopadhyay, Wendy Cunningham, Carl Dahlman, Eduardo Doryan, Marito Garcia, James Hanna, Barbara Larraneta, Daniel Lederman, Danny Leipziger, Ernesto May, Marcelo Olarreaga, Lant Pritchett, Jamil Salmi, Luis Serven, Wesley Yin, Shahid Yusuf, and others at the Chief Economist's Retreat in November 2001.

The report benefited immensely from authors who prepared background papers. These authors include Andreas Blom, Magnus Blomström, Mariano Bosch Mossi, Martin Carnoy, Ed Feser, Andrew Foster, Leonardo Garnier, Pinelopi Goldberg, Claudia Goldin, Lauritz Holm-Nielsen, Caroline Hoxby, Hanan Jacoby, Vanus James, Juan J. Jimeno, Larry Katz, David Mayer, Walter Park, Nina Pavcnik, Maurice Schiff, Simon Schwarztman, Emmanuel Skoufias, Maximo Torero, and Yanling Wang.

The authors would like to thank those whose insight, comments, and suggestions proved valuable in putting this report together. These contributors include Daron Acemoglu, Eduardo Bitran, Jose Joaquin Brunner, Paul David, Jean Guinet, Alan Kreuger, Stephen Machin, Ramon Marimon, Christina Paxson, Andres Rodriguez-Clare, and Gilles Saint-Paul.

Finally, we'd like to thank Lee Morrison, Anne Pillay, Patricia Soto, and the World Bank's Office of the Publisher for production and dissemination support.

Any errors or omissions in the report are the sole responsibility of the authors and should not be attributed to any of the above individuals or the institutions they represent.

Abbreviations

CEPR	Centre for Economic Policy Research
CIMO	Integral Quality and Modernization Program (Mexico)
DHS	Demographic and Health Surveys
ECLAC	Economic Commission for Latin America and the Caribbean
ENIGH	Encuesta Nacional de Ingresos y Gastos de Los Hogares (Mexico)
EE	Eastern Europe
EPZ	Export processing zone
EU	European Union
FDI	Foreign direct investment
FTZ	Free trade zone
GDP	Gross domestic product
GRI	Government research institute
HE	Higher education
HRDC	Human Resource Development Council (Malaysia)
HRDF	Human Resource Development Fund (Malaysia)
IBRD	International Bank for Reconstruction and Development
ICT	Information and communications technology
ILO	International Labour Organization
IPRs	Intellectual property rights
LAC	Latin America and the Caribbean
MIT	Massachusetts Institute of Technology
MNC	Multinational corporation
NAFTA	North American Free Trade Agreement
NBER	National Bureau of Economic Research
NIC	Newly industrialized country
NIS	National innovation system
NPV	Net present value
OECD	Organisation for Economic Co-operation and Development
PL	Public laboratories
PPP	Purchasing power parity
PRO	Public research organization
PRR	Private rate of return
R&D	Research and development
RCA	Revealed comparative advantage
S&T	Science and technology system

SBTC	Skill-biased technological change
SITC	Standard Industrial Trade Classification
SMEs	Small and medium-size enterprises
SRR	Social rate of return
STPC	Science and Technology Policy Council (Finland)
STPS	Department of Labor and Social Welfare (Mexico)
TFP	Total factor productivity
TIMSS	Third International Mathematics and Science Study
TQM	Total Quality Management
TRIPS	Trade-Related Intellectual Property Rights
UNAM	Universidad Nacional Autónoma de México
UNCITRAL	United Nations Conference on International Trade Law
UNESCO	United Nations Educational, Scientific and Cultural Organization
WBES	World Business Environment Surveys
WTO	World Trade Organization

The authors are the sources for all figures and tables in this book unless otherwise noted.

CHAPTER 1

Introduction and Summary: Skills Upgrading and Innovation Policies

O VER THE LAST 50 YEARS, THE WORLD HAS INCREASINGLY BECOME DIVIDED into two clubs—those of rich and of poor countries. What is most striking is that the increasing bimodal distribution of income is due not to concentration of the factors of production, such as capital, but rather of knowledge. The North has continued to generate new technologies that statistical studies suggest drive at least half of economic growth, while most of the South has been unable to take full advantage of them. Latin America for the most part finds itself in the less desirable club. Between 1950 and 2000, the annual per capita income in OECD countries tripled from US$7,300 to $23,000 (hereinafter, all dollar values in US$). The Latin America and the Caribbean region's (LAC) income level grew much less during this period—just doubling from $3,000 in 1950 to $6,200 in 2000. So the ratio of LAC's average income to the developed-country average fell from more than 40 percent in 1950 to about 25 percent in 2000, with much of the divergence occurring during the last quarter century. This should perturb policymakers in the region.

The trend is of special concern since the newly industrialized countries (NICs) of Asia—as well as other countries, such as Finland, that are closer to LAC in resource endowments—were able to achieve dramatic

technology-driven increases in living standards across the same period. In fact, the central lesson of our flagship study of 2001, *From Natural Resources to the Knowledge Economy*, was that what distinguished the successful resource-abundant countries (Australia, Canada, and the Scandinavian countries) from the disappointing LAC experience was precisely their ability to learn from abroad—their national innovative capacity. This report looks more carefully at what it takes for countries, and more centrally, for firms, to learn how to learn. The key ingredients in the success of these countries are, first, that they early on recognized the need for an explicit, efficient, and sustained policy to move the private sector to the technological frontier, and second, that they engaged in one of the most rapid and dramatic build-ups of national human capital in human history.

Education is vital for at least two reasons. First, it has always been a critical complement to technological advance.

Even as late as 1950, the United States was perhaps the only country where the median individual leaving school was a high school graduate. By the time countries in Europe—seeing the rapid rise of the United States as an economic powerhouse—learned their lesson, the United States had expanded its lead over Europe in tertiary education, and most European countries have only recently begun closing this gap. The East Asian countries appear to have learned the lesson much more quickly—the Republic of Korea, for example, has secondary and tertiary education indicators that are already better than those of many European countries. In most other countries—including much of Latin America—this recognition has come more slowly. Emerging evidence suggests that the knowledge transfer benefits of foreign direct investment (FDI) and trade liberalization, for example, are enhanced by higher stocks of human capital.

Technological change in the 20th century has been increasingly biased in favor of skilled workers and appears to be the largest force driving the increasing skilled/unskilled wage differential in the industrialized countries. This has been true for so long that people now think that technical change has always favored more skilled or educated workers. But this was not always the case: for example, technical change in 18th-century Britain displaced skilled artisans. There is some evidence that the skill-biased character of technological change has accentuated in the last decades, partially as a result of the so-called information and communications technology (ICT) revolution (de Ferranti and others, 2001).

This report focuses not only on the gaps facing Latin America in both education and technology, but especially on the interactions between the two. The central premise of the report is that skills and technology interact in important ways, and this relationship is a fundamental reason for the large observed differences in productivity and incomes across countries. Indeed, numerous studies have shown that differences in per capita income depend more on differences in total factor productivity (TFP) than on differences in primary factor accumulation.[1] And this report argues that skills upgrading, technological change, and their interaction are major factors behind total factor productivity growth.

The report shows that skill-biased technological change is indeed being transferred today at faster speeds to LAC countries, as elsewhere, insofar as they are now more open to trade and FDI flows and have increased the level of education of their work force. In chapter 2 we present empirical evidence that technological change has been complementary with skill levels in Latin America in the last two decades, as it has been the case in more developed countries. We also show that, as a result, firms have substantially increased the demand for educated workers in the region, particularly workers with tertiary education, and this rise in the demand for educated workers has bid up their relative wages, as has been happening in first world countries.

This technological transformation appears to be intimately related to patterns of integration in the world economy. Trade and FDI have facilitated the transmission of technological change across borders. Also, firms in sectors with higher exposure to trade and FDI are subject to more competitive pressures. Adopting and adapting more advanced technologies and hiring and training more educated workers is one way to respond to this pressure to become more productive. Finally, these changes have

affected countries differently and at different points in time. Increases in the demand for skills associated with the adoption of new technologies have taken place primarily in countries with levels of human capital above a minimum threshold. In addition, the patterns observed in most Latin American countries in the 1990s are similar to those observed in Chile in the 1980s, suggesting the existence of long-term cycles associated with technological progress in the relative demand for more skilled workers, depending on when countries opened up to trade and FDI competition.

Such a process is thus creating both challenges and opportunities. Demand for higher skills, and in particular for workers with tertiary education, is rising faster than demand for less skilled workers in most of the region. Hence the challenge: inequality in wages tends to increase as long as major inequalities in access to education remain, and the lack of skills may become an effective constraint for fast and efficient technology transfer and thus for potential growth.

But also the opportunity: the increased potential demand for education offers the possibility to accelerate productivity growth in the economy by closing the educational and technological gaps that Latin American countries exhibit with respect to their peers. To achieve this, policy must respond swiftly so that this potential demand for higher and better education is actually translated into higher and better educational levels of the work force and higher productivity at the firm level.

Focusing on skills upgrading, technological change, and their interactions helps us to discipline thinking about the currently confused issues surrounding the so-called knowledge economy. In box 1.1 and figure 1.1 (elaborated upon in Gill 2002) we present a simple graphic representation of the interaction between technology and skills that we follow to organize the discussion of skills upgrading and technological change throughout the report.

Productivity, Educational, and Technology Gaps in Latin America and the Caribbean

In chapter 2 we compare the performance of countries in Latin America in terms of productivity, skills, and technology with the performance of an "average country in the world," of the East Asian "tigers," and of a group of successful natural resource—based economies. Because the countries we want to compare are at different stages in development, we calculate their expected level of achievement given their per capita income levels and compare it

FIGURE 1.1

The Knowledge Economy Simplified

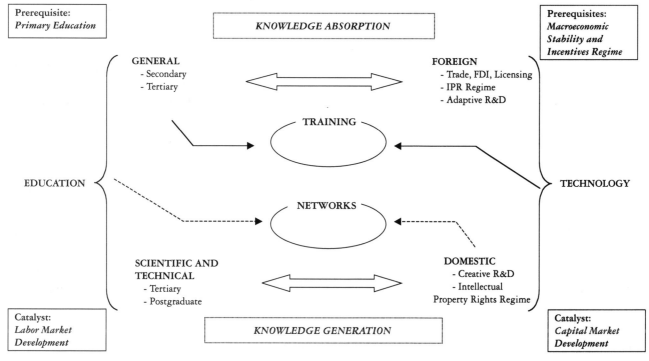

Source: Gill (2002).

to their actual level of achievement so that the estimated gaps are relative to the level of development of each country. We find that, in the aggregate, Latin America suffers from significant deficits in productivity, skills, and technology. (See figure 1.2 and table 1.1).

As mentioned, productivity differences between countries and between firms within countries are profoundly affected by differences in skills and technology.[2] It is therefore no surprise that the East Asian tigers, which exhibit well-above-average rates of TFP growth, also outperform Latin America on measures of technology and skills. The same is true for some of the successful natural resource–based economies. Within Latin America, the best-performing country, Chile, concurrently had positive increases in productivity, substantial skill upgrading, and increases in all indicators associated with technology transfer and innovation.

Since there is no perfect measure of skills, we consider the evolution of educational attainment of the adult population (measured as average years of education) and the evolution of enrollment rates. Over the course of the last two decades, the mean years of education of the adult population aged 25 and older has gone up by 1.7 years in the region

(from 4.1 to 5.8 years). On average, however, Latin American adults have 1.4 fewer years of education, and East Asian adults have 0.4 more years of education than would be expected for their income levels. This gap in the *stock* of educational attainment is a reflection of relatively slow and sometimes inadequate education investments in the past. It is therefore particularly worrying to observe that the *flow* of new educated workers is also inadequate. The region has large deficits in enrollment, particularly at the secondary school level (figure 1.3), as well as a problem with the quality of education. Latin America has an aggregate deficit of around 20 percentage points in net secondary enrollment and 10 percentage points in gross tertiary enrollment given its average income level, while East Asia has surpluses of more than 17 and 5 percentage points, respectively, and successful natural resource–based economies of 6 and 14.[3] Finally, we discuss the quality of the students "produced" at each level of education, as given by the performance of Latin American students and adults on international standardized tests. The evidence here is more limited, as most Latin American countries do not participate regularly in international tests, but the available data reflect yet another

BOX 1.1

Unlocking Productivity: The Knowledge Economy Decomposed

The center of the action in figure 1.1 is the firm, where coordinated decisions on skills recruitment, training, adoption of technologies, research and development (R&D), and innovation are undertaken. At the left we have the formal education system progressing from basic to tertiary and postgraduate education. At the right, a set of channels for transmission of foreign technologies and policy instruments and institutions to foster the adoption, adaptation, and creation of new methods of organization, production, and marketing by firms (what we call for short the "technology system"). Generalized basic education and macroeconomic stability appear as prerequisites for a meaningful and sustained process of adoption, adaptation, and creation of modern technologies by firms. Skills acquired through secondary and tertiary education enable firms to adopt and adapt existing technologies in a more efficient manner and to train their workers. Skills developed at the postgraduate level—especially but not exclusively in fields such as science and engineering—allow firms to create and develop new technologies.

Openness to trade and FDI, and, more generally, competitive pressures, create an environment that fosters innovation and training by firms and facilitates transfer of foreign technologies. Licensing and circulation of brains are crucial channels for such a transfer. Well-designed government incentives and support to training and R&D activities by firms—intellectual property rights (tax incentives, competitive matching grants, ICT infrastructure, and legal framework)—on top of a supply of well-educated workers and a competitive environment, are instrumental to bring these activities, which produce significant externalities, closer to their social optimum. Well-regulated labor and capital markets are also important catalysts, but countries aiming to close productivity gaps should not wait to launch efforts until these conditions are met; these become criti-

cal obstacles for productivity growth only later in the educational and technological transitions.

For the system to work efficiently it is not only important to develop the individual components, policies, and instruments, but to ensure that they are properly "linked" through effective networks that help overcome coordination and informational asymmetries problems. As an integrated system builds up, societies transit from technological stagnation, through a process in which individuals and firms engage increasingly in knowledge absorption (through skills upgrading, and adoption and adaptation of technologies), to one in which a significant number of them engage also in knowledge creation (development of new technologies and basic science). As mentioned below, however, this process does not advance at the same pace in all sectors or firms. Leaders are critically important (see box 1.3).

Our report is divided into two sections that conform to this diagram. In the first section (chapters 2 and 3) we present evidence of the complementarities between technology and skills in Latin America, using household-, firm-, and country-level data, and measure the gaps of Latin America in skill levels and upgrading and in technological inputs and outputs with respect to other countries, with special reference to the East Asian Tigers and successful natural resource abundant countries (such as Canada, Australia, and Scandinavian countries). Technology and skills are important factors in development, and Latin America is in short supply of both. In the second section (chapters 4 through 7), the policy implications of this analysis are presented. Chapters 4 and 5 look at education and training policies, while chapters 6 and 7 focus on technology policies and knowledge networks, respectively.

Source: Gill (2002).

serious deficit. Not only do Latin American countries (other than Cuba) underperform relative to an income-adjusted benchmark, they often underperform relative to much poorer countries.

We also use three sets of factors to assess the technology gap. First, we examine the degree to which Latin American countries are exposed to foreign imports, in particular

imports of capital goods, make payments to license foreign technologies, and receive FDI. Import penetration as a share of GDP is lower than expected, and import penetration of capital goods, which often embody new technologies, is about one-sixth of that in the East Asian tigers. While Latin America enjoyed an advantage over East Asia in terms of computer imports in 1980, that position was reversed by

FIGURE 1.2

The Latin America and the Caribbean Region's Deficits in Technology and Education Relative to East Asia (1980–99)

Income-adjusted comparisons

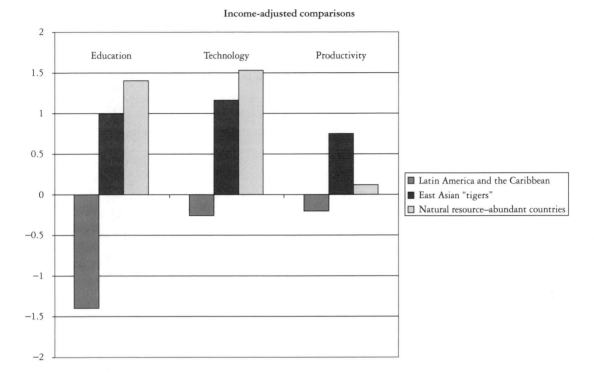

1990, and there are no indications that Latin America is closing that gap. FDI is, on average, higher in Latin America than in East Asia as a proportion of FGDP. However, this also reflects a greater preference for licensing—the contractual transfer of technology, which provides technology in a more accessible manner than FDI—in many Asian countries.

Second, we evaluate the development of the ICT sector as an essential complementary instrument to develop technological capabilities and we show that LAC's gap relative to East Asia has more than tripled during the 1990s.

Third, we focus on domestic spending on research and development (R&D) and payments for licensing, relative to the benchmark for countries of their levels of income, but also with respect to the performance of superstars such as Finland, Korea, Israel, or Ireland, and to the extraordinary returns generated on innovation investments. The most striking result is the low level of R&D conducted by firms. This is partly due to weak supporting institutions such as credit markets, ICT infrastructure, or government policies toward fomenting innovation (IPRs, competitive subsidies, and tax incentives for private R&D, and so on). It also reflects that until the recent opening of LAC economies to competition and foreign ideas, firms had neither the moti-

vation nor the ability to look outside for relevant technologies. Partly for historical reasons and partly to compensate for the low private sector effort, governments have tended to have a disproportionately high level of participation in total financing and implementation of R&D (a large part of the latter being concentrated in public universities).

Finally, though far more difficult to benchmark, the use of innovation-related resources and human capital is highly inefficient in the region. The overall coordination of universities, research centers, and the productive sector is poor, implying that the little R&D investment that is done is employed relatively inefficiently, with lower results in terms of patents and impact on growth than in the case of comparable countries or the OECD. Thus, not only does Latin America lag in terms of the total amount of R&D relative to GDP, but a relatively large share of that R&D is undertaken by the public sector and has less spillover on private R&D than in other latitudes. As a consequence, R&D spending in Latin America is not only small, but is less concentrated in *applied* research and development and has less effect on patents and productivity growth than what we observe in OECD countries and in the Asian tigers (see chapters 2 and 7),

TABLE 1.1

The Gaps That Matter Most

	OBSERVED LAC MEAN	INCOME-ADJUSTED DEFICIT IN LAC	OBSERVED EAST ASIAN TIGER MEAN	INCOME-ADJUSTED SURPLUS IN EAST ASIAN TIGERS	OBSERVED NRA COUNTRY MEAN	INCOME-ADJUSTED SURPLUS IN NRA COUNTRIES
Productivity						
TFP growth per year (1990–99)	0.45	−0.21	1.42	0.76	0.78	0.12
Education						
Mean years of education, population aged 25+	5.8	−1.4	9.7	1.0	11.1	1.4
Net secondary enrollment rate (percent)	46.7	−18.7	93.3	17.8	93.2	6.0
Gross tertiary enrollment rate (percent)	20.0	−10.0	47.3	5.1	67.0	14.0
Third International Mathematics and Science Study (TIMSS) score (points)	387	−81.2	584	86.3	524	+ (n.s.)
Technology						
Capital goods imports as a fraction of GDP, 1999 (percent)	7.7	−3.6	29.5	18.1	12.6	2.0
Domestic R&D expenditures per worker (1995 US$)	35.6	−26.4	329.5	116.5	725.4	152.5
Patents registered in the U.S., 1996–2000 average (per million)	0.8	−1.5	54.4	48.3	114.8	80.9
Mean number of computers per 1,000 workers	37.7	− (n.s.)	172.0	+ (n.s.)	404.2	+ (n.s.)

Note: The regional "deficits" or "surpluses" are calculated as the weighted sum of the difference between the observed value and the predicted value from an OLS ordinary least squares regression on log per capita income for all outcomes except TFP growth and imports of capital goods. For TFP, the means and the predicted value are given by the weighted world average, without a regression. For imports of capital goods the explanatory variable is GDP. The regional means, deficits, and surpluses for imports of capital goods are weighted by GDP; those for the mean years of education, net secondary enrollment rates, gross tertiary enrollment rates, TIMSS scores, and the number of computers are weighted by population; the measures of domestic R&D and patents, finally, are weighted by the working-age population aged 25 and older. "n.s." indicates that the deficit or surplus is not statistically significantly different from zero (at the 5 percent level). The East Asian tiger economies included in the sample are Hong Kong (China), Republic of Korea, Malaysia, and Singapore. Data for Hong Kong are not available for TFP growth, imports of capital goods, or R&D expenditures; data on Singapore are not available for net secondary enrollment rate, and imports of capital goods; data on Malaysia are not available for R&D expenditures. The natural resource–abundant countries included in the sample are Canada, Australia, New Zealand, Finland, Norway, and Sweden.
Sources: Data on TFP from Loayza, Fajnzylber, and Calderón (2002); data on educational attainment of adults from Barro and Lee (2002); data on enrollment rates from UNESCO; data on TIMSS scores from TIMSS; data on imports, imports of capital goods, GDP, GDP per capita, and population from World Bank databases; data on R&D and patent registration from Lederman and Saenz (2002).

FIGURE 1.3

A Problem in Many LAC Countries: Massive Deficits on Secondary Education

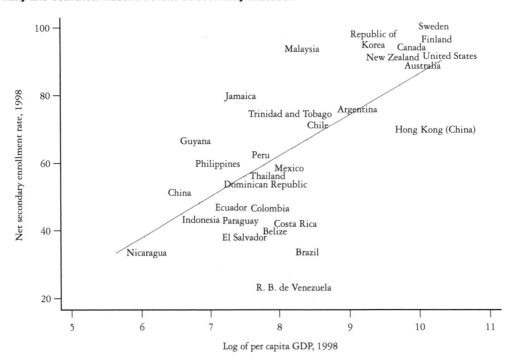

even when benchmarked by their respective average per capita income.

The overall picture that emerges is thus one of LAC countries not having given innovation and science and technology a central role in their development strategies until very recently. As a result, while their levels of indicators of technology absorption and innovation have increased, these countries have fallen behind more aggressive economies such as the Asian tigers, Israel, Ireland, and Finland. No doubt the opening of the LAC countries has given them greater access to various technologies developed abroad. However, as we argue throughout this report, merely having access to technology need not be enough for rapid sustainable growth. The critical question is what capabilities and institutions these countries need to use these technologies efficiently and eventually to steer themselves onto a path of innovation-based development, which allows for sustainable long-term growth.

From Financing Gaps to Productivity Gaps: Closing the Gap in Education and Technology in a Synchronized Way

The 1980s and 1990s in Latin America and the Caribbean were marked by a struggle with twin deficits: a budget gap and a trade gap. Fiscal and monetary policies kept center stage. It would not be an exaggeration to state that countries of the region have mostly accepted the wisdom of balancing the budget and ensuring external balance through conservative monetary and exchange rate policies. But, with few exceptions such as Chile, these decades have also been marked by sputtering growth engines—which in turn reflects low annual average rates of productivity growth. With productivity growth accepted as the *sine qua non* of sustained economic growth, Latin America's challenge is shifting from closing the financing gaps to closing the productivity gaps.

Just as the financing gap had two closely related components (the so-called twin deficits—fiscal and current account), productivity gaps can be thought of as having two equally symbiotic components—skills and technology. In the same way that the financing gaps must be closed together to ensure sustainability, skill and technology gaps must be reduced *simultaneously* in order to reduce productivity gaps in an efficient way.

The experience of countries in Latin America and around the world appears to condemn countries that attempt to close education and technology gaps in an unsynchronized

manner to low or erratic economic growth. The reason is the strong complementarity between technology and skills that lies behind skill-biased technological change because of three facts. First, skilled workers are needed to implement new technologies because skilled workers are more adept at dealing with change. The second is the phenomenon of "directed" technological change—the availability of more skilled workers in developed countries has created incentives for firms to develop new technologies that are more skill-intensive (Acemoglu, 2001). Directed technical change requires an even greater need for *speed* in the upgrading of education systems in developing countries, as the skill-biased nature of technological change is poised to continue. Third, skilled workers, engineers, and scientists are required to produce significant adaptations of existing technologies and even more to create new ones. Even plain adoption and diffusion of existing technologies require a minimum generalized level of education of the work force (at least some secondary education) and of training and R&D in firms.

Thus, countries with low levels of education remain in a trap of technological stagnation, low growth, and low demand for education (a reason why basic education must be highly subsidized everywhere). Conversely, countries may strongly subsidize tertiary education, but if they do not open to trade and FDI and firms are not subject to competitive pressures that stimulate technological progress, and hence demand for education, they will find out that a high proportion of their educated emigrate and that they must keep or increase the level of subsidization to compensate for weak effective demand. In a similar vein, low levels of R&D in firms may easily become an effective limitation to adoption of new technologies and innovation and hence to the growth of demand for education; while efforts by the government to subsidize R&D may fail to achieve their goals when low levels of education prevail and/or the economies are not open to trade and FDI and firms face no competitive pressures to innovate. A background paper for this report (Gill 2002) compares a set of Latin American and non–Latin American countries, some of which have been highly successful in synchronizing their educational and technological policies and developing educational and technological capabilities in a balanced way, and some that have not. The paper's conclusions are summarized in box 1.2.

The implication for countries of Latin America and the Caribbean and elsewhere is that they can close skill and technology gaps more productively, that is, with stronger effects

BOX 1.2

Lessons in Contrast: Exploiting Technology-Skill Complementarities

A background paper for this report (Gill 2002) explored a comparison of a set of five Latin American (Brazil, Costa Rica, Chile, Peru, and Mexico) and five non–Latin American countries that, at some moment of their development, shared both similarities and dissimilarities in educational and technological policies (China, Korea, Finland, Spain, and Singapore) to illustrate how and why some policy regimes have proven to be more successful than others in capturing the complementary environment in which skills and technology can boost productivity. The conclusions of such an exercise reinforce the basic messages of this report:

- Countries that neither increase education levels nor approach the technological transition in a sequenced manner suffer poor productivity outcomes:

  - Opening up to foreign technology will not help much in aggregate productivity, if education levels are kept low (or highly skewed), given the complementarity between technology and skills. These countries run the risk of not only facing skill bottlenecks, but also of exacerbating earnings inequality.

  - Heavily investing and subsidizing R&D would not pay back in higher productivity growth either in closed economies (which do not provide competitive pressures for firms to innovate and do not facilitate transfer of technologies through trade and FDI) or in those with low levels of education of most of the working force. (Brazil's past history is a prime example of such an imbalanced educational and technological policy that did not pay off in the last decades.)

- Countries that have increased their average education levels but do not institute policies that facilitate tech-

nology transfers also experience low productivity growth. However, it is easier for such countries to increase productivity—an opening up of the economy to foreign trade, investment, and knowledge flows results in increased productivity growth almost immediately. The contrasting experience of Peru in the 1980s and 1990s is a case in point.

- Countries that both increase education levels and increase technology transfers, but do so mostly through direct public sector provision (of education, training, and R&D) also appear to do poorly in productivity outcomes. These countries face a difficult challenge of increasing private sector participation in developing new technologies and delivering education and training. Mexico is a prime example, where the main challenge today is to effectively link the high levels of public R&D with a boost to private R&D.

- Countries that have increased education levels and that have done so by building a broad base of primary and secondary schooling, and at the same time have encouraged the adoption and adaptation of new technologies by private sector firms through openness, should focus most of their attention on strengthening their support to private R&D and stimulating knowledge networks, through improved linkages between universities and firms and among firms, both within the country and internationally, extending tertiary schooling, and supporting postgraduate programs, particularly in sciences and engineering. Chile is a good example of a country in this stage.

Source: Gill (2002).

on productivity and hence economic growth—and indeed with less effort—if their policies in these two areas are *synchronized.*

The need for synchronization implies that phases of the educational transition (from low basic and secondary education levels and quality to high levels of secondary and tertiary education) and the technological transition (from reliance on adopting simple foreign technology to major

adaptations and creation of new technologies) should match one another. Thus there is no "one size fits all" recommendation: policy priorities should depend on where precisely the country is located, at a given moment of time, on the educational and technological transitions from "knowledge absorbing" toward "knowledge creating" societies, and what imbalances it shows in progress in those areas. The report thus offers a road map for policymakers and private sector actors to identify policy priorities and actions to correct imbalances and accelerate educational and technological progress in a synchronized way. The section on Closing the Technology and Productivity Gaps and tables 1.2–1.4 provide a simplified version of such a road map.

Students, Workers, and Firms: The Major Actors of Educational and Technological Progress

In this report we focus our analysis on the major actors of the educational and technological process: students, workers, and firms. They are the ones that accumulate and use knowledge to spur productivity and growth. Families, schools, universities, research centers, and government institutions and policies are just facilitators—though of critical importance—of the process of skill and technological upgrading in a society. Both the main actors and the facilitators must face the right incentives to contribute in an efficient way to this process.

Students and workers will not accumulate enough knowledge if they are not offered (or cannot identify) high-quality education and training and see no prospects of profitable employment for educated/skilled workers. What they need in today's world of rapid skill-biased technological change are abilities to "learn," to adapt, to innovate, to work in teams, and to relate to a wide variety of actors. It is not excessively specialized, "technical" education, at least not until tertiary or postgraduate studies, and even then basic scientific knowledge in their areas and development of "problem solving" abilities are more important than mastering specific techniques that may fast become obsolete.

Students and workers need information about the quality of education and training offered by the diverse suppliers (hence the importance of state exams, sound accreditation processes, labor observatories) and credit availability to overcome liquidity constraints (and in the case of poor families outright subsidies to overcome high short-term opportunity costs). Credit and information are especially important in tertiary education, in order to convert the potential demand created by rapidly rising wage premiums for workers with tertiary education into effective demand and higher enrollment, particularly in the best private and public universities.

Having the right incentives for public schools and universities, as well as for teachers, is also crucial. Too often public resources follow the schools and the teachers, and not the students. Currently used criteria for allocation of

resources to public schools and universities generate perverse incentives in many countries in the region. Education is definitely not just a question of the number of schools and teachers. We found too many cases in the region in which large increases in expenditures in public education in the last decades were not matched by a corresponding increase in coverage or quality.

The firm is at the center of the process of skill upgrading and technological change. A firm makes decisions on the skills of its work force (through recruitment and on-the-job or external training) and the technology it uses (through adoption, adaptation, or creation) in an integrated way. At the micro level the skill–technology complementarities are just too obvious. It is educators, economists, and policymakers who sometimes miss the point. Indeed, we found that firms that are more aggressive in adopting, adapting, or creating new technologies are also those that recruit higher skills and invest more in training. Firms that do not change technologies do not train. Firms that invest in R&D do more training. Not surprisingly, firms that both innovate and train are the ones that show higher productivity growth (of course, causality runs both ways here, as usual). Incentives are critical. We found that firms more exposed to foreign competition (whether of imports or in export markets) recruit higher skills (and pay them better) and spend more in training, licensing, and R&D.

A critically important finding is then that the level of training by firms depends more on the competitive pressures they face, and their incentives to adopt, adapt, and create new technologies, as well as on the level and quality of education of the labor force they can hire, than on subsidies for training (see chapter 5). In particular, firms in Latin America and the Caribbean find little value in technical education and training services offered by large public agencies, generously financed by earmarked taxes. This is an area in which reform has been under way in many countries (Chile, Mexico, and Uruguay are ahead of the curve in this area) in the region, but still a lot remains to be done. Good educational and technology policies are good training policies. Existing training services must become more competitive. And earmarked taxes for training should either be allocated in a competitive way through matching grant schemes (to both in-firm and external training) or to improved coverage and quality of general education.

Flexible labor markets are important for firms to be able to rapidly restructure the skill composition of their labor force in response to requirements of new technologies. Rigid labor markets delay the pace of adoption of new technologies and adaptations by firms.

Similarly, access to risk capital is also critical for firms engaging in larger R&D and skill upgrading efforts. Hence the importance of deep and more sophisticated financial markets—and, specifically, the need to develop venture capital funds—for countries wishing to step up efforts in adaptation and innovation.

The Role of Government Policy

The previous discussion highlights the fact that although students, workers, and firms are the main actors in the process of accumulation and productive use of knowledge, and that a variety of facilitating institutions or firms that supply educational, training, and technological services pop up spontaneously in the *right environment*, there is a critically important role for government policy in these areas. First, governments must create the *right environment* through stimulating openness to foreign trade and FDI, facilitating the development of deep and sound financial markets and flexible labor markets and applying effective competition policies. Only in such an environment are firms willing and able to engage in adoption, adaptation, and creation of new technologies and in recruiting higher skills and training.

Second, as indicated, credit and information constraints, as well as opportunity costs for poor families, may inhibit potential demand for education to be converted into effective demand. Government support to create widespread student loan systems; targeted educational vouchers, scholarships, and subsidies for students of poor families; and state exams, labor observatories, and accreditation systems to deal with asymmetric information problems are critical policy actions to overcome imperfections in educational and training markets. Appropriate governance and funding allocation rules for public schools and universities are essential to create the right incentives in public educational systems. Supply constraints are still important in many countries in basic education, especially in rural areas.

Third, knowledge creation and diffusion is characterized by imperfect appropriability and high spillovers; that is to say, the social value is much higher than the private value and, thus, in the absence of effective subsidies or protection, firms and markets will produce less than what is socially optimal. In particular, the literature finds that the social value of private R&D exceeds its private value for a multiple of

3 in developed countries and that R&D should probably be increased by a factor of 2 to 10 in developing countries. Hence, a variety of policies and instruments have been designed and implemented everywhere to support the process of knowledge creation and diffusion: intellectual property rights; tax incentives or subsidies to private R&D and/or training; and the creation of specialized public (or public/private) educational, scientific, and technical institutions.

The report analyzes design issues for some of these instruments and where, when, and under which conditions these interventions seem to have been more successful. It finds, for example, that tax incentives for private R&D are effective only in countries with a strong tax system characterized by few exemptions and high enforcement. Transparent and competitive matching grants schemes may be more effective in most LAC countries under present circumstances. The most important conclusion, however, is that effective interaction (through so-called innovation networks) is as important as the individual design and development of institutions and policy instruments to support the process of knowledge creation and diffusion.

The Critical Importance of Effective Innovation Networks

The importance of sectoral, national, and international "innovation networks" (or clusters) arises not only from the strong links that exist between education and technology, but from the nonmarket character of many of the institutions and organizations that are active participants in these areas and the significant "informational asymmetries" that characterize the processes of knowledge creation, diffusion, and absorption. We find that the Latin America and the Caribbean region not only lags in the level of stocks and flows of educational and technological capital, but also often uses them poorly owing to a faulty incentive framework and to lack of integration of the countries' "national innovation systems" (NIS) (see figure 1.4 and chapter 7).

Linkages between universities and private sector firms are important even at the early stages of technological catch-up, when most firms are primarily engaged in the adoption and minor adaptations of foreign technologies. (At this stage of development, universities and public research institutions are likely to be the only institutions where scientific research and technological knowledge are acquired in a significant way, and thus they are critical supports for leading firms and sectors that engage in more significant adaptations or even

FIGURE 1.4
A Simple National Innovation System (NIS)

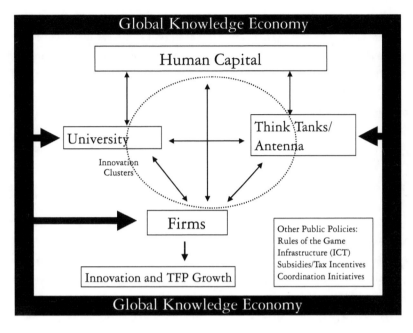

in the creation of technologies.) Strengthening those links becomes even more important in the second phase, in which a large number of firms begin to be engaged in major adaptations and leaders engage more in creation. However, a number of institutional design problems can blunt the incentives for firms and universities to interact, and public policy can play a very important role in redressing them.

Latin American countries may want to start by paying close attention to designing policies that strengthen incentives for such collaboration. Collaboration is ineffectual owing not only to problems of asymmetric information (firms do not know well what universities can indeed offer, and universities do not know well what firms need), but also because of bad incentives. Of particular importance are issues of intellectual property rights of research results obtained in universities and through public funding (individual researchers must benefit from a substantial part, but universities or independent research centers need to share to compensate for the financial and institutional risks they incur in supporting these activities) as well as other incentives embedded in the structure of benefits and promotions within universities and public research centers. In Latin America and the Caribbean some degree of cultural reticence must also be overcome, on the part of public universities as well as firms. Public policy supporting private R&D and training might give some preference to joint university (or independent research

centers)/firms skills upgrading and R&D efforts, to help overcome some of the asymmetric information and coordination problems.

More generally, the so-called National Innovation System can hardly be called a "system" in Latin American countries and it produces little innovation. It is not—nor should it be—strictly national either. Sectoral and international dimensions are critical.

Firms interact with other firms in a variety of ways—and proximity (or virtual clusters) can reduce the transactions costs of these interactions and improve the speed and quality of the flow of information among them. More important, as there are significant spillovers arising from in-firm training and R&D efforts, sectoral clusters help internalize in many ways these externalities (by setting cooperative skill upgrading and R&D efforts and establishing "rules of the game" among private actors), thereby providing a boost to these activities. They also help address the asymmetric information and coordination problems that plague the relationships of market and nonmarket actors in knowledge creation and diffusion activities. Indeed, sectoral innovation systems or "clusters" can be developed in a rather independent way (the innovation system in copper mining may have very little that intersects with that of agricultural exports or of fisheries or forestry in Chile, or elsewhere). They require the development of specialized skills and R&D efforts (which is not to say that success stories may not spill over to other sectors, as happened in Finland with the Nokia case or in the U.S. mining industry in the last century). Governments can and should support efforts of such emerging innovation clusters. However, attempts to create clusters from scratch have often backfired and there are no clear policy design recipes that can be followed. Evidence shows that existing successful clusters seem to be the result of private entrepreneurship that benefits from a positive business environment: open trade regimes, strong domestic legal and financial institutions, and sound educational and technology policies. Most successful experiences suggest that well-designed support policies for R&D and skills upgrading, of a general nature and coverage, might be efficiently implemented through existing and incipient sectoral clusters and somewhat tailored to their specific needs.

As important, any successful National Innovation System must have an international dimension. Knowledge creation and diffusion is essentially an international phenomena. Most new knowledge will continue to be produced in a handful of advanced countries, where the largest stocks of human capital and innovation networks exist, and, thus, both firms and national education and innovation systems must effectively link with them if they want to succeed in adopting, adapting, and creating technologies in an efficient way. Thus, national educational systems in Latin America and the Caribbean must be well connected with the best educational systems abroad. These links are especially critical at the tertiary and postgraduate level. Linking up local universities and autonomous research centers with world-class institutions can be relatively straightforward and yield a high payoff.

The ability of domestic firms to network with foreign ones will usually require that the domestic firm already have some degree of indigenous technological capability. This makes it difficult to come up with general policies that can jump-start such linkages, other than removing regulatory hurdles to FDI, or other export or import regulations that prevent domestic firms from integrating with global chains. However, successful sectoral innovation clusters have to be connected with their peers abroad. Government policy might especially support some skill upgrading and R&D initiatives of existing sectoral clusters that have such an international enhancing dimension.

Finally, as a lot of knowledge is "disembodied" and can hardly be transmitted (in spite of ICT progress) without personal interaction, the international circulation of skilled workers and students is a critical aspect of a successful National Innovation System. Study-abroad programs and temporary emigration of workers is a major and highly efficient source of technological transfer. Clearly brain drain hurts the country of origin in the short run because in most developing countries education is publicly funded and migration represents a drain on resources. But even brain drain can be turned into a gain, as witnessed by the critical role of the Indian engineers in Silicon Valley for the subsequent development of the domestic software industry or the Chinese or Jewish diasporas for the rapid technological catch-ups of China and Israel.

Closing the Skill Gaps

As mentioned, new technologies have particularly increased the productivity of educated workers, which means that skill upgrading now should have a larger effect on growth rates than it did before. The region must then close the skill gaps as fast as possible. Chapter 4 shows that by 1960 the region had levels of education comparable to those of East Asian countries and many peripheral European countries. Those countries, however, engaged in more rapid educational transitions and thus we observe today major gaps in Latin America, as indicated above.

Most successful episodes of educational upgrading—the United States between 1850 and 1950, Korea and the Scandinavian countries since World War II—have all followed a sequential pattern of upgrading, first building up universal basic education, then broad secondary education, and finally generalized access to universities. Educational transitions are discussed in chapter 4 and represented in figure 1.5, in which the top part shows the transition followed by most OECD and East Asian countries. The figure shows that while most countries sought to gradually build the mean level of general education. others focused on tertiary education.

Public Policy and Funding in Most Countries in Latin America Should Focus on Expanding Secondary Education, while Facilitating Private Expansion of Tertiary Education

The increasing returns to secondary and tertiary education suggest that the technological transition will require more workers of this skill level. However, as mentioned before, the most distinctive feature of the Latin America and

FIGURE 1.5

Educational Transitions

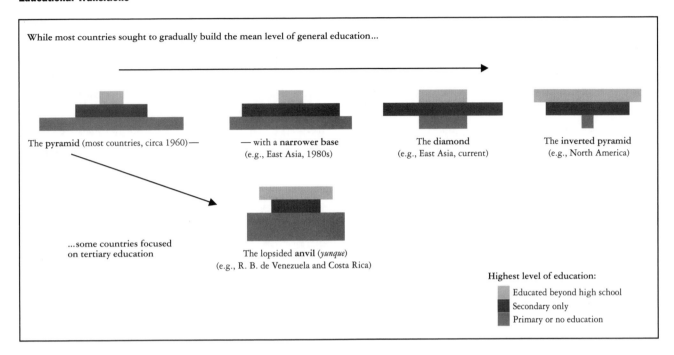

While most countries sought to gradually build the mean level of general education...

The pyramid (most countries, circa 1960)—   — with a **narrower base**
(e.g., East Asia, 1980s)

The diamond
(e.g., East Asia, current)

The inverted pyramid
(e.g., North America)

...some countries focused
on tertiary education

The lopsided **anvil** (*yunque*)
(e.g., R. B. de Venezuela and Costa Rica)

Highest level of education:

Educated beyond high school

Secondary only

Primary or no education

Caribbean region's average educational landscape is a large shortfall in secondary-educated workers, compared to mild deficiencies at the tertiary level given its level of development. In this sense, the region has followed an "unbalanced" educational path, when compared with OECD and Asian countries. This pattern makes poor use of the intrinsic complementarities within the educational system since it reduces the efficiency of tertiary education (as there is a narrower talent pool from which to select students for tertiary education). It also makes poor use of the complementary relationship between the educational and the technological transition of a country, as a widespread coverage of secondary education has been found to be a condition for countries to fully reap technological spillovers from FDI and trade. It is also likely to be unsustainable since it exacerbates inequality. The lesser deficit, and the higher private returns to tertiary education may suggest that public policy (and in particular the allocation of public resources) should focus more on increasing secondary education, while at the same time facilitating the private expansion of tertiary education.

This general pattern notwithstanding, some countries in the region—in particular Chile, Argentina, Uruguay, and many of the English-speaking Caribbean countries—have done a better job on secondary education and their educational push should now center more on broadening atten-

dance to tertiary education. In the other extreme, there are laggards that still need to focus most of their efforts on improving coverage and quality of basic education.

The Best Ways to Expand Access to Education Vary with Bottlenecks Faced

Are students completing primary school and not enrolling in secondary school, or are they dropping out midway through secondary school? Low enrollment levels may themselves reflect either insufficient effective demand by individuals, or insufficient supply of educational opportunities. The demand for more education by individuals should be closely related to the demand for more educated workers by firms: as relative wages rise, we would expect young people to seek more schooling. This demand for more schooling by individuals may fail to materialize, however, because of credit constraints, uncertainty about the returns to education, and other information market failures. In other cases, the problem may lie not with the demand for education by individuals, but with the supply in the education system. The number of slots in a public university may be fixed (as there is not enough cost recovery and most countries face fiscal constraints), and in rural areas in some countries there may simply be no secondary schools. The appropriate mix of policies will therefore be country-specific, and should be determined after a careful analysis of bottlenecks, demand, and supply constraints in the education market.

We find in several countries in the region indications of both supply constraints and insufficient effective demand for secondary education. Such insufficient demand for secondary schooling may be related either to insufficient demand by firms and to high opportunity cost of schooling. Policies that promote technological change have the potential to increase the returns to schooling and the willingness by young men and women to defer entrance into the labor market. So will those that improve quality, and hence returns of secondary education. And, as an important motivation to finalize secondary school lies in the possibility to proceed to tertiary education and reap the benefits associated with the high wage premiums for workers with higher education, students must know that they will have a fair chance to get a university education (see below). Programs that subsidize the cost of secondary schooling for students from poor families, such as conditional cash transfers like those in the Progressa program in Mexico or the Bolsa Escolha in Brazil, may also be effective in overcoming gaps between perceived moderate returns to secondary education and high opportunity costs of forgone employment.

Insufficient supply of secondary school infrastructure appears to be a problem in rural areas in many Latin American countries and even in urban areas in some. In these settings, programs to increase the availability of schooling facilities are required.

We also find that, in many countries in the region, the main constraint for private universities is effective demand, while that for subsidized public universities is supply. Although there is high *potential* demand for private universities, because of the high returns, this does not necessarily translate into high *effective* demand because of liquidity constraints and information asymmetries. Student loan and targeted scholarship programs hold promise, if they are well designed. Providing households with information about the quality of private providers (through state exams for graduates, labor market observatories, and sound accreditation programs) will help them make better choices and, by reducing uncertainty and bridging information gaps, may increase effective demand.

In contrast, public universities are heavily subsidized in many countries and, as a consequence, face unmet effective demand. Increasing aggregate budgets to public universities is generally not a feasible or desirable solution,

given fiscal shortages in most countries. In many countries, where costs per student are inordinately high by international standards, there are significant possibilities of increases in enrollment for a given budget. In most, higher cost recovery, if coupled with widening credit and targeted scholarship programs to relieve liquidity constraints, would be an efficient way to increase coverage. This obvious course of action, however, appears to be constrained by the same political economy forces that led in the first place to unbalanced educational transitions and high subsidization of tertiary education for the elites and middle classes. In such cases, there is at least the need to transfer public resources according to performance, thus creating appropriate incentives for efficiency, and for increases in coverage and quality.

Training Policies Have in General Overemphasized Public Provision and Underemphasized the Importance of Good Technology and Education Policies

Chapter 5 considers training and lifelong learning policies, identifying several broad types of technical education and training systems in Latin America and the Caribbean, including the classic corporatist "Latin American Model" (for example, the approach followed by Brazil, Colombia, and Peru) and the approaches adopted by countries such as Chile (which relies on training incentives to firms) and Mexico (which relies more on public sector provision of training). We examine the relative benefits of these models—and other approaches found in East Asia and OECD countries—with the aim of drawing out the most appropriate policy mix for the region in the coming decades. Using firm survey data for 22 Latin American countries and comparing the findings to data for selected OECD and East Asian countries, we find that the public provision of technology-oriented training is generally viewed as relatively inefficient and irrelevant.

Evidence from evaluations in East Asia indicates that well-run schemes such as tax rebates are effective in increasing in-service training, but the evidence from within and outside LAC overwhelmingly indicates that education levels of workers and introduction of new technologies are the most important correlates of in-service training. The main lesson is that LAC countries should view "training policy" as not just subsidizing or providing training, but also increasing the demand for training through appropriate technology-related policies, and increasing the trainability of workers through appropriate education policy. Education seems to be the most important enabler of training, and technology change its most important instigator. The main reform needed for explicit training policies is a change in the existing public-private balance in training provision. Many LAC countries (most notably Chile, Uruguay, and Mexico) have been progressing in this direction, but much still remains to be done.

Lifelong Learning Has Always Been Important

Lifelong learning is necessitated by the obsolescence of general skills acquired in schools, as compared with retraining, which is necessitated by the obsolescence of specific skills acquired on the job or through technical education. The report addresses the following question: Has the labor market changed so that the emphasis on lifelong learning is now greater than it was before? The evidence from six LAC countries appears to indicate that it has not: the "new economy" may not be that different from the old one. There is no doubt that rapid technological change, especially skill-biased technological change, requires constant retraining. But even if lifelong learning is more important now than ever before, the main policy implications are in fact for *education* systems. And the implications are that schools should teach how to learn, not occupation-specific skills, and the importance of secondary vocational education should decline over time as occupation-specific learning gets pushed up to tertiary levels.

Closing the Technology and Productivity Gaps

The Progressive Stages of Technological Evolution and the Synchronized Phasing of Educational and Technological Policies

In chapter 6 we identify the instruments and policies for technology acquisition and development, and evaluate their impact on productivity. Firms usually begin their technological catching-up by adopting more modern technologies in a rather straightforward fashion, though in many cases even this requires some skills upgrading and R&D to appropriately select and adapt technologies to local conditions. Later on many successful firms begin to do major adaptations, which require stepping up efforts in skill upgrading (through recruitment and training) and significant R&D investments. Finally, the most successful firms, especially when competing internationally, require major innovations and development of new technologies to keep a competitive edge. For this, they require highly specialized skills and major investments in R&D. Progressively, major adaptations

and innovations cannot be done in-house but in the largest of firms and thus require effective "innovation networks," at least at a sectoral level.

However, it must be kept in mind that even in developed countries most of the firms are fundamentally adopting or adapting with just a few doing cutting-edge innovation. To wit: it has been estimated that 86 percent of France's technological progress is purchased from abroad, the remainder being generated locally (Eaton and Kortum, 1999) and that resources dedicated to "adoption" in the United States, widely recognized as the innovation leader, exceed those dedicated to innovation at the frontier by a factor of roughly 30:1 (Jovanovic, 1997).

For the sake of convenience, we offer a stylized view here of the technological transition that countries pass through. The choice of policies and instruments, we argue, depends on their levels of technological and educational achievement—country conditions and endowments. Technological progress and innovation is a process and evolves over time as conditions change. We thus attempt to classify the countries of Latin America according to these rubrics, and draw appropriate policy lessons for each stage of the technological evolution.

"Plugging In": The First Stage in Modern Technological Transitions

We consider a country to have entered the "plugging in" stage when most of its firms are in a state of relative technological stagnation and it takes the conscious decision to accelerate the transfer of new technologies by achieving full coverage of basic education, opening to trade, FDI and ITC, facilitating licensing and skilled labor circulation, and more generally, creating a competitive environment for firms that induce innovation and skills upgrading. Transiting through this stage will unleash a significant increase in potential demand for education by rapidly raising premiums for secondary and tertiary education. Most countries in Latin America and the Caribbean have already gone successfully through this stage.

Access to global markets exposes firms to newer products and processes—which leads to a process of technological imitation and some adaptation—the first step toward any catch-up. However, technology adoption is not an easy and costless activity; even the first stage of adoption—selecting the right technology—implies an ability to gather relevant information and make astute judgments. And quite often it requires at least some minor adaptations to the quality of local inputs and other local conditions.

For countries that find themselves farthest from the technological frontier (such as Haiti), the cornerstone of their technology policy should be their education policy—a push toward getting to the threshold level of basic education coupled with an open trade policy and deregulation of markets that enforces market discipline and discourages rent-seeking behavior, understanding that the lower the educational levels the lower the benefits from trade and FDI.

As countries transit through this stage, however, improvements in the quality of basic education and increased coverage of secondary education begin to increase in importance, as does beginning to step up efforts to attract FDI, particularly through institutional shortcuts such as special regimes for export promotion zones. Copyright and trademark protection and some form of patent protection do need to be considered at this stage to facilitate technology transfer from abroad. Specific support programs to skill upgrading and R&D efforts in emerging innovation clusters, normally in sectors with traditional comparative advantage such as those based on natural resource endowments, may have high payoffs. It is also important to engage as early as possible in telecommunications sector reform, to increase competition and coverage, and the development of a friendly Internet legal framework to increase connectivity. Countries at the upper end of this stage include Nicaragua, Guatemala, Bolivia, Honduras, and Paraguay (see table 1.2).

Catching Up—Moving toward the Technological Frontier
The first stage is followed by a relatively long period of "catching up," in which most firms are busily engaged in technological transfer and catch-up, but where innovations are still scarce. A natural boost to making the transition to this next stage is usually received when firms move from domestic to export markets and when they are exposed to significant levels of competition. Demand for workers with higher education is high, but these countries still face a large secondary education gap. Skill needs become more specialized, as does the policy environment. As a country transits through this stage a larger fraction of firms engage in skills upgrading through training and in R&D for adaptation of foreign technologies, reflecting the need to take better advantage of local resources or to modify the technology to better suit local conditions.

TABLE 1.2

First Stage

EDUCATION		
GENERAL CONDITIONS		POLICY PRIORITIES
Basic	Low coverage	1. Increase public spending to increase coverage of basic education
Secondary	Low demand	
Tertiary	Low demand	2. Institutional reform to increase efficiency and quality

TECHNOLOGY		
GENERAL CONDITIONS		POLICY PRIORITIES
Trade	Low	Increase openness to trade by simplifying structure of protection
FDI	Low	Promotion of FDI through EPZs
IPR	Low	Copyright and trademark protection
R&D	Low	Regulatory reform to reduce disincentives for R&D
		Selective subsidies to private R&D
ICT	Low	Telecomunications sector reform and friendly ICT legal framework
Networks	Nonexistent	Public support to emerging innovation clusters

First priority for these countries, in educational policy, is to close the large secondary education gap. As explained earlier, to achieve this countries need to overcome remaining supply constraints (mainly in rural sectors), improve the quality of secondary education to increase expected returns and effective demand, and target subsidies to poor families to compensate for the high opportunity costs of schooling. But, as an important motivation to finish secondary education is to be able to proceed to tertiary education and reap the high wage premiums, the countries also need to put in place a well-designed system of credit (and information) for tertiary education, so that students from poor families know they have a fair chance to proceed to tertiary education if they indeed finalize secondary school.

Countries in this bracket, in which a large number of firms need to transition from simple adoption to more complex adaptations, are likely to benefit from more active promotion of technological transfer and adaptation. Further encouraging trade and FDI by engaging in bilateral and multilateral agreements that ensure market access, and improving the investment climate through active promotion policies (as practiced by Costa Rica) will accelerate the pace of technology transfer. Technology diffusion and significant adaptations, as well as creation by an emerging set of leaders, should be fostered by implementing a patent protection regime that is trade-related intellectual property rights

(TRIPS)–consistent, but not as strict as to impose high short-run costs in terms of slower diffusion; by fully developing the ICT sector, and by establishing a broader policy of support for private R&D and training through competitive grant systems, in lieu of the previously more focused support to a few innovation clusters.

It is also important at this stage to improve incentives for university/firms cooperation in R&D and specialized skills upgrading. As mentioned earlier, chapter 7 finds that most of R&D in Latin America and the Caribbean is currently being done by the public sector and universities without enough links and spillovers on R&D by firms and specialized private agencies, in sharp contrast with what happens in more successful countries, and that many of them still have generously financed public or tripartite training institutes that tend to get behind the technology curve.

Labor market flexibility and deep financial sectors (in particular, access to venture capital) become more important in this stage as an increasingly larger number of firms engage in technological and skills upgrading.

Most Latin American countries, such as Brazil, Colombia, Costa Rica, the Dominican Republic, El Salvador, Panama, the República Bolivariana de Venezuela, and the English-speaking Caribbean countries, are in different phases of this stage. Thus, in summary, the central priorities for most LAC countries at present are closing fast the gap in secondary education while continuing to expand tertiary education, and at the same time creating better incentives for private R&D and training, including an overhaul of present predominantly publicly funded and executed R&D and training schemes (see table 1.3).

Joining the League of Innovators

Firms that have been present in global markets—adapting existing technologies and selling the resulting products at lower cost than their competitors—find margins eroding as new low-wage entrants take away market share. Sustaining a position in global markets then necessitates a leap forward into creating new products and processes (which is greatly facilitated by the acquired knowledge), as well as capital accumulation, from the adapt-and-export stage. Countries in this tier normally have full coverage of secondary education for new cohorts of workers and rapidly increasing enrollments in tertiary education. Postgraduate programs begin to flourish. As expected, the United States and Japan are far ahead of the rest of the world.

TABLE 1.3

Second Stage

EDUCATION		
GENERAL CONDITIONS		POLICY PRIORITIES
Basic	High coverage	1. Increase resources and efficiency in secondary education
Secondary	High demand	2. Facilitate access to higher education (through student loans and state accreditation and exams)
	Low coverage	
Tertiary	High demand	3. Improve cost recovery and allocation of resources to public universities according to performance
	Low coverage	

TECHNOLOGY		
GENERAL CONDITIONS		POLICY PRIORITIES
Trade	Increased	Trade agreements to guarantee market access
FDI	Increased (Maquilas and natural resources)	Active promotion / Improvement of investment climate
IPR	Low	Increase protection of intellectual property rights (TRIPS consistent)
R&D	Low	Establish competitive subsidy schemes to promote private R&D
ICT	Low	Development of ICT infrastructure
Networks	Incipient	Promote university-firm linkages
	Fragmented	Increase support to emerging innovation clusters

What is noteworthy is that newly advanced countries such as Korea, Israel, and Finland find themselves in this first tier also. Despite frequent references to such nations as "new entrants" to the league of innovative economies, the notion of suddenly "arriving on the scene" is misconceived. Firms in these countries have been engaged in making product and process improvements for many years. It is also true, however, that there appear to be "turning" points in many cases, when investments in R&D by firms and patent registration (just to mention two major indicators of technological innovation) accelerate at a vary rapid pace and such cases seem to be related to a major push by governments and private sectors to create a fully integrated "innovation system." Such countries appear as outliers in terms of their efforts in R&D and their outcomes in terms of patents when benchmarked with respect to their income level (see figure 1.6). Such efforts are typically associated with very high overall productivity growth and, as chapter 7 stresses, the rates of return appear to justify these investments (see figure 1.7).

Countries in this stage need to cope with the large fraction of students who, having finished secondary education, are demanding access to tertiary education. Student-loan programs must become massive, targeted scholarships need to

FIGURE 1.6

Superstars in R&D

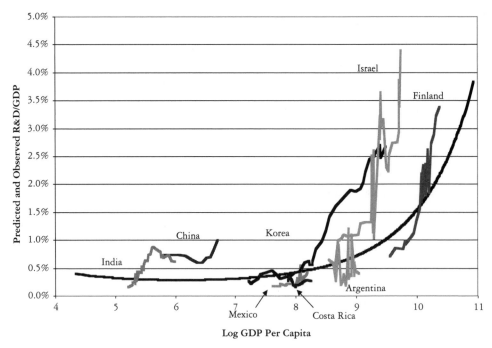

Source: Lederman and Maloney (2002)

FIGURE 1.7

Returns to R&D and Physical Capital

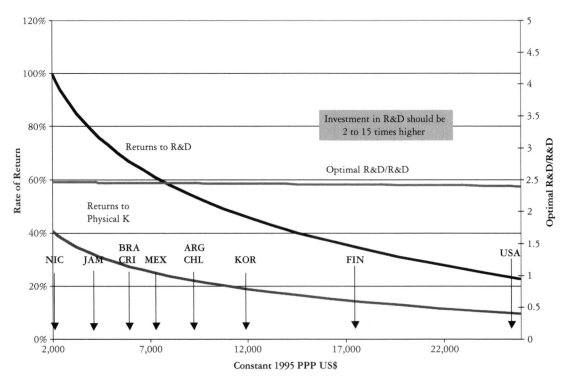

be increased substantially, and information systems (state exams, labor observatories, accreditation systems) need to be substantially strengthened. Postgraduate systems, particularly in sciences and engineering, must receive a strong push.

With the distance to the technological frontier narrowed even more, technology policy gets even more complex. The objective now is to stimulate the creation of new technologies by a large number of firms and enlarge the fraction of those that engage in major adaptations of foreign technologies (most will continue to transfer and adapt technologies from abroad). Advancing to the innovation stage requires a significant leap forward in private R&D. On the part of firms, it necessitates large investments in in-house R&D activity or close cooperation with universities and independent research centers. Governments must support these efforts by stepping up in a considerable way subsidies through competitive matching grant systems, establishing tax incentives for R&D, increasing the financing and provision of basic research, strengthening intellectual property rights, deepening credit markets, and continuing to upgrade ICT-related infrastructure to world class levels.

At this stage much of technological advance is tacit (embedded in individuals) rather than coded (available on "blueprints"), and so issues related to labor mobility and cooperative networks of firms and institutions of higher learning and research (sectorally, nationally, and internationally) assume even greater importance. A coherent and stage-dependent innovation and R&D framework is essential to successfully reach the creation stage. Most of all, the incentives facing all actors have to be clearly aligned and a coherent, integrated innovation system must be in place. This has not happened in the Latin America and the Caribbean region.

The evidence of the impact of a well-designed system is clear. Evidence presented in this report shows that patent rights, public funding, and human capital stimulate private R&D in OECD and East Asian countries. Private R&D and public R&D in turn stimulate domestic patenting and foreign transfer of technology, which contribute to the stocks of domestic and foreign-generated knowledge capital, which in turn lead to higher productivity. Such links, especially those from public R&D to private R&D, are found to be weaker in Latin America and the Caribbean than elsewhere.

Indicators for Chile and Mexico suggest that they are just in the first stages of this phase, but have not yet engaged in the kind of dramatic takeoffs that Korea, Israel, and

Finland made when they had a similar level of income, or that India and China appear on the way to making. Other countries, such as Argentina and Uruguay, have not only not taken off in terms of innovation in spite of a high level of human capital, but they are also far behind the "normal" countries at their level of income. As chapter 6 notes, many LAC countries have today the level of tertiary education that the NICs, Finland, and Israel had at the beginning of the 1980s during their takeoff period and hence it would appear timely for them to make a big push in policies to encourage private RD investment (see table 1.4).

The transition that we have sketched above should be viewed as a continuous process, though there appear to be some significant nonlinearities in the path followed by many successful countries, particularly when shifting to the innovation phase: a concentrated push in innovation policies and a corresponding exponential increase in private R&D, patents, and productivity growth. And progress through the different stages of this transition may be quite uneven among sectors, as well as among firms in each sector. (See box 1.3.)

TABLE 1.4

Third Stage

EDUCATION		
GENERAL CONDITIONS		POLICY PRIORITIES
Basic	High coverage	1. Significantly increase resources for higher education (credit/scholarships)
Secondary	High coverage	
Tertiary	High demand	2. Develop postgraduate programs, specially in sciences and engineering
	Medium coverage	3. Strengthen state accreditation and exams
		4. Further improve cost recovery and allocation of resources to public universities

TECHNOLOGY		
GENERAL CONDITIONS		POLICY PRIORITIES
Trade	High	Trade agreements to guarantee market access
FDI	High (including industries intensive in R&D)	Active promotion
IPR	Increased	Increase protection of intellectual property rights to OECD levels
R&D	Increased	Strengthen private R&D competitive subsidies and tax incentives, and public R&D spending
ICT	Increased	Advance to OECD levels
Networks	More developed	Promote integration of a strong national innovation system with international links
	Better integrated	

19

BOX 1.3

The Importance of Diversity and Leaders

In this report we insist on the importance of balanced, bottom-up, and synchronized educational and technological transitions. Obviously, however, this does not mean that all students and workers must have the same level of education and skills or that all firms in an economy will be in the same phase of the technological transition.

Diversity is always important and in the fields of knowledge and technological progress, more than in others, leaders play a critical role. Thus, even in countries that still have low coverage of their basic education there are a few universities that train the elites and conduct research—and they would rather be good and play a useful social role. There is, of course, the question of whether in such a case the state should subsidize higher education for the elites—as most LAC countries do—and the answer is: of course not. But the state may well give loans or fellowships to the few students from poor families who can complete secondary school so that they have a fair chance of proceeding to tertiary education; it may also support joint applied research projects that effectively link these universities with firms.

As important, even in economies in which the large majority of firms may be stagnant, in technological terms, or just adopting foreign technologies in a straightforward way, there will be some doing major adaptations and even significant technological innovations. This is most likely the case in sectors in which the country has for long had a comparative advantage, as is the case with those based on natural resources. It is important that government policies support such leadership efforts even in countries that are lagging overall in the technological transition. Hence, supporting skill upgrading and technological efforts in incipient sectoral innovation clusters should be part of educational and technological policies even in countries that are in the first stages of the educational and technological transition.

Natural resource–based sectors are especially important, as even when technological transfers from abroad are possible, they normally require significant adaptations to the characteristics of indigenous natural resources and their particular environmental conditions. Major examples can be found in the successful development of fresh fruits or salmon in Chile or cut flowers in Colombia. Even more, there is very little R&D in tropical agriculture (or health) in OECD countries for obvious reasons, so in these areas either we do it or productivity growth will likely stall. Our 2001 flagship publication, *From Natural Resources to the Knowledge Economy* (de Ferranti and others, 2001), of which the present report is a natural outgrowth, presented strongly the case that Latin American countries' historically lackluster performance in comparison to other more successful natural resource–based economies (such as Scandinavian countries, Australia, New Zealand, Canada, and the United States), had a lot to do with the fact that they did not invest—and still do not invest—enough in skills and R&D in these sectors.

Something similar may happen in some service sectors such as marketing, finance, and others that require significant adaptations to local tastes, culture, and institutions. Contrary to popular belief, one may expect more R&D in primary and service sectors, as compared to manufacturing sectors in which straightforward transfer of technologies is more possible, at least in the initial stages of the technological transition.

Summing Up

One of the abiding mysteries in development economics has been why poor countries have not aggressively exploited the immense global stock of knowledge to accelerate growth. Increasingly the literature focuses on shortcomings in national innovative capacity. High levels of human capital and exposure to foreign technologies—for instance through trade, FDI, licensing, and the international circulation of skilled workers—are critical not only in their own right, but also vitally in how they complement each other. As countries seek to accelerate the pace of technological progress, ensuring that the right human capital is available and coordinated effectively with technological policies becomes central.

The evidence clearly shows that the higher-performing countries that made a transition to full partners in global innovation—Israel, Finland, Korea, for example—have dramatically increased both their level of human capital and their investments and policies for innovation in a concerted fashion. In addition to getting the basics right in terms of plugging in to the global knowledge economy, they also came to terms with two fundamental issues affecting every country following in their footsteps.

First, knowledge as a commodity is plagued with extraordinary market failures and hence the market will not generate the optimal level of innovation. To repeat, serious analysts argue that the United States should probably increase its R&D by a factor of 4 and we offer evidence that LAC is also even further below optimal. Furthermore, the institutions created to resolve these market failures—universities, government laboratories, intellectual property rights—lie, by definition, outside the market and hence are not coordinated by the price mechanism.

Second, a critical aspect of the process of development is that firms, and the country as a whole, "learn to learn." In particular, increasing the technological absorptive capacity of the firm has required a supportive set of policies and institutions ranging from well-designed fiscal incentives and subsidies to the active promotion of collaboration through incubators, technological parks, and clusters; to the creation and coordination of industrial consortia that share the costs and risks of R&D and skill upgrading and serve as learning laboratories for less advanced firms; and to establishing antennas for identifying ideas from abroad.

Both considerations demand an integrated approach and a coordinative and even leading role for government. At a minimum the state needs to ensure a consistent and coherent set of incentives to ensure that the institutions created to address market failures collaborate fruitfully with firms. In the highly successful countries, governments have not been shy about financing and undertaking R&D that has broad spillovers.

Not all countries are at a stage where undertaking such policies is feasible. It probably does not make sense to contemplate broad government financing of R&D if the economy remains closed, if basic institutional integrity is in doubt, or as the report has stressed, if the required human capital is absent. That

said, the successful countries have consistently taken an active approach to integration in the world economy—upgrading the learning and training capacity of firms, selectively financing private R&D, encouraging the licensing of foreign technologies, protecting intellectual property rights, stimulating the development and access to ICT and progressively deepening and tuning up their National Innovation Systems rather than passively waiting for multinational corporations or imports to transfer technology. Thus engagement in the long process of undertaking the necessary institutional reforms needs to start early in the development process.

Though arguments for traditional "industrial policy" have largely been discredited, a government's role in providing the necessary innovation and skill upgrading–related complements to previous reforms provides a challenging policy agenda over the next decades. An active and efficient "innovation policy" is required, and though many of its components and institutions should be neutral across sectors, some need to be tailored to support emerging innovation clusters in particular sectors. As this report will show, most countries in the Latin America and the Caribbean region lag in almost every dimension of educational and technological achievement. As a region, to rephrase Pasteur's quote, our collective mind is not yet prepared to take advantage of the unpredictable technological opportunities that the new millennia will present us.

Endnotes

1. See de Ferranti and others (2001, chapter 3), Hall and Jones (1999), Parente and Prescott (2000).

2. Of course, differences in skills and "technology" do not explain away all differences in productivity levels. Differences in quality of institutions, depth of financial sectors, macro/fiscal performance, among others well known in growth studies, contribute in an important way to such differences. See Loayza, Fajnzylber, and Calderón (2002).

3. It is important to note, however, that low net enrollment rates at the secondary level are partly the result of high repetition rates and late entry into primary school.

CHAPTER 2

The Gaps That Matter Most

THE CENTRAL PROPOSITION OF THIS REPORT IS THAT SKILLS AND TECHNOLOGY interact in important ways, and are a fundamental reason for the large observed differences in productivity across countries. Focusing on *gaps* in productivity, technology, and education is a natural way of considering differences in welfare across nations, and goes back (at least) to the work of economic historian Alexander Gerschenkron. (Gerschenkron, 1962; see also Fagerberg, 1994). But estimating the size of gaps is not an easy matter for a number of reasons. First, data are not always available on appropriate measures of productivity, skills, and technology and, when they can be found, these data are often plagued with measurement error. Second, different countries are at different stages in development: a simple comparison of the educational attainment of adults in the United States and Peru is obviously not very informative, but one of Peru and Thailand may be. Much of the early work by Gerschenkron and others analyzed the gaps between "leader" and "technologically backward" countries. In this chapter, we take a different approach. Most of the evidence we present assesses whether countries in Latin America and the Caribbean have high (or low) levels of productivity, skills, and technology for their levels of per capita income. The estimated gaps are therefore gaps *relative* to the level of development. They provide a *benchmark* for countries in Latin America (box 2.1).

Throughout this chapter and in much of the report, we particularly stress the comparison between Latin America and two sets of economies: the successful East Asian "tigers," including Hong Kong (China), Korea, Malaysia, and Singapore; and a group of countries abundant in natural resources, including Canada, Australia, New Zealand, Finland, Norway, and Sweden. The comparison with the East Asian tigers is a natural one because both sets of countries started at a similar level of development in the 1960s. In last year's report, *From Natural Resources to the Knowledge Economy*, we stressed that many countries in Latin America have a comparative advantage in natural resources. For this reason, the comparison with other countries abundant in natural resources is also informative.

The Productivity Gap

Table 2.1 summarizes total factor productivity (TFP) growth for a sample of countries in the OECD and all developing regions for the four decades between 1960 and 2000 (Loayza, Fajnzylber, and Calderón, 2002). (The top panel presents simple averages across countries, while in the bottom panel the averages have been weighted by a country's GDP.) Specifically, we present the results of a Solow decomposition of output growth into the contributions of capital, labor, and productivity growth. Note that this is the simplest possible Solow decomposition: it does not control for changes in the "quality" of labor (for example, if the mean education level of the labor force rises), or changes in the "quality" of capital (for example, if new technologies

Benchmarking Latin America

We benchmark countries by running a linear OLS regression of the outcome in question (for example, the net secondary school enrollment rate, or the number of patents registered) on the log of per capita income. Countries that are significantly below the regression line are then taken to have a deficit or gap. More complicated formulations, which control for time or year effects affecting all countries, rely on more general functional forms and, when necessary, control for variables other than GDP, or use estimation methods other than OLS (for example, count-data techniques for regressions on patents), are also possible. Some results from these more complex approaches to benchmarking are presented in later chapters in the report.

The sample in the regressions in this chapter includes *all* of the countries in the world for which data are available. Regressions are generally weighted by population or GDP, as detailed in the notes at the foot of each figure. Unweighted OLS estimates provided similar benchmarks. In this chapter, Latin America is therefore benchmarked against the "weighted average" country in the world, although we will often stress the comparisons between Latin American countries and those in East Asia, especially the "tiger" economies (Hong Kong [China], Korea, Malaysia, and Singapore), and a group of countries that are abundant in natural resources (Australia, Canada, Finland, New Zealand, Norway, and Sweden).

are embodied in capital). All increases in skill, increases in technology, as well as any interaction effects between skill and technology on growth will therefore be captured by this measure of TFP.

Total Factor Productivity Growth in Latin America Has Been Low in the Last Two Decades

Table 2.1 shows that the last two decades have not been good for Latin America. Focusing on the GDP-weighted averages, Latin America had the highest rates of productivity growth of any developing region in the pre-1980 period and, in a fashion similar to Eastern Europe, the Middle East and North Africa, and Sub-Saharan Africa, very low or negative growth

rates of TFP in the post-1980 period. By contrast, TFP growth in the last two decades has been high in East Asia and South Asia. Table 2.2 presents the same information, by country. Table 2.2 clearly shows the differences between Latin America, East Asia, and the natural resource–abundant countries: in Latin America, only Chile had robust TFP growth rates in both the 1980s and 1990s, while Argentina, Bolivia, Costa Rica, and Uruguay had respectable growth rates of TFP in the 1990s. Korea and Singapore were good performers among the East Asian tigers, while Finland and Norway also did well.[1]

The Skill Gap

Latin America is falling behind in the global TFP leagues. What explains this? We first examine differences in skills. Since there is no perfect measure of skills, we consider three components. We start off with a discussion of the *stock* of educational attainment of the adult population in Latin America. We then consider the *flow* of skilled workers in the region, as given by current enrollment at various levels in the education system. Finally, we discuss the *quality* of the students "produced" at each level of education, as given by the performance of Latin American students and adults on international standardized tests.

Workers' Educational Attainment in Many Latin American Countries Is Low

Over the course of the last two decades, the mean years of education of the adult population aged 25 and older has gone up by 1.7 years in Latin America (from 4.1 to 5.8 years). But educational attainment in many Latin American countries is still very low. Figure 2.1 presents a scatter-plot of the mean years of schooling of the labor force aged 25 and older relative to per capita GDP, as well as the corresponding regression line. (Note that here, as throughout this chapter, the regression includes all of the countries in the world for which data are available—in this case 105 countries. We do not show all the country labels on the graph to make it more easily legible.) Figure 2.1 shows that many Latin American countries—especially Venezuela, Colombia, Costa Rica, Brazil, El Salvador, Honduras, Haiti, and Guatemala—have large education deficits. The comparison between Latin America and the more successful East Asian countries is revealing: Malaysia, Costa Rica, and Brazil all have approximately the same level of GDP per capita: despite this similarity, the mean years of education of Malaysian adults (7.9)

TABLE 2.1

TFP Growth Rates in Latin America Were Negative in the 1980s and Low in the 1990s

A: UNWEIGHTED AVERAGE

	ANNUAL GROWTH RATES OF TOTAL FACTOR PRODUCTIVITY			
	1960–69	1970–79	1980–89	1990–99
East Asia and Pacific	0.93	1.26	1.25	1.30
Eastern Europe	−0.17	−0.17	0.43	0.07
Latin America and the Caribbean	1.16	0.47	−1.60	0.47
Middle East and Northern Africa	1.12	0.84	−1.24	0.58
OECD	1.92	1.10	0.88	0.94
South Asia	0.71	−0.08	1.49	1.38
Sub-Saharan Africa	0.40	0.37	−0.79	−0.14
East Asian tigers	1.32	1.09	1.32	1.83
Natural resource–abundant countries	1.75	1.12	0.83	0.90

B: GDP-WEIGHTED AVERAGE

	ANNUAL GROWTH RATES OF TOTAL FACTOR PRODUCTIVITY			
	1960–69	1970–79	1980–89	1990–99
East Asia and Pacific	1.14	1.28	2.27	2.01
Eastern Europe	−0.17	−0.27	0.52	0.3
Latin America and the Caribbean	1.50	1.15	−0.93	0.45
Middle East and Northern Africa	1.14	−1.62	−1.12	0.85
OECD	2.09	0.85	1.10	0.56
South Asia	0.46	−0.39	2.27	1.72
Sub-Saharan Africa	1.54	−0.55	−0.88	−0.43
East Asian tigers	1.79	1.03	2.18	1.42
Natural resource–abundant countries	1.68	0.93	0.76	0.78

Source: Authors' calculations using data from Loayza, Fajnzylber, and Calderon (2002).

is almost two years higher than that of Costa Rican adults (6.0), and more than three years higher than that of Brazilian adults (4.6). All of the comparison natural resource–abundant countries outside Latin America are above the regression line, having education levels above those that would be predicted for their income levels. There are also Latin American high performers: Peru, Thailand, and Colombia have very similar income levels, but Peruvian adults have more than one more year of schooling than their Thai counterparts (7.3, compared to 6.1 years), and more than 2 years more schooling than Colombians (5.1). On average, however, Latin American adults have 1.4 years *fewer* years of education, while adults in the East Asian tiger countries have 1.0 *more* years of education, and those in the natural resource–abundant countries have 1.4 *more* years of schooling than would be expected for their income levels.[2] As we will discuss in chapter 4, these differences are a result of the patterns of much faster skill upgrading in East Asia and in some Scandinavian countries than in Latin America since 1960.

In Latin America, the Distribution of Education among Adults Appears to Be Less Equitable than That in the East Asian Tigers and the Natural Resource–Abundant Countries

The mean years of educational attainment of adults is only a summary statistic. Two countries with the same mean could have very different underlying distributions: in country A, a "medium" level of attainment could be the result of large numbers of adults with primary and tertiary education, and only a small fraction with secondary education, whereas in country B the same level of attainment could be the result of a very large number of adults with secondary education. Table 2.3 therefore presents estimates of the fraction of adults with no schooling, some primary schooling, some secondary schooling, and some university for countries in Latin America, the East Asian tigers, and the group of natural resource–abundant countries in 2000. The table clearly shows that the distribution of education among adults is very different in the three sets of countries: in 2000, Latin America had much higher fractions of adults with no schooling, or

TABLE 2.2

In the 1980s and 1990s, Growth Rates of TFP Were High in Chile and Low in Most Other Latin American Countries

	ANNUAL GROWTH RATES OF TFP			
	1960–69	1970–79	1980–89	1990–99
Latin America	1.50	1.15	-0.93	0.45
Argentina	1.37	0.21	−1.75	2.81
Bolivia	−0.25	0.23	−1.63	1.88
Brazil	1.69	2.15	−0.21	−0.42
Chile	1.31	0.31	2.29	2.22
Colombia	1.66	1.76	−0.06	−0.39
Costa Rica	0.73	0.29	−1.13	1.80
Dominican Republic	0.74	0.92	−0.39	1.66
Ecuador	0.38	3.59	−1.03	−0.87
El Salvador	1.05	−0.82	−3.92	1.05
Guatemala	1.55	1.56	−1.39	0.70
Guyana	0.89	−0.65	−3.85	−3.91
Haiti	−0.97	−0.29	−2.54	−1.99
Honduras	0.89	1.46	−0.91	−1.24
Jamaica	2.06	−1.46	0.22	−2.10
Mexico	1.66	1.13	−1.60	0.31
Nicaragua	1.66	−3.53	−3.53	0.22
Panama	2.32	−0.71	−2.18	1.12
Paraguay	0.78	1.86	−1.27	−1.46
Peru	1.35	0.34	−2.45	0.83
Trinidad and Tobago	2.86	1.75	−2.26	−0.25
Uruguay	0.66	1.71	−0.06	2.02
Venezuela, R.B. de	1.50	−1.30	−2.79	−0.00
East Asian tigers	1.79	1.03	2.18	1.42
Hong Kong (China)				
Korea	2.03	0.96	2.53	1.30
Malaysia	0.79	1.46	0.42	0.98
Singapore	1.82	0.89	2.01	2.62
Natural resource–abundant countries	1.68	0.93	0.77	0.78
Australia	1.67	0.30	0.96	1.31
Canada	1.45	0.98	0.32	0.15
Finland	1.70	1.44	2.08	1.15
New Zealand			−0.34	0.70
Norway	2.24	2.10	0.96	2.09
Sweden	1.65	0.79	0.90	0.58

Note: Calculations based on annual data, so that figures for each country are GDP-weighted decade averages.
Source: Authors' calculations using data from Loayza, Fajnzylber, and Calderon (2002).

only some primary schooling compared to the tigers or natural resource–abundant countries. There are also differences in the distribution of educational attainment for countries with the same mean years of schooling. Malaysia and Panama both have 7.9 mean years of schooling, but in Malaysia 43.0 percent of the population has some secondary schooling only, and only 7.5 percent has some tertiary education, whereas in Panama 28.5 percent of the population has some secondary schooling only, and 19.8 percent has some university. In Venezuela, the fraction of adults with some university education is not much lower than that in the Scandinavian countries, even though the mean years of schooling of a

Venezuelan adult is only one-half that of a Scandinavian adult. To a large extent, these differences are a result of the highly inequitable distribution of educational attainment in some Latin American countries.

Some Latin American Countries Appear to Be Undergoing "Unbalanced" Educational Transitions

In chapter 4 we show that the bulk of skill upgrading between 1960 and 2000 in Latin America took place at the tertiary level, while the bulk of skill upgrading in East Asia took place at the secondary level. (The picture for the natural resource–abundant countries is more mixed, as many of

FIGURE 2.1

Most Latin American Countries Have Low Levels of Educational Attainment of Their Adult Population

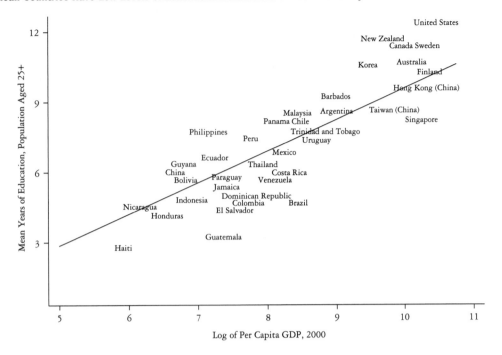

Note: The line corresponds to the predicted years of schooling from a weighted regression on log per capita GDP and a constant, with the weights given by the population aged 25 and older in a country. The sample size for the regression is 105 countries. Some country names have been omitted to make the figure more legible.

Source: Authors' calculations using data from Barro and Lee (2002).

them were already further in their education transition in 1960.) As a result, some Latin American countries—especially Costa Rica, the Dominican Republic, El Salvador, and Venezuela—seem to be following "unbalanced" educational transitions: although most adults in these countries still have primary education or less, so much upgrading took place at the tertiary level, and so little at the secondary level, that by 2000 there were fewer adults with only secondary school education than adults with tertiary education.[3] As we will discuss in detail in chapter 4, unbalanced educational transitions are likely to have negative consequences in terms of the long-term sustainability of educational transition, inequality, and the ability to upgrade technologies.

The educational attainment of the population in a country is the result of the accumulated flow of investments in schooling in earlier decades. Present enrollments determine how stocks will evolve in the future. New cohorts will be most of the labor force in the next decades. We now turn to a discussion of contemporaneous investments in education by looking at the enrollment rates in primary school, secondary school, and tertiary institutions.

Most Latin American Countries Do Not Have a Gap in Net Enrollment in Primary School

Primary school is the necessary building block for all educational upgrading. Benchmarking Latin America in terms of net primary enrollment rates suggests that the region as a whole does not "underperform" on this dimension.[4] (The net enrollment level is given by the fraction of children of primary school age who are enrolled in primary school.) Still, there are countries such as some of the poorer countries in Central America, and regions within other countries, such as parts of the south in Mexico and the Northeast in Brazil, where primary enrollment rates are still low, and should continue to be a focus for government policy.

Most Latin American Countries Have Massive Deficits in Net Enrollment in Secondary School...

Although the Latin American picture regarding net primary enrollment rates is encouraging, the same cannot be said about net secondary enrollment rates. Overall, the region has a *massive* deficit in secondary enrollment. Figure 2.2

TABLE 2.3

Compared to East Asia and the Natural Resource–Abundant Countries, Latin America
Has Low Levels and an Unequal Distribution of Educational Attainment among the Adult Population

		FRACTION OF THE ADULT POPULATION			
	YEARS OF SCHOOLING	NO SCHOOL	SOME PRIMARY	SOME SECONDARY	SOME TERTIARY
Latin America	5.8	17.9	50.1	20.3	11.8
Argentina	8.5	5.8	49.6	24.9	19.7
Bolivia	5.5	1.4	39.8	46.9	11.9
Brazil	4.6	21.3	56.8	13.5	8.4
Chile	7.9	5.3	42.9	36.0	15.8
Colombia	5.0	19.8	48.9	21.4	9.9
Costa Rica	6.0	9.4	60.7	11.3	18.6
Cuba	7.8	5.8	40.3	42.6	11.3
Dominican Republic	5.2	25.6	46.8	13.1	14.5
Ecuador	6.5	17.8	45.2	18.3	18.7
El Salvador	4.5	35.0	45.6	8.8	10.6
Guatemala	3.1	47.1	37.6	9.5	5.8
Haiti	2.7	54.4	32.3	12.3	1.0
Honduras	4.1	25.9	57.0	10.6	6.5
Jamaica	5.2	3.4	54.5	38.0	4.1
Mexico	6.7	12.4	47.3	29.0	11.3
Nicaragua	4.4	31.6	43.0	16.5	8.9
Panama	7.9	11.3	40.4	28.5	19.8
Paraguay	5.7	9.8	63.8	18.1	8.3
Peru	7.3	13.8	35.7	28.1	22.4
Trinidad and Tobago	7.6	5.1	46.3	44.1	4.5
Uruguay	7.3	3.2	52.2	32.1	12.5
Venezuela	5.6	15.7	56.6	9.7	18.0
East Asian tigers	9.7	10.2	23.5	47.4	18.9
Hong Kong (China)	9.5	10.7	26.6	47.4	15.3
Korea	10.5	8.0	16.7	49.5	25.8
Malaysia	7.9	13.9	35.6	43.0	7.5
Singapore	8.1	12.6	28.3	48.5	10.6
Natural resource–abundant countries	11.1	1.7	21.1	38.6	38.7
Australia	10.6	2.2	24.4	43.6	29.8
Canada	11.4	1.7	18.6	26.6	53.0
Finland	10.1	0.4	29.2	47.3	23.2
New Zealand	11.5	0.0	32.2	26.3	41.6
Norway	11.9	1.2	11.5	62.5	24.8
Sweden	11.4	2.0	17.7	57.2	23.1

Note: Regional averages are weighted by the population aged 25 or older in a country.
Source: Authors' calculations based on data from Barro and Lee (2002).

presents a scatter-plot of the net enrollment rate in secondary school. The figure clearly shows that many Latin American countries are well below the regression line. In table 2.4, we tabulate the secondary enrollment deficit, defined as the difference between the observed secondary enrollment rate and its predicted value, for the sample of countries. The table shows that Latin America has a deficit of almost 19 percentage points in secondary enrollment. By contrast, the East Asian tigers have a surplus of almost 18 percentage points, and the natural resource–abundant countries have a surplus of 6 percentage points. Within Latin America, the biggest deficits are those of Brazil (36 points), Venezuela (42 points), and Costa Rica (24 points). By comparison, many of the countries in the English-speaking Caribbean, including Barbados, Guyana, Jamaica, and Trinidad and Tobago, have net secondary enrollment rates that are substantially higher than expected for their income levels.

FIGURE 2.2

Many Countries in Latin America Have *Massive* Deficits in Secondary Enrollment

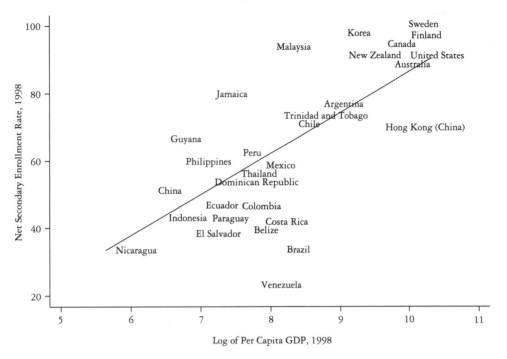

Note: Secondary enrollment data for Korea and Nicaragua are for 1997; for Venezuela are for 1996; for Colombia, Guyana, Hong Kong (China) and the Philippines are for 1995; and for Indonesia are for 1994. All other data are for 1998. The net secondary enrollment for Brazil has been calculated from the PNAD household surveys. Net enrollment rates for all other countries are from UNESCO. Countries with net secondary enrollment ratios above 100 were not included in the regression. The line corresponds to the predicted net secondary enrollment rate from a weighted regression on log per capita GDP and a constant, with the weights given by the population in a country. The sample size for the regression is 116 countries. Some country names have been omitted to make the figure more legible.

Source: Authors' calculations, based on data from UNESCO.

... Reflecting, in Part, Problems in the Primary School System

Because net secondary enrollment rates are a measure of the fraction of children of secondary-school age who are in secondary school, countries with high rates of repetition or late entry into *primary* school will generally tend to have low net enrollment rates in *secondary* school. A comparison of the net enrollment rates with the *gross* secondary enrollment rate, given by the fraction of children of secondary-school age who are enrolled in school, regardless of the school *level* they attend, can shed some light on this. In a population-weighted regression of the gross enrollment rate on the log of per capita GDP and a dummy variable for Latin America, the coefficient on this dummy is negative but insignificant. (The coefficient is −4.8, with a standard error of 4.2). This suggests that some of the observed problems of coverage in

secondary school in Latin America are a reflection of inadequate progression earlier on. As we discuss in chapter 4, Latin American countries have problems with *both* progression within primary school and continuation of primary school graduates on to secondary school.

Large Deficits in Tertiary Enrollment

In addition to the deficit in secondary enrollment, many Latin American countries also have relatively low enrollment rates at the tertiary level. Figure 2.3 presents a scatter-plot of the gross enrollment rate at tertiary institutions for countries in Latin America, East Asia, and the group of natural resource–abundant countries. As a whole, the Latin American deficit at the tertiary level is about 10 percentage points. Table 2.4 shows that Belize, Brazil, and Trinidad and Tobago all have particularly large deficits in the region, while

TABLE 2.4

Many Countries in Latin America Have Massive Secondary Enrollment Deficits, and Some Have Smaller Tertiary Enrollment Deficits

	SECONDARY NET ENROLLMENT DEFICIT	TERTIARY GROSS ENROLLMENT DEFICIT
Latin America	**−18.7**	**−10.0**
Argentina	−1.2	6.0
Belize	−22.8	−27.4
Bolivia		9.5
Brazil	−36.3	−20.9
Chile	1.2	−1.7
Colombia	−14.1	−6.5
Costa Rica	−23.9	0.0
Cuba		
Dominican Republic	−3.6	0.1
Ecuador	−8.4	−3.4
El Salvador	−18.1	−4.0
Guatemala		−12.5
Guyana	17.6	−3.6
Haiti		−2.8
Honduras		1.0
Jamaica	22.8	−13.9
Mexico	−8.4	−12.6
Nicaragua	−6.3	5.8
Panama		3.5
Paraguay	−13.9	−12.5
Peru	2.2	3.0
Trinidad and Tobago	4.7	−28.1
Uruguay	−6.0	−3.1
Venezuela	−42.2	−2.5
East Asian tigers	**17.8**	**5.1**
Hong Kong (China)	−17.4	−24.9
Korea	19.3	24.1
Malaysia	26.2	−21.9
Singapore		−9.9
Natural resource– abundant countries	**6.0**	**14.0**
Australia	1.9	27.1
Canada	7.8	6.6
Finland	4.9	27.7
New Zealand	7.3	13.6
Norway	9.7	7.2
Sweden	−0.1	21.0

Note: Regional averages are population-weighted.
Source: Authors' calculations based on data from UNESCO.

Argentina and Bolivia have high tertiary enrollment rates for their income level. Also noteworthy is the fact that the countries in the English-speaking Caribbean, which generally did well in terms of enrollments in secondary school, often have large tertiary enrollment gaps. By comparison, both the East Asian tigers and the natural resource–abundant countries have surpluses in tertiary enrollment.

Latin American Students and Adults Perform Poorly on International Tests

How well youth in Latin American countries are prepared to participate productively in the economy depends on both the number of years they stay in school and how much they learn in each year of school. Most Latin American countries do not participate regularly in international tests, but there are some exceptions: eighth-grade students in Colombia participated in the 1995 Third International Math and Science Study (TIMSS) test, and eighth-grade students in Chile participated in the 1998 TIMSS. Fifteen-year-olds in Brazil and Mexico participated in the OECD's PISA international tests. Chilean adults also participated in OECD tests of adult literacy. Finally, a large number of countries in Latin America participated in the OREAL (OREAL 2001) tests of third- and fourth-graders in primary school. However, because the OREAL tests were not administered to countries outside the region, they cannot be used to compare the performance of Latin American students with that of their counterparts in East Asia or elsewhere.

The sum of the evidence on the performance of Latin American students on international tests suggests that, in addition to the gap in terms of the *quantity* of education, both measured as the stock of educated adults and the flow of students from various schooling levels, Latin America has a serious *quality* deficit. Figure 2.4 shows that both Colombia and Chile were among the worst performers on the TIMSS, performing substantially worse than countries of similar income levels, and at about the same level as much poorer countries: the mean math score in Chile was almost 140 points below the score of Hungary, and below the score of Indonesia, a substantially poorer country. The mean math score in Colombia was also about 140 points below that of Thailand, and well below that of Iran, a country with lower per capita income. Brazil and Mexico were the two worst performers in the PISA test of 15-year-olds, well below similar-income countries such as Poland and Latvia, and well below their predicted performance from a regression of scores on spending on education per student.[5] Figure 2.5, finally, shows that Chile, the only participating country in Latin America in tests of adult literacy, had the lowest quantitative scores, well below those of Eastern European countries of similar income levels.[6] For any given level of education, Chilean adults appear to have learned less than their counterparts in Poland, Slovenia, Portugal, Ireland, the Czech Republic, and a number of OECD countries.

FIGURE 2.3

Some Countries Also Have Large Deficits in Tertiary Enrollment, although These Are Generally Smaller

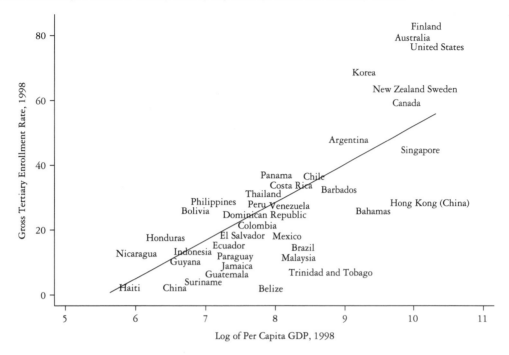

Note: Tertiary enrollment data for Barbados, Belize, Bolivia, Colombia, Costa Rica, the Dominican Republic, Ecuador, Guatemala, Guyana, Haiti, Hong Kong (China), Indonesia, Korea, Malaysia, Nicaragua, Panama, Paraguay, Singapore, and Venezuela are for 1997. The line corresponds to the predicted gross tertiary enrollment rate from a weighted regression on log per capita GDP and a constant, with the weights given by the population in a country. The sample size for the regression is 161 countries. Some country names have been omitted to make the figure more legible.

Source: Authors' calculations, based on data from UNESCO.

Most Latin American Countries Do Not Have a Low Stock or Flow of Scientists and Engineers for Their Income Level

As we discuss in chapters 6 and 7, the number of scientists and engineers is an important input into the production of domestic R&D and is therefore of interest in its own right. In figure 2.6, we present a scatter-plot of the number of scientists and engineers per 10,000 workers as a function of per capita GDP. The figure suggests that some Latin American countries, particularly El Salvador, Colombia, and Venezuela, have relatively few scientists and engineers for their income levels. Others, including Bolivia, Peru, and Costa Rica, have a relative abundance of scientists and engineers.

Latin American countries generally do not appear to have too small a *stock* of scientists and engineers for their income levels.[7] Figure 2.7 shows that enrollment levels in science and engineering as a function of gross tertiary enrollment levels are not low for the "average" Latin American country either.[8] The figure shows that there is no clear relationship between overall enrollment levels and enrollment in sciences and engineering. Latin American countries are scattered widely: Chile and Costa Rica both have high tertiary enrollment rates, but the fraction of students in science and engineering is much higher in Chile. A similar comparison can be made for El Salvador and Colombia, both of which have middle-level enrollment rates, with El Salvador having a much higher fraction of students in science and engineering.

In sum, Latin America has a profound skill gap in relation to many of its competitors in East Asia, and in comparison with the many other countries with abundant natural resources. In most countries, the mean years of education of the adult population is low. The enrollment gap in the region is particularly severe at the secondary school level, although some countries also appear to have a gap at the tertiary level. On the positive side, there does not appear to be a problem with the composition of university graduates: as a whole, the

FIGURE 2.4

Colombian and Chilean Secondary School Students Perform Badly on International Tests

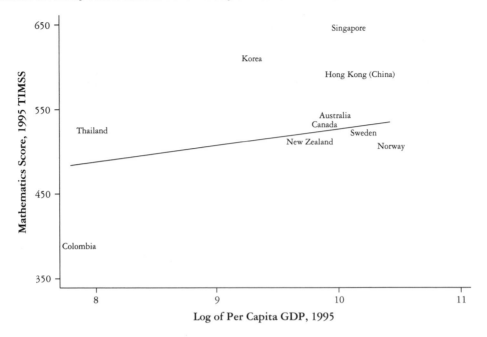

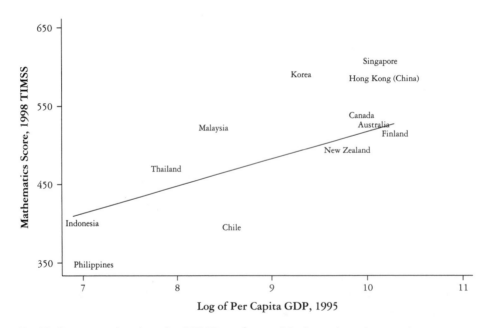

Note: The line corresponds to the predicted TIMSS score from a weighted regression on log per capita GDP and a constant, with the weights given by population. The sample size is 39 for the 1995 TIMSS, and 37 for the 1998 TIMSS. Some country names have been omitted to make the figure more legible.

Source: Authors' calculations, based on TIMSS data.

region does not have a deficit in the stock or flow of scientists and engineers. Finally, the gap in terms of the quantity of education is further aggravated by the poor quality of education, as made apparent by the low performance of Latin American students on international tests.

The Technology Gap

We next turn to a discussion of the extent to which countries in Latin America appear to have a technology gap. We first present evidence of the degree to which Latin American countries are exposed to foreign imports, especially imports

FIGURE 2.5

Chilean Adults Also Do Badly on International Tests of Literacy

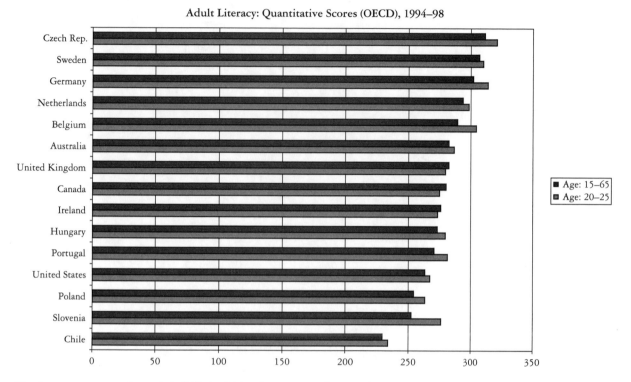

Adult Literacy: Quantitative Scores (OECD), 1994–98

Note: Scores are an average of scores for individuals with less than upper secondary, complete upper secondary, and complete tertiary. These three scores were equally weighted when constructing the average score in order to abstract from differences in labor force composition across countries.

Source: Author's calculations, based on data from OECD (2000).

of capital goods, make payments to license foreign technologies, and receive foreign direct investment (FDI). We also pay special attention to imports of computer equipment, as these are likely to be particularly intensive in high technology. This first part of the analysis therefore summarizes the degree to which countries in Latin America are likely to have access to foreign technologies from the "leader" countries. In the second part of this section we focus on domestic spending on R&D by the public and private sectors, which is necessary for the absorption and adaptation of foreign technologies, as well as for the creation of new technologies. Finally, we consider the number of patents registered by Latin American inventors in their own countries and the United States.

Latin American Countries Receive Fewer Imports than East Asian Countries, and Fewer Imports of Capital Goods

Imports of goods from countries that are more advanced technologically have the potential to be an important source of

new technology for developing countries. Table 2.5 shows that countries in Latin America generally have low import penetration: the GDP-weighted mean import penetration is more than four times as high in the East Asian tiger countries as in Latin America, and almost twice as high for the group of natural resource–abundant countries. Import penetration is particularly low in two of the largest Latin American economies—Argentina and Brazil. Larger economies generally have lower rates of import penetration, and it is conceivable that Latin America's lower import penetration is driven by the relatively large size of some economies. In practice, however, this does not explain the deficit in import penetration in Latin American countries.[9] Also, the fraction of imports that comes in the form of capital goods is much lower in Latin America than in the East Asian tigers or the natural resource–abundant countries. Much new technology is "embodied" in imports of capital goods, so this shortfall may be particularly damaging to Latin America in terms of technology transfer.

FIGURE 2.6

Some Latin American Countries Appear to Have Low Numbers of Scientists and Engineers for Their Income Levels, but Others Do Not

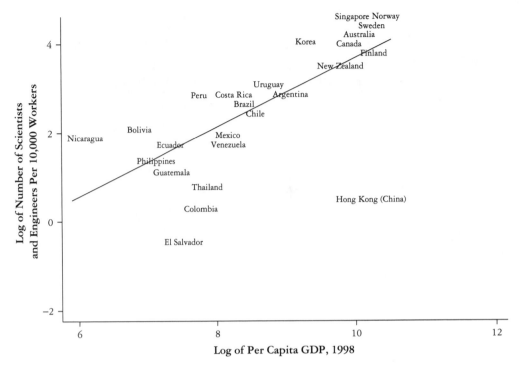

Note: The line corresponds to the predicted number of scientists and engineers from a weighted regression on per capita GDP and a constant, with the weights given by the population aged 25 and older in a country. The sample size for the regression is 110 countries. Some country names have been omitted to make the figure more legible.

Source: Authors' calculations, based on data from Park (2002) for the number of scientists and engineers, and World Bank databases for per capita GDP levels.

There is a Great Deal of Variation in FDI Penetration Within Latin America

Table 2.5 shows that the levels of FDI in a number of Latin American countries are comparable to those in the East Asian tiger or natural resource–abundant economies elsewhere. However, there is a great deal of variation. In Latin America, Bolivia, Chile, and Nicaragua all attract a great deal of FDI relative to the size of their economies, while FDI penetration is low in Colombia, Peru, and Uruguay. Within East Asia, FDI penetration is very high in Singapore and Malaysia, but negligible in Korea, which has actively pursued high-technology imports and technology licensing but has not similarly encouraged FDI. By contrast, Singapore has relied a great deal on FDI as the source of its technological miracle. Foreign direct investment is also high in Finland and Sweden. One thing that is not clear from the FDI penetration statistics in table 2.5 is whether the *composition* of FDI varies across the three sets of countries, or

across countries within Latin America. This is potentially an important consideration, as different forms of FDI may contribute more or less to technological upgrading in the host economy.

Latin American Countries Also Spend Relatively Little on the Licensing of Foreign Technologies

Licensing involves the contractual transfer of knowledge between firms. Given that licensing provides knowledge in a more accessible manner than FDI, many countries such as Brazil, India, Mexico, and Japan have in the past actively discriminated against direct investment by firms and favored technology licensing. In practice, as table 2.5 shows, there is considerable variation in the amounts that countries spend on technology licensing. Worryingly, table 2.5 shows that by this measure of technology transfer Latin America is also far behind many of its potential economic competitors.

FIGURE 2.7

Most Countries in the Region Do *Not* Appear to Have an Important Deficit in the Fraction of University Students Enrolled in Science and Engineering

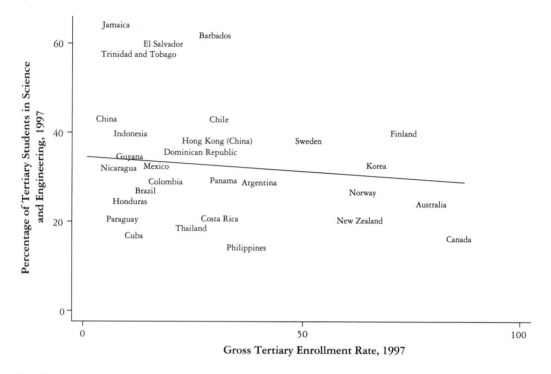

Note: Tertiary enrollment data for Barbados, Belize, Bolivia, Colombia, Costa Rica, Dominican Republic, Ecuador, Guatemala, Guyana, Haiti, Hong Kong (China), Indonesia, Korea, Malaysia, Nicaragua, Panama, Paraguay, Singapore, and Venezuela are for 1997; science and engineering data for Barbados, Indonesia, Jamaica; Nicaragua, Philippines and Trinidad and Tobago are for 1996; for Argentina, Brazil, China, Honduras, and Panama are for 1995; and for Hong Kong (China) is for 1994. The line corresponds to the predicted percentage of students in science and engineering from a weighted regression on the gross tertiary enrollment rate and a constant, with the weights given by the population in a country. The sample size for the regression is 117 countries. Some country names have been omitted to make the figure more legible.

Source: Authors' calculations, based on data from UNESCO.

In the Late 1980s, East Asia Opened Up an Important Lead in Computer Penetration over Latin America...

Imports of computer equipment are a clear sign of transfer of advanced technologies. In recent work, Caselli and Coleman (2001) explore cross-country differences in the adoption of computer technology. Figure 2.8 uses these data to calculate population-weighted means of the country-specific values of computer imports (in 1995 U.S. dollars) for a large sample of Latin American and East Asian countries. The main message of figure 2.8 is abundantly clear: until 1980, Latin America had an edge over East Asia in computer penetration. By 1990, however, this situation had been reversed, so that the population-weighted mean computer penetration in East Asia was about three times that found in Latin America.

...Which Did Not Shrink in the 1990s

The data used by Caselli and Coleman end in 1990. To investigate whether the digital divide between East Asia and Latin America shrank in the 1990s we turn to data on the number of personal computers per 1,000 population for the 1988–99 period. These data, which are only available for a handful of countries in Latin America, confirm that some countries in East Asia—particularly Korea, Hong Kong (China), and Singapore—already had a serious lead on Latin American countries in the sample in 1988: the number of computers per 1,000 population was roughly 10 times as high in Singapore as in Mexico, Argentina, or Chile, and 15 times as high in Hong Kong as in Brazil. By 1999, this number was 10 to 20 times as high as at the beginning of the period in virtually every country in the sample. However, there is no consistent evidence of digital convergence between

TABLE 2.5

Countries in Latin America Have Low Import Penetration, Low Penetration of Capital Goods, and Low Levels of Royalty Payments

| | PERCENTAGE OF GDP | | | |
	IMPORTS GOODS AND SERVICES	CAPITAL GOODS IMPORTS	NET FDI	ROYALTY PAYMENTS
Latin America	19.10	7.69	3.33	0.15
Argentina	11.42	4.16	2.72	0.16
Belize	63.78	14.45	1.86	
Bolivia	25.09	9.88	10.81	0.06
Brazil	12.13	4.18	4.39	0.17
Chile	30.79	7.45	2.46	0.07
Colombia	20.42	4.31	1.62	0.07
Costa Rica	46.08	11.74	3.56	
Dominican Republic	39.33		5.65	0.19
Ecuador	30.80	4.58	4.28	0.40
El Salvador	42.71	6.90	3.75	0.19
Guatemala	27.88	8.74	1.84	
Honduras	56.37	15.35	3.44	0.22
Jamaica	55.05	8.84	4.21	0.94
Mexico	33.23	14.75	2.52	0.16
Nicaragua	81.17	18.79	7.53	
Panama	38.93	13.14	7.43	0.33
Paraguay	35.37	8.86	2.00	0.04
Peru	17.86	4.59	2.72	0.10
Uruguay	20.71	4.97	0.93	0.05
Venezuela	17.03	6.64	3.39	0.00
East Asian tigers	83.77	29.51	2.95	0.47
Hong Kong (China)	145.26	41.60	−20.40	
Korea	42.20	10.75	0.74	0.47
Malaysia	104.36	49.95	4.94	0.47
Singapore	161.45	78.29	6.93	
Natural resource–abundant countries	34.09	12.59	5.07	0.37
Australia	22.31	7.44	1.99	0.29
Canada	40.78	17.95	5.62	0.43
Finland	29.27	10.50	6.81	0.31
New Zealand	32.75	11.14	3.75	0.64
Norway	32.83	9.34	3.91	0.18
Sweden	37.83	10.67	8.91	0.50

Note: Data on imports and capital goods imports are from 1999; data on royalties are for 2000; data on FDI are the mean for the 1998–2000 period. The East Asian tiger average for FDI does not include Hong Kong (China) because of the high volume of FDI investments flowing from Hong Kong to mainland China in the late 1990s. Regional averages are weighted by GDP in the corresponding year.
Source: World Bank and UNESCO databases.

the East Asian and Latin American countries in the sample. Chile narrowed the gap with Singapore somewhat, but Malaysia did so even more rapidly. In 1999 there were about six times as many computers per person in Hong Kong as in Mexico and Argentina—just as in 1988. And the growth in computer penetration was particularly impressive in China (albeit starting from a very low base). The two panels in figure 2.9 clearly show that the digital divide between East Asia and Latin America did not narrow significantly in the 1990s.

The gap in information and communications technology (ICT) between Latin America and East Asia is also apparent in other measures. Figure 2.10 presents a "summary" measure of ICT, which is a composite of the number of computers, Internet hosts, main telephone lines, and cell phones, all normalized by the population of a country.[10] The figure shows that the high performers in East Asia—Singapore, Malaysia, Korea—are well ahead of countries in Latin America. Within Latin America, countries can be grouped into those with reasonably "high" levels of ICT infrastructure (Chile, Argentina,

FIGURE 2.8

In the 1980s East Asia Opened Up a Big Lead over Latin America in the Degree of Computer Penetration

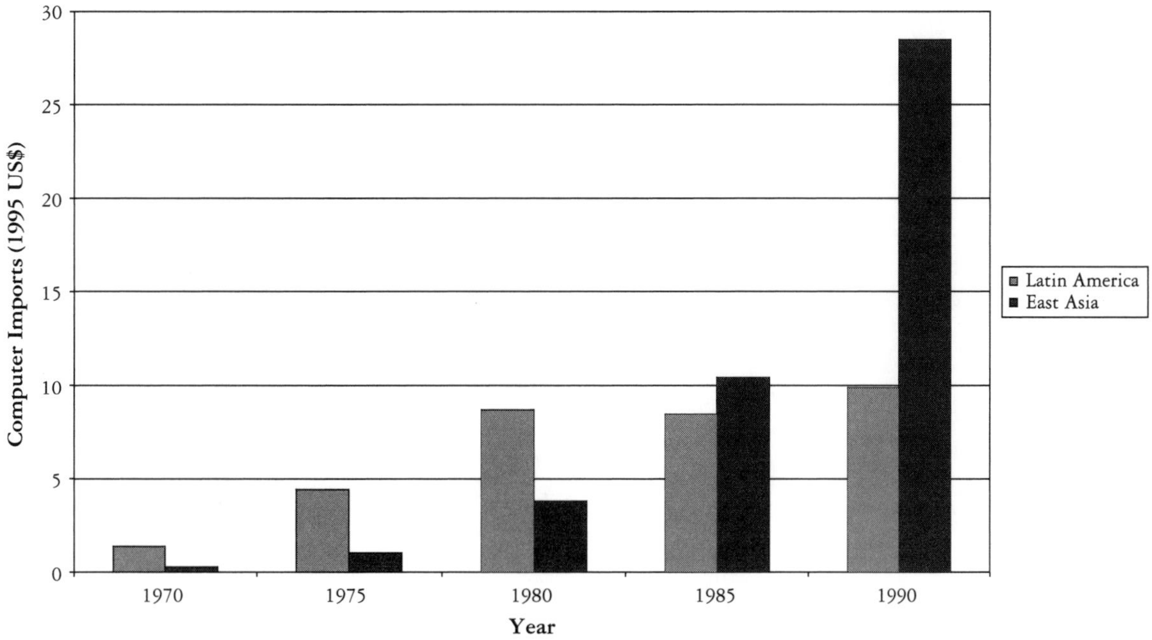

Note: Regional averages are population-weighted, and are in 1995 US$. The Latin American sample includes Argentina, Barbados, Bolivia, Brazil, Chile, Colombia, Costa Rica, the Dominican Republic, Ecuador, El Salvador, Guatemala, Guyana, Haiti, Honduras, Jamaica, Mexico, Nicaragua, Panama, Paraguay, Peru, Trinidad and Tobago, Uruguay, and Venezuela; the East Asian sample includes Fiji, Hong Kong (China), Indonesia, Malaysia, Papua New Guinea, Philippines, South Korea, Singapore, and Thailand.

Source: Authors' calculations, based on data from Caselli and Coleman (2001).

Costa Rica, Colombia, Venezuela, Brazil, and Mexico), those with "medium" levels (Peru, Trinidad and Tobago, Uruguay, and Ecuador), and those with relatively "low" levels (mostly countries in Central America, as well as Bolivia and Paraguay).

Domestic technology is a complement to access to foreign technology—especially (but not only) for countries that are relatively close to the global technology frontier. But as we discuss in chapters 6 and 7, even countries that rely mainly on technology developed abroad need some domestic R&D to adapt imported technologies. We next turn to a discussion of two measures of domestic technology: R&D expenditures and patent applications.

Workers in Latin America Have Access to Less Domestic R&D Capital Stock than Those in Korea or Singapore, or in the Natural Resource–Abundant Countries

R&D expenditures are a measure of the domestic "effort" the public and private sectors are making to close the

technology gap. Table 2.6 shows that Latin American workers have less R&D capital available than those in Korea and Singapore, as well as those in natural resource–abundant countries. Within Latin America, Brazil, Chile, and Peru all have relatively high ratios of R&D to GDP (although these are still considerably below those in Korea and Singapore, as well as the Scandinavian countries).

The amount of R&D capital per worker rises with per capita income, and it is therefore important to benchmark R&D expenditures. Figure 2.11 graphs the log of R&D expenditures per worker as a function of the log of per capita GDP for a sample of Latin American, East Asian, and natural resource–abundant countries. The figure shows a worrying picture for Latin America: all of the countries in the region except Brazil are below the regression line. By contrast, all of the East Asian tigers and the natural resource–abundant countries are on or above the line.

FIGURE 2.9

The Digital Divide between East Asia and Latin America Did Not Shrink in the 1990s

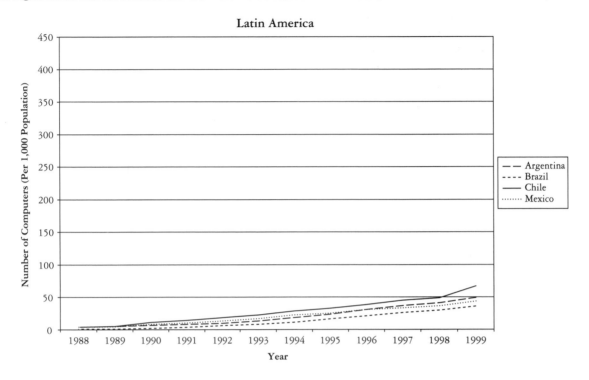

Latin America

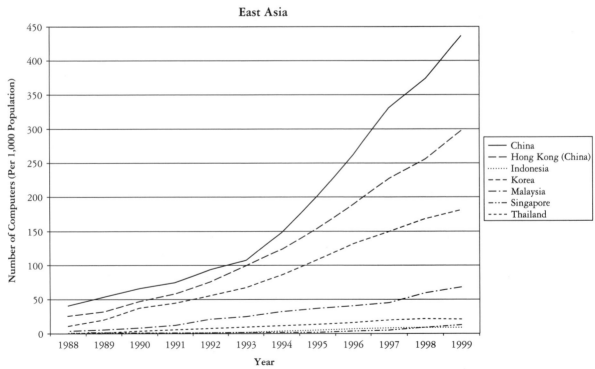

East Asia

Source: Authors' calculations based on data from the International Telecommunications Union.

FIGURE 2.10

Latin America Also Lags behind East Asia in Other Measures of ICT Infrastructure

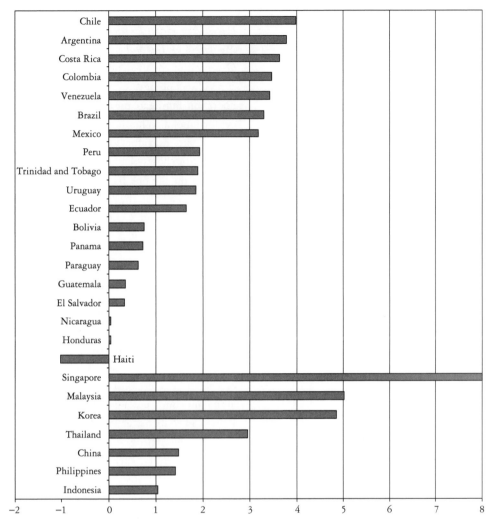

Source: Lederman and Xu (2001).

The Number of Patents Registered by Residents of Most Latin American Countries Is Low

R&D expenditures are geared toward innovation, and the number of patents registered by the residents of a country provides some measure of the "success" of these expenditures. Patent registrations are therefore a critical measure of domestic inventive activity in a country.[11] In chapters 6 and 7 we show that patent stock capital, a measure of the depreciated number of inventions available in an economy at any given point in time, has a positive effect on TFP. Table 2.7 presents summary statistics on the number of patents registered per million inhabitants in a sample of Latin American, East Asian, and natural resource–abundant countries. The table presents two sets of statistics: the number of patents registered by residents of a country in their own country, as well as the number of patents registered by residents of this country in the United States (both per million inhabitants). The advantage of the measure of patents registered in the United States is that it abstracts from differences in the stringency of examination and granting rates of patents across countries. In so doing, it arguably provides a measure of innovative activity of patents of similar "quality" (within a given technology field) across countries. The shortcoming of this measure is that it also reflects, in part, the expected likelihood that inventors of a given country will sell their product in the U.S. market, and may therefore be contaminated by trade

TABLE 2.6

Latin American Workers Have Small Amounts of R&D Expenditures

	TOTAL R&D PER WORKER	R&D (PERCENTAGE OF GDP)
Latin America	35.6	0.5
Argentina	54.5	0.4
Bolivia	5.1	0.3
Brazil	58.0	0.6
Chile	44.2	0.7
Colombia	10.0	0.2
Costa Rica	15.6	0.3
Ecuador	2.2	0.1
El Salvador	15.8	0.3
Guatemala		0.2
Mexico	20.7	0.4
Nicaragua	1.1	0.1
Panama	18.2	0.4
Peru	2.3	0.6
Uruguay	31.1	0.1
Venezuela	18.7	0.5
East Asian tigers	329.6	2.2
Hong Kong (China)		0.3
Korea	434.0	2.8
Malaysia	22.8	0.2
Singapore	628.2	1.1
Natural resource–abundant countries	725.4	1.9
Australia	521.6	1.7
Canada	507.4	1.6
Finland	1300.9	2.5
New Zealand	291.2	1.1
Norway	956.8	1.8
Sweden	1709.7	3.4

Note: Regional averages of private and public R&D are weighted by the number of workers in a country; R&D as a fraction of GDP is weighted by GDP size.
Source: R&D data from Park (2002) and Lederman and Saenz (2002).

and other flows across countries.[12] Moreover, the relatively high cost may further discourage inventors from poor countries from registering a patent in the United States.

Table 2.7 shows that patent registrations in Latin American countries are low by comparison with those of the East Asian tiger and natural resource–abundant countries. The four countries with the highest rates of patent activity in Latin America—Argentina, Chile, Costa Rica, and Venezuela—all have registrations in the United States that are very far below those of Singapore, Korea, and Hong Kong (China), as well as in relation to countries such as Finland and Sweden. Are the levels of patent registration in Latin American countries low for their level of GDP per capita? Figure 2.12 suggests that this is indeed the case: most Latin American countries, including Argentina, Brazil, Mexico, and Chile,

have patent registration rates that are lower than expected for their levels of per capita income.

Latin American Countries Do Poorly by Aggregate Measures of Technology

Given all of the evidence on the deficit in individual measures of technology, it is no surprise that Latin America does poorly on aggregate measures as well. Figure 2.13 shows the evolution of a technology index constructed on the basis of 19 standard indicators for Latin America and other regions.[13] The figure shows that the technology gap between Latin America on the one hand, and the OECD and East Asian tiger economies on the other more than tripled in the 1990s. Even Eastern and Central Europe did better than Latin America, a fact that can be seen more clearly in the lower panel, which graphs the same measures without the OECD and East Asian tigers.

In sum, compared to East Asia, Latin American countries appear to have less access to technologies from abroad: import penetration is lower, the fraction of imports that are capital goods is also lower, licensing payments are smaller, and computer penetration and ICT infrastructure is below that of the more successful East Asian and natural resource–abundant countries. Taken together, this suggests that Latin American countries are receiving less technology transferred from "leaders" close to the global technology frontier than their competitors. Latin American countries also have low levels of domestic R&D and they register few patents—even controlling for their income levels. In practice, this means that a worker in Finland, Sweden, Korea, or Singapore will be operating with more advanced technologies, both domestic and foreign, than his or her counterpart in Brazil, Argentina, or Mexico.

Conclusion: Benchmarking Latin American Performance

Latin America has profound deficits in productivity, skills, and technology. Table 2.8 summarizes some of the most salient gaps we have discussed in this chapter. The table presents the mean level of a given outcome in Latin America, and the gap in this outcome—where the gap is defined as the difference between the observed value in the region and the expected value for its income level. For comparison, we also present similar statistics for the East Asian tiger economies (Korea, Hong Kong [China], Malaysia, and Singapore) and the natural resource–abundant countries

FIGURE 2.11

Latin American Countries Also Have Low Levels of R&D Per Worker

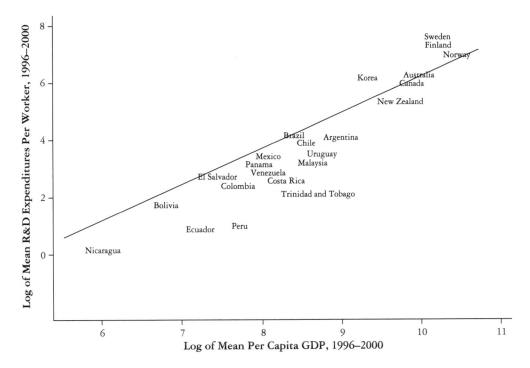

Note: The line corresponds to the predicted log of the stock of domestic R&D in 1996–2000 from a weighted regression on the log of per capita GDP and a constant, with the weights given by the number of working-age adults in a country. The sample size for the regression is 73 countries. Some country names have been omitted to make the figure more legible.

Source: Authors' calculations based on data from Lederman and Saenz (2002).

(Canada, Australia, New Zealand, Finland, Norway, and Sweden). Table 2.8 presents a stark picture indeed. Latin America has low TFP growth relative to the East Asian tiger countries, and relative to other natural resource–abundant countries. Moreover, controlling for their levels of per capita income, Latin America also has profound *deficits* in all four measures of educational attainment, and all four measures of technology. By contrast, both the East Asian tigers and the natural resource–abundant countries have *surpluses* in *all* of these measures.

Table 2.8 shows the depth of the productivity gap in the region: annual TFP growth in Latin America between 1990 and 1999 was a mere 0.45 percent, compared to the global average of 0.66, the East Asian tiger average of 1.42 percent, and the natural resource–abundant country average of 0.78 percent.

Productivity differences between countries and between firms within countries are profoundly affected by differences in skills and technology. It is therefore no surprise that the

East Asian tigers, which had well-above-average rates of TFP growth, also outperform Latin America on measures of technology and skills. Within Latin America, the best-performing country, Chile, concurrently had positive increases in productivity, substantial skill upgrading, and increases in foreign and domestic technology. As we will show in chapter 3, there is also evidence that firms that increase their productivity in Latin America often do so in a context of technological upgrading and increases in the demand for skilled workers.

The deficit in educational attainment in Latin America is profound. Latin American adults of working age have almost one-and-a-half fewer years of schooling than would be expected. This gap in the *stock* of educational attainment is a reflection of inadequate investments in the past. It is therefore particularly worrying to observe that the *flow* of new educated workers is inadequate: Latin America has very large deficits in enrollment, particularly at the secondary school level, as well as a problem with the quality of education. In

TABLE 2.7

Residents of Most Latin American Countries Have Low Rates of Patent Registration in Their Own Countries as Well as in the United States

	DOMESTIC PATENTS TO RESIDENTS (PER MILLION INHABITANTS)	U.S. PATENTS TO RESIDENTS (PER MILLION INHABITANTS)
Latin America	2.07	0.80
Argentina	4.65	1.83
Bolivia	0.41	0.22
Brazil	2.33	0.72
Chile	2.43	1.09
Colombia	0.44	0.27
Costa Rica		2.10
Ecuador	0.15	0.19
El Salvador	0.10	0.11
Honduras	0.30	0.48
Mexico	0.90	1.00
Nicaragua	0.41	0.08
Panama	2.17	0.46
Peru	0.38	0.19
Trinidad and Tobago	1.33	0.70
Uruguay	1.66	1.17
Venezuela	1.58	2.02
East Asian tigers	187.0	54.4
Hong Kong (China)	1.53	27.8
Korea	283.6	81.0
Malaysia	1.54	1.80
Singapore	113.1	48.4
Natural resource– abundant countries	83.8	114.8
Australia	96.1	49.0
Canada	26.8	138.3
Finland	133.6	160.0
New Zealand	80.4	38.3
Norway	71.7	66.0
Sweden	184.3	208.6

Note: The figures are the mean number of patents registered per year in the 1996–2000 period.
Source: Authors' calculations, based on data from World Bank databases (domestic patents to residents), and data from Lederman and Saenz (2002) (U.S. patents to residents).

chapter 3 we show that there have been very sharp increases in the demand for more skilled workers in Latin America in the last two decades. In order to compete with the East Asian tigers or with other countries with a comparative advantage in natural resources, both of which have high levels of educational attainment, enrollment, and quality, governments in Latin America need to put in place policies that will allow young people to acquire more high-quality education.

Did Latin America always have such a profound deficit in educational attainment? In Figure 2.14 we graph the gap in the years of completed schooling of the adult population

in Latin America, the East Asian tigers, and the set of natural resource–abundant countries, by decade, between 1960 and 2000. The figure clearly shows that Latin America has had a deficit since 1960—a deficit that became particularly acute between 1970 and 1980. In 1960, adults in the East Asian tiger economies also had almost three-quarters of a year of schooling fewer than would be expected for their income level. The difference is, however, that the tigers gradually reduced this deficit, so that by 2000 they had a surplus of almost a full year of schooling. The natural resource–abundant countries, finally, have always had a surplus in educational attainment—a surplus that has grown over time. In chapter 4 we discuss in detail the differences in the educational transitions among Latin America, East Asia, and the natural resource–abundant countries, focusing on both changes in the mean and the distribution of educational attainment.

Access to technology, both foreign and domestic, is low in Latin America. Import penetration is lower than expected, and import penetration of capital goods, which often embodies new technologies, is about one-quarter of that in the East Asian tigers. The average Latin American worker has only one-tenth as much domestic R&D capital available as the average worker in the tiger economies, and one-twentieth as much as a worker in the natural resource–abundant countries. And residents of Latin America register far fewer patents domestically and in the United States than their East Asian or Scandinavian counterparts. Workers in Latin America also have access to fewer computers. With the exception of the measure of computer penetration, these differences in innovation activity among the three sets of countries can be explained only very imperfectly by the difference in their per capita incomes. In chapters 6 and 7 we return to these differences in the level of technology between the two regions.

What can we say about changes in the technological gap in Latin America over time? Figure 2.15 graphs decade averages in the gap in the number of patents per worker registered in the United States for Latin America, the East Asian tigers, and the set of natural resource–abundant countries intervals between the 1960s and the 1990s. As with the comparable figure for the mean years of schooling, figure 2.15 shows that the East Asian tigers turned a deficit into a surplus, while the natural resource–abundant countries increased the size of their surplus in patents. In Latin America, meanwhile, the deficit in patents has remained essentially unchanged.

FIGURE 2.12

The Rates of Patent Registration by Latin American Inventors Are *Low* for Their Levels of Per Capita Income

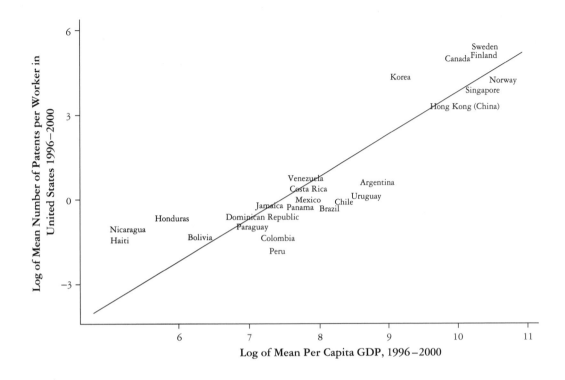

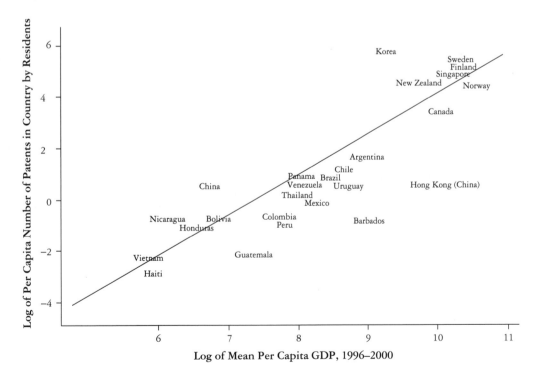

Note: The number of patents has been multiplied by one million.

Source: Authors' calculations based on data from World Bank databases and Lederman (2002).

FIGURE 2.13

The Widening of the LAC Technology Gap: Regional Comparisons of Index Scores

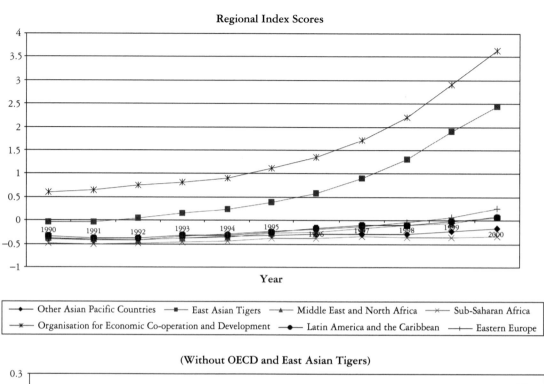

Regional Index Scores

Legend:
- ◆ Other Asian Pacific Countries
- ■ East Asian Tigers
- ▲ Middle East and North Africa
- ✕ Sub-Saharan Africa
- ✴ Organisation for Economic Co-operation and Development
- ● Latin America and the Caribbean
- ┼ Eastern Europe

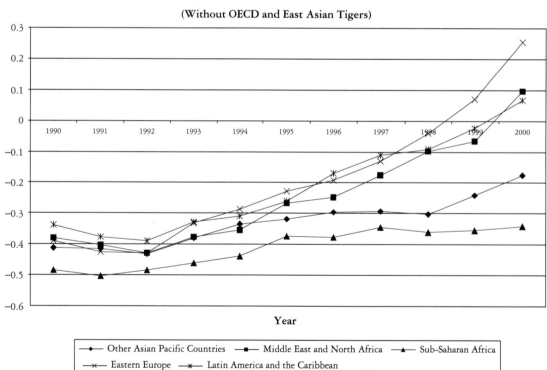

(Without OECD and East Asian Tigers)

Legend:
- ◆ Other Asian Pacific Countries
- ■ Middle East and North Africa
- ▲ Sub-Saharan Africa
- ✕ Eastern Europe
- ✴ Latin America and the Caribbean

Source: Guasch and Brehon (2002).

TABLE 2.8

The Gaps That Matter Most

	OBSERVED LAC MEAN	INCOME-ADJUSTED DEFICIT IN LAC	OBSERVED EAST ASIAN TIGER MEAN	INCOME-ADJUSTED SURPLUS IN EAST ASIAN TIGERS	OBSERVED NRA COUNTRY MEAN	INCOME-ADJUSTED SURPLUS IN NRA COUNTRIES
Productivity						
TFP growth per year (1990–99)	0.45	−0.21	1.42	0.76	0.78	0.12
Education						
Mean years of education, population aged 25+	5.8	−1.4	9.7	1.0	11.1	1.4
Net secondary enrollment rate (percent)	46.7	−18.7	93.3	17.8	93.2	6.0
Gross tertiary enrollment rate (percent)	20.0	−10.0	47.3	5.1	67.0	14.0
TIMSS score (points)	387	−81.2	584	86.3	524	+ (n.s.)
Technology						
Capital goods imports as a fraction of GDP, 1999 (percent)	7.7	−3.6	29.5	18.1	12.6	2.0
Domestic R&D expenditures per worker (1995 US$)	35.6	−26.4	329.5	116.5	725.4	152.5
Patents registered in the United States, 1996–2000 average (per million)	0.8	−1.5	54.4	48.3	114.8	80.9
Mean number of computers per 1,000 workers	37.7	− (n.s.)	172.0	+ (n.s.)	404.2	+ (n.s.)

Note: The regional "deficits" or "surpluses" are calculated as the weighted sum of the difference between the observed value and the predicted value from an OLS regression on log per capita income for all outcomes except TFP growth and imports of capital goods. For TFP, the means and the predicted value is given by the weighted world average, without a regression. For imports of capital goods the explanatory variable is GDP. The regional means, deficits, and surpluses for imports of capital goods are weighted by GDP; those for the mean years of education, net secondary enrollment rates, gross tertiary enrolment rates, TIMSS scores, and the number of computers are weighted by population; the measures of domestic R&D and patents, finally, are weighted by the working-age population aged 25 and older. n.s. means that the deficit or surplus is not statistically significantly different from zero (at the 5 percent level). The East Asian tiger economies included in the sample are Hong Kong (China), Korea, Malaysia, and Singapore. Data for Hong Kong are not available for TFP growth, imports of capital goods, or R&D expenditures; data on Singapore are not available for net secondary enrolment rate, and imports of capital goods; data on Malaysia are not available for R&D expenditures. The natural resource–abundant countries included in the sample are Canada, Australia, New Zealand, Finland, Norway, and Sweden.
Source: Data on TFP from Loayza, Fajnzylber, and Calderón (2002); data on educational attainment of adults from Barro and Lee (2002); data on enrollment rates from UNESCO; data on TIMSS scores from TIMSS; data on imports of capital goods, GDP, GDP per capita, and population from World Bank databases; data on R&D and patent registration from Lederman and Saenz (2002).

FIGURE 2.14

Between 1960 and 2000, the East Asian Tigers Turned a Deficit in the Mean Years of Schooling into a Surplus, while the Deficit in Latin America Did Not Change

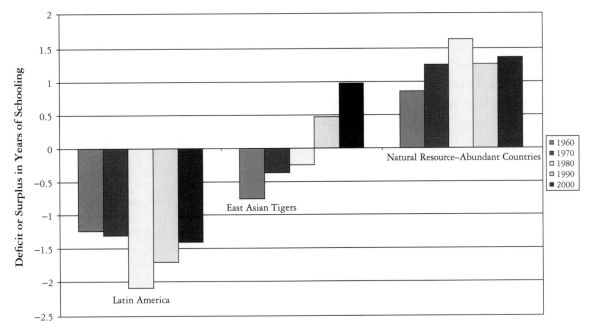

Source: Authors' calculations based on data from Barro and Lee (2002).

FIGURE 2.15

Between the 1960s and the 1990s, the East Asian Tigers Turned a Deficit in the Mean Number of Patents Per Worker Registered in the United States into a Surplus, while the Deficit in Latin America Did Not Change

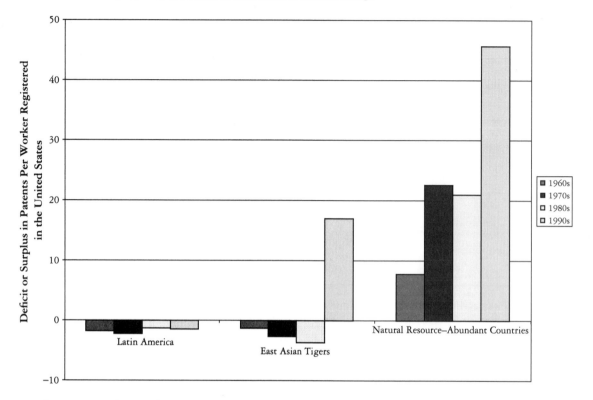

Source: Authors' calculations based on data from Lederman and Saenz (2002).

Chapters 6 and 7 discuss these technological transitions and the implications they have for countries in Latin America.

In order to reduce poverty, Latin American countries must grow. Firms must increase their productivity to compete in global marketplaces. As we will show in the following chapters, the *interaction* between technology and skill is critical to setting countries in Latin America on a higher growth path, fueled by a virtuous cycle of technological upgrading, increases in the demand for skill, skill upgrading, and further technological improvements.

Endnotes

1. The 1980s were not a good time for Latin America, with many countries mired in the recessions associated with the Debt Crisis. Loayza, Fajnzylber, and Calderón (2002) concede that their estimates may *under*estimate TFP growth in the 1980s, and *over*estimate TFP growth in the 1990s—because adjustments of the true rate of utilization of labor and capital stocks, using rates of unemployment and hours worked, may be imperfect.

2. In a population-weighted regression of the mean years of schooling of the population aged 25 and older on the log of per capita GDP and a dummy variable for Latin America for a sample of 105 countries in the world, the coefficient on the Latin American dummy is −3.82, with a standard error of 1.66. In a corresponding regression with an East Asian dummy, the coefficient is 0.80, with a standard error of 0.28.

3. The same pattern can also be observed in Thailand.

4. In a weighted regression of net primary enrollment rates on the log of per capita GDP and a dummy variable for Latin America, the coefficient on the Latin American dummy is 4.3, with a standard error of 3.7.

5. The PISA results also show that students scoring in the top 10 percent of all students taking the mathematics test in Mexico and Brazil score below the OECD mean, and even the top 5 percent of students in Brazil only score *at* the OECD mean. See Carnoy (2002).

6. PISA separately reports scores for individuals with less than upper secondary, complete upper secondary, and complete tertiary education (OECD 2001). To abstract from differences in the distribution of educational attainment in the population, we construct a mean, with equal weight given to these three scores. Of course, to the extent that

there are differences across countries in the distribution of educational attainment *within* these large categories, so that the mean Chilean adult with less than a completed secondary education has fewer years of education than his or her counterpart in (say) Poland, this is only an imperfect adjustment for underlying differences in educational attainment across countries.

7. When we include a Latin American dummy in the global regression of the number of scientists and engineers per 10,000 workers on per capita GDP, the coefficient on the Latin American dummy is clearly insignificant (the coefficient is 0.85, with a standard error of 4.52).

8. In a population-weighted regression of enrollment in science and engineering as a function of overall enrollment rates and a dummy variable for Latin America, the coefficient on the Latin American dummy is −4.1, with a standard error of 3.4.

9. In an OLS regression of import penetration on log GDP and a constant, for a sample of 152 economies, most Latin American economies, including (but not only) Argentina, Brazil, Venezuela, Colombia, Chile, and Peru, are below the regression line, while Korea, Taiwan (China), Malaysia, Hong Kong (China), and Singapore are above the line. Economies in Latin America and the Caribbean with higher-than-expected rates of import penetration are Barbados, Belize, Dominica, Guyana, Honduras, Jamaica, Nicaragua, St. Kitts and Nevis, St. Lucia, St. Vincent and the Grenadines, and Trinidad and Tobago.

10. The four variables are aggregated by factor analysis, after imputing missing values with other variables such as GDP per capita. In 1997, the resulting index has a range between 8.83 (Norway) and the Democratic Republic of Congo (−1.17); in Latin America, the lowest value is for Haiti (−1.0), and the highest for Chile (4.0). See Lederman and Xu (2001).

11. See especially the review by Griliches (1990).

12. See Grossman and Helpman (1991). In practice, both measures of patent activity are highly correlated in the data set we use: The GDP-weighted correlation coefficient is 0.89, significant at the 1 percent level.

13. Guasch and Brehon (2002).

CHAPTER 3

How Technology and Skills Interact: The Evidence for Latin America and the Caribbean

THE CENTRAL MESSAGE OF THIS REPORT IS THAT THE INTERACTION BETWEEN technology and skill is critical in determining growth, productivity, and the distribution of earnings. This is of particular relevance today, given the wave of rapid technological change in the United States and other OECD countries—technological change that has been complementary with skill. Chapter 2 showed that Latin America has profound deficits in both education and technology—in this chapter we turn to a dynamic picture of *changes* in Latin America, focusing primarily on the 1980–2000 period. We make use of the macroeconomic, firm-level, and household-level data in the region (box 3.1), and show that technology and skills interact in important ways in Latin America.

The chapter makes the following four points:

- There is a great deal of evidence of a wave of technological change that is complementary with skill in Latin America. As a result, firms have substantially increased the demand for educated workers in the region, especially workers with university education. The rising demand for educated workers has bid up the relative wages of these workers.

- This technological transformation appears to be intimately related to patterns of integration in the world economy. Trade and foreign direct investment (FDI) have facilitated the transmission of skill-biased technology across borders. Also, firms in sectors with higher exposure to trade and FDI are subject to more competitive pressures. Using more advanced technologies and hiring more educated workers is one way to respond to this pressure to become more productive.

- Increases in the demand for skills associated with the adoption of new technologies have primarily affected countries with levels of human capital above a minimum threshold level.

- There appear to be long-term cycles in the relative demand for more skilled workers associated with technological progress. The patterns observed in most

Latin American countries in the 1990s are similar to those observed in Chile in the 1980s.

The Rising Demand for Skilled Workers in Latin America

In Many Countries in Latin America, the Relative Wages of Workers with Tertiary Education Have Been Rising over Time...

We start off with an analysis of data from labor force surveys. The six panels in figure 3.1 show measures of relative supply and relative wages for workers with tertiary and secondary education for Argentina, Bolivia, Brazil, Chile, Colombia, and Mexico (see box 3.2). All series have been normalized, so that the relative wages and relative supplies are given a value of 100 in the first year for which data are available.[1] Figure 3.1 shows that in all of the countries except

BOX 3.1
Data Sources

Three different sources of data are used in this chapter: household-level data, firm-level data, and macro-level data. Each of them has its strengths and shortcomings, hence informing different aspects of the questions we are interested in. This box briefly discusses what these strengths and shortcomings are.

Many countries in Latin America regularly collect large household or labor force surveys. These surveys provide reliable, detailed information on the "skills" of the labor force, in particular on education levels, and these are fairly comparable across countries. For our purposes, the main disadvantage of the household-level data is that they do not collect information about the level of technology in the economy or across different firms. However, because relative wages are a signal, they can be used to make inferences about the demand for workers with different amounts of skill, and about how these differences in demand relate to changes in technology.

Firm-level surveys frequently contain direct information on technology upgrading by firms, including variables such as investments in different forms of capital equipment, import of foreign materials, and use of patents. Unfortunately, these surveys only collect information on firms in the manufacturing sector, and cannot therefore be used to analyze technology and skill upgrading in other sectors, such as services. Moreover, there is often very little information on the skill level of the workforce employed by firms, which is generally divided into "production" and "non-production" workers, rather than by education level.

Information on trade, foreign direct investment and other variables of interest is only available at a more aggregate level—for example, by country or industry. These data do not therefore have the richness associated with micro-level data, but they do cover a larger number of countries and time periods.

Most of the original work presented in this chapter uses household-level data, while the analysis based on firm-level data draws from the work of other authors. The table below provides more details on these household data, their sampling frequency, and the periods covered by each of them.

Household-Level Data Sources

	SURVEY	FREQUENCY	PERIOD COVERED
Argentina	Survey of Greater Buenos Aires	Yearly	1986–2000
Bolivia	Encuesta Integrada de Hogares	Yearly	1989–95
	Encuesta Nacional de Empleo	Yearly	1996–97
	Encuesta Nacional de Hogares	Yearly	1999–2000
Brazil	Pesquisa Mensal de Emprego	Monthly	1982–99
Chile	Encuesta de la Universidad de Chile	Yearly	1966–99
Colombia	Encuesta de Ingresos de los Hogares	Quarterly	1982–2000
Mexico	Encuesta Nacional de Empleo Urbano	Quarterly	1987–99

Note: Some of these surveys use a rotating panel scheme for data collection (Argentina and Mexico), but we do not make use of this feature and treat the data as a series of cross-sections.

Chile the wages of workers with tertiary education rise steadily relative to those of workers with secondary education. In Chile, meanwhile, the relative wages grew by 27.2 percent in the 1980s, and fell by 13.5 percent in the 1990s. In spite of these common patterns, however, figure 3.1 also shows that the *magnitude* of changes in relative wages varies a great deal by country. Calculating growth rates for the series, and focusing on the 1990s, the relative wages of workers with tertiary education increased by an incredible 72.9 percent in Colombia, by 48.3 percent and 45.4 percent in Mexico and Bolivia, and "only" by 19.7 percent and 11.7 percent in Argentina and Brazil, respectively.

... in Spite of Their Increasing Relative Abundance...
The second striking feature of figure 3.1 is the fact that in all of the countries except Brazil, this increase in relative wages took place in spite of an *increase* in the relative supply of workers with tertiary education. The biggest increase in relative supply in the 1990s occurred in Mexico (34.0 percent), which makes the magnitude of the change in relative wages there even more remarkable. The relative supply of workers with tertiary education increased by little in Colombia (7.2 percent), and moderately in Argentina (25 percent), Bolivia (20.9 percent), and Chile (16.9 percent). In Brazil, the relative supply of workers with tertiary education fell

FIGURE 3.1

The Relative Wages and Relative Supply of Workers with *Tertiary* Education Increased Substantially in Most Latin American Countries

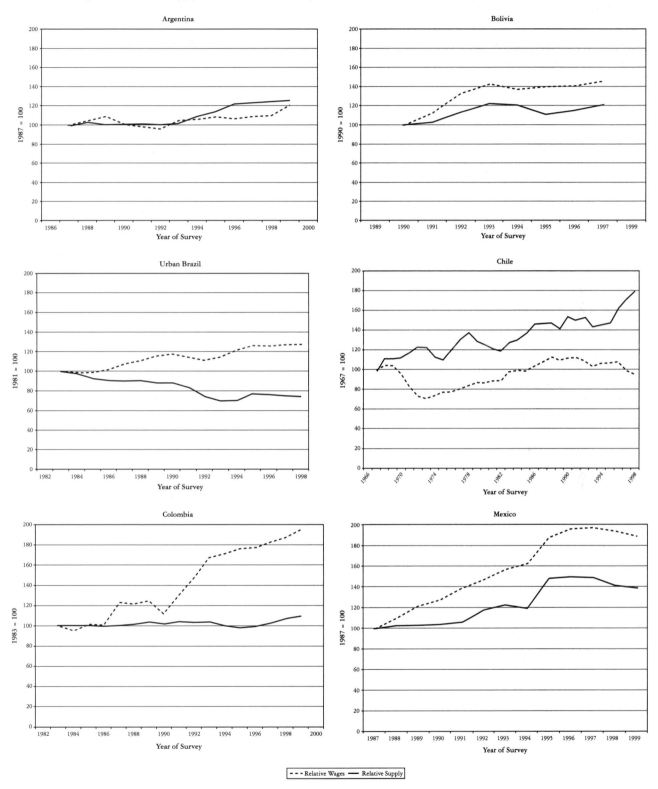

Note: Relative wages and supply series are three-year moving averages.
Source: Sánchez-Páramo and Schady (2002), based on the labor force surveys.

Measuring Education, Relative Wages, and Relative Supply

Much of the analysis in this chapter is concerned with differences in the relative wages and supply of workers with different amounts of education. This box briefly discusses how workers are assigned across education groups and explains how relative wages and supply measures are constructed.

Education measures: Two issues need to be considered concerning the assignment of workers to different education groups and the interpretation of such a classification. First, education systems vary across countries, so that a person who has completed secondary school in Chile has not necessarily spent the same number of years in school as a person who has completed secondary school in Mexico. The table below provides a schematic summary of the education system in the countries of interest.

Education Levels and Years of Schooling

	YEARS		
COUNTRY	PRIMARY	SECONDARY	TERTIARY
Argentina[a]	7	5	3–5
Bolivia	8	4	3–5
Brazil	8	3	3–5
Chile[b]	8	4	3–5
Colombia	5	6	3–5
Mexico	6	6	4–5

a. The Argentine system changed in 1997–98 to primary (6 years), lower secondary (3 years), and upper secondary (3 years). This change does not affect the analysis since we focus exclusively on individuals aged 25 and above.
b. Individuals born prior to 1950 were educated under a different system in Chile (primary, 6 years; secondary, 6 years; post-secondary, 3–5 years). This change was taken into account when assigning individuals to different education groups based on their years of schooling.

Second, workers can be assigned across education groups according to different criteria. The two most common criteria in the literature have been those of partial or full completion of a certain education level. For instance, a person with seven years of education in Mexico would be considered a primary school graduate and hence assigned to the primary school category if the full completion of a level criteria were used for classification. On the other hand, since she has some secondary school, she would be assigned to the secondary school category if the partial completion criteria were used instead.

An alternative method of classification is proposed in this chapter that, in a sense, combines the two described above. Specifically, individuals are assigned to two different education groups: The group corresponding to the highest education level they have completed and the group corresponding to the next education level they can complete. Weights are then constructed that reflect the individual's relative progress between both education levels.

This procedure can best be illustrated with an example. Consider again an individual with seven years of education in Mexico. As described above, this person will have completed her primary studies plus one year of secondary studies, and will therefore be included in both the "primary education" and "secondary education" groups. Notice that secondary school requires a total of six years of schooling in Mexico, out of which she has only completed one. This implies that she has completed one-sixth of secondary school. She is therefore given a weight of 1/6 when including her in the secondary education group and a weight of 5/6 (1 minus 1/6) when including her in the primary education group.

There are two reasons why this seems a preferable way of assigning workers to schooling categories. First, in many Latin American countries large shares of the population have only a few years of education. In that context, restricting the analysis to only those individuals who have actually completed at least one education level would miss a significant fraction of the population. Similarly, assigning these individuals to the no-education group would also be misleading, since most of them do have some education. Second, a substantial amount of the educational progress that takes place in developing countries over time occurs *within* rather than *between* levels. This skill upgrading would be missed altogether if workers were assigned to education categories corresponding to the levels they have completed or begun. The proposed procedure, by contrast, accounts for these within-category changes with changes in the weights that are assigned.

Relative wages and supply measures. Once workers have been assigned to different education groups, relative wage and supply measures are constructed as follows. Relative wages for workers in education groups i and j in year t are calculated as the difference in their average (log) hourly wages:

(1) $W^t_{i,j} = $ log (hourly wage)$_{it}$ – log (hourly wage)$_{jt}$,

where i = tertiary or secondary, and j = secondary or primary, respectively. Similarly, the relative supply in year t is calculated as the ratio of the percentage share of groups i and j in the labor force:

(2) $S^t_{i,j} = $ (% education level i in labor force in year t)/ (% education level j in labor force in year t)

Finally, we restrict the sample to males and females aged 25–60. Within this group labor force participants—employed and unemployed workers, defined in the standard way—are considered when constructing labor supply measures, while only salaried workers are considered when constructing wage measures.

by 7.3 percent, a change that can be explained by increases in the number of workers with secondary education in the absence of comparable increases in those with tertiary education.

...Which is Strong Evidence of Demand-side Changes Favoring Workers with Tertiary Education

The relative wages of skilled and unskilled workers are a signal of the relative demand for and supply of skills in an economy. In the absence of changes in relative demand favoring skilled workers, we would expect the relative wages of skilled workers to *fall* because of their increasing relative abundance. In all of the countries in our analysis except Brazil we find increases in both the relative wages and the relative supply of workers with tertiary education. This is strong evidence of demand-side changes favoring workers with tertiary education in the region. Indeed, these patterns suggest that the demand-side shifts towards workers with tertiary education would have to be so large as to more than offset the downward pressure on wages that results from their increasing relative abundance. Separate graphs that break down these changes by sector suggest that the increase in relative demand for workers with tertiary education has taken place in both manufacturing and services.

There Have Been Increases in the Supply of Workers with Secondary Education Relative to Workers with Primary Education in Latin America...

Turning next to workers with secondary and primary education, figure 3.2 shows clear increases in the relative supply of workers with secondary education: In the 1990s, the rel-

ative supply of workers with secondary education went up by more than 18 percent in every country, with particularly sharp increases in Bolivia (39.6 percent), Colombia (32.8 percent), Mexico (29.2 percent), and Argentina (29.1 percent). In Brazil, there has been a notable increase in the relative supply of workers with secondary education since 1994 (26.7 percent). In Chile, the most dramatic skill upgrading at this level took place in the 1980s, with an increase of 63.1 percent. These changes reflect widespread public efforts to increase secondary school enrollments in virtually every country in Latin America.

...and a Decrease in Their Relative Wages in a Number of Countries

Figure 3.2 also shows that the relative wage of workers with secondary education fell over the period in a number of countries. As with figure 3.1, and focusing on the 1990s, the magnitude of these changes varies a great deal by country—from a very small decrease in Colombia (–0.4 percent), to much larger decreases in Argentina (–32.3 percent) and Brazil (–20.3 percent). Only in two countries did the relative wage of workers with secondary education actually increase over the period—by 8.9 percent in Mexico, and by a staggering 375 percent in Bolivia. A combined look at figures 3.1 and 3.2 makes obvious that the wages of workers with secondary education in every country but Bolivia and Mexico therefore fell relative to *both* workers with primary education and those with tertiary education. The evidence on changes in relative demand for workers with secondary education by firms is therefore unclear in every country except Bolivia and Mexico.

FIGURE 3.2

The Relative Supply of Workers with *Secondary* Education Increased Substantially in Latin America

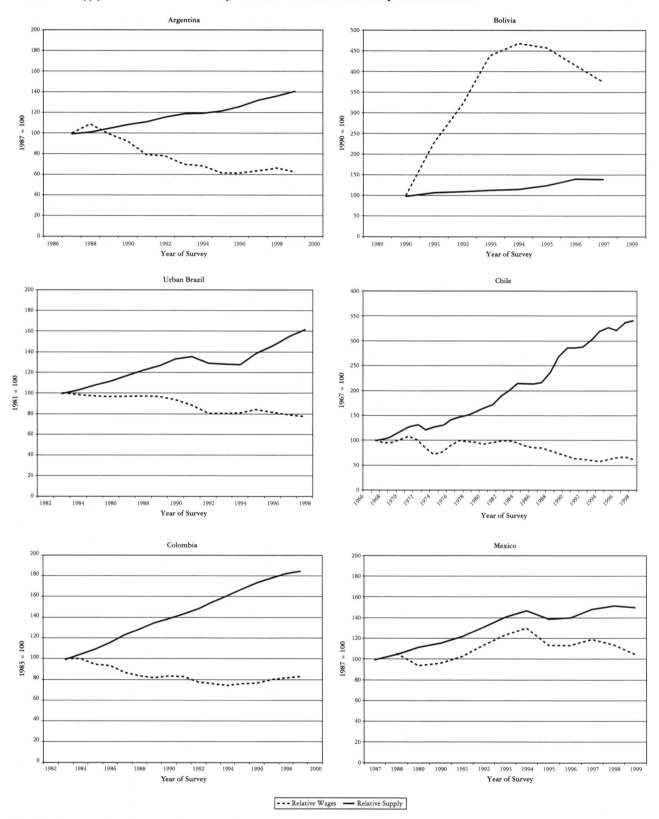

Note: Relative wages and supply series are three-year moving averages.
Source: Sánchez-Páramo and Schady (2002), based on the labor force surveys.

Changes in Relative Wages Can Be Decomposed into Changes in Relative Demand and Relative Supply...

Because relative wages are determined by relative demand and supply, changes in relative wages can be decomposed into changes in relative demand and changes in relative supply (box 3.3). To do this, assumptions have to be made about the value of σ, the parameter for the elasticity of substitution between workers with more or less education. This elasticity of substitution is a measure of how sensitive the quantity demanded of workers with a given level of education is to changes in their relative price, and is related to the ease with which one kind of worker can be substituted for another in production. Figure 3.3 presents a series of graphs of the evolution of relative demand for workers with tertiary education for values of the elasticity of substitution between 1 and 3—the values that are commonly thought to be "reasonable" for developing countries. The *value* of relative demand at any point in time is not a meaningful concept, so all of the series have been normalized to zero for the first year in which data are available (See Murphy, Riddell, and Romer (1998), especially pp. 27–28). On the other hand, *changes* in log relative demand over time, given by the slope of the lines, measure shifts in the demand schedule, and can be compared across time periods and countries.[2]

...Which Generally Confirms the Sharp Increases in Relative Demand for Workers with Tertiary Education

Figure 3.3 confirms that, no matter what the chosen value for the elasticity of substitution, there is evidence of increases in relative demand for workers with tertiary education in the late 1980s and in the 1990s in Argentina, Bolivia, Colombia, and Mexico. In Chile, the steep demand-side shifts favoring skilled workers took place in the late 1970s and in the 1980s, with the overall pattern in the 1990s being essentially flat. In Brazil, the estimated demand-side shifts are much more sensitive to the choice of σ, the parameter for the elasticity of substitution. As with the relative wage series in figure 3.1, figure 3.3 shows that the magnitude of the demand shifts favoring workers with tertiary education varied a great deal by country, and over time. In Colombia and Mexico, firms appear to have increased the demand for workers with tertiary education particularly sharply. In a background paper prepared for this report, Sánchez-Páramo and Schady (2002) show that these demand changes are as large or larger than those that occurred in the United States.[3] In Brazil, meanwhile, demand shifts were anemic. As we discuss later on in this chapter, new technolo-

gies flow primarily to countries with skill levels above a minimum threshold level. The absence of demand shifts for more educated workers in Brazil may itself have been determined by the fact that education levels in the country were very low.

A Similar Decomposition also Shows that There Have Been Increases in Relative Demand for Workers with Secondary Education in Most Countries

Because the relative supply and relative wages of workers with secondary education over those with primary education have generally moved in opposite directions in Argentina, Brazil, Chile, and Colombia, it is not clear *a priori* whether there have been demand-side shifts favoring workers with secondary education. Figure 3.4 presents the results of a decomposition of the relative wages of workers with secondary education. The results vary substantially from country to country. In Bolivia, there was a massive demand-side shift favoring workers with secondary education over workers with primary education in the 1990s. In Argentina and Brazil, the pattern of demand-side changes is quite sensitive to the choice of σ. However, abstracting from two crisis periods (1988–90 in Argentina, and 1990–92 in Brazil), the overall pattern seems to be of a moderate increase in relative demand for workers with secondary education. The time series for the other four countries appear to be closely related to those found for tertiary-educated workers. Figure 3.4 suggests a consistent increase in demand for workers with secondary education in Colombia. In Bolivia, Chile, and Mexico, a period of increasing relative demand for secondary-educated workers (1990–94 in Bolivia, 1974–85 in Chile, and 1988–93 in Mexico) is followed by a flattening or fall in relative demand. This is precisely the pattern found for workers with tertiary education.

Skill-Biased Technological Change in Latin America

The evolution of relative wages and supply make clear that firms in Latin America sharply increased the demand for more educated workers. We now show that the household-level data, firm-level data, and aggregate country-wide data are all most consistent with an explanation of the demand shifts that stresses the complementarity between technology and skill.

Demand-side Shifts Favoring Skilled Workers Could Be the Result of Any One of a Number of Economic Reforms

The 1980s and 1990s were a period of profound changes in much of Latin America: Formerly closed economies opened

BOX 3.3

Constructing Relative Demand Shifts: What Needs to Be Assumed and Why

Changes in the relative wages of workers with different education levels are a function of changes in the relative demand for and the relative supply of these workers, as well as of the elasticity of substitution between workers with different education levels. This elasticity is a measure of the ease with which one kind of worker can be replaced for another in production. For instance, if the elasticity of substitution between engineers and technicians is high, a small increase in the relative wage of engineers would lead to a large substitution out of engineers and into technicians, whereas if the elasticity is low changes in the wages of engineers would lead to little substitution between both types of workers. More formally, if σ, the parameter for the elasticity of substitution, is equal to x, a 1 percent increase in the relative wage of engineers is associated with an x percent decrease in the quantity demanded of engineers relative to technicians. These ideas can be modeled simply as follows. Under the assumption of a common elasticity of substitution (CES), relative wages have to satisfy the condition:

(1) $\mathrm{Log}[w_1(t)/w_2(t)] = (1/\sigma)[D(t) - \log\{x_1(t)/x_2(t)\}]$

where $w_1(t)/w_2(t)$ is the ratio of relative wages, $x_1(t)/x_2(t)$ is the ratio of relative supplies, σ is the elasticity of substitution between workers in the two education levels, and $D(t)$ is the time series of relative demand shifts (Katz and Murphy 1992).

Since both $D(t)$ and σ are unknown parameters, additional assumptions about either the behavior of $D(t)$ or the value of σ are necessary in order to construct a time series of relative demand shifts using (1). Two different approaches have been proposed in the literature for this purpose. First, a working value of σ can be estimated if relative demand shifts are assumed to follow a linear trend by running a regression of the (log) relative wages on the (log) relative supplies and such a trend as follows:

(2) $\mathrm{Log}[w_1(t)/w_2(t)] = \alpha + (1/\sigma)\ \text{time trend}$
$- (1/\sigma)\log\{x_1(t)/x_2(t)\}$

The value of σ can then be recovered from the coefficient on relative supply and plugged into (1) after rearranging terms to obtain:

(3) $D(t) = \sigma\log[w_1(t)/w_2(t)] + \log\{x_1(t)/x_2(t)\}$

where all of the parameters on the right-hand side are now "given." Unfortunately, because all of the series for the countries we analyze in this report are rising (or falling) almost monotonically, estimates of σ conditional on a time trend are highly imprecise (with t-statistics of one or lower), and often wildly improbable, rendering this first approach invalid.

The second approach relies on assumptions about σ rather than on assumptions about the behavior of $D(t)$, thus avoiding econometric estimation. In particular $D(t)$ is then estimated *directly* from (3) under plausible values of σ. In this chapter σ is assumed to vary between 1 and 3, which is the range of international estimates summarized in Katz and Autor (1999).

An additional concern with simple estimates of σ and $D(t)$ obtained from equations (2) and (3) is the changing composition of the workforce. The five countries in the sample are relatively advanced in their demographic transitions. The fraction of workers who are older is therefore higher in later than in the earlier years. Older workers generally earn more than younger workers, and a life-cycle model of earnings determination suggests that the wage gap between more and less educated workers should also increase with age (Mincer 1974; Heckman, Lochner, and Todd 2001). The observed increase in the relative wage of the skilled could, therefore, be a product not of the changing supply or demand for educated workers, but rather of the changing age profile. Many countries in Latin America are also witnessing important changes in the participation of women in the labor force. If the difference in wages by education is larger (or smaller) for women than for men, this too could distort uncorrected estimates of $D(t)$. Again following Katz and Murphy, compositional changes in the labor force were controlled for by holding age and gender distributions constant over time in each country. Specifically, for any education group, average share of total employment were calculated for 14 age-gender cells *over the entire period* and these weights were then used to construct mean wages for an education group in any given year.

Source: Katz and Murphy (1992).

FIGURE 3.3

The Demand for *Tertiary* Workers Increased in Every Country except Brazil

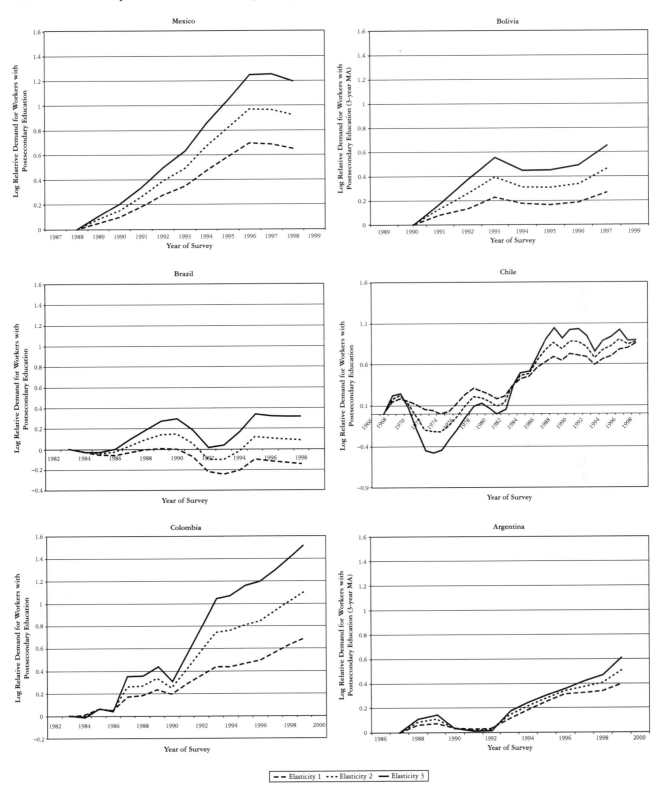

Note: Demand series are three-year moving averages.
Source: Sánchez-Páramo and Schady (2002), based on the labor force surveys.

FIGURE 3.4

The Demand for *Secondary* Workers Increased in Every Country except Argentina and Brazil

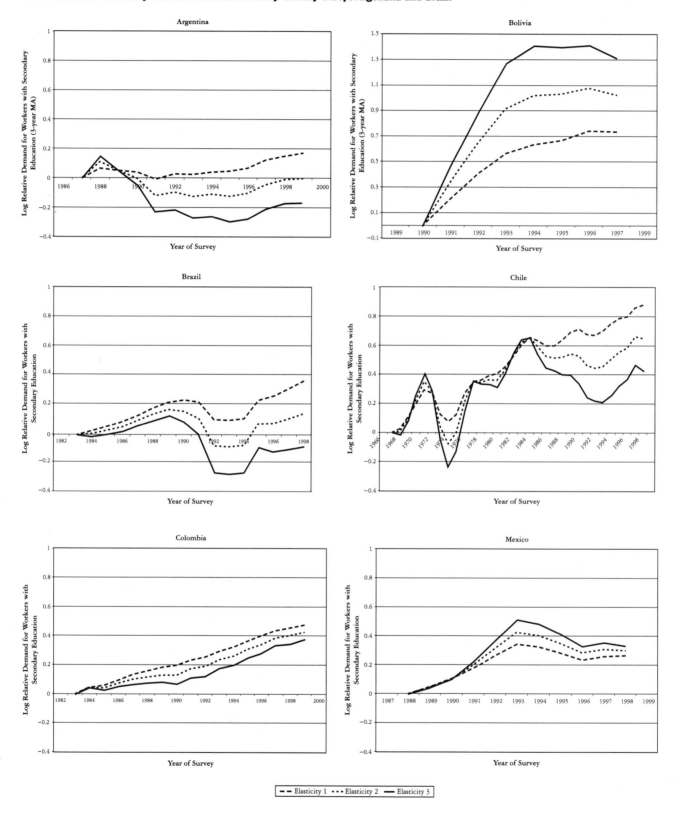

- - - Elasticity 1 · · · Elasticity 2 —— Elasticity 3

Note: Demand series are three-year moving averages.
Source: Sánchez-Páramo and Schady (2002), based on the labor force surveys.

up to trade and FDI; Latin American firms were forced to raise their productivity to compete in the global marketplace; in some countries, modest attempts were made to reform labor markets. All of these changes could potentially explain the rising demand for skilled workers in the region. As it turns out, the patterns we observe are not consistent with an explanation based on product demand shifts, such as those predicted by the Heckscher-Ohlin (H-O) model of international trade, or with changes resulting from labor market reform. Rather, the evidence is most consistent with the effect of skill-biased technological change on the relative demand for workers with different amounts of skill.

Labor Market Reforms Do Not Explain the Patterns Observed in Latin America

The impact of labor market reforms on the relative demand for skilled workers is likely to have been modest simply because the magnitude of these reforms in Latin America was modest. Proposals to increase labor market flexibility in Latin America in the 1980s and 1990s often faced substantial opposition, making them difficult to implement. In fact, while most countries in the region carried out profound trade and financial reforms, only a few actually introduced substantial changes to their labor legislation during the 1990s (Gill, Montenegro, and Dömeland 2002). Moreover, although generally intended to increase labor market flexibility, reforms were not always successful at achieving this. A paper by Behrman, Birdsall, and Szekely (2001), which graphs the evolution of various indexes of reform in Latin America, including a composite measure of labor market reform, suggests that labor markets were, on average, no more flexible in the 1990s than in the 1980s.

Trade Reforms Could Explain Many of the Patterns We Observe

Product demand shifts associated with trade reforms in Latin America seem like a more serious contender for the observed increases in relative demand. Trade liberalization in a country will generally have two effects. First, it will change the relative price of goods produced in different sectors. This, in turn, will have an effect on the relative size of sectors, and on the relative wages of workers with different levels of education. Specifically, in a two-sector economy with different skill intensities, the H-O theorem of international trade predicts that trade reform in a skill-abundant country will increase the relative price of goods produced in the

skill-intensive sector. The accompanying Stolper-Samuelson theorem predicts that this change in product prices will be translated into an increase in the wages of workers in the skill-intensive sector of the economy. Since the skill-intensive sector, by definition, employs more skilled workers, changes in product demand should therefore lead to an aggregate rise in the wages of skilled labor in a skill-intensive country. It is not clear *a priori* whether Latin American countries are relatively skill-abundant or relatively skill-scarce.[4] Also, in many Latin American countries tariff protection was highest in sectors that employed the highest fraction of unskilled workers.[5] As a result, tariff declines were largest in sectors that were relatively skill-unintensive.[6] Trade liberalization therefore reduced the relative price of goods produced by the skill-unintensive sector, and this could have translated into a reduction in the relative wages of the unskilled through Stolper-Samuelson effects.

The second effect of trade reform is that it facilitates the transmission of technology across borders. Decomposing skill upgrading into within-sector and between-sector components provides an empirical test to distinguish between H-O-Stolper-Samuelson and skill-biased technological change: The critical prediction of an H-O-Stolper-Samuelson type explanation is that economy-wide skill upgrading is a result of an increase in the relative size of skill-intensive sectors. This, in turn, increases the aggregate demand and the relative wage of skilled labor. Because skilled workers are now relatively more expensive, however, we would expect to see *within-sector* substitution *away* from skilled labor and into unskilled labor. By contrast, skill-biased technological change is consistent with within-sector increases in both the relative wage and employment share of skilled workers.

A standard way of considering the importance of these two competing explanations for the increasing demand for skilled workers is to decompose the change in the aggregate wage bill, given by the product of employment and the wage, into between-industry and within-industry components.[7] Within-industry changes in the wage bill can then be attributed to skill-biased technological change or skill-biased capital accumulation, while between-industry changes in the wage bill can be attributed to increases in the relative size of skill-intensive sectors.[8]

The Bulk of Skill Upgrading in Latin America Has Taken Place within Industries...

We turn again to the household data for Argentina, Bolivia, Brazil, Chile, Colombia, and Mexico, and disaggregate the wage and employment data into the greatest number of sectors possible—from 13 in Bolivia to 75 in Mexico. The results from this decomposition are presented in table 3.1. The top panel considers changes in the share of the wage bill for workers with tertiary education (as a fraction of the wage bill for workers with secondary and tertiary education), while the bottom panel considers changes in the share of the wage bill for workers with secondary education (as a fraction of the wage bill for workers with primary and secondary education). Table 3.1 shows clearly that the bulk of the increase in the aggregate wage bill for workers with tertiary education took place *within* industries. The fractions vary by country—from 72 percent in Argentina to 122 percent in Bolivia (within-industry changes larger than 100 percent are possible if there are decreases in the relative size of the skill-intensive sectors). In Mexico, despite the greatest number of sectors in the data, which should allow for a more accurate measurement of shifts across sectors, fully 95 percent

of the observed skill upgrading can be explained by within-sector changes. In Chile, the labor force survey data shows that just over 90 percent of the skill upgrading in the 1980s took place within sectors.[9] The picture for changes in the secondary wage bill in table 3.1 is, if anything, even clearer: 90 to 150 percent of the increase in the wage bill for workers with secondary education took place *within* industries.[10]

... Which Is Consistent with Skill-biased Technological Change or Capital-skill Complementarity, But Not with H-O-Stolper-Samuelson Effects of Trade Reform

Within-industry upgrading is consistent with skill-biased technological change, or with a complementary relationship between capital and skill together with a falling relative price of capital. Empirically, skilled labor and capital do appear to be complements (Berman, Bound, and Griliches 1994). Capital is likely to have become relatively more abundant and cheaper in Latin America as a result of trade liberalization,

TABLE 3.1

The Bulk of Changes in the Wage Bill for Tertiary Workers and Secondary Workers Occurred *within* Industries

| | | | TERTIARY | | | |
	PERIOD	NUMBER OF SECTORS	INITIAL S_t	CHANGE IN S_t (ANNUALIZED – % POINTS)	CHANGE DUE TO WITHIN-INDUSTRY CHANGES (ANNUALIZED – % POINTS)	CHANGE DUE TO BETWEEN-INDUSTRY CHANGES (ANNUALIZED – % POINTS)
Argentina	1986–89 and 1997–99	25	53.0	1.8	1.3	0.5
Bolivia	1989–91 and 1997–99	13	59.7	1.8	2.2	−0.4
Brazil	1982–83 and 1987–89	48	60.9	−0.1	−0.1	0.0
	1987–89 and 1997–99	48	60.6	−0.2	−0.2	0.0
Chile	1977–79 and 1987–89	39	51.0	1.2	1.1	0.1
	1987–89 and 1997–99	39	60.8	0.1	0.2	−0.1
Colombia	1982–83 and 1988–89	34	48.6	−0.1	0.0	−0.1
	1988–89 and 1998–99	34	48.2	1.1	0.9	0.2
Mexico	1987–89 and 1997–99	75	36.6	2.1	2.0	0.1

| | | | SECONDARY | | | |
	PERIOD	NUMBER OF SECTORS	INITIAL S_s	CHANGE IN S_s (ANNUALIZED – % POINTS)	CHANGE DUE TO WITHIN-INDUSTRY CHANGES (ANNUALIZED – % POINTS)	CHANGE DUE TO BETWEEN-INDUSTRY CHANGES (ANNUALIZED – % POINTS)
Argentina	1986–89 and 1997–99	25	45.9	1.0	0.9	0.1
Bolivia	1989–91 and 1997–99	13	48.2	3.7	3.6	0.1
Brazil	1982–83 and 1987–89	48	43.7	1.6	1.5	0.1
	1987–89 and 1997–99	48	49.4	0.6	0.9	−0.3
Chile	1977–79 and 1987–89	39	63.5	1.0	1.1	−0.1
	1987–89 and 1997–99	39	72.4	0.6	0.6	0.0
Colombia	1982–83 and 1988–89	34	51.3	1.3	1.4	−0.1
	1988–89 and 1998–99	34	56.7	1.4	1.3	0.0
Mexico	1987–89 and 1997–99	75	48.8	0.6	0.7	−0.1

Note: The wage bill for tertiary workers, S_t, is the wage bill of tertiary workers as a fraction of the wage bill for secondary and tertiary workers, while the wage bill of secondary workers, S_s, is the wage bill for secondary workers as a fraction of the wage bill for primary and secondary workers.
Source: Sánchez-Páramo and Schady (2002).

rising FDI, and other developments that have increased investment. A careful analysis of the changes in the use of skilled labor by Colombian firms between 1983 and 1998 (which takes into account the effect of the changing price of capital) suggests that skill upgrading has been driven both by capital-skill and technology-skill complementarity (Kugler 2002). In general, however, the changes in the price of capital in Latin America and in other developing countries appear to be much too small to account for the observed changes in the demand for skilled workers (Berman and Machin 2000).

Given the rising relative cost of skilled workers, table 3.1 leaves little doubt that the observed increases in demand for skilled workers in Latin America are inconsistent with H-O-Stolper-Samuelson explanations. This is not to say that trade has not had an important influence on the evolution of relative wages in Latin America. Rather, as we show below, trade has worked as a vehicle whereby skill-biased technologies have been transferred to Latin America, rather than through H-O-Stolper-Samuelson effects.

Patterns of Skill Upgrading at the Tertiary Level Are Similar across Different Countries in Latin America

Another piece of evidence suggestive of skill-biased technological change comes from the similarity of patterns of skill upgrading across countries, especially among workers with tertiary education. Insofar as skill-biased technologi-cal change is *pervasive*, we would expect to find a positive correlation between the degree of skill upgrading across sectors in different countries. In table 3.2, we present weighted correlations of the changes in the employment share of workers with tertiary education (upper panel) and that of workers with secondary education (lower panel). Because the patterns we observe in Chile *in the 1980s* resemble those in other countries *in the 1990s*, we correlate employment shares for Chile in the 1980s with those for Argentina, Brazil, Colombia, and Mexico in the 1990s.[11] (We do not include the data for Bolivia because the classification for sectors and industries was not comparable.) If there were no relationship between the pattern of skill upgrading in different countries, we would expect half of these correlations to be positive, and the other half negative. Instead, 9 of the 10 correlations for workers with tertiary education, and (less impressively) 6 of the 10 correlations for workers with secondary education are positive.[12] Consider the implications of this: Despite profound differences in the productive structure of the five countries, skill upgrading at the tertiary level appears to have taken place in the same sectors. There was particularly large skill upgrading in professional and financial services, education and welfare, and government.[13] These results are highly suggestive of technological changes that affected some sectors more than others, and which were transmitted to Chile in the 1980s and to the other countries in the region in the 1990s.

TABLE 3.2

By and Large, Skill Upgrading at the Tertiary Level Occurred in the Same Sectors in Chile in the 1980s and in Other Latin American Countries in the 1990s...

	ARGENTINA	BRAZIL	CHILE	COLOMBIA
Brazil	−0.251			
Chile	0.314	0.508		
Colombia	0.154	0.409	0.543	
Mexico	0.115	0.315	0.322	0.298

...while the Picture for Upgrading at the Secondary Level Varied a Great Deal More from Country to Country

	ARGENTINA	BRAZIL	CHILE	COLOMBIA
Brazil	−0.186			
Chile	−0.028	0.190		
Colombia	−0.020	0.138	0.163	
Mexico	−0.376	0.085	0.611	0.291

Note: These are cross-country correlations of within-industry changes in the proportion of workers with tertiary education as a percentage of workers with tertiary and secondary education (top panel), and corresponding correlations for the proportion of workers with secondary education as a percentage of workers with secondary and primary education (bottom panel). Changes for Argentina, Brazil, Colombia and Mexico are measured between 1988/89 and 1998/99. Changes for Chile are measured between 1978/79 and 1988/89. Bolivia is not included because data by industry are not disaggregated enough. Observations are weighted by industry employment shares averaged over time and across all countries.
Source: Sánchez-Páramo and Schady (2002).

Firm-level Data Show That Plants Using Foreign Technology Increased the Demand for Skilled Workers in Chile...

We continue our analysis of the complementary relationship between technology and skill in Latin America by turning to the firm-level data. These data have the advantage of often including direct measures of technology, but the disadvantage of covering only manufacturing, and not the service sector. Pavcnik (2002) shows that between 1979 and 1986 the relative wages, employment shares, and wage bill of skilled workers all went up in Chile. These patterns closely mirror those observed in the labor force survey data, and provide further strong *prima facie* evidence that firms were increasing the relative demand for workers with tertiary education. Moreover, skill upgrading in Chile took place at the same time as heavier investments and increased use of foreign technology by firms (measured by foreign technical assistance, patent use, and import of foreign materials). The results in table 3.3 show that plants that used foreign technical assistance, patented technology, and imported materials all had a significantly higher wage bill share of skilled

TABLE 3.3

In Chile Firms That Were Exposed to New Technology from Abroad Also Upgraded Skills

SKILL UPGRADING REGRESSIONS, CHILE, 1979–86	DEPENDENT VARIABLE: SHARE OF SKILLED WORKERS IN THE WAGE BILL	
	(1)	(2)
Ln (Capital/Value Added)	.021**	.022**
	(.001)	(.001)
Ln (Value Added)	.046**	.049**
	(.001)	(.001)
Foreign Technical Assistance Indicator	.021**	
	(.005)	
Patent Indicator	.016**	
	(.002)	
Imported Materials Indicator	.047**	
	(.003)	
Foreign Technical Assistance Cost/Value Added		.196**
		(.063)
Patent Cost/Value Added		.004**
		(.001)
Imported Materials/Materials		.087**
		(.007)
R² (Adjusted)	.480	.480
Number of Observations	26,513	26,513

Note: All regressions include area, industry, and year indicators. Huber-White standard errors are in parentheses. ** indicate significance at a 5 percent level.
Source: Pavcnik (2002)

workers in Chile. This is highly suggestive of technology-skill complementarity: Firms with access to foreign technology demanded more skilled workers, and increased the share of skilled workers in the wage bill—all of this, in spite of their rising relative wages.[14] The Chilean data also show that the relationship between technology and skill varied considerably with the skill distribution of plants. Specifically, the impact of technology was negligible for firms that originally had few skilled workers, but important for skill-intensive plants. As we discuss in the final section of the chapter, similar differences can also be found across *countries* in Latin America, with new technologies flowing primarily to countries with higher mean levels of education of their population.

...as Well as in Mexico, Colombia, and Brazil

The patterns observed in the firm-level data in Chile are reasonably similar to those observed elsewhere in Latin America.[15] The relative wages of skilled to unskilled workers are higher in Mexico among firms that upgraded their technology through licensing arrangements (Harrison and Hanson 1999). A background paper for this report by Mayer and Foster (2002) shows that the returns to education were higher in municipalities that had larger firms—firms that are often thought to be more technologically advanced compared to smaller ones (see box 3.4). In Colombia, the firm-level data show increases in both the relative cost of skilled labor, and the intensity of use of skilled labor in production in the 1980s and 1990s (Kugler 2002). In Brazil, finally, firms with a highly schooled labor force were more likely to be exporters. Insofar as exporters are more technologically sophisticated than non-exporters, this result supports the conclusion that more skilled labor is needed to competitively use sophisticated technology (Corseuil and Muendler 2002).

Firms with Exposure to Foreign Technology Are Also More Likely to Complement This with Their Own R&D

Firms often have to adapt foreign technology to make it appropriate to their particular (skill) endowments. Increased competition from imports and potential access to foreign markets that require higher technical sophistication also provide strong incentives for firms both to adapt the latest available technology and to innovate. As a result, exposure to foreign technology is an important incentive for firms to invest in their own R&D activities. Recent work comparing R&D activities in Mexican firms before and after the

BOX 3.4

Scale, Technological Change, and Human Capital: Manufacturing and Development in Mexico

In a seminal paper, Foster and Rosenzweig (1996) show that during the Green Revolution in India the returns to primary and secondary education increased in areas where technological change, measured by adoption of new, more productive seeds was largest and fastest, and that those increases in turn induced private investments in education. Following a similar approach, Mayer and Foster (2002) combine municipal-level information on manufacturing firms in Mexico for 1989 and 1993 with demographic information from the 1990 Population Census and the 1995 Population Count to study these issues. In order to do this they use scale, defined as the average number of workers per manufacturing firm in each municipality, as a proxy for technology—that is, larger-scale firms are assumed to be more technologically advanced firms—after arguing that "scale and its rate of change are natural technological indices in manufacturing."

Their main findings can then be summarized as follows. First, scale appears to be highly correlated with municipal levels of skills and net migration flows, suggesting that firms that use more advanced technologies do indeed locate in skill-abundant areas. Second, the returns to human capital (education) are higher where scale is higher, suggesting that increased demand for skills by these firms translates into higher wages for skilled workers. Finally, higher returns to education are positively and significantly correlated with increases in schooling and school attendance, suggesting that individuals acquire more education when it pays to do so. Hence, to the extent that scale does in fact proxy for technology, there seems to be evidence of a virtuous relationship between technology and human capital.

Source: Mayer and Foster (2002)

North American Free Trade Agreement (NAFTA) finds that the export orientation of a firm and the tariff levels in a sector were both important determinants of a firm's own R&D efforts in 1999, but not in 1992 (Meza and Mora 2001).

The Relationship between Technology Transfer, the Rising Demand for Skills in Latin America, and Patterns of Integration into the Global Economy

Firms using foreign materials and technology invested in complementary R&D efforts, and increased their demand for skilled workers. We now present more evidence on the effect of patterns of integration of Latin America into the global economy on the observed changes in relative demand.

Integration into the Global Economy Facilitated the Transfer of Skill-biased Technologies to Latin America …

The 1980s and 1990s were a period of increasing trade liberalization, rising foreign direct investment (FDI), and more flexible licensing arrangements for many countries in Latin America. Figure 3.5 shows very large decreases in tariffs for some of the countries in our analysis—Colombia and Argentina in the 1980s, Brazil in the early 1990s. By and large, Chile and Mexico had liberalized tariffs earlier. Figure 3.6 shows dramatic increases in FDI in the mid-1990s in Brazil and Mexico. As we discuss in box 3.5, the patterns we observe in the evolution of relative wages in Latin America are quite similar in character to those found in the United States and other OECD countries. It thus seems likely that some of the technological changes that account for the rising wage of skilled workers in OECD countries, in particular in the United States, were transmitted through trade, FDI and licensing, and helped determine the evolution of relative wages in Latin America. Since the technological changes in the United States were complementary with skill, we would expect new technologies adopted in Latin America also to favor more educated workers.

… as Can Be Seen from an Analysis of the Relationship between Changes in Demand and Changes in Import Penetration

To analyze the relationship between the skill upgrading and trade in Latin America, we disaggregate the data for the manufacturing sector in a country into industries, and pool these data to create an unbalanced panel. We then regress relative demand, the relative wage bill, relative wages and the relative employment share on measures of import penetration, the foreign R&D stock, and a decomposition of this foreign R&D stock into a measure of volume and one of composition of the trade flows. (We focus on the comparison between workers with tertiary education and those with secondary

FIGURE 3.5

Tariffs Decreased and Import Penetration Increased in a Number of Latin American Countries in the 1980s and 1990s

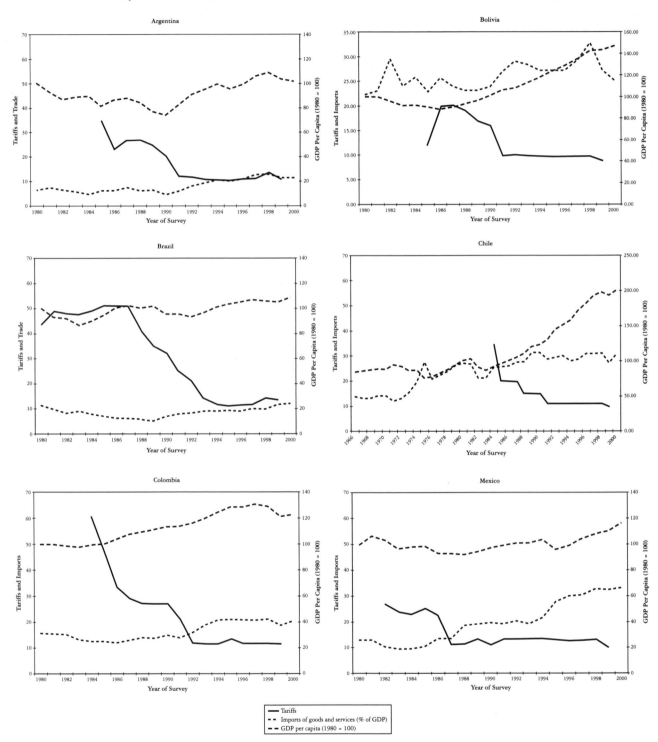

Sources: GDP data from the *World Development Indicators,* The World Bank. Trade and tariffs data from the Research Group; The World Bank (using WTO, IDB CD-ROM database; and *Trade Policy Review Country Report,* various issues, 1990–2000; UNCTAD, *Handbook of Trade Control Measures of Developing Countries Supplement,* 1987; *Directory of Import Regimes,* 1994; World Bank, *Trade Policy Reform in Developing Countries since 1985,* WB Discussion Paper #267, 1994; *The Uruguay Round: Statistics on Tariffs Concessions, Given and Received,* 1996 and *World Development Indicators, 1998–2000;* OECD, *Indicators of Tariff and Non-Tariff Trade Barriers,*1996; IDB, *Statistics and Quantitative Analysis Data,* 1998.

FIGURE 3.6

FDI Flows Increased Significantly in a Number of Latin American Countries

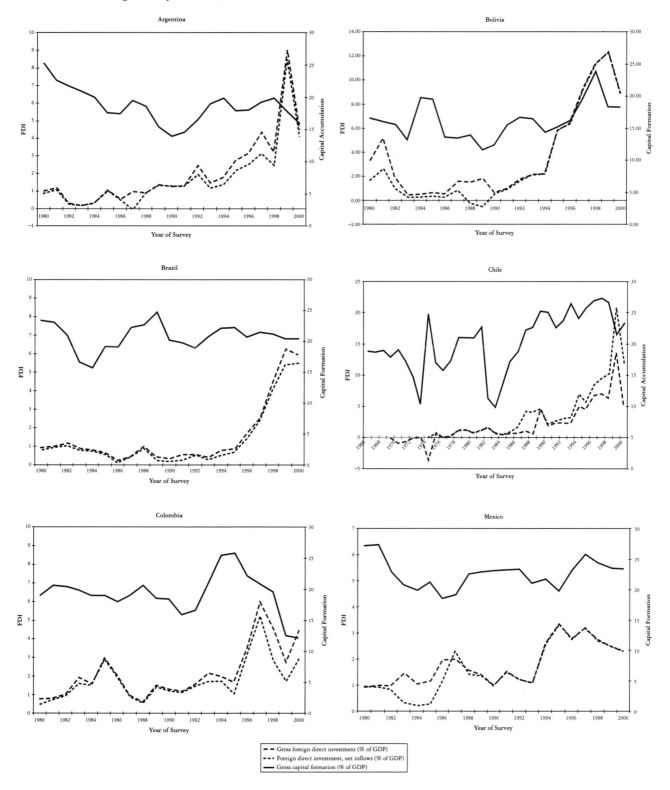

Source: *World Development Indicators*, selected years.

BOX 3.5

Evidence of Skill-Biased Technological Change in the United States and other OECD Countries

There is substantial evidence for the United States and other OECD countries that the increases in the relative wages of more educated workers observed in the last 25 years are to a large extent associated with skill-biased technological change (SBTC). This box reviews this evidence, paying special attention to those papers whose approach and methodology we follow in this chapter to assess the extent of SBTC in Latin America.

The literature on SBTC and its effect on the demand for skilled workers has followed two approaches. First, estimates of changes in the relative demand for skilled workers are often constructed using a simple model of (relative) supply and demand for skilled and unskilled labor, where relative wage changes that cannot be explained by changes in relative supply are assumed to be associated with changes in relative demand (see box 3.3). Second, the degree to which skill upgrading has taken place *within* sectors and *within* firms is then used to assess the extent to which these changes in relative wages are associated with SBTC.

Katz and Murphy (1992) apply the demand-and-supply framework described above to study changes in the structure of wages in the United States during 1963–87. They report that increases in the wages of more educated and more experienced workers are driven by changes in the demand for these workers associated with skill-biased technological change.

Autor, Katz, and Krueger (1998) study the same phenomenon using data on computerization as a proxy for skill-biased technological change. They find evidence that the growth of demand for more educated workers is associated with rapid skill upgrading within detailed industries, and that this upgrading is greater in more computer-intensive industries.

Berman, Bound, and Machin (1998) and Machin and Van Reenen (1998) discuss the extent to which there is evidence of SBTC in countries other than the United States. The first paper investigates whether R&D intensity is related to increases in the demand for more skilled workers in the United States and other OECD countries, and concludes that SBTC is an international phenomenon. The second paper analyzes within-industry changes in the wage-bill for skilled workers. The authors argue that not only did the proportion of skilled workers increase in most industries in most countries, but the magnitude of these increases was also correlated across countries. Specifically, increases in the demand for skilled workers were particularly large in capital-intensive industries, and in industries with the highest degree of computer usage.

Source: Katz and Murphy (1992); Autor, Katz, and Krueger (1998); Berman, Bound, and Machin (1998); Machin and Van Reenen (1998).

education, as this is where we observe the clearest patterns in relative wages, employment shares, and demand.)

Data on imports, and on the R&D content of these imports are only available for three countries in our sample—Chile, Colombia, and Mexico—and only for the manufacturing sector. Moreover, since all our series are trending upwards, we have to de-trend the data to avoid a spurious correlation between our measures of relative demand, or relative wages, or relative employment, and the foreign R&D stock. We do this by removing a country-industry specific linear time trend from all variables. We then regress the dependent variable (relative wages, relative demand, the wage bill, or the employment share) in industry i in country c at time t on the measure of imports, foreign R&D, or the decomposition of the imports in this industry-country

cell, lagged by one period. The results are summarized in table 3.4.

In the first panel, the explanatory variable is import penetration—where import penetration is defined as total imports in an industry over value added. Table 3.4 shows that increases in import penetration are consistently associated with increases in skill upgrading—regardless of whether this upgrading is measured in terms of relative wages, demand, wage bill, or employment share of workers with tertiary education. In the second panel, the explanatory variable is a measure of the foreign R&D stock available in an industry-country-year cell. This measure, developed by Schiff, Wang, and Olarreaga (2002) can be thought of as a measure of import penetration by industry, when the imports are weighted by their R&D content.[16] Once again, the results

TABLE 3.4

There Is More Skill Upgrading, Measured by the Relative Wages, Relative Employment Shares, and Relative Demand for Tertiary Workers, in Countries and Industries That Have Higher Import Penetration, Especially of Imports That Are Intensive in R&D

	RELATIVE WAGES	RELATIVE DEMAND	WAGE BILL	EMPLOYMENT SHARE (HOURS)	EMPLOYMENT SHARE (WORKERS)
MODEL 1					
Imports (% VA)	0.049***	0.087***	0.018***	0.006***	0.005**
	(0.011)	(0.023)	(0.006)	(0.002)	(0.003)
N	375	375	375	375	375
Prob > Chi^2	0.000	0.000	0.000	0.000	0.000
MODEL 2					
Foreign R&D stock	0.138***	0.282***	0.051***	0.011***	0.009***
	(0.012)	(0.027)	(0.007)	(0.003)	(0.003)
N	375	375	375	375	375
Prob > Chi^2	0.000	0.000	0.000	0.000	0.000
MODEL 3					
Trade volume (imports)	0.041***	0.065***	0.016***	0.002	0.001
	(0.011)	(0.023)	(0.006)	(0.002)	(0.002)
Trade composition (R&D index)	0.044***	0.119***	0.015***	0.019***	0.021***
	(0.012)	(0.028)	(0.007)	(0.003)	(0.003)
N	375	375	375	375	375
Prob > Chi^2	0.000	0.000	0.000	0.000	0.000

Source: Sánchez-Páramo and Schady (2002).

show that increases in foreign R&D stock are consistently related to increases in skill upgrading within industries. Moreover, the relatively larger magnitude of the coefficients suggests that the composition of imports, not just the volume, is important. In the third panel, we disaggregate changes in the foreign R&D stock in an industry into changes in *volume* and changes in *composition* (increases in the R&D content of imports, holding constant the volume), and regress skill upgrading on both of these measures.[17] The results show that both measures, but particularly the measure of trade composition, are important determinants of skill upgrading in Chile, Colombia, and Mexico. Put differently, it is not just the amount of trade but whom you trade with that matters—so that imports from countries and industries that are intensive in R&D are particularly important as an impetus for skill upgrading.[18] Earlier work by Machin and Van Reenen (1998) shows that there is a strong association between industry-level R&D intensity and the wage bill for skilled workers in a sample of OECD countries (including Denmark, France, Germany, Japan, Sweden, the United States, and the United Kingdom). The results in table 3.4 are consistent with a pattern whereby foreign R&D, transmitted through trade, increases the relative wages, employment shares, and demand for workers with tertiary education in Latin America. In a

background paper commissioned for this report, Pavcnik and others (2002) show that there is also evidence of sector-specific skill-biased technological change transferred through trade (box 3.6).

The Level of Skill in a Country Is an Important Determinant of Technology Transferred from Abroad

Up to this point, this chapter has focused on the extent to which technology has determined the demand for workers with more or less education in Latin America. We now consider the reverse question: Can low levels of skill be a constraint to technology transfer through trade and FDI? We find a great deal of evidence that the answer to this question is "yes," suggesting a circular relationship between skill upgrading and technology transfer: Technological innovation increases the demand for skilled workers and, as we will show in chapter 4, can result in increases in educational attainment. This, in turn, can further stimulate the demand for new technology by firms. Some countries may therefore enter a virtuous cycle of upgrading of both technology and skill—a cycle that results in higher productivity and higher growth rates. Countries with very low skill levels, by contrast, may be unable to attract sufficient levels of FDI, and

BOX 3.6
Trade Liberalization and Sector-Specific Skill-Biased Technological Change in Brazil

Recent work by Pavcnik and others (2002) investigates the relationship between trade liberalization and the relative wages of workers with different amounts of education in Brazil, a country that experienced a profound reduction in tariffs in the late 1980s. Because of differences in tariff levels across industries before the reform, this reduction in tariffs affected some industries more than others, and at different times, which makes it possible to convincingly estimate the effect of changes in import penetration or tariffs on changes in wages across industries.

In Brazil, as in many other countries, workers in certain industries are paid a wage premium that cannot be explained by their education or experience. The underlying reasons for this premium are not clear, although it may be related to differences across industries in working conditions, nonwage compensation, or unionization affecting relative wages. In addition, there is a wage premium to *skill* that varies across industries: highly educated workers are paid more in some industries than in others, and these patterns do not necessarily correspond to the patterns in overall industry wage premia. How did trade liberalization affect the industry-specific wage premium to skill? Pavcnik and others show that while the overall industry wage premium was not affected by trade liberalization, the industry wage premium for skill was significantly related to reductions in tariffs. Specifically, a one percentage point reduction in tariffs is associated with about a 0.2 percent

increase in the wage premium paid to educated workers. These are comparatively large effects, as more than half the industries in the sample cut tariffs by more than 50 points between 1987 and 1998 in Brazil.

What explains these surprising findings? First, they point to rigidities in the Brazilian labor market: if educated workers were perfectly mobile across industries, we would expect them to switch out of the industries with falling wage premia for skill and into those with rising premia. Second, the results are consistent with a pattern of sector-specific skill-biased technological change. There is considerable evidence from around the world that technological innovations from a "leader" country transmitted through trade to a "follower" country have the largest effect on productivity in firms that are in the same industry in both countries (see, for example, Keller 2002). It therefore seems plausible that in Brazil new technologies were adopted primarily in those industries that faced the biggest reductions in tariffs. These technologies likely had two impacts on firms in these industries: they raised productivity, and some of these productivity increases were passed on to workers in the form of higher wages. However, because new technologies were skill-biased, they particularly increased the productivity and wages of skilled workers, rather than of the average worker in an industry.

Source: Pavcnik and others (2002)

the amount of technology transferred through trade may also be low. Moreover, what little technology is transferred may be quite inappropriate because it was developed for the highly skill-intensive workforce of the "leader" countries. As a result, expected productivity improvements may not materialize (Acemoglu and Zilibotti 2001). These countries may also be unable to generate technological upgrading through domestic R&D, as this is by its very nature a skill-intensive process. In the absence of policy reforms, countries with very low levels of skill may therefore be trapped in a vicious cycle of little technology transfer, no domestic innovation, low returns to education, low productivity, and stagnant growth prospects.

Differences in the Degree of Computer Penetration between Latin America and East Asia Are Explained by Differences in Education and Trade Exposure ...
We begin our discussion of the effect of human capital on technology transfer with an analysis of the relationship between computer penetration, trade, and human capital. To do this, we return to the data from Caselli and Coleman we referred to in chapter 2. The main finding of Caselli and Coleman's analysis is that computer adoption is strongly associated with high levels of human capital (even after controlling for differences across countries in income per worker), and with *manufacturing* trade with the OECD. To estimate the extent to which these two variables can explain

differences in the pattern of computer penetration between Latin America and East Asia, we perform a simple calculation: We predict what the change in computer penetration in Latin America between 1980 and 1990 would have been if Latin America had had the mean changes in education and manufacturing trade with the OECD observed in *East Asia*. The results from these calculations suggest that computer penetration would have increased by *a greater amount* in Latin America than it did in East Asia during the 1980–90 period if Latin America had had the East Asian patterns of skill upgrading and trade.[19]

...as Can Differences within Latin America

In chapter 2 we showed that computer imports within Latin America varied a great deal—even for countries with the same level of income. For example, the value of computer imports per worker in 1990 was more than twice as high in Panama as in Ecuador, despite their comparable per capita incomes, while the level of computer penetration in Brazil was the same as in Honduras, despite the very large income differences.[20]

What explains these differing patterns of computer penetration within Latin America? Table 3.5 reproduces some of the regressions in the Caselli and Coleman study, when the sample is limited to countries in Latin America. The results show that differences in computer penetration within Latin America are explained by differences in two factors, and two factors only. First, the level of education, specifically the fraction of the population with primary school and (especially) secondary school education. At the means of the other variables, a one-standard deviation (13.5 percentage point) increase in primary education increases computer imports by about 39 percent, while a one-standard deviation (10.5 percentage point) increase in secondary education almost doubles computer penetration (an increase of 95 percent). These effects are much larger than those for the world as a whole, suggesting that primary and secondary schooling levels are better predictors of the adoption of new technologies in Latin America than elsewhere. The second variable that is a significant predictor of computer penetration is the amount of trading in the manufacturing sectors with OECD countries. Countries in Latin America that trade with the technological leaders, especially in manufacturing, have significantly higher propensities to upgrade their technologies. This effect is also larger in the Latin American sample than in the global sample. At the means of the other variables, a one-standard deviation increase in manufacturing imports from the OECD increases the degree of computer penetration in Latin America by about 90 percent.[21] None of the other variables—the level of income or investment

TABLE 3.5

Countries in Latin America with More Skilled Workers Are Better Prepared to Adopt New Technologies

	DEPENDENT VARIABLE: LOG OF COMPUTER IMPORTS PER WORKER, 1970–90	
	COEFFICIENT	STANDARD ERROR
Log income per worker	0.350	0.437
Log investment per worker	0.269	0.337
Fraction with primary education	**0.025***	**0.012**
Fraction with secondary education	**0.063****	**0.016**
Fraction with tertiary education	0.004	0.035
Log manufacturing imports from OECD per worker	**0.636***	**0.303**
Log non-manufacturing imports from OECD per worker	−0.117	0.189
Log manufacturing imports from non-OECD per worker	−0.192	0.341
Log non-manufacturing imports from non-OECD per worker	−0.125	0.177
Fraction speaking English	−0.997	0.585
Property rights (1–10)	0.098	0.075
Agriculture share in GDP	−0.013	0.014
Manufacturing share in GDP	0.004	0.016
Government spending share in GDP	−0.015	0.018
R-squared	0.772	
Number of countries	23	
Number of observations	82	

Note: All regressions include year fixed effects. Estimation technique is Random Effects (RE).
* significant at the 5 percent level; ** significant at the 1 percent level.
Source: Schady (2002), based on data from Caselli and Coleman (2001).

per worker, measures of the composition of the economy, property rights, and trade other than manufacturing trade with OECD countries—is a significant predictor of technological upgrading through increased computer imports in Latin America during the 1970–90 period.

There Is Also a Complementary Relationship Among FDI, Trade, and Human Capital

The analysis of computer penetration shows that high-technology imports flow primarily to countries with high levels of secondary school attainment. Empirical work on FDI finds a similar pattern: Technologies transferred through FDI increase productivity in the host country only in cases involving countries where the mean level of education is about two years of secondary school.[22] Other studies have found a strong (positive) interaction between imports of machinery and secondary school enrollment in determining growth rates.[23] There is also evidence specific to Latin America suggesting that FDI is directed primarily at countries and regions with high levels of human capital. For every additional year of schooling in 1985, countries in Latin America received almost half a percentage point more FDI as a fraction of GDP during the 1985–98 period. In Mexico, states with higher levels of human capital receive more FDI—even after controlling for distance to the United States border (de Ferranti and others 2002, pp. 93–103). The maquiladoras in northern Mexico and the Dominican Republic employ workers with higher mean levels of education than the population average, especially women with secondary schooling Cunningham (2002). Finally, trade with developed countries has a particularly large impact on TFP in Latin America when trade takes place in R&D-intensive sectors in the exporting country, and when there is a high degree of human capital in the recipient country (Schiff and Wang 2002).

Long-Term Cycles in the Demand for Skilled Workers and Technology?

The Experiences of Different Countries in Latin America over the Last 20 Years Were "Determined" by Their Potential Capacity to Receive and Effectively Use New Technologies ...

Because new technologies are complementary with skills, the initial levels of technology and education, as well as the speed with which these levels changed over time, have played an important role in determining the returns to education, and the ability to rapidly absorb new technology transferred through trade, FDI, and licensing.

... with Chile Moving a Decade or More before Other Latin American Countries

In this context, the case of Chile is instructive. Differences in the patterns of relative demand, technological change, integration in the world economy and productivity between Chile, on the one hand, and other countries in Latin America, on the other, are noteworthy as Chile undertook many "Washington Consensus" type reforms well before other countries in the region. Of the six countries we analyzed extensively with the labor force survey data, an "ad hoc" ranking of the degree of global integration and structural transformation of the economy would put Chile highest, then Mexico, followed by Argentina, Bolivia, Brazil, and Colombia (these last four, in no particular order). This ranking of countries by macroeconomic reforms—reforms that should have a critical influence on the degree to which countries are able to adopt technologies from abroad, for example—can be mapped reasonably well onto the series of changes in relative demand for workers with tertiary education for the five countries in our sample. We pursue this line of thought in figure 3.7, in which we superimpose the demand series for $\sigma = 2$ for Argentina, Bolivia, Brazil, Colombia, and Mexico on the longer Chilean series. Figure 3.7 suggests that countries in Latin America are at different stages in a long-term cycle of changing relative demand for workers with different amounts of skill. (The "years" on the x-axis are not the same across countries, precisely because our hypothesis is that different countries are at different stages in this cycle of relative demand.) This is more apparent if we visually "smooth out" deviations from long-term trends that are caused by macroeconomic crises.

Understanding long-term patterns in relative demand, productivity, and growth has profound implications for the development of countries in the region. In the early 1970s, Chile started off with reasonably low education and technology levels, limited access to international technology, and low returns to education. Between 1975 and 1990, it opened up to trade and FDI, both of which served to transmit technology from the "leader" countries. As this technology was applied by firms, these increased their demand for skilled workers and the wages they were willing to pay them. In consequence, wage inequality increased—temporarily (table 3.6). In response to the sharp wage differentials

FIGURE 3.7

The Long-Term Cycles in Relative Demand in Latin America ($\sigma = 2$)

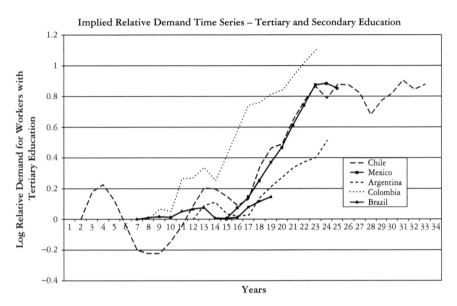

Source: Sánchez-Páramo and Schady (2002).

TABLE 3.6

Wage Inequality Increased with Increases in Demand for Skilled Workers

	ARGENTINA	BOLIVIA	BRAZIL	CHILE	COLOMBIA	MEXICO
	GINI COEFFICIENT OF MONTHLY WAGES (FIVE-YEAR AVERAGES)					
1965–70				0.447		
1970–75				0.419		
1975–80				0.453		
1980–85			0.545	0.484	0.392	
1985–90	0.396		0.559	0.504	0.371	0.352
1990–95	0.377	0.456	0.557	0.469	0.402	0.403
1995–99	0.388	0.458	0.548	0.461	0.416	0.430

Source: Sánchez-Páramo and Schady (2002), based on household and labor force survey data from each country.

associated with education, young men and women in Chile acquired more education before entering the labor market. Mean education levels increased and this, in turn, kept the returns to education from increasing further. Productivity also increased substantially: Between 1985 and 2000 value added per worker grew by 71 percent. Within a 20-year period, Chile made the transition from a country that was arguably in a low technology–low education equilibrium to one at the medium technology–high education equilibrium—at least by regional standards. Indeed, by 2000 it had both the highest educational attainment and the highest degree of technological sophistication in the region.[24] This transformation helps explain the increases in firm productivity, the steady growth, and the recent improvements in wage inequality in Chile. They also explain why, with a more

educated workforce, a much larger fraction of the workforce can benefit from the high returns to education than before.

Where does the cycle go from here? Although Chile was able to import much of the technology it needed in the 1980s and early 1990s from abroad, it may now need to place an increasing amount of effort into developing its domestic technological capacity. Undoubtedly, Chile is closer to the world's technological frontier now than it was 20 years ago—even though the frontier has itself shifted farther out. Indeed, in some sectors, Chile may itself need to push out the frontier in order to stay competitive. These distinctions between countries that are more or less far away from the global technological leaders have important implications for the design of policies for domestic innovation structures. We return to these in chapters 6 and 7.

Conclusion

In this chapter we have made a number of points about the relationship between technology and skills in Latin America. The most important include the following:

- There has been an increase in the demand for skills in Latin America, in particular the demand for workers with university education. This increase in demand has not been matched by equivalent increases in the supply of highly educated workers, so that overall relative wages of workers with tertiary education have gone up relative to those of workers with secondary education.
- Most of the increase in the demand for skills is a result of the transfer of skill-biased technologies to Latin America.
- Improved access to these technologies, as well as growing competitive pressure to use them, can be linked to trade opening and new FDI flows. However, new technologies were transferred primarily to countries with reasonably "high" levels of human capital.
- Many of the changes observed in Argentina, Bolivia, Colombia, Mexico, and (less clearly) Brazil in the 1990s closely resemble the experience of Chile in the 1980s. As we showed in chapter 2, Brazil has by far the lowest level of skills of any of the countries in our sample. This may be the reason why skill-biased technologies have not been adopted to a significant degree in Brazil, and may be a plausible explanation for the differences between the Brazilian and (more general) Latin American patterns.

The Relationship between Technology and Skills and the Patterns It Generates Has Important Implications for Education Policy

Countries need a broad base of workers with secondary education to be able to access new technologies. Given that most countries in the region exhibit a large gap at the secondary level, substantial improvements in secondary enrollment and graduation rates will be required in order to create such a base. Also, new technologies appear to be complementary with skills, in particular with tertiary education. Although countries in the region do not exhibit as large a gap at the tertiary level as they do at the secondary level, the job is far from done. As a result, Latin American countries will have to concentrate heavily on improving the education level of their population, increasing the number of workers with sec-

ondary *and* tertiary education, if they are to remain as competitive players in global markets. Chapter 4 discusses different policy interventions aimed toward achieving these goals, as well as some successful experiences in the region that can serve as guidelines for the reformers to come.

Endnotes

1. This section is based on Sánchez-Páramo and Schady (2002). Since our sample sizes are relatively small, in particular in Argentina, Bolivia, Chile, and Colombia, and especially when we consider workers with university education, we graph three-year moving averages for the values of relative supply and wages in a given year.

2. For example, the fact that the demand series for $\sigma = 3$ for Colombia is steeper for the 1990–93 period than for the 1993–96 period provides evidence that the relative demand for workers with tertiary education grew more quickly in the first three years of the decade. Similarly, the fact that the demand series for $\sigma = 3$ for Colombia for the 1990–93 period is steeper than the corresponding demand series for Argentina, Bolivia, Brazil, Chile, and Mexico shows that demand grew by more in Colombia than elsewhere.

3. Sánchez-Páramo and Schady (2002) calculate changes in a manner comparable to those found in Autor, Katz, and Krueger (1998).

4. For one thing, the degree of skill-abundance varies a great deal from country to country. Insofar as most trade of most Latin American countries is with the United States or other OECD countries that are relatively more skill-abundant, we would expect trade reform to lead to a decrease in the wage premium associated with education in Latin America.

5. On Brazil, see Pavcnik and others (2002); on Colombia, Attanasio, Goldberg, and Pavcnik (2002); on Mexico, Hanson and Harrison (1999).

6. In Brazil, for example, an industry with 10 percentage points more unskilled labor could expect to see, on average, a four point bigger reduction in tariffs between 1987 and 1998. A regression of the annual change in tariffs against the share of unskilled workers in 1987 yields a coefficient of -3.97 for the share of unskilled workers (*t*-statistic = -1.88). See Pavcnik and others (2002, p. 13).

7. As proposed by Berman, Bound, and Machin (1998), changes in the wage bill share of workers with tertiary education are decomposed as follows: (1) $\Delta Sn = \sum_i \Delta Sn_i \overline{W_i} + \sum_i \Delta W_i \overline{Sn_i}$, where Sn is the wage bill share of tertiary (skilled) workers defined as $Sn = \dfrac{w_s S}{w_s S + w_u U}$, and W_i is the wage bill share of industry i defined as $W_i = \dfrac{WB_i}{\sum_i WB_i}$, where S is workers with tertiary education (or skilled), U is workers with secondary education (or unskilled), W_s is wages of workers with tertiary education, W_U is wages of workers with secondary education, WB is the wage bill, i is an industry index and an overstrike indicates an average between the initial and final periods considered. Industry wage bill shares are then used as industry-specific weights in (1), so that the first term captures within-industry changes in the wage bill share and the second term captures between-industry changes. In other

words, the first terms holds industry-specific weights constant and the second term holds within-industry wage bill shares constant.

8. See Autor, Katz, and Krueger (1998); Katz and Autor (1999); Berman, Bound, and Machin (1998); and Berman and Machin (2000).

9. Similar estimates based on firm-level data for Chile for the 1979–86 period suggest that 66 percent of the changes in the wage bill occurred within very detailed four-digit ISIC industries (Pavcnik 2002).

10. Calculations based on a United Nations classification of industrial employment into "non-production" (skilled) and "production" (unskilled) workers for the 1980s show a similar pattern for the six Latin American countries for which data are available: The proportion of the change in the wage bill of non-production workers that takes place *within* industries is 51 percent in Uruguay, 62 percent in Venezuela, 69 percent in Guatemala, 84 percent in Colombia, 103 percent in Peru, and 153 percent in Chile. See Berman and Machin (2000, p. 29).

11. Observations are weighted by the sector employment shares averaged over time and across countries, in a similar fashion to the correlations for industrialized countries presented in Berman, Bound, and Machin (1998).

12. The fact that none of the correlation coefficients is significant is probably not surprising given that we only have 11 comparable sectors across countries.

13. To identify the sectors most affected by skill upgrading at the tertiary level, we pooled the data for Chile in the 1980s with the data for other countries in the 1990s, and regressed the within-sector change in the employment share on a set of country and sector indicator variables. See Berman, Bound, and Machin (1998) for a similar approach.

14. Pavcnik's results for Chile are not robust to the inclusion of plant fixed effects, raising the possibility that some unobserved differences across plants explain both skill upgrading and technology adoption. However, it is quite possible that measurement error and the comparatively small number of years in the plant-level panel are responsible for the lack of significance of the technology measures in the plants fixed-effects regressions.

15. Firm-level data for Mexico between 1992 and 1999 also show that firms that adopted new technology paid higher wages to workers from all skill groups, but especially semi-skilled workers. The Mexican data also show that there is a positive, significant correlation between a firm-level measure of Total Factor Productivity (TFP) and the employment share of high-skilled workers. See Lopez-Acevedo (2002).

16. Schiff, Wang, and Olarreaga (2002) define North-foreign R&D in industry i of developing country c, as $NRD_{ci} = \sum_j a_{cij} RD_{cj} = \sum_j a_{cij} \left[\sum_k \left(\frac{M_{cjk}}{VA_{cj}} \right) RD_{jk} \right]$, where $c(k)$ indexes developing (OECD) countries; j indexes industries; M, VA and RD denote imports, value added, and R&D, respectively; and a_{cij} is the input-output coefficient (which measures the share of imports in industry j that is sold to industry i in country c). Data on import input-output flows are not available, so they are proxied by domestic input-output flows in the estimation. Sales of imports for final consumption are excluded from the estimation.

17. This methodology closely follows that in Coe, Helpman, and Hoffmaister (1997).

18. These results are from Sánchez-Páramo and Schady (2002).

19. Specifically, we regress the difference in the log of computer penetration between 1980 and 1990 on changes in the education variables between 1970 and 1980 and changes in manufacturing trade with the OECD between 1980 and 1990 for the sample of *Latin American* countries, and then multiply the coefficients from this regression by the mean change in these covariates in *East Asian* countries over the period. (Changes in human capital are lagged to limit the extent to which the changes in education could themselves have been caused by changes in technological penetration.) This calculation, which is similar in character to the standard Oaxaca-Blinder decomposition used by labor economists, gives a sense of the changes in computer penetration we would have expected to see in Latin America if there had been changes in education and trade of the magnitude of those observed in East Asia. The results should be treated with caution, as the regression in changes only has 22 Latin American observations, while the mean changes in East Asia are an average of only 9 observations.

20. According to these data, Jamaica, Panama, Chile, and Costa Rica are all positive outliers within the Latin America region, having higher levels of computer penetration than would be predicted for their (regional) income levels.

21. Note that, as Caselli and Coleman point out, the significance of this result is *not* driven by the inclusion of computers in the measure of manufacturing imports, as computing equipment is a miniscule fraction of total trade with both OECD and non-OECD partners. Also, Caselli and Coleman (p.7) point out that for the global sample the effect of manufacturing imports from the OECD remains significant even after a host of related variables—bilateral-trade-weighted measures of distance from the leading world exporters, measures of FDI inflows, the black market premium, and the Sachs-Warner openness measure—are included in the regression. Moreover, none of these additional variables is itself a significant predictor of computer penetration. Unsurprisingly, given the obvious time trend in computer penetration, all of the year dummies are highly significant. Still, the results in table 3.5 are remarkable, as much as anything else, when we consider all of the variables that do *not* have an effect on computer penetration in Latin America.

22. Xu (2000). Earlier work by Borensztein, De Gregario, and Lee (1998, p. 126) reaches similar conclusions. The authors write that there are "strong complementary effects between FDI and human capital on the growth rate of income," a result that is "consistent with the idea that the flow of advanced technology brought along by FDI can increase the growth rate of the host economy only by interacting with that country's absorptive capability," although the threshold level of secondary school in Borensztein, De Gregario, and Lee (1998) is somewhat lower than that estimated by Xu.

23. Romer (1993), cited in Borensztein, De Gregario, and Lee (1998, p. 127).

24. Chile had the largest amount of private R&D and the largest number of computers available per worker of any country in the region, and was second-highest in the number of patents registered in the United States, after Argentina.

CHAPTER 4

Closing the Skills Gap: Education Policies

I N EARLIER CHAPTERS WE ARGUED THAT LATIN AMERICA HAS A PROFOUND GAP in skills. Latin American adults have almost one-and-a-half fewer years of education than would be expected for their levels of per capita income, and enrollment rates at the secondary and tertiary levels are both low as well. Moreover, the quality of Latin American education is deficient, and students from the region (with the exception of those from Cuba) do poorly on international tests.

Chapter 3 showed that technological upgrading, such as that which is transmitted through trade and FDI, is a key reason why firms have increased the demand for skilled workers, and have bid up their relative wages. We also argue that policies enabling young men and women in Latin America to meet this increase in demand by seeking more schooling should be a key objective of government policy.

In this chapter, we consider policies to close the skill gap in Latin America. The chapter moves from an analysis of the *labor* market, which determines the relative wages of individuals with different amounts of schooling, to an analysis of the *education* market. Does the education system in a country produce an adequate amount and mix of skilled workers? Specifically, the chapter considers two sets of issues. First, we consider the *speed* and *distribution* of skill upgrading for countries in the region. Second, we discuss appropriate policies for secondary school and for the university system. We leave aside

concerns about primary education—both because most Latin American countries do not appear to have a deficit in primary enrollment for their income level, and because skill-biased technological change in the region has particularly raised the demand for workers with secondary and tertiary education.[1]

The key messages of this chapter are three.

- Latin America needs to close the skills gap *quickly* if it is to be competitive in the global marketplace. New technologies have particularly increased the productivity of educated workers, and employers are passing on some of these productivity increases in the form of higher wages. There is a direct link between this relationship of education and wages at the *individual* level, and the relationship of education and aggregate income at the *country* level (Krueger and Lindahl 2001).

This means that skill upgrading should have a larger effect on growth rates now than before. Positive externalities associated with education may further augment the impact of schooling on growth.

- There is very limited potential for "leapfrogging" education levels. The most successful episodes of educational upgrading—the United States between 1850 and 1950, Korea and the Scandinavian countries since World War II—have all followed a pattern of bottom-up upgrading, first building up basic education, then secondary education, and finally university. A balanced education transition ensures that the most gifted students go to university, is likely to minimize inequality, and takes advantage of the complementarities between the phases in an *educational* transition and those in the *technological* transition of a country. A number of Latin American countries appear to have been following "unbalanced" educational transitions—increasing the coverage of university without ensuring a large pool of secondary school graduates. Expanding the coverage of secondary school is therefore the biggest priority for most countries in the region. However, policies that enable students to attend university are also important, both because there are high returns to tertiary education, and because the option value of going to university is one of the main incentives for completing secondary school.

- Both the quality of education and the nature of the skills learned in school have important consequences for wages and productivity. Higher quality education will make workers more productive, increase the rate of return to education, and provide an incentive for further private investments in education. In a rapidly changing environment, schools and universities should teach general, problem-solving skills that enable young men and women to "learn how to learn" throughout their lives.

The rest of the chapter proceeds as follows. We first consider the evolution of educational attainment in the region, focusing in particular on countries with different transition paths. The second half of the chapter then applies a supply-demand framework to the analysis of the secondary school and university systems. In the final section we discuss policy implications.

Educational Transitions: The How

Educational Transitions: Pyramids, Anvils, and Diamonds

In this chapter we refer to the process of skill upgrading through the formal school system as an "educational transition." This transition entails changes in both the *mean* and the *distribution* of educational attainment. In figure 4.1 we present some stylized shapes for the underlying distribution of schooling for countries at different stages in their educational transitions. As we will show, these correspond to the paths followed by countries in Latin America, East Asia, and Scandinavia.

- When the mean years of schooling is low, the distribution of educational attainment in countries tends to

look like a pyramid. The base, corresponding to the fraction with no schooling or with some primary schooling only, is wide. The middle section, corresponding to the fraction with some secondary schooling, is thin but fatter than the top, which corresponds to adults with some tertiary education. Virtually all of the countries we consider in this report found themselves at this phase in 1960.

- As they moved from the first stage of the transition to the second, some countries upgraded from the bottom up. These countries gradually increased the proportion of adults with some secondary schooling by decreasing the number who had no schooling or only primary education. The resulting distribution still looks like a pyramid—albeit one with a much thinner base and a much fatter middle. This stage corresponds to East Asian tigers and Finland in 1980, and to many Latin American countries in 2000.

- When countries move from the second phase of the transition to the third, so much mass is shifted from the base to the middle that the distribution resembles a diamond. More adults have some secondary schooling than those with only some primary schooling or less. Finland, Norway, Sweden, and all of the East Asian tigers except Malaysia (but none of the Latin American countries) have diamond distributions.

- Some Latin American countries, including Costa Rica, the Dominican Republic, Ecuador, El Salvador, and Venezuela, as well as Thailand in East Asia, have evolved along a different path. These countries "squeezed from the middle" in moving beyond the first phase: The base got thinner and the top wider, while the middle was relatively unaffected. The resulting distribution resembles a lopsided anvil rather than a pyramid, with the bulk of the population with only some primary schooling or less, but more individuals with tertiary education than secondary schooling only.

- Finally, access to university in some countries has become so widespread that more adults have university education than either secondary or primary school only. For example, in the United States and Canada more than half the adult population has some university education. The distribution of educational attainment in these countries resembles an inverted pyramid.

FIGURE 4.1

Education Transitions

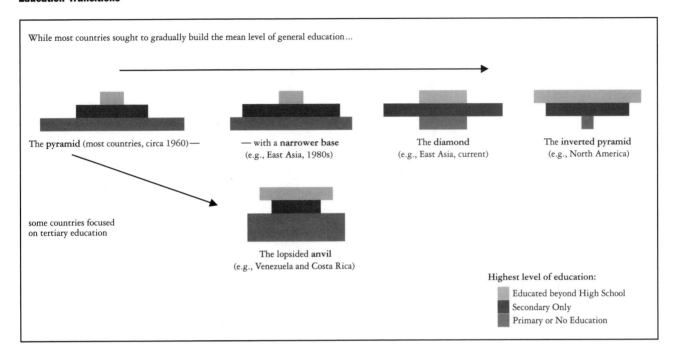

In 1960 the Distribution of Educational Attainment in Latin America, East Asia, and the Countries of the European "Periphery" Resembled a First-phase Pyramid

In 1960, the first point at which we have comparable education statistics for a large cross-section of countries, educational attainment was low in Latin America, East Asia, and some countries on the European periphery such as Finland and Spain. The mean years of schooling in 1960 among the population aged 25 or older was 5 or below in every East Asian country in the sample, and less than 3.5 in Korea, Malaysia, Singapore, and Taiwan (China). In Latin America, mean educational attainment was also 5 years or fewer in every country, and 2.5 years or fewer in Mexico, Venezuela, and a number of countries in Central America. In Spain, meanwhile, the mean years of schooling was 3.6, and in Finland it was 5.4. In every one of these countries in East Asia, Latin America, and the European periphery, more than three-quarters of the population had only primary schooling or less.[2] Figure 4.2 illustrates these similarities by graphing the distribution of educational attainment in 1960 in Korea, Brazil, and Spain. The figure shows that both the mean years of schooling and the distribution of schooling were similar in all three countries.

The Story of the East Asian Tigers and Finland: Fast, Bottom-up Upgrading

Although the starting points were similar, the evolution of educational attainment was not. Figure 4.3 and table 4.1 show that between 1960 and 2000 the mean years of schooling went up by more than 4.5 years in Hong Kong (China), Korea, Malaysia, Singapore, Taiwan (China), and Finland. In the most remarkable transformation, Korea more than *tripled* the mean years of schooling of adults to 10.5—a level well above those of most European countries.

How did these countries achieve such a remarkable performance? In all of them, skill upgrading began with improvements at the bottom. Take the examples of Korea and Finland. Between 1960 and 1980, the fraction of adults with only primary education or less fell by more than 30 percentage points in both Korea and Finland. Meanwhile, the corresponding fraction of adults with only some secondary education increased by more than 25 percentage points in both countries. In terms of the schematic distributions in figure 4.1, Korea and Finland both moved from the first to the second stage of their educational transitions by squeezing the base of the pyramid, fattening the middle section, and leaving the top largely unchanged.

FIGURE 4.2

The Distribution of Educational Attainment Was Similar in Brazil, Spain, and Korea in 1960

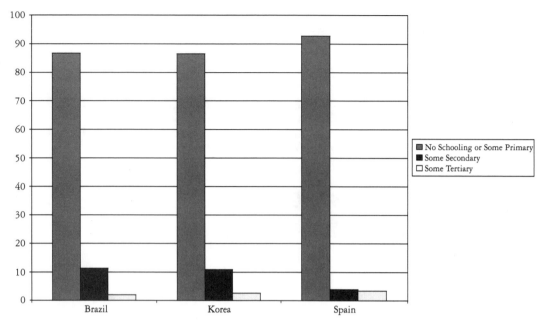

Source: Authors' calculations, based on data from Barro and Lee (2002).

Between 1980 and 2000, the fraction of adults with only some primary education or less fell by an additional 32 percentage points in Korea, and by 22 points in Finland. This second wave of upgrading above the primary school level was more evenly divided between increases in the fraction of adults with some secondary education only, and increases in the fraction of adults with some tertiary education. That is, both Korea and Finland moved from the second to the third phase of their educational transitions by again squeezing the base of the pyramid, further fattening the middle, and increasing the size of the top. As a result of this 40-year process, by 2000 there were more adults with secondary education in both countries than adults with primary schooling or less. Upgrading skills from the bottom, Korea and Finland had made the transition from a pyramid to a diamond. As table 4.1 shows, so had Hong Kong (China), Singapore, and Taiwan (China)—and Malaysia was not far behind.

The Story of Most Latin American Countries:
Slow, Top-down Upgrading
Overall, skill upgrading between 1960 and 2000 was much less impressive in Latin America. Some countries did have large increases in attainment: In both Mexico and Peru the mean years of schooling of adults went up by 4.3 years. But table 4.2 shows that in many countries the changes were

small: In Brazil, Bolivia, and Guatemala the educational level of adults went up by fewer than 2 years, and in another 13 countries changes were 3 years or fewer.

Not only did Latin American countries fall behind the East Asian tigers and Finland in terms of the *mean* educational attainment of the workforce, the *pattern* of transitions was also different. In 1960, there was (on average) one worker with tertiary education for every 5 to 10 workers with secondary education in most countries in Latin America and East Asia. Between 1960 and 2000 this ratio of workers with tertiary education to those with secondary education *quadrupled* or more in Bolivia, Chile, Costa Rica, Ecuador, El Salvador, Guatemala, Panama, and Venezuela, and *tripled* or more in Argentina, Brazil, Dominican Republic, Honduras, and Peru. The bulk of Latin American countries upgraded skills by making the distribution of education more skewed. The only exceptions to this pattern were Mexico, Cuba, and the English-speaking countries of the Caribbean (Guyana, Jamaica, and Trinidad and Tobago). By contrast, skill upgrading was much more egalitarian in the East Asia tiger countries. The ratio of tertiary-educated workers to those with secondary education was essentially unchanged in Hong Kong (China), Malaysia, and Taiwan (China). In Singapore, this ratio increased, but was still lower in 2000 than anywhere in Latin America except Haiti and

FIGURE 4.3

Fast, Balanced Transitions in the East Asian Tigers and Finland

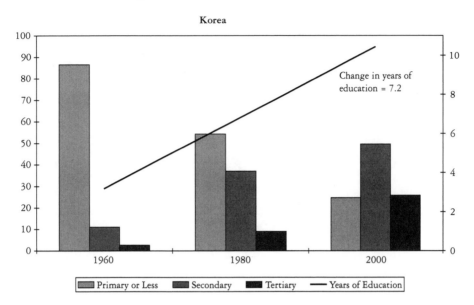

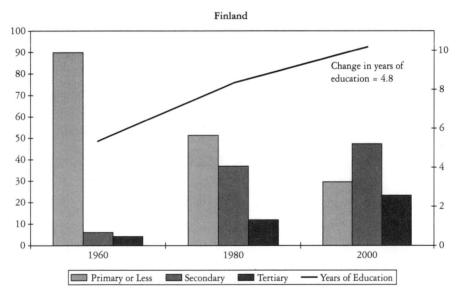

in the English-speaking countries of the Caribbean, and in Korea it went up only after 1990—once the country had education levels that were higher than those found in most OECD countries. In Finland, finally, the ratio of tertiary-educated workers to those with secondary education actually *decreased* between 1960 and 2000. Mean educational attainment thus went up by more, and the dispersion of educational attainment went up by less in the East Asian tigers and Finland than in Latin America.

Where does this leave Latin American countries in their educational transitions in 2000? Figure 4.4 shows that in

some countries, such as Mexico, one of the region's star performers in terms of skill upgrading, the mean and the distribution of education attainment in 2000 were similar to those of Korea *two decades earlier*, while in others, such as Colombia, which had done comparatively little skill upgrading, the mean and distribution in 2000 were similar to those in Korea *three decades earlier*. Over the course of four decades, Mexico had fallen behind Korea by 20 years, and Colombia had fallen behind by 30.

Other countries, including Costa Rica, the Dominican Republic, Ecuador, El Salvador, and Venezuela, upgraded

TABLE 4.1

From Pyramid to Diamond in East Asia and Scandinavia

COUNTRY	YEAR	YEARS OF SCHOOLING	NO STUDIES+ PRIMARY	SECONDARY	TERTIARY
Korea	1960	3.2	86.5	10.9	2.6
	2000	10.5	24.7	49.5	25.8
Taiwan (China)	1960	3.3	84.8	11.0	4.2
	2000	8.5	39.9	41.1	19.1
Singapore	1960	3.1	76.6	23.4	0.0
	2000	8.1	41.0	48.5	10.6
Hong Kong (China)	1960	4.7	77.9	17.4	4.7
	2000	9.5	37.3	47.4	15.3
Finland	1960	5.4	89.9	6.0	4.1
	2000	10.1	29.6	47.3	23.2
Sweden	1960	7.6	58.6	33.9	7.5
	2000	11.4	19.7	57.2	23.1

Note: Countries in East Asia and Scandinavia are sorted (separately) by the change in mean years of schooling between 1960 and 2000.
Source: Authors' calculations, based on data from Barro and Lee (2002).

primarily at the tertiary level, so that their educational transitions were unbalanced. As figure 4.5 shows, in terms of the stylized transitions in figure 4.1, these countries had made the transitions from a fat pyramid to an anvil. Table 4.3 shows that in all of them, there were fewer adults with only secondary school than those with only primary school or with some tertiary education.

Educational Transitions: The (Uncertain) Why

What accounts for the differences between Latin America, Finland, and the East Asian tigers, as well as differences within Latin America? We next turn to a discussion of the way in which demand, supply, and institutions may affect the speed and distribution of the education transition.

The Demand Side ...

Whether technologies favor workers with primary school, secondary school, or university education can obviously have an effect on the patterns of educational transition. Households respond to price signals—including the signals sent by relative wages. In a well-known study on India, Foster and Rosenzweig (1996) show that the Green Revolution increased the returns to education and this, in turn, prompted households to seek further schooling in those areas most suited for the new technologies. A background paper for this report by Mayer and Foster (2002) shows that households in Mexico are also responsive to the rising rates of return to schooling.

Latin American countries generally have a comparative advantage in natural resource extraction and processing,

while East Asian countries do not. Production processes involving natural resources may favor workers with tertiary education—mining or petroleum engineers, scientists in biotechnology—over secondary school graduates. By contrast, firms in East Asian countries, building on more traditional manufacturing processes, may have demanded a workforce with only secondary schooling. This idea has some appeal, although it is hard to test because of the lack of labor force data from many countries prior to the 1980s. Also, it does not explain the *similarities* in the education transition patterns between Venezuela, where oil extraction dominated the economy, and Costa Rica, a country with fewer natural resource endowments.

The "unusual" amount of skill upgrading at the tertiary level relative to the secondary level in some Latin American countries may itself be a response to the rapidly rising returns. In Chile and Colombia gross tertiary enrollment rates more or less doubled between 1980 and 1995, at a time of rising relative wages of workers with tertiary education. However, there are also counter-examples: between 1980 and 1995 tertiary enrollments did not increase by much in either Mexico or Brazil, despite the fact that these countries also saw rising returns to university. Moreover, in some Latin American countries such as Argentina and Mexico the biggest increases in tertiary enrollment rates took place between 1970 and 1985, well before the increases in the demand for educated workers associated with the transfer of skill-biased technologies through trade and FDI. One way of reconciling these varying patterns within the region is by

TABLE 4.2

From Pyramid *toward* Diamond in Some Latin American Countries

COUNTRY	YEAR	YEARS OF SCHOOLING	NO STUDIES+ PRIMARY	SECONDARY	TERTIARY
Malaysia	1960	2.34	91.2	7.2	1.5
	2000	7.88	49.5	43.0	7.5
Spain	1960	3.64	92.7	3.9	3.4
	2000	7.25	53.0	30.7	16.2
Mexico	1960	2.41	94.3	4.3	1.4
	2000	6.73	59.7	29.0	11.3
Peru	1960	3.02	87.7	9.7	2.6
	2000	7.33	49.5	28.1	22.4
Cuba	1960	3.79	93.7	4.3	1.9
	2000	7.78	46.0	42.6	11.3
Panama	1960	4.26	82.1	15.4	2.6
	2000	7.90	51.8	28.5	19.8
Argentina	1960	4.99	85.4	11.6	3.0
	2000	8.49	55.4	24.9	19.7
Trinidad and Tobago	1960	4.19	88.0	10.9	1.0
	2000	7.62	51.4	44.1	4.5
Chile	1960	4.99	75.5	22.4	2.1
	2000	7.89	48.2	36.0	15.8
Jamaica	1960	2.46	94.1	5.5	0.5
	2000	5.22	57.8	38.0	4.1
Guyana	1960	3.50	97.0	2.5	0.5
	2000	6.05	60.0	36.0	4.0
Honduras	1960	1.69	95.8	3.5	0.6
	2000	4.08	82.9	10.6	6.5
Paraguay	1960	3.35	91.8	6.9	1.2
	2000	5.74	73.6	18.1	8.3
Nicaragua	1960	2.09	92.7	4.7	2.5
	2000	4.42	74.7	16.5	8.9
Uruguay	1960	5.03	78.1	16.8	5.1
	2000	7.25	55.4	32.1	12.5
Colombia	1960	2.97	86.4	11.9	1.9
	2000	5.01	68.7	21.4	9.9
Haiti	1960	0.70	95.6	4.2	0.2
	2000	2.67	86.7	12.3	1.0
Brazil	1960	2.83	86.7	11.3	2.0
	2000	4.56	78.0	13.5	8.4
Guatemala	1960	1.43	95.9	3.6	0.5
	2000	3.12	84.7	9.5	5.8
Bolivia	1960	4.22	68.7	27.5	3.7
	2000	5.54	70.7	14.9	14.4

Note: Countries are sorted by the change in mean years of schooling between 1960 and 2000.
Source: Authors' calculations, based on data from Barro and Lee (2002).

underlining that the increase in demand for tertiary education by individuals could only translate into more schooling where institutions, especially the university system, were responsive. As we discuss below, it is likely no coincidence that Chile and Colombia, two countries with a sharp increase in enrollments *concurrent* with the increase in the wage premia to tertiary graduates, had also reformed their university system.

... the Supply Side ...

Even the most casual glance at the comparison between Latin America and East Asia suggests that both the speed and balance of transitions can be affected by government "effort." All of the East Asian tiger economies made education a priority. Korea is a good example: The country's government emphasized the *sequential* expansion of the education system, focusing first on enrollments in primary schools

FIGURE 4.4

Balanced but Slow Transitions in Some Latin American Countries

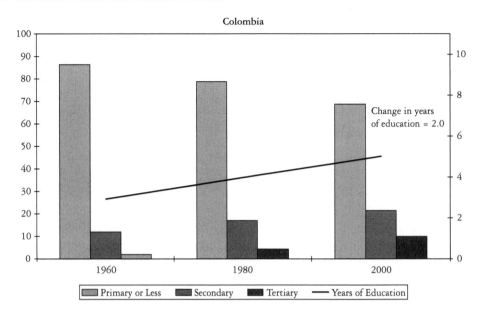

Colombia

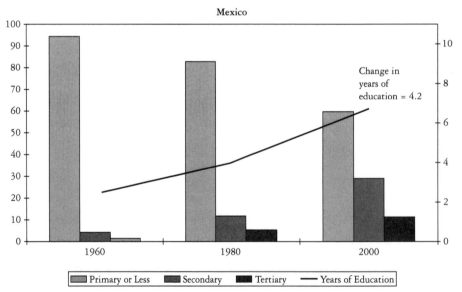

Mexico

(between 1950 and 1970), then on enrollments in secondary schools (between 1970 and 1985), and finally on access to university (especially, since 1990) (Gill and Patrinos 2002; Kim 2001). Within Latin America, the clearest example of how a supply push can make a difference is Cuba. In 1950, the gross secondary enrollment in Cuba was about 5 percent; by 1965, it had reached 23 percent, and continued to rise to 42 percent in 1975; by 1985 it had reached 82 percent, the highest level in Latin America at the time, bar none (Reimers 2001). No other Latin American country has gone through a comparably rapid expansion of the secondary school system.

More "effort" does not always mean more money. In describing the success of the Cuban school push, Carnoy (2002) underlines the change in "the level of expectations in the society as a whole regarding what students are expected to learn in school." Indeed, aggregate public resources do not seem to explain much of the difference between Latin America and East Asia. Table 4.4 shows that, on average, Latin American governments spend a *higher*

FIGURE 4.5

Unbalanced and Slow Transitions in Other Latin American Countries

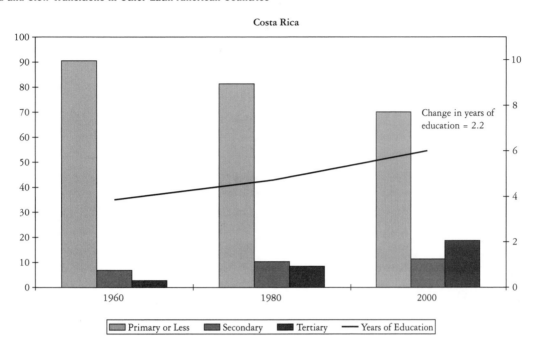

Costa Rica

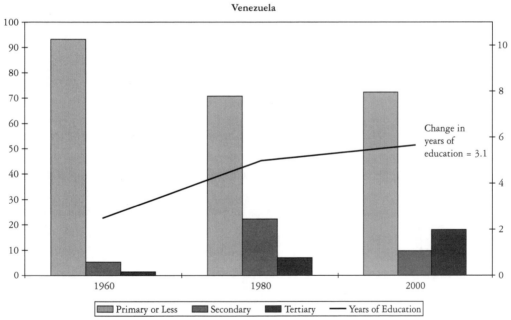

Venezuela

fraction of GDP on education than those in East Asia (although private expenditures on education may be higher in East Asia than in Latin America). Moreover, within Latin America there is no clear relation between high levels of expenditure and good education outcomes—again with the exception of Cuba, which both spends a lot on education and has some of the most impressive outcomes in terms of both the quantity and quality of schooling.

Broad public expenditure aggregates are notoriously difficult to compare. In some countries, they include spending by the central government and regional governments only, which will be misleading in heavily decentralized systems. Also, they may or may not include items such as retirement pay for teachers, transfers to private institutions, and expenditures by entities outside the Ministry of Education, such as Social Fund programs which repair or build school

TABLE 4.3

From Pyramid to Anvil in Other Latin American Countries

COUNTRY	YEAR	YEARS OF SCHOOLING	NO STUDIES+ PRIMARY	SECONDARY	TERTIARY
Thailand	1960	3.4	94.5	4.9	0.6
	2000	6.1	79.5	9.3	11.3
Ecuador	1960	2.9	91.5	7.1	1.4
	2000	6.5	62.9	18.3	18.7
Venezuela	1960	2.5	93.2	5.3	1.5
	2000	5.6	72.3	9.7	18.0
Dominican Republic	1960	2.4	96.5	2.7	0.8
	2000	5.2	72.5	13.1	14.5
El Salvador	1960	1.7	95.0	4.6	0.5
	2000	4.5	80.6	8.8	10.6
Costa Rica	1960	3.7	90.5	6.8	2.7
	2000	6.0	70.1	11.3	18.6

Note: Countries in Latin America are sorted by the change in mean years of schooling between 1960 and 2000.
Source: Authors' calculations, based on data from Barro and Lee (2002).

TABLE 4.4

Education Spending as a Fraction of GDP Is *Not* Low in Most Latin American Countries

	1980	1985	1990	1995
Latin American Economies	3.73	3.53	2.94	4.37
Argentina	2.67	1.47	1.12	3.33
Belize	2.38	4.71	4.81	5.31
Bolivia	4.42	1.99	2.47	5.93
Brazil	3.60	3.78		5.07
Chile	4.63	4.38	2.67	3.10
Colombia	1.86	2.89	2.52	3.67
Costa Rica	7.76	4.45	4.58	4.64
Cuba	7.19	6.27	6.55	6.78
Dominican Republic	2.16	1.59		1.92
Ecuador	5.59	3.70	3.08	3.44
El Salvador	3.90		1.98	2.19
Guatemala	1.81	1.56	1.39	1.70
Guyana	9.79	9.79	4.83	4.29
Haiti	1.48	1.18	1.46	
Honduras	3.19	4.17		3.62
Jamaica	6.96	5.40	5.37	6.35
Mexico	4.73	3.94	3.73	4.87
Nicaragua	3.38	5.93	3.44	3.71
Panama	4.90	4.55	4.93	5.22
Paraguay	1.51	1.50	1.12	3.36
Peru	3.09	2.86	2.29	2.94
Trinidad and Tobago	3.97	6.05	3.97	3.64
Uruguay	2.29	2.83	3.08	2.81
Venezuela	4.40	5.08	3.14	
East Asian Economies	2.45	3.42	2.24	2.60
Indonesia	1.72		1.04	1.40
Korea	3.73	4.45	3.45	3.68
Malaysia	6.04	6.61	5.45	4.68
Philippines	1.72	1.35	2.90	2.96
Singapore	2.84	4.40	3.01	2.98
Thailand	3.42	3.79	3.59	4.14
Vietnam			2.06	2.99

Note: Regional averages are population-weighted.
Source: Authors' calculations using World Bank databases.

infrastructure in many Latin American countries. For all of these reasons, comparisons of broad expenditure aggregates should be treated with caution.

If there are large differences across countries in terms of how they account for education spending, and if these differences remain more or less constant within a country over time, estimating the effect of *changes* in spending on *changes* in enrollment or attainment may provide more accurate results.[3] Figure 4.6 presents a scatter-plot of the changes in educational attainment of adults (in years of education) between 1980 and 1995 as a function of changes in expenditures (as percentage points of GDP). The figure shows no clear relationship between the two. Colombia increased its education spending by two percentage points, while Ecuador decreased it by two points. In spite of these differences, both countries had small increases in mean years of schooling (just over one year). Mexico and Guatemala both left their levels of expenditure unchanged, but in Mexico the mean years of schooling grew by three years, and in Guatemala by one year only. Assuming there were no major changes in the quality of the schooling delivered, Mexico and Ecuador would seem to be getting a lot more for their additional education spending than Guatemala and Colombia.

Perhaps the most fair assessment of the relation between expenditures and changes in mean educational attainment in Latin America is that increases in expenditure, whether public or private, can only make a difference if additional monies are used well. One consideration is the level—primary, secondary, tertiary—that receives the additional

FIGURE 4.6

There Is No Clear Relationship between Changes in Education Expenditure and Changes in Attainment in Latin America

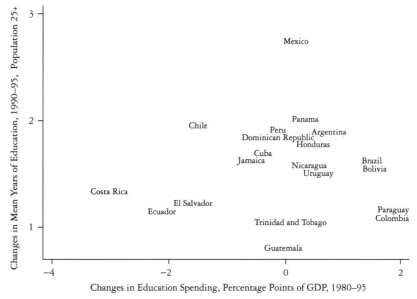

Source: Authors' calculations based on World Bank and UNESCO data.

resources. Cross-country comparisons of the *composition* of education expenditures across levels are even more hazardous than comparisons of expenditure *aggregates*. But it is likely no coincidence that within Latin America the ratio of expenditures on tertiary education to primary and secondary school expenditures is *highest* in Venezuela and Costa Rica, two countries with the largest secondary school gaps (together with Brazil) but essentially no gaps in tertiary enrollment.[4] A second consideration is how resources are used within a given education level—specifically if programs are structured so that they relieve a clearly identified constraint to the acquisition of further schooling. This is the subject of the second half of this chapter, where we discuss policies for secondary school and universities.

... and Institutions

No matter what the ultimate effect of additional expenditures on outcomes, the deeper question is why governments in some countries have been willing to tax their citizens to provide a majority of people with education, and why some have spent additional resources on egalitarian interventions, such as increases in secondary school enrollments, rather than elite interventions, such as high-quality university education for a privileged few. There is no simple answer to this question. Some authors have stressed higher levels of

equality as an explanation for the differences in educational attainment between Latin America and North America.[5] This clearly has some appeal in accounting for differences between Latin America and the East Asian tigers as well, given the much higher levels of inequality of income and other assets in the former in 1960. The focus on inequality may also do well in explaining the patterns found in some countries, such as Brazil, with high levels of inequality, and an unequal distribution of education. Brazilian public universities, in particular, have often been described as a system of "elite formation." Yet other countries are a puzzle, including Costa Rica (where income inequality is low, but the distribution of education is skewed), or Chile (with relatively high levels of income inequality, but reasonably broad access to mass secondary schooling) (Reimers 2001). Ultimately, the dynamics of educational transitions seem to be highly country-specific. In some countries (such as Argentina, Chile, and Uruguay), reasonably broad coalitions emerged which supported mass schooling in the first half of the 20th century; in others, such as Cuba, Korea, or Taiwan (China), authoritarian governments saw mass schooling as integral to the construction of a new national identity; and in yet others, no such consensus emerged, so that the speed of educational transition was slow, and the pattern often unbalanced.

Educational Transitions: Policy Implications

Differences in educational transitions pose a public policy challenge. What is the appropriate role for government in stimulating the pace and the pattern of transitions? We argue below that public investments should focus on expanding the coverage and quality of the secondary school system in most countries in Latin America. In addition, to facilitate the transition to university, government policy should help individuals overcome market failures.

A Balanced Education Transition

The case for a balanced education transition for Latin America rests on three arguments: ensuring that the most gifted students go to university, minimizing inequality, and taking advantage of the complementarities between the phases in an *educational* transition and those in the *technological* transition of a country.

- *A small base of secondary school graduates means that the most able are often excluded from university*. Education is cumulative: one must graduate from secondary school in order to go to university. Having few secondary school graduates therefore means a small pool of university candidates. When university students are drawn from this small pool, many of the most gifted students cannot go to university.

- *Unbalanced transitions may perpetuate inequality*. Latin America is the most unequal region in the world, and unbalanced transitions can perpetuate inequality. The bi-modal "anvil" distributions of educational attainment relegate the bulk of the workforce to low-skill, low-wage jobs, while a privileged few earn the high wages that come with a university education.[6] Because of the close relationship between schooling and earnings, an unequal distribution of *education* tends to perpetuate an unequal distribution of *income*.

- *Sequential* technological *upgrading requires a high fraction of the workforce to have secondary schooling*. As we discussed in chapter 3, mass secondary schooling is an important determinant of the ability of countries to attract trade and FDI with a high technological content, and to benefit from the spillovers from these investments.

In education, as elsewhere, history holds important lessons for Latin America. Three are particularly important. The first

lesson is that the countries that upgraded skills most successfully did so from the bottom-up. Like Korea a century later, the United States went through three sequential "waves" of skill upgrading, involving large increases in primary enrollment in the mid-19th century, in secondary enrollment between 1910 and 1940, and in university enrollment after World War II. It is hard to overstate the importance of these "transformations," especially the transition to mass secondary education. It gave the United States a huge lead in educational attainment over other industrialized countries, and provided the essential building block that made the United States the most successful economy of the 20th century (see box 4.1). The second lesson is that forging a broad consensus is a *sine qua non* for the reforms necessary for a fast, balanced educational transition. Governing elites in Latin America have traditionally viewed education as elite formation, and have limited access to education as a means of controlling the distribution of economic resources and wealth. The complementary relationship between technology and education means that educated workers are ever-more important as the key to high productivity and high growth rates. Insofar as this more closely binds the economic well-being of *elites* to access to education by *non-elites*, it may broaden the support for policies that increase the coverage and quality of the education system. The third lesson is that, even if the most necessary reforms to education for many Latin American countries involve those that raise enrollment levels in secondary school, countries cannot afford to disregard tertiary education. There is considerable *interdependence* across education levels. Parents send their children to secondary school in part because of the option value of a university education. Reforms that help more children from disadvantaged backgrounds enter university may therefore also raise secondary school enrollment levels. We now turn to a discussion of precisely what policies are most necessary at the secondary school and university levels in Latin America.

Understanding the Education Market: Secondary School

Understanding whether the bottleneck in secondary education is on the demand or supply side of the market is an important first step to designing appropriate policies. In addition, careful consideration must be given to the extent to which there are incentive problems that result in wasteful education spending.

BOX 4.1

Expanding Secondary School: The Great Transformation of American Education

In education, as elsewhere, history holds important lessons for Latin America. Between 1910 and 1940, secondary schooling expanded greatly in the United States. In 1910, 10 percent of youths were high school graduates, but by 1930 the median youth had a high school diploma. This transformation gave the United States a large lead over other industrialized countries in the level of education of its work force—a lead that persisted for a long time: As late as 1962, for example, only 15 percent of British 17-year-olds were in school, while the high school graduation rate in the United States was almost 70 percent.

What explains this "Great Transformation" of American education? Recent work by Goldin (1999, 2001) provides a number of insights. First, prior to mass secondary enrollment, the rate of return to secondary school was very high in the United States. This rate of return was high, in part, because high schools in the United States successfully transformed themselves from institutions that only prepared youths for college, to programs that taught their students skills—such as accounting, typing, shorthand, and algebra—that were valued in the workplace. Such high rates of return provided youths with the incentive to seek further schooling—even those who did not

intend to go on to college. Second, school administrators and others waged a successful campaign to convince youths and their parents that high schools offered them something of value. Third, the low levels of inequality and the egalitarian features of the schooling system in the United States, which did not encourage early, rigid tracking of students, facilitated mass secondary enrollments. Lastly, the Great Depression substantially reduced the employment prospects of youths, and thus reduced the opportunity cost of schooling. As Goldin explains, "the Great Depression may have had one positive effect: it enticed youth to stay in school." Differences in the opportunity cost of schooling also help explain why the "high school movement" lagged in the agricultural areas of the South, as well as the industrial areas of the North and Midwest.

The massive expansion of secondary school enrollments in the United States substantially brought down the high school wage premium. As the premium fell, employers in turn hired more high school graduates in occupations that had previously been filled by unskilled workers.

Source: Goldin (1999, 2001).

Direct Private Costs, Opportunity Cost, and Demand-side Constraints to Secondary School

Demand-side constraints to secondary education can arise for three reasons. First, the direct private costs of schooling may be an impediment. Second, the opportunity cost of going to school, in terms of foregone wages, may be high. Third, the "rate of return" to secondary schooling may be low.

In general, direct private costs are much less of an impediment at the secondary school level than at the university level. Calculations based on the ENIGH survey in Mexico, for example, suggest that direct private cost, including school fees, school supplies such as textbooks and pencils, uniforms, and transportation, are less than 10 percent of household income per capita—both for households in the poorest income quartile, as well as for those in the richest income quartile. The fact that the fraction of expenditures is relatively constant across quartiles is indirect evidence that the poor are receiving a worse-quality education. The Mexican

figures are probably low by regional standards, but direct private costs are unlikely to be a critical reason for the low secondary enrollments in many countries in the region.

While the opportunity cost of sending a child to primary school is generally thought to be low, this is not the case for children of secondary school age. Child labor is a reality in all but the wealthiest Latin American countries, and teenage children can supplement household income by working in the informal sector, or as agricultural laborers. Table 4.5 provides estimates of the ratio of the hourly wages earned by 15- to 19-year-olds in urban areas in 12 Latin American countries to those of median wages for the population aged 15 to 70, as well as the ratio of unemployment rates among youths to those in the overall population. The table shows that the wages earned by youths are generally between one half and three quarters of median wages. The probability of unemployment of 15- to 19-year-olds is much higher than those observed in the overall population, and this will also

TABLE 4.5

The Opportunity Cost of Attending Secondary School Appears to Be *High* in Most Latin American Countries

	WAGE RATIO		UNEMPLOYMENT RATIO	
	MALES	FEMALES	MALES	FEMALES
Argentina	0.61	0.53	2.67	2.54
Brazil	0.44	0.54	2.80	2.74
Chile	0.52	0.62	3.12	3.12
Colombia	0.72	0.73	2.68	2.35
Dominican Republic	0.65	0.72		
El Salvador	0.86	0.71	1.38	1.14
Honduras	0.72	0.72	1.93	1.84
Mexico	0.66	0.69		
Nicaragua	1.11	0.74		
Paraguay	0.59	0.46		
Peru	0.55	0.58		
Venezuela	0.64	0.62	2.40	2.89

Note: The wage ratio is the ratio of median wages of 15- to 19-year-olds to the median wages of 15- to 70-year-olds; the unemployment ratio is the ratio of the unemployment rate of 15- to 19-year-olds to the unemployment rate of 15- to 70-year-olds.
Source: Authors' calculations based on data in Cunningham (2002).

be a factor in any reasonable calculation of the opportunity cost of secondary schooling.[7] Still, table 4.5 suggests that the opportunity costs of schooling are not low, at least in urban areas.

Further evidence of the importance of the opportunity cost of schooling comes from careful analyses of patterns of school enrollment and work of children during macroeconomic crises in Latin America. The theory of human capital suggests that macroeconomic crises will have counter-acting effects on child schooling: On the one hand, crises limit opportunities in the labor market, and thus depress the opportunity cost (which should lead to more schooling), on the other hand crises reduce household income and may make borrowing constraints more binding (which should lead to less schooling). In practice, the negative effects of crises on schooling in Latin America are, at most, moderate: In Brazil, schooling decisions are largely unaffected by aggregate economic conditions, while children in Mexico and Peru are less likely to drop out of school during a crisis. The counter-cyclical relationship between schooling and aggregate income provides further evidence that the opportunity cost of schooling is an important determinant of secondary school enrollments in a number of Latin American countries.[8]

The high opportunity cost of secondary schooling in Latin America is a serious concern because the rate of return to secondary schooling is low in many countries. Table 4.6 shows that this rate of return is 6 percent or lower in Argentina, Colombia, and Mexico. It is not clear what

TABLE 4.6

High Rates of Return to Tertiary Education, and Modest Rates to Secondary School in Most of Latin America

	"RATE OF RETURN" TO SECONDARY SCHOOL	"RATE OF RETURN" TO TERTIARY EDUCATION
Argentina	0.05	0.11
Bolivia	0.08	0.14
Brazil	0.19	0.19
Chile	0.08	0.22
Colombia	0.05	0.18
Mexico	0.06	0.13

Note: The rate of return is approximated by the wage increment divided by the number of years in a cycle.
Source: Authors' calculations based on data from the labor force surveys.

discount rate households use when they compare investments in schooling with other investments. For one thing, this discount rate is likely to be higher for poorer households. Table 4.6 suggests, however, that investments in secondary school may not be an economically sensible decision for children in some Latin American countries unless there are improvements in quality, additional increases in the demand for secondary school workers by firms, or high transition rates from secondary school to university.

Access and Supply-Side Constraints to Secondary School

Inadequate access to school and teacher shortages can both be supply constraints to schooling. In some areas, especially rural areas, there may simply be no school available. The extent to which lack of school infrastructure explains low enrollment levels can often be approximated with administrative data—for example, by comparing the distribution of the school-aged population from a census with the distribution of school facilities. Many household surveys also have community modules that ask informants about the presence of certain facilities, including schools, in a community. Focusing on rural areas, 79 percent of communities with 500 people or fewer in Peru reported having a primary school, but only 17 percent had a secondary school. In those communities where there was no secondary school the mean time to walk to a neighboring school was about one hour and 15 minutes, and in 10 percent of communities the time was three hours or more.[9] Clearly, lack of school infrastructure could be a constraint to secondary school enrollments in rural areas in Peru.

The Problem of Low Education Quality

The low performance of Latin American students on international tests is evidence of the low quality of education

TABLE 4.7

There Is Generally Little Variation in Primary School Student Performance on Test Scores within Latin America, with the Exception of Cuba

	MEDIAN SCORES ON UNESCO – OREAL TEST, 1997			
	THIRD GRADE LANGUAGE	THIRD GRADE MATHEMATICS	FOURTH GRADE LANGUAGE	FOURTH GRADE MATHEMATICS
Cuba	343	351	349	353
Argentina	263	251	282	269
Chile	259	242	286	265
Brazil	256	247	277	269
Venezuela	242	220	249	226
Colombia	238	240	265	258
Bolivia	232	240	233	245
Paraguay	229	232	251	248
Mexico	224	236	252	256
Peru	222	215	240	229
Dominican Rep.	220	225	232	234
Honduras	216	218	238	231

Source: Carnoy (2002, table 7).

throughout the region. School quality is important in its own right, since it determines how much children learn for a given year of education. Higher quality schooling may also reduce repetition rates and free up resources for further expansions in coverage.

The OREAL-UNESCO exams tested third- and fourth-graders in 12 Latin American countries on language and mathematics. These tests show that there appears to be relatively little variation in the education quality of primary school across countries in the region, with the exception of Cuba, which outperforms every country in Latin America by a wide margin. Table 4.7 shows that in language as well as mathematics, and among third-graders as well as fourth-graders, Cuban students score at least 70 points more than students in the next-highest scoring country. By contrast, the difference between the mean score in this next-highest scoring country and the *worst* performer in the region is never more than 50 points. There are no comparable tests for secondary school students covering a large number of countries in the region, but the equally low scores of Chilean and Colombian students on the TIMSS suggests a widespread problem with quality at the secondary school level.

There is little consensus among academics or policymakers about the most effective interventions to improve school quality—in Latin America, or elsewhere.[10] In a background paper prepared for this report, Carnoy (2002) writes that "historically, nations have not been successful in improving the average amount that students learn in, say, fourth or eighth grade, but they have been very successful in

bringing a high proportion of their young population to complete levels of schooling available to only a few in the past." Still, there is some agreement that education systems in Latin America have generally spent too much on recurrent expenditures, especially teacher salaries, and too little on capital expenditures. Filmer and Pritchett (1999), for example, argue that school inputs are systematically biased in favor of those valued by teachers over those valued by students. This would suggest the need for policymakers to reallocate spending from the wage bill to complementary inputs such as textbooks and classroom material. Most studies also find that teachers are critical in the learning process, but the relation between "observable" teacher characteristics (such as education, experience, and salary levels) and learning outcomes (such as performance on tests) is weak (Hanushek 2002). Teacher motivation and ability are critical, but how best to improve them is unclear.

Should educators give higher priority to policies that seek to improve the *quantity* or *quality* of secondary schooling? Fortunately, there may be no quantity-quality trade-off. Higher quality schools attract more students, and countries in Latin America with higher mean enrollment levels do not appear to have lower quality. Figure 4.7 graphs the mean test score on OREAL-UNESCO tests as a function of enrollment levels. The figure shows that there is no clear relationship between these two outcome measures: For example, Argentina and Peru both have high enrollment rates, but Argentina outperforms both Peru and Venezuela, a country with a relatively low enrollment rate, in terms of test scores.

FIGURE 4.7

There Is No Clear Relationship between Education Quality and Quantity in Latin America

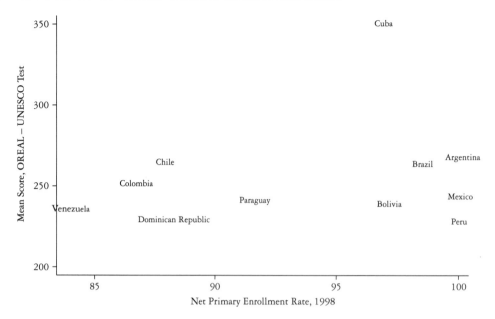

Within countries, too, there is some evidence that school access and quality are complements rather than substitutes (Hanushek 1995).

Incentives and Institutional Reforms

A recent review of the literature concludes that "developing countries spend hundreds of billions of dollars each year on education, and there is ample evidence that these funds are used inefficiently" (Glewwe 2002, p. 475). In Latin America, too, education outcomes in many countries continue to be poor, both in terms of quantity and quality, in spite of substantial expenditures. This has led many policymakers to consider deep reforms of the *incentives* in the education system as a possible remedy. Many of these reforms are designed to hold schools and teachers accountable for learning outcomes.

Reforms to align incentives generally fall into one of two categories: (i) those in which the government conditions budget transfers on outcomes, including capitation schemes, and schemes in which schools or teachers with superior performance are rewarded with bonuses; and (ii) those in which greater control is given to parents, either in the form of participation and decisionmaking power over the allocation of school budgets, or with a voucher that allows them to select a school. All of these have been tried in Latin America, and all of them hold promise—although more systematic

evaluation needs to be conducted to establish the conditions under which these policies can be most effective.

Capitation schemes transfer resources to schools in direct proportion to the number of students they enroll (rather than in proportion to the number of teachers, or in accordance with historical budgeting rules). In Brazil, a substantial portion of public resources for education for subnational levels of government have been distributed on the basis of student enrollment since 1998, under the financing mechanism called the *Fundo de Manutenção e Desenvolvimento do Ensino Fundamental e de Valorização do Magistério* (FUNDEF). State and municipal governments contribute an earmarked proportion of their revenues, and these resources are then distributed on the basis of the number of primary education students enrolled. As each subnational government *contributes* to FUNDEF, but obtains *receipts* from the fund only to the extent that it has enrolled students, the new legislation created an incentive to subnational governments to enroll as many primary education students as possible. This new financing scheme is credited with substantially increasing primary enrollment levels in Brazil (World Bank 2002).

Performance-based financing has been implemented in a number of countries in Latin America. In Mexico, under the *Carrera Magisterial* program, teacher pay is linked to several measures, including performance on the job (as evaluated by the principal), scores on a test taken by the teacher, student test scores, and teacher education and experience. The program is voluntary, but more than 60 percent of eligible teachers have participated in it. A recent evaluation of the program suggests that students in classes taught by teachers participating in the *Carrera Magisterial* program have about 2 percent higher scores on Mathematics tests (Lopez-Acevedo 2002, p. 28). In Chile, the *Sistema Nacional de Evaluación del Desempeño de los Establecimientos Educacionales Subvencionados* (SNED) gives monetary bonuses to schools chosen for their outstanding performance—whereby schools are selected primarily in terms of student performance on a nationwide test. The SNED is innovative in a number of ways: It only compares schools serving similar populations (to control for the fact that children from better-off economic backgrounds generally do better on tests); it considers both the performance *level* and *changes* in performance of schools; and it rewards *all* teachers within a high-performing establishment. While its nationwide coverage makes it difficult to convincingly estimate the impact of the SNED on student outcomes, it appears to have improved the accountability of schools and teachers (See particularly Mizala and Romaguera 2002).

Other reforms have sought to directly empower parents. In El Salvador, schools in the Community-Managed Schools Program (*Educación con Participación de la Comunidad*, or EDUCO) are managed autonomously by community education associations (*Asociaciones Comunales para la Educación*, or ACES). The Ministry of Education contracts these ACES to deliver a given curriculum to an agreed number of students. The ACES are then responsible for hiring and firing teachers, closely monitoring performance, and equipping and maintaining schools. The EDUCO program is credited with a rapid expansion of schools to rural areas, with diminished student absences, and with a significant improvement in students' language skills (Jimenez and Sawada 1999). A similar program in Nicaragua is also thought to have positive effects on the learning outcomes of children (King and Ozler 2000).

Vouchers are perhaps the most radical solution to the incentive problem in the delivery of education services. Vouchers make education resources portable, and thus allow parents to "vote with their feet" by sending their children to a school of their choice. Chile has had a nationwide voucher program since 1981. The Chilean voucher program was implemented in the context of a larger reform that transferred schools from the Ministry of Education to municipalities, gave municipal schools a per-student transfer, and gave private (non-tuition-charging) subsidized schools the same per-student payment as public schools. The Chilean experience has been the subject of intense analysis, but little consensus exists about the extent to which the reforms as a whole improved student outcomes.[11] More recently, careful analysis of a randomized experiment with a voucher program in Colombia (*Programa de Ampliación de Cobertura de la Educación Secundaria*, or PACES) suggests that the program resulted in a reduction in repetition rates among participants (See Angrist and others 2002).

Misaligned incentives are pervasive in the provision of education services. Principal–agent problems can be found at every link in the delivery chain—between Ministry of Education officials and school administrators, between principals and teachers, and (most important) between parents and teachers. Reforms that seek to find innovative solutions to these problems in Latin America, be they those attempting to link finance with performance or those giving parents greater control over resources, should continue to be tried and carefully evaluated.

Putting the Pieces Together: Patterns of Secondary School Attainment in Latin America

How can we assess the relative importance of demand, supply, quality, and incentive problems in explaining the low levels of secondary school attainment in a country? To consider this, we turn to data from the Demographic and Health Surveys (DHS). The advantage of the DHS is that they apply the same questionnaire in all countries. Moreover, and unlike most labor force surveys, they collect data for both urban and rural areas.

In figure 4.8, we graph the probability that persons aged 20 to 29 have completed at least a given number of years of schooling, ranging from 1 to 9 years, separately for urban and rural areas in Guatemala (1999), Nicaragua (1998), and Peru (2000).[12] The figures include a vertical line corresponding to completion of primary school. (The sample includes those who are still in school as well as those who have dropped out.) A comparison of the figures shows large differences across countries: In Peru more than 90 percent of youths in urban areas have completed at least primary school, while in Guatemala and Nicaragua the numbers are below 80 percent. The graphs also show that attainment is much lower in rural areas than in urban areas in all of the countries. In the rural areas of Guatemala and Nicaragua a quarter of youths have no schooling whatsoever.

FIGURE 4.8

Patterns of Educational Attainment in Guatemala, Nicaragua, and Peru

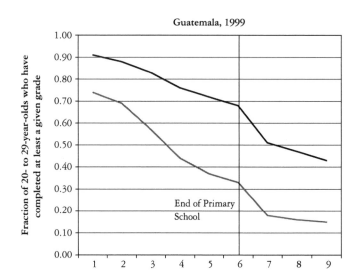

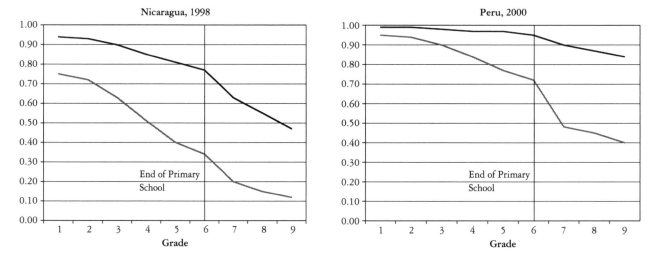

Note: The rural schedule is shaded in lighter color, and is always below the urban schedule.

Source: Authors' calculations based on data from Filmer (2000).

Two features of the graphs are helpful in determining whether the low attainment levels of youths are driven by problems of inadequate demand or inadequate access: The steady decline in the number of youths who have completed at least a given number of years of schooling, and the sharp kinks associated with transition from one schooling level to another observed in some countries.

Schools generally teach all grades within a level—for example, a primary school will teach all grades in primary, while a secondary school will teach all grades in secondary. The steady decline in attainment within a given schooling

level cannot therefore be a result of the lack of access. On the other hand, this decline could be explained by the rising opportunity cost of schooling. To see this, consider two facts. First, the number of years of schooling a child can complete is related to his or her age. Put differently, 20- to 29-year-olds who have completed only one year of schooling will, on average, have dropped out of school at a younger age than those who have completed two. Second, the wage that children can command also rises steadily with age. The steady decline in attainment may therefore reflect the rising opportunity cost of schooling: It may not pay off to drop out after

92

completing only one or two years of schooling, because these children would be very young, but it may pay off to drop out for older children who have completed a few more years—especially, if the quality of education is low.

What about the kinks in attainment that coincide with one's completion of primary school? These are particularly obvious in the rural areas of Guatemala and Peru. As we showed in our analysis of the Peruvian data, primary schools are generally available in most settings, both urban and rural, but secondary schools may not be. As a result, a disproportionate number of children drop out of school in the transition from primary to secondary school. These kinks are therefore highly suggestive of supply-side constraints. Alternatively, they could be the result of particularly large wage premia to completing the last year of schooling within a given level—graduation or so-called "sheepskin" effects.[13] This seems unlikely, however, as sheepskin effects are generally thought to be lower in rural than in urban areas because of the higher fraction of the rural population in non-wage employment.

Comparing graphs in a country for two years can also give one a sense of how demand and supply constraints have evolved over time. In figure 4.9, we present graphs for Colombia using the 1990 and 2000 DHS. The figure shows that both the urban and rural schedules pivoted counter-clockwise: A higher fraction of 20- to 29-year-olds have completed more years of schooling in 2000 than in 1990. On the other hand, conditional on completing the primary cycle, the *transition* to secondary school does not appear to have become much easier in 2000 than in 1990, especially in rural areas. Figure 4.9 therefore suggests that increases in the demand for schooling, rather than improvements in access, explain the bulk of the improvements in educational attainment in Colombia in the 1990s.

Using Demand-Supply Diagnostics to Inform the Design of Policies

These diagnostics provide a useful first step to considering policies to improve schooling outcomes. In many countries in Latin America, there are limited (if any) secondary school facilities in rural areas. Under these circumstances, investments in school infrastructure can have very high returns (see box 4.2). More innovative solutions such as long-distance education may also hold promise. The *TeleSecundaria* program in Mexico is an interesting example of this approach. Finally, innovative reforms to better align incentives with learning outcomes within the education system should be implemented, and carefully evaluated.

FIGURE 4.9

Supply and Demand Factors in the Evolution of Educational Attainment in Colombia, 1990–2000

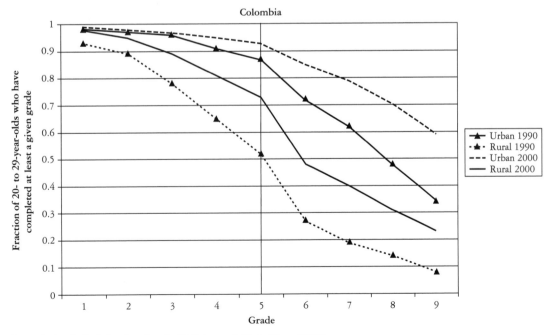

Source: Authors' calculations based on the DHS data available in Filmer (2000).

BOX 4.2

The Returns to Investments in School Infrastructure: Evidence from Peru and Indonesia

A number of studies have assessed the impact of spending on school infrastructure in the developed and developing world. The majority of studies in developing countries have found a positive impact of these investments in school facilities on learning outcomes (Hanushek 1995). Two recent papers on Indonesia and Peru confirm that there can be high returns to investments in school infrastructure. In addition, both studies make obvious the value of impact evaluations in assessing the effectiveness of education interventions, and in designing future programs and policies.

Between 1992 and 1998, the Peruvian Social Fund (FONCODES) spent in excess of US$100 million building and renovating school infrastructure, mainly primary schools, in rural areas in Peru. Paxson and Schady (2002) show that these funds were generally well targeted to poor communities, and had a large impact on the enrollment levels of young children aged 6 to 11. They estimate that every sol (about 60 cents of a U.S. dollar, at the December 1992 exchange rate) spent on school infrastructure increased enrollment rates by between 0.75 and 2.5 percentage points in districts with an initial enrollment rate of 85 percent. These are large impacts, considering that about a quarter of children lived in districts with enrollment rates equal to or less than 85 percent in 1993.

Duflo (2001) estimates the impact of a program that built about 61,000 schools in Indonesia between 1973 and 1978. She finds large improvements in school attainment and in the wages of adults exposed to the program. Duflo estimates that each primary school constructed per 1,000 children led to an average increase of between 0.12 and 0.19 years of education, and a 1.5 to 2.7 percent increase in wages.

Source: Hanushek (1995); Paxson and Schady (2002); Duflo (2001).

BOX 4.3

Conditional Cash Transfers: The Impact of PROGRESA in Mexico

Conditional cash transfer programs can be an effective education intervention when high opportunity cost keeps children from attending school. There are a number of conditional cash transfer initiatives in Latin America, including programs in Brazil and Colombia, but perhaps the best known is PROGRESA in Mexico. The education component of PROGRESA provides monetary transfers to families that are contingent on the regular attendance of children at school. So as to offset the opportunity cost of schooling, the benefit levels rise with the grade a student is attending, and are highest in secondary school. Benefits are also higher for girls than for boys, in recognition of the lower secondary school attendance rates among girls. PROGRESA has been shown to have significant effects on enrollment: on average, poor children who benefited from PROGRESA completed almost one-half more years of schooling than they would have in the absence of the program, with somewhat larger impacts among girls.

PROGRESA also shows the importance of evaluation in program design. In its first phase, once a list of eligible poor communities had been developed, communities were selected to receive PROGRESA transfers by randomization. This design allowed for highly credible evaluation of the impact of PROGRESA on schooling outcomes.

Source: Schultz (2001); Behrman, Sengupta and Todd (2001).

much incentive to seek more schooling. The demand for educated workers by firms is often determined by the degree to which there is technological change, so reforms to liberalize trade regimes, encourage FDI, and facilitate licensing of technologies may therefore *unleash* the demand for schooling.[14] Firms will also be willing to pay secondary school graduates higher wages if there are improvements in school quality—improvements that raise the productivity of secondary school graduates.[15] And where the opportunity cost of schooling is high, conditional cash transfer programs such as PROGRESA in Mexico and Bolsa Escola in Brazil can be used to subsidize education and successfully raise enrollments (see box 4.3).[16]

Often, however, the problem appears to be that the demand for secondary schooling is low. If firms do not demand workers with a secondary school education, the returns will be low, and young men and women will not have

Understanding the Education Market: Universities

Enrollments in tertiary education in Latin America have grown steadily since the 1950s, and very rapidly in some countries since the 1980s. Tables 4.8 and 4.9 show gross tertiary enrollment rates for a sample of Latin American countries. Table 4.8 shows that between 1980 and 1995 enrollment rates more than doubled in Chile and Colombia, and increased substantially in Argentina, Panama, and Peru. Despite these increases in enrollment, the relative wages of workers with university education have continued to grow,

suggesting a large unmet demand by firms for these most skilled workers. This section discusses how Latin American countries can best put in place policies that will allow more students to access university education.

A Segmented Market

Until mid-century, university enrollment was essentially an affair of the public sector for most countries in Latin America. Since then, there have been important changes.[17] Figure 4.10 shows that the increase in overall enrollments has been accompanied by a rising market share of private institutions

TABLE 4.8

Tertiary Enrollments Have Been Growing since the 1970s...

LATIN AMERICA, GROSS RATES OF ENROLLMENT IN TERTIARY EDUCATION, 1970–97

COUNTRY	1970	1975	1980	1985	1990	1995	1996–97
Argentina	13.4	26.6	21.8	35.7	38.1	36.2	—
Brazil	4.7	10.1	11.1	10.3	11.2	14.5	—
Chile	9.1	14.8	12.3	15.6	21.3	28.2	31.5
Colombia	—	—	8.6	10.9	13.4	15.5	—
Jamaica	—	—	6.7	4.4	6.8	7.8	—
Mexico	5.4	10.2	14.3	15.9	14.5	16.0	—
Nicaragua	—	—	12.4	8.8	8.2	11.5	—
Panama	—	—	20.8	24.5	21.5	30.0	—
Paraguay	—	—	8.6	9.1	8.3	10.1	—
Peru	—	—	17.3	22.4	30.4	27.1	—

—Data not available.
Source: UNESCO and World Bank database.

TABLE 4.9

...And Have Continued to Grow in the 1990s

LATIN AMERICA, GROSS RATES OF ENROLLMENT IN TERTIARY EDUCATION, 1990–97

COUNTRY	1990	1991	1992	1993	1994	1995	1996	1997
Argentina	—	38.1	—	—	36.2	—	—	—
Bolivia	21.3	21.7	—	—	—	—	—	—
Brazil	11.2	11.2	10.9	11.1	11.3	—	14.5	—
Chile	—	21.3	24.2	26.5	27.4	28.2	30.3	31.5
Colombia	13.4	14.0	14.6	14.7	15.4	15.5	16.7	—
Costa Rica	26.9	27.6	29.4	29.9	30.3	—	—	—
Cuba	20.9	19.8	18.1	16.7	13.9	12.7	12.4	—
Dominican Republic	—	—	—	—	—	—	22.9	—
Ecuador	20.0	—	—	—	—	—	—	—
El Salvador	15.9	16.8	17.2	17.0	18.2	18.9	17.8	—
Guatemala	—	—	8.3	8.1	8.4	8.5	—	—
Haiti	—	—	—	—	—	—	—	—
Honduras	8.9	8.9	9.2	9.0	10.0	—	—	—
Mexico	14.5	14.1	13.6	13.9	14.3	15.3	16.0	—
Nicaragua	8.2	8.1	8.9	—	—	11.5	11.5	11.8
Panama	21.5	23.4	25.3	27.3	27.2	30.0	31.5	—
Paraguay	8.3	—	—	10.3	10.1	10.1	10.3	—
Peru	30.4	32.0	31.5	28.0	26.8	27.1	25.7	25.8
Uruguay	29.9	30.1	27.2	—	—	—	29.5	—
Venezuela, RB	29.0	28.5	—	—	—	—	—	—

—Data not available.
Source: World Bank 2001a.

95

FIGURE 4.10

The Rising Share of the Private Sector in the University Market

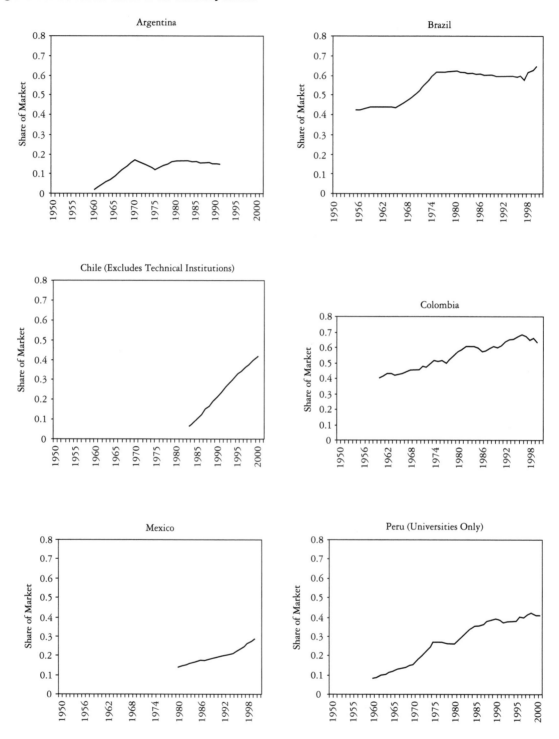

Source: Schwartzman (2002), World Bank (2002) for Colombia.

FIGURE 4.11

Private Tertiary Education Is More Expensive to Households

Direct Costs for User (Tuition)

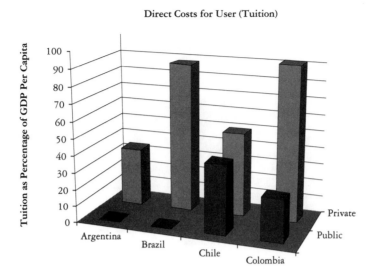

Source: Schwartzman (2002), World Bank (2002) for Colombia.

in every country for which data are available. In many countries, the rising demand for university education prompted governments to deregulate the university market, abolishing what had been a public sector monopoly, and allowing for some competition between private and public providers. The private sector now accounts for more than half of the university market in Brazil and Colombia, and for more than a third in Chile and Peru.

Private providers generally charge much higher fees than public universities. In figure 4.11, we use administrative data to calculate these differences. The figure shows that tuition costs in Argentina and Brazil are essentially zero in the public sector, but large in the private sector. Tuition payments in public universities are substantial in Chile and Colombia, two countries that have reformed their university systems, although they are still much lower than in the private sector (especially in Colombia).[18] Similar estimates based on the household survey data for Peru, Guatemala, and Mexico also suggest that the difference in cost between the public and private sectors is large, especially once costs above and beyond tuition are taken into account.

In most countries in Latin America, then, there are large differences in fees between the public and private university systems. These differences in costs have led to a *rising*

demand for a limited number of seats in public universities, along with a *falling* demand for seats in some private universities. In Brazil, the number of applicants per seat in public universities grew from 5.7 to 8.9, while that in private universities fell from 2.9 to 1.9 between 1990 and 2000. By some estimates, more than half the seats in private universities in Colombia are unfilled. These numbers are simple averages. In practice, there is a great deal of *heterogeneity* in providers, especially those in the private sector, in terms of the types of institutions, diplomas and disciplines, as well as in the quality of the services they offer. As a result, the demand for university slots in the most prestigious private universities in virtually all Latin American countries continues to be high.

When there is excess demand, rationing becomes necessary. Private universities have relied on a combination of high fees and entrance exams, and public universities on a combination of entrance exams and quotas to assign seats.[19] All of these make it more difficult for poorer students to attend university: Poorer students have fewer resources, are less likely to have access to credit, will generally have attended lower quality secondary schools, and will therefore do worse on university entrance exams. Despite the increase in aggregate enrollments, university education is often something

FIGURE 4.12

Conditional on Enrollment, Students from Poorer Households Are Less Likely to Attend Private Universities

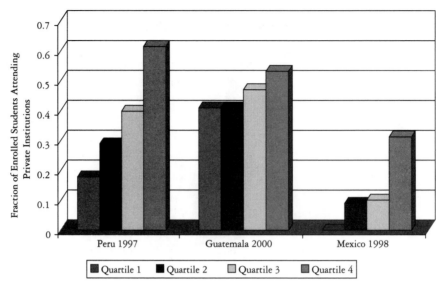

Sources: Peru: Encuesta Nacional de Hogares (ENAHO); Guatemala: Encuesta de Condiciones de Vida (ENCOVI); Mexico: Encuesta Nacional de Ingresos y Gastos de Los Hogares (ENIGH).

that only the better-off can afford in Latin America. Seventy percent of all university students in Brazil, and 50 percent of those in Colombia, belong to the highest income quintile; a further 20 percent in both countries comes from the second-highest income quintile. Moreover, poor students who attend university are less likely to attend *private* universities. Figure 4.12 shows that, of those who enroll, virtually no students in the poorest consumption quartile attend private university in Mexico, compared to about 30 percent in the richest quartile. In Guatemala and Peru there is also a clear relationship between household welfare and the probability that enrolled students attend private university. Youths from poorer households are much less likely to go to university and, for those who do, are much less likely to attend a private institution.

Direct Private Costs, Opportunity Cost, Information Flows, and the Demand-side Constraints to University Expansion: the Story of the Private Sector

Unlike secondary school, the pay-offs to tertiary education are high in most Latin American countries. Of course, the direct costs of private university to individuals are also high. But a calculation of the net present value of tertiary education that combines the data on costs in figure 4.11 with estimates of the returns in table 4.6

suggests it is a good economic investment in Brazil, Chile, and Colombia—even with a high discount rate of 10 percent. In Argentina, where the returns to university education are lower, the picture is less clear, and is sensitive to the choice of discount rate.

Low university enrollments by poor households in spite of the high returns to tertiary education suggest that liquidity constraints may be binding. A background paper for this report by Jacoby and Skoufias (2002) uses household survey data to estimate the extent to which liquidity constraints are an impediment to university enrollment in Mexico. The authors distinguish between "transitory" income (proxied by current income), "permanent" income (proxied by measures of family background and education), and the opportunity cost of schooling (approximated by variation in local labor market conditions, both across states, and over time, such as before and after the Mexican Peso Crisis). Jacoby and Skoufias show that, conditional on graduation from secondary school, current parental income is a good predictor of tertiary attendance. In other words, households with similar permanent income, and facing similar labor market conditions, are less likely to send a child to university if they had a bad year. These differences in tertiary attendance rates can then plausibly be attributed to the effect of binding credit constraints.

In addition to credit constraints, information problems may help explain the low demand for private universities relative to public universities in the region. Some households, perhaps especially households with lower mean education levels, may only be partially aware of the returns to education. In the United States, a public information campaign about the economic benefits associated with education appears to have been one of the reasons for the expansion in high school enrollments in the first half of the century (see box 4.1). The large increase in the number of private providers in tertiary education may also make it difficult for households to discriminate between high quality and low quality establishments and programs.[20] The quality of university education is hard to measure without information on wage differentials by university, or an exit exam for university graduates. Faced with uncertainty about the quality of providers, risk-averse households may sensibly under-invest in private tertiary education.

Limited Resources, Low Efficiency, and the Supply-side Constraints to University Expansion: the Story of the Public Sector

Limited budgets are the main constraint to expanding enrollment in public universities. The gap in secondary school attainment, the need to upgrade skills from the bottom up, and the fact that the bulk of university entrants in Latin America are (and will continue to be) relatively well-off all make it hard to justify an aggregate expansion in the budget of public universities.

More money may not be the solution, but cost recovery and better use of existing funds would help. In many Latin American countries, public universities are inefficient in terms of the amount of time it takes a given student to graduate. This is a serious drain on resources, as every spot occupied by a student who takes more than the required years to complete a program could have been filled by another applicant who was turned away from university. In Colombia, only somewhere between 50 and 60 percent of an entering class graduates on time in both the public and private sectors. This "internal efficiency" of the public sector will almost certainly be lower in countries where tuition at public universities is essentially nonexistent. Anecdotal evidence suggests that many students at the *Universidad Nacional Autónoma de México* (UNAM) and similar free-of-charge universities are often enrolled for eight years or longer.

Science, Humanities, and the Content of Tertiary Education in Latin America

In addition to concerns about coverage, there is considerable debate about the *content* of instruction at tertiary institutions in Latin America—in particular, about the extent to which universities are producing "too many" students in the humanities and social sciences, and "too few" students in the hard sciences and engineering. There is no evidence that the "knowledge economy" has particularly increased the demand for scientists and engineers—in Latin America or elsewhere. Rather, it is the returns to general problem-solving skills, as well as to (harder to measure) attributes such as flexibility, adaptability, and "client skills" that have increased substantially.

General, Problem-Solving Skills are Most Valuable in the "New Economy"

In the United States, increases in the demand for skilled workers have been linked to the profound effects of computerization and other technological changes on workplace organization. In these countries, the "new" skills demanded entail the ability to perform complex tasks—tasks that require non-algorithmic reasoning, cognitive work, and managerial skills, rather than increases in the demand for very specialized "scientific" skills (see box 4.4). The wages of computer programmers and others with scientific or "new economy" skills have *not* gone up disproportionately in the United States (Card and DiNardo 2002). We find a similar pattern in Mexico, one country in which the labor force survey asks workers about the subject they studied in university. There is a small skill premium to scientific studies at the secondary level, and a small premium to non-scientific studies at the tertiary level. As figure 4.13 shows, however, these premia did not change between 1987 and 1999, suggesting that the increase in demand for workers with tertiary education in Mexico has favored scientists and humanists alike.

Evidence that the demand for "scientific" skills has not gone up disproportionately can also be found in employer surveys. Recent surveys in Thailand and Costa Rica both suggest that employers are much more concerned with the general education level and the ability of their employees to learn on the job than with specific skills such as mathematics and computer proficiency—even among firms in the technology sector in Costa Rica.[21] In Thailand, fully 80 percent of employers in the manufacturing sector and

BOX 4.4

How Information Technology Has Changed the Workplace: Evidence from the OECD

In a background paper commissioned for this report, Carnoy (2002) considers the changes in production that have taken place as a result of the "new information economy" and the relevance they have for Latin American countries. One of the features he stresses is changes in workplace organization: "The organization of production and of economic activity... has changed from mass standardized production to flexible customized production, and from vertically integrated large organizations to vertical disintegration and horizontal networks between economic units." Moreover, Carnoy reasons that "the effect of individualization and differentiation (of production) is to separate more and more workers from 'permanent' full-time jobs in stable businesses that characterized post–World War II development in Europe, Japan, the United States, and other industrialized countries." He concludes that "as post-industrial economies and governments adjust to new realities, employment growth, not displacement, dominates. There will be plenty of jobs in the future, and many of them will be high-paying jobs."

The earliest research on the effect of ICT on workplace organization in the United States was an analysis of Tammany Bank by Levy and Murnane (1996). Since then, much of the econometric evidence for the United States has focused on the increasing returns to worker characteristics other than education, experience, gender, and industry affiliation in the past two decades. These characteristics, unobservable to the econometrician but observed by employers, are often though to capture traits such as "people skills," the capacity to work in teams, multi-task, work successfully without supervision, show initiative, and be entrepreneurial. Two recent papers go back to Levy and Murnane's focus on the complementarity between ICT and organizational changes within firms. They suggest that recent technological changes in information and communication technology have profoundly redefined the ways in which firms employ workers in different tasks.

Assar Lindbeck and Dennis Snower (2000) argue that firms in industrialized countries are restructuring to change from "Tayloristic" organizations (characterized by specialization of tasks) to "holistic" organizations (characterized by job rotation, integration of tasks, and learning across tasks). Computerized access to information has provided employees with better information about the work of others within an organization, as well as about customers. As a result, employees have become more involved with each others' work, and have been better able to respond to rapidly changing customer needs. Also, the introduction of flexible machine tools and programmable equipment has made the capital equipment itself more versatile, and better capable of performing a variety of tasks. In response, workers using this capital equipment have become more versatile as well. Finally, a steady increase in the human capital of workers in OECD countries has resulted in "human capital deepening" (allowing workers to better perform particular tasks), as well as "human capital widening" (allowing firms to reorganize workers so that they multitask). Lindbeck and Snower argue that a variety of managerial innovations—for example, Total Quality Management (TQM) and just-in-time production—exploit these changes in workplace organization.

Timothy Bresnahan, Erik Brynjofsson, and Lorin Hitt (2002) also focus on the profound impact of information technology on workplace organization: "Firms do not simply plug in computers or telecommunications equipment and achieve service quality or efficiency gains. Instead they go through a process of organizational redesign and make substantial changes to their product and service mix." Based on a combination of formal modeling, econometric work, and case study interviews with firm managers, they argue that there are profound complementarities between information technology, workplace organization, and product innovation—and that it is these complementarities that drive skill-biased technological change. Frequently, investment in new ICT involves a second round of innovation. Unlike direct investments in ICT, which can (to a large extent) be bought ready-made off the shelf, these second-order "organizational co-inventions" are highly firm-specific. The result of this is much greater heterogeneity and turnover of firms, a greater degree of market instability, and profound changes in worker demand. Simple tasks (record-keeping, simple calculating, individual transactions) are automated, while the premium on complex tasks (tasks that require non-algorithmic reasoning, cognitive work, and managerial skills) increases dramatically. Bresnahan and his co-authors conclude that the information revolution has actually resulted in a "cluster of inventions," including computerization, computer-enabled organizational change, and computer-enabled forms of output.

Source: Carnoy (2002); Levy and Murnane (1996); Lindbeck and Snower (2000); Bresnahan, Brynjofsson, and Hitt (2002).

FIGURE 4.13

The Wages of Workers with "Scientific" Degrees Relative to Those with "Humanistic" Degrees in Mexico Have Not Changed in the 1990s

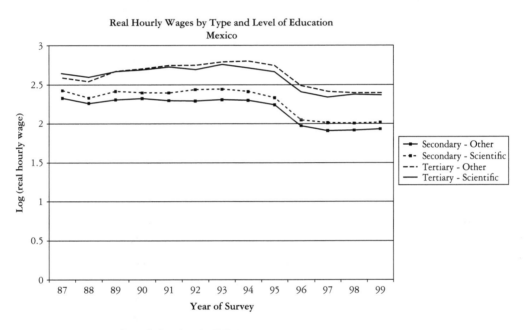

Real Hourly Wages by Type and Level of Education
Mexico

Source: Sánchez-Páramo and Schady, based on the ENEU surveys.

100 percent in the service sector considered the "ability to learn" important, compared to only 7 percent in manufacturing and 60 percent in the service sector who stressed computer literacy. Many more employers listed reading as an important skill than mathematics, again in both manufacturing and non-manufacturing jobs. In Costa Rica, employers in the technology sector were twice as likely to stress "learning speed" as "specific knowledge." In an evolving workplace, with a rapid pace of technological change, schooling that teaches workers to "learn how to learn" will be most valuable.

Putting it Together: Supply, Demand, and Policies to Reform Tertiary Education in Latin America

High quality tertiary education in Latin America pays off—for individuals, who will earn higher wages, and for countries, which will enjoy higher growth rates. How best to reform the university system in a given country will (obviously) depend on its institutional setup—but some policy reforms apply to a large number of countries.

The fundamental challenge for the public university system is making better use of existing resources. This entails a combination of policies: cost recovery, increasing the fraction

FIGURE 4.14

Cost Recovery in Public Universities Is Low in Many Latin American Countries

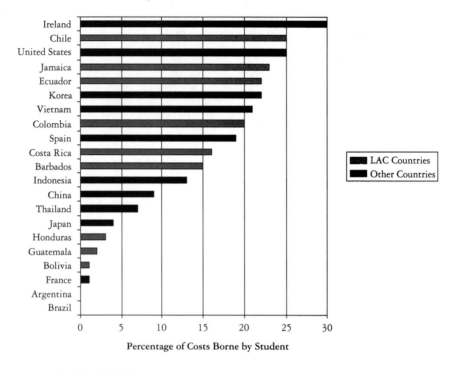

Source: World Bank (2002).

of students admitted to university, improvements in efficiency, and better allocation of resources across public universities.

Cost recovery through fees is very low in some Latin American countries. Figure 4.14 shows the fraction of costs borne by students in public universities in a cross-section of countries. The figure shows that in some Latin American countries, such as Chile, Jamaica, Ecuador, Colombia, and Costa Rica, this fraction is comparable to that in the United States, Ireland, or Korea. In other countries, such as Honduras, Guatemala, and Bolivia, it is very low, and in Argentina and Brazil it is essentially zero. Low cost recovery has serious implications for the coverage, quality, and sustainability of the public university system. Where politically possible, Latin American countries with low degrees of cost recovery in the public system should attempt to introduce fees. Increases in tuition and other fees should be implemented hand in hand with a program of student loans or well-targeted scholarships.

Reforms to increase tuition tend to be politically difficult to implement (as shown by the crippling strike at the UNAM in Mexico). Reducing unit costs is an alternative way of increasing the coverage of the public university system. Per-student costs are alarmingly high in the public university system in some Latin American countries. The most

egregious example is Brazil, where the unit costs of the public university system are staggering. Per-student costs in 1998 are estimated to have been above US$8,500, about 6 times the per-student costs in other "expensive" public systems such as those in Venezuela and Costa Rica, and almost 10 times those in Argentina.[22] An alternative summary measure of the real economic cost of education is expenditure per student as a proportion of GDP per capita. By this measure, educating students is 10 times as expensive in federal universities in Brazil as it is in Spain, and 5 times as expensive as in the United States.[23] Reducing per-student costs should clearly be a priority for the public university system in Brazil-even if this entails some drop in quality. Simply opening the doors of the federal universities to a larger number of students may be the single most important reform of the university system in Brazil.

The third set of reforms that are promising for the public university system are those seeking to improve internal efficiency. Performance-based financing, which ties transfer of public monies to measures such as per-student cost, graduation rates, time to graduation, and others hold promise. In Chile, for example, the funding formula whereby resources are transferred to public and private universities incorporates the fraction of the 27,500 highest-scoring students in a national academic test which a given university can attract.

The fundamental challenge for an expansion of the private university system in most Latin American countries is overcoming the liquidity constraints faced by poor households. The scholarship programs that exist in most Latin American countries cover only a very small fraction of students, and are often regressive. In Mexico, the probability that a student enrolled in university receives a scholarship *rises* with income. Estimates based on the 1998 ENIGH survey suggest that, of those enrolled, no student in the poorest income quartile received a scholarship, compared to 8.3 percent of students in the richest income quartile. These figures are noteworthy because the probability of enrollment was itself about *40* times higher for households in the richest income quartile than those in the poorest. In many Latin American countries, well-targeted scholarships for able, poor students and student loan programs both hold considerable promise. Box 4.5 provides some recommendations for setting up effective student loan

---

BOX 4.5

Student Loan Schemes

Many hopeful graduates from secondary school are keen on continuing on to university. In countries where university education is not free of charge, however, they may be unable to do so because of the upfront living and tuition costs. University education is clearly a good investment for many secondary school graduates. One might therefore expect the private sector to offer student loans. But information asymmetries between the lender and borrower (for example, about a student's ability, or the effort he or she will put into his studies), and the absence of seizable collateral (unlike loans on a car, or a house, which can be repossessed by a bank) limit private sector provision in the absence of some government intervention. This has resulted in provision by the public sector in many countries.

Public sector efforts to provide student loans can be a serious drain on the public purse, for at least two reasons. The first is that interest rates are often subsidized, and the second is that repayment rates are often low. A systematic (if by now outdated) review of student loan programs in Latin America by Albrect and Ziderman (1991) concluded that only 25 percent of costs are recovered, compared to over 70 percent in Scandinavian countries. Low-cost recovery provides a substantial subsidy to beneficiaries. Since student loan schemes are generally not targeted, student loan schemes in many countries essentially work like poorly targeted scholarships.

Although the bulk of the experience with student loan schemes in Latin America has not been a success, there are exceptions. The *Sociedad de Fomento a la Educación Superior* (SOFES) in Mexico is an interesting case. Mexico has a long-standing tradition with student loan schemes, including a program in the northern state of Sonora which has been in operation since 1981 (Blom and Paqueo 2002). SOFES is a relatively new program, less than five years old, which provides loans to about 10,000 students per year. In the scheme, private universities buy shares into the student loan company, which is capitalized by the government of Mexico and the World Bank. Participating universities on-lend SOFES funds to students on unsubsidized terms. The universities are responsible for all interaction with the students. If more than 10 percent of the portfolio is non-performing, the university either replenishes SOFES with the lost amount or becomes ineligible for further funds. This institutional setup features several aspects that should help achieve sustainability, including (i) clearly stated objective of financial sustainability, which allows administrators to provide loans without subsidy, and provides them with credible corrective measures in case of non-servicing of debt; (ii) strong incentives for collection in institutional setup; (iii) frequent information-gathering about borrowers' prospects for repayment; (iv) frequent interaction with the borrower, which helps build a culture of repayment; (v) monetary incentives for the education institutions to provide relevant, quality education to the student; and (vi) infusion of private capital, which is critical given the high potential demand for student financing in Mexico.

To date, SOFES has had single-digit default rates. The SOFES program has only been in operation for five years, and is therefore relatively new, and perhaps untested. Yet SOFES holds important lessons for other countries developing student loan schemes in Latin America.

Source: Albrecht and Ziderman (1991); Blom (2002); Blom and Paqueo (2002).

---

schemes, as well as a description of an innovative program in Mexico.

The second problem of the private university market, namely the information asymmetry between providers and consumers, could be minimized with an accreditation system for private universities, and an information campaign that provides data to the public about the relative performance of various tertiary institutions, both public and private, in terms of learning and labor market outcomes. The challenge of an accreditation system is providing minimum standards without limiting entry into the market by legitimate providers. Chile is a good example of a well-functioning accreditation board in Latin America (see box 4.6). The challenge of a public information campaign about university performance, whether in terms of test scores of graduates or their labor market performance is to disseminate comprehensible information widely. The *Provão* system in Brazil tests every graduating student in over a dozen disciplines and publishes mean results by institution. This system has allowed potential students and their families to make reasonable inferences about the quality of instruction (see box 4.6).

Conclusion: Priorities for Education Upgrading in Latin America

This chapter has discussed the main constraints to skill upgrading through the formal schooling system in Latin America, as well as the broad direction of policies to overcome them. Some of the most important conclusions of the chapter include the following:

- Skill-biased technological change means there is a bigger premium to education in terms of wages, productivity, and growth now than before. Latin American countries therefore need to close the education gap with East Asia and the OECD *quickly*.
- Countries that have most successfully closed the skill gap have done so from the bottom up. Many Latin American countries have given insufficient attention to secondary education in their education transitions. This is perhaps the most serious constraint to an "intelligent integration" of Latin American countries into the global economy.
- The main problem with Latin American education systems is not insufficient aggregate spending, but the quality of spending. Appropriate policies for secondary school and tertiary education can only be

designed with a clear understanding of the nature of constraints—specifically, whether these are primarily on the demand or supply side of the education market. Institutional reforms that better align incentives with outcomes, including capitation, teacher compensation schemes that reward better teachers, parent participation in schools, and school competition may also hold promise.

- Low demand for more education by individuals is a serious concern at the secondary school level. Insufficient demand for schooling is related to insufficient demand by firms, to the low quality of education, and to the high opportunity cost of schooling. Policies that promote technological change have the potential to increase the returns to schooling and the willingness by young men and women to defer entrance into the labor market. Improvements in the quality of secondary school should also increase the demand for education. Finally, programs that subsidize the cost of schooling, such as conditional cash transfers, can also be effective.
- Insufficient supply of secondary school infrastructure is a problem in rural areas in some Latin American countries. In these settings, programs to increase the availability of schooling facilities can hold promise.
- The main constraint to an expansion of the private university system is on the demand side of the market. There is high *potential* demand for private university because of the high returns, but this does not necessarily translate into high *effective* demand because of liquidity constraints and information asymmetries. Student loan and targeted scholarship programs hold great promise, if they are well designed. Providing households with information about the quality of private providers may also help them make better choices.
- The main constraint to an expansion of the public university system is on the supply side of the market. Increasing aggregate budgets to public universities is generally not a feasible or desirable solution. Cost recovery, increases in enrollment for a given budget, and policies that tie the transfer of public resources to performance should all be considered.

In much of Latin America, firms have increased their demand for more educated workers in the last two decades.

BOX 4.6

Minimizing Information Problems about Private University Providers: Experiences from Latin America

Lack of information about the quality of private university providers is a serious constraint to expansion of the coverage of the university system in Latin America. There are two approaches to minimizing information asymmetries between providers and consumers: accreditation of private providers and the provision of information about learning or labor market outcomes.

Chile has a well-functioning accreditation system developed as a response to an increasingly heterogeneous offer of private tertiary education. This quality assurance system has proved successful in two ways: (i) establishing a quality stamp through external institutional and programmatic evaluation procedures; and (ii) creating a culture of self-evaluation in which institutions continuously benchmark teacher qualifications, curricula, and learning facilities with competitors and thus stimulate competition. The accreditation is voluntary but more than 35 universities and 106 programs have or are currently applying for accreditation, which points to the importance of being accredited.

The reason for the success of the Chilean accreditation scheme appears to be related to the fact that the system is voluntary, not excessively onerous, and relatively free of bureaucracy. Unfortunately, other accreditation schemes in the region have sometimes been "captured" by entrenched interests such as the administrators of public universities seeking to protect their market position. In Venezuela, IESA, a dynamic private institute of business administration, had to wait several years to receive the official approval from the Council of Rectors for a new MBA program designed and delivered together with the Harvard Business School. The Brazilian Institute of Applied Technology (IAT), the most prestigious private engineering school in the country, faced similar problems getting accreditation. And in Nicaragua, the University of Mobile in Alabama was denied a license to operate by the Council of Rectors keen on protecting the public universities from competition.

The second way countries have attempted to correct information asymmetries is through standardized graduation tests, or information about the wages and employment prospects of university graduates. In Brazil, the *Exame Nacional dos Cursos*, or *Provão*, has raised public awareness about quality in tertiary education. This standard, nationwide exam measures the performance of graduates in over a dozen disciplines. The results are disaggregated by institution, and published. As such they serve as a *de facto* comparative indicator of the quality of graduates, and, by inference, the quality of instruction and education.

Since its inception in 1996, the Provão has grown both in coverage and influence. The first exam covered only three disciplines (Administration, Engineering, and Law). The very existence of the Provão provoked strong opposition from segments of both the students and the professoriate, including boycotts and threats of disruptions at exam sites. Such opposition has not continued, especially given the interest of the press and the general public in the results. In its fourth year, the Provão is now widely accepted.

The most notable effect of the Provão has been to provide much greater information on the quality of individual degree programs to potential students, thereby creating more savvy educational consumers. Private institutions, many of which felt wrongly deprived of prestige by the wealthier, research-oriented public universities, now have an objective means of demonstrating the quality of their course programs. Several well-known public universities have degree programs whose Provão scores were disappointing; these are now struggling to save their reputations as the leaders in the field.

Students are voting with their feet thanks to the Provão. Applicants now routinely inquire about Provão performance, and schools that do well highlight this information in their informational literature. Those private institutions whose scores have been consistently high have almost universally reported increasing applications. Also, private universities, which have now proven their quality, are attracting talented professors away from public institutions.

"Labor market observatories" provide an interesting complement to graduation tests. The Chilean government, with support from the World Bank, is in the process of developing such an observatory to regularly provide consumers with information on the labor market performance of graduates from different tertiary institutions.

Source: Blom and Holm-Nielsen (2002); World Bank (2000, 2002).

Having a more educated workforce is a *sine qua non* of competitiveness and high productivity. Designing policies that will allow young men and women to seek more schooling, and to take advantage of the higher wages paid to educated workers is the challenge facing Latin American education systems.

How best to upgrade the skill levels of a population means different things for different countries. Haiti and some countries in Central America should focus on increasing the coverage of the primary schooling system. For Brazil, continued increases in primary education and secondary education should be the priority. Secondary education should also be the priority for most other Latin American countries—especially countries such as Venezuela, Costa Rica, Colombia, and others with alarmingly low secondary attainment for their income levels. Jamaica, Trinidad and Tobago, and other countries in the English-speaking Caribbean have managed impressive secondary school attainment, but comparatively low enrollments at tertiary institutions. Chile is at or very close to the world technology frontier in a number of sectors such as fruit cultivation, vineyards, and salmon farming, yet it has only 6 percent as many Ph.D. scientists per million people as Korea, and 2.5 percent as many as Finland.[24] In addition to necessary improvements in secondary school and university, the comparatively low number of Ph.D. students, especially in the hard sciences, may be a real source of concern in Chile.

The relative emphasis on different policies will vary depending on the stage at which countries find themselves in their education transitions. Because there is a lot of interdependence across education levels, however, governments must often work at many levels in the education system. Consider a poorly performing university system. Part of the problem may be that secondary school graduates do not have the content knowledge and learning ability to be successful in university. Policies that improve secondary school quality may therefore decrease repetition at the university level. Consider also a poorly performing secondary school system, with many dropouts before graduation. Part of the problem may be that children leave school because they consider it highly unlikely that they will be accepted by a university (or that they will be able to pay for it). Policies that increase transition rates from secondary school to university may therefore reduce dropouts throughout secondary school.

A careful understanding of the education market within a given level is the key to improving schooling outcomes.

More resources may help, but often they make little difference. This is not to say that education expenditures do not matter, but rather that *how* money is spent matters a great deal. Policies should focus on alleviating a given constraint to the acquisition of more schooling, and on improving incentives. Sometimes, effective policies may be under the purview of the ministry of education—for example, programs to build school infrastructure, provide teaching materials, or regulate the university system. At other times, reforms to the safety net could be important, as with the creation or expansion of conditional cash transfer programs that reduce the opportunity cost of schooling. And in yet other circumstances policies that increase the demand for more educated workers, including trade reform and legislation that encourages the flow of technologies from abroad may hold the biggest promise.

Endnotes

1. This is not to say that Latin American countries do not have problems with their primary school systems—in terms of both coverage and quality. Indeed, many countries, especially some of the poorer countries in Central America, are still far from achieving 100 percent primary enrollment levels. The point is, rather, that the region as a whole does not have a primary enrollment deficit for its income level, whereas it has deep deficits in secondary and tertiary education.

2. In Brazil, Mexico, Peru, and Venezuela, 40 percent or more of the population had no schooling whatsoever, while the comparable figures in Korea, Malaysia, Singapore, and many Central American countries were in excess of 60 percent.

3. This is equivalent to sweeping out any fixed effects in a regression. However, if there is a lot of measurement error in these data, the first-differenced results could be less, not more, accurate than the results from a regression in levels.

4. Authors' calculations, based on data from UNESCO and the World Bank. These ratios are an average of the ratios for the 1980–95 period.

5. Mariscal and Sokoloff, in Haber (2000).

6. Bolivia, Costa Rica, Ecuador, and Venezuela all have higher mean years of schooling than Jamaica, but much higher fractions of the population with no schooling whatsoever. In all of the East Asian tiger countries, the "diamond" distribution of educational attainment is bunched around the middle, with large fractions of the workforce having secondary schooling.

7. In a simple formulation, the opportunity cost would be given by the expected wage, defined as the product of the observed wage and the probability of employment.

8. A summary of evidence can be found in de Ferranti and others (2000); on Brazil, see also Neri and Thomas (2000); on Mexico, see Cunningham and Maloney (2000); on Argentina, see Cunningham and Maloney (2000), and España, Parandekar, and Savanti (2002); on Peru, see Schady (2002).

9. Authors' calculations, based on the 2000 ENAHO survey.

10. See, for example, Hanushek (1995), Kremer (1995), and Glewwe (2002).

11. See, among others, Hsieh and Urquiola (2002); Contreras (2001); Gauri (1998); McEwan (2000); and Mizala and Romaguera (1999).

12. The graphs we present are based on the tabulations in Filmer (2000).

13. On sheepskin effects, see Lam and Schoeni (1993) and Strauss and Thomas (1996) on Brazil, and Schady (2003) on the Philippines.

14. In some countries, the possibility of international migration may also increase the demand for schooling even when the domestic returns to education are low. This may be part of the explanation for the high observed rates of secondary schooling in countries in the English-speaking Caribbean.

15. Policies that increase the demand for educated workers by firms or improve quality will become particularly important if the expansion of secondary school enrollments places downward pressure on the relative wages of secondary school graduates.

16. For a review of demand-side financing initiatives in Latin America, see Patrinos (2002).

17. Much of this section draws on background notes by Blom and Yin (2002), and Frydman (2002).

18. A breakdown of the direct private cost of a year of university education by low-priced, middle-priced, and high-priced public and private universities in Brazil, Chile, and Mexico shows very large differences in these costs in Brazil and Mexico, and much smaller differences in Chile. See Frydman (2002).

19. There are exceptions. In Argentina, for example, access to public universities is essentially unrestricted. See Frydman (2002, p.8).

20. In Brazil, for example, the mean quality is lower and the dispersion higher in private than in public universities.

21. On Thailand, see Abelmann and others (2001); on Costa Rica, Garnier (2002).

22. IPEA (2000); Schwartzman (2002, p. 25); World Bank (2000, pp. 30–31).

23. The high per-student costs in federal universities in Brazil are, in part, a reflection of very low ratios of students to academic staff. This ratio (9.2) is lower than that in *any* other country for which data are available. There are more than twice as many students per academic staff in Italy, the Netherlands, Switzerland, or Ireland as in Brazil.

24. These figures are from Brunner (2001, p. 12).

CHAPTER 5

Closing the Skills Gap: Training Policies

T HE PRECEDING CHAPTER DISCUSSED POLICIES TO CLOSE THE GAP IN RELATIVELY general skills acquired in schools, colleges, and other institutions of learning. This chapter focuses on skills acquired in the workplace, referring to them as "training," though it also addresses vocational-technical education in schools. What is equally important is the shift in the unit of analysis from the household to the firm. A quick look at figure 1.1 in chapter 1 can help in understanding why training is treated specially: education-technology complementarities are fundamental to an understanding of the "knowledge economy," and **training** and **networks** play a critical role in this regard. In the most general terms, training may be seen as efforts by firms and workers to customize the skills acquired in schools and colleges to the specific technologies in use. This emphasis on actively increasing the complementarity between education and technology explains why training is positioned between education on the left and technology on the right in the figure. Gill (2002) explains this approach to the knowledge economy, and the role of education, technology, training, and networks in more detail.

This chapter addresses the issue of training policy in Latin America and the Caribbean, using this interpretation of training as a device to increase the complementarity between skills and technology. It is not a comprehensive analysis of training in the region; there are competent surveys that meet that criterion, such

as CINTERFOR/ILO (2001), Callart (2001), Zuniga (2001), and Guerrero (2002). Like many of these assessments, this chapter concludes that the movement of reform in many countries of the region is indeed in the right direction. But there remains a considerable unfinished agenda.

Interpretations of *training as a link between education and technology* conform well with the evidence, and have important implications for the design of training policy. Using this approach, this chapter makes three main points:

- A summary of the evidence gleaned from surveys of firms and households in Latin America and the Caribbean indicates that firms invest in formal training more when they adopt new technologies and—when they do so—more educated workers are more likely to receive this training. That is, the evidence points to strong complementarities between education

and firm-sponsored training, and between technology and firm-sponsored training.

- Matching this evidence of complementarities to the design of training systems in Latin America and the Caribbean indicates that in many of the countries there is considerable potential for increasing the effectiveness of training systems. The proposed tenet is that "training policy" should be seen as consisting of three components: education policy, technology policy, and incentives for firms to formally train their workers. Education and technology policies are treated in other chapters in this report, but policymakers interested in improving training outcomes should view these three systems as symbiotic.

- In assessing training policy, this chapter argues for an increased emphasis on providing learning rather than vocation-specific skills in schools, and a shift away from publicly sponsored vocational education in schools or industry-level vocational training institutes to well-designed training incentives to firms. The evidence summarized in chapter 3 and the associated imperative to have a workforce capable of facilitating technological progress calls for (a) a shift of vocational education from the secondary to the post-secondary level; (b) a shift in the balance between public and private providers of training toward the latter; and, based on reform experience, (c) a shift away from coercive training legislation toward fiscal incentives to firms. This chapter also contains general guidance on how this can be done, but the specifics are better left to more detailed country-level training policy assessments.

This chapter first summarizes the training policy design in countries of Latin America and the Caribbean, contrasting the "Latin American model" of vocational training with other approaches. We then summarize the evidence on skills and training in Latin America and East Asia, drawn from enterprise surveys. The determinants of in-service training are then analyzed, drawing mainly on a paper commissioned for this report that utilizes firm panel data from Mexico (Tan and Lopez-Acevedo, 2002). The issue of lifelong learning is also briefly examined, with illustrative evidence from Brazil, Colombia, and Mexico using household survey data. The concluding section summarizes the tentative policy priorities that, when augmented by country-level analysis, could provide useful guidance to policymakers engaged in the difficult task of improving training systems in the region.

Vocational Education and Training Systems in Latin America

Training policies recognize that training is the most important linkage between education and work, and generally aim to strengthen this link. But government efforts to do so have varied considerably.

Education and Training Systems around the World

Figure 5.1 illustrates different education and training systems around the world, based on ILO (1999). At the risk of oversimplification, and emphasizing that all of these systems are constantly changing, five basic approaches can be distinguished:

- The *Japanese system* may be the most simple in design. Students completing basic education go on to

general secondary education; from there, they go either to firms that provide training upon initiation, or to tertiary education.

- The *American system* is similar in that there is no "streaming" until after secondary education, but is different in its reliance on postsecondary education for facilitation of transition to work. Students completing secondary education go on to community colleges, polytechnic institutes, and universities, which provide both general and professional training.

- The *French system* is marked by vocational streaming that starts at the secondary level. Students going into (school-based) vocational-technical education are prepared for entry into the labor market, and those going into the humanistic-scientific stream are prepared for higher education.

- The *German system* is based on a long tradition of apprenticeships; for a (diminishing) majority of secondary school students, instruction is "dual," in that it consists of a school-based general instruction, and firm-based occupation-specific training regulated by industry guilds. The German model is distinguished by a system of qualifications that are regulated by guilds, which provide a broad equivalency between graduates of the academic and the dual subsystems.

- The *Latin American* system of training is a hybrid of the French and German systems. In the most simple terms, it is identifiable by its reliance on autonomous vocational training institutes for a set of students completing basic education as a bridge to the labor market, general (humanistic-scientific) education at the secondary level as a bridge to tertiary education for another, and school-based vocational education for the others (Callart 2000). Most secondary-level students not streamed into the academic tract are expected to receive vocational instruction in training institutes under tripartite—employer, labor union, and government—auspices, funded by an earmarked tax on enterprises. The streaming thus takes place at an early stage, and there are few opportunities to go back into a stream that would allow going on to tertiary education.

As can be seen in figure 5.1, training systems have to be assessed in relation to education systems, and not in isolation. Examining **training** systems more closely, three types can be distinguished (see table 5.1): cooperative, enterprise-based,

FIGURE 5.1

Education and Training Systems around the World

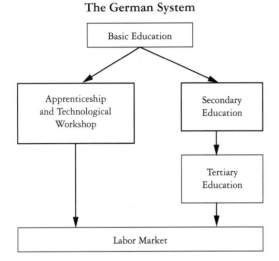

The German System

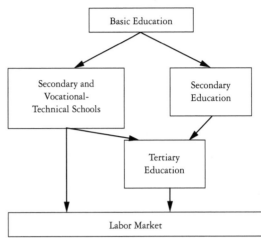

The French System

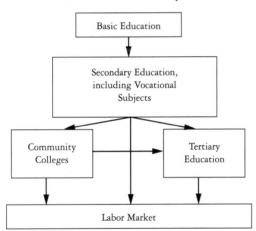

The North American System

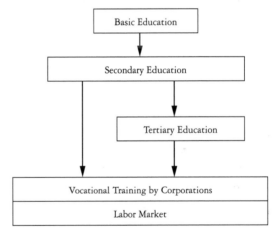

The Japanese System

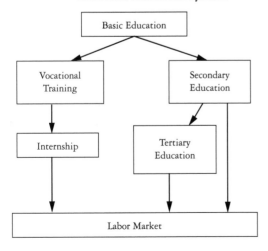

The Latin American System

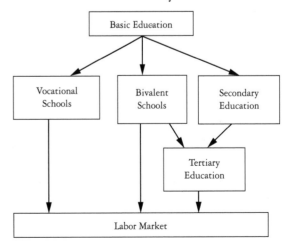

The Mexican System

TABLE 5.1

A Typology of Training Systems

TYPE	EXAMPLE COUNTRIES	MAIN FEATURES
Cooperative		
Employer-led	Germany, Austria, Switzerland, *Brazil*	Pressure to train workers resulting from cooperation between employer federations, the state, and labor unions
State-led	*Barbados, Colombia, Jamaica, Paraguay, Peru, Venezuela*	Pressure to train workers resulting from tripartite cooperation
Enterprise-based		
Corporate	Japan	Firms take responsibility for training workers, who stay with firms for long periods
Voluntarist	United States, United Kingdom	Little or no institutional pressure on firms to provide training
State-driven		
Demand-led	Korea, Singapore, Hong Kong (China), Taiwan (China), Malaysia, *Chile*	State plays a leading role in coordinating training, but operates in an open and competitive environment
Supply-led	France, East European countries, *Mexico*	State plays a leading role in providing training, with little or no pressure on employers to train

Source: ILO (1999).

and state-driven. Within each of these three categories, there are two categories, depending on whether it is the employer or government that leads the training effort, whether there are societal or government pressures to train, and whether the role of government is largely provision of training, or its finance. What is noteworthy is that there are no Latin American countries where training systems may be classified as enterprise-based.

It is important here to distinguish between vocational education and vocational training (see Gill, Fluitman, and Dar 2000, for more details). While vocational *education* is classroom-based, and should be considered part of the (government-sponsored or regulated) schooling system, vocational *training* takes place outside of the formal schooling cycle. The clearest example of the latter is workplace training of workers, sponsored by enterprises. The Latin American system—with its reliance on taxpayer-funded *training institutes* managed by governments and employers—attempts to establish a hybrid of these two forms of skill accumulation.

Main Features of the Latin American Model

The prototype of the autonomous vocational training institute was Brazil's SENAI, founded in 1942 for industry, and the SENAC, SENAR, and SENAT—for services, agriculture, and transport, respectively—which were founded some years later. A training levy—collected by the government on behalf of employer federations—was earmarked for financing these training institutes. Students completing basic education in schools were streamed into general secondary education (regulated or run by the Ministry of Education) or these vocational training institutes (run by employer federations). For the latter, the prospects for reentry into the education system were slim.

Over the next three decades, many countries followed Brazil's example with similar enterprise-funded vocational training institutes, but with the difference that they were run by governments; in other words, they were *public institutions*. During the 1950s and 1960s, six countries introduced such institutes: SENA in Colombia (1957), INCE in Venezuela (1959), SENATI in Peru (1961), INA in Costa Rica (1963), INACAP in Chile and SENAP in Ecuador (1966). In the 1970s, more countries introduced such institutes: SNPP in Paraguay (1971), INFO in Honduras and INTECAP in Guatemala (1972), and IFARHU in Panama (1973).

By the 1990s, vocational training institutes in 14 Latin American countries that had such systems (Argentina, Barbados, Brazil, Colombia, Costa Rica, the Dominican Republic, Ecuador, Guatemala, Haiti, Honduras, Jamaica, Paraguay, Peru, and Venezuela) enrolled more than 5 million people (about half of this enrollment was in Brazil), equivalent to about a third of secondary enrollment in the same countries. As a result of the dominance of this mode of training, the ratio of enrollments in vocational training and vocational education courses to those in general secondary education in Latin America is more than double that in other developing-country regions, with more students enrolled in training institutes and centers than in vocational schools. This ratio has fallen, as secondary enrollment in schools has increased considerably during the last decade in LAC. But in most of these countries, this system remains an important part of the apparatus to close skill gaps between LAC and industrialized countries.

Over time, three main changes have taken place.

- In some countries, the definition of "basic education" has been changed to include more years of formal schooling. In Brazil, for example, basic education (after which streaming into vocational institutes and secondary schools takes place) has been increased from six years to eight.
- In other countries, vocational education has been introduced in secondary schools, leaving open the prospects of going on to postsecondary education institutions. In Argentina and Chile, for example, a sizable fraction of secondary school enrollment is vocational.
- In countries where vocational training institutes were run by governments, some have introduced an element of competition (see CINTERFOR/ILO 2001 for a detailed account of the changes introduced in most countries). The most extreme version of this is Chile, where INACAP lost its special status and became just another training institution that had to compete with other public and private training institutions.

Because of differences in original design and the changes that have taken place over the last two decades, while the 12 countries that are classified as falling into the "Latin American mode" of training have elements in common, there are important differences in the roles of government, employers, and workers among these countries. Today, the most notable exceptions to the "basic Latin American model" in the region may be Mexico, Uruguay, and Chile, which have over time adopted approaches that can be better classified as variants of, respectively, the American and French models of vocational education and training.

Chile's reforms since the mid-1970s are especially illustrative. It broke away from the Latin American mold in 1976, when it created a system in which the government replaced free training in the national training institute (INACAP) with tax rebates for training in enterprises. More than 2000 private training agencies (universities, schools, centers, consulting firms, and others) compete to sell their services to private firms and government programs (see Espinoza, 1997; and Cox Edwards, 2000). Mexico's system of vocational training relies more on vocational

education than other Latin American countries; almost 40 percent of students leaving primary school are streamed into vocational and vocational-general hybrid (called "bivalent") schools. Public institutes such as those in the CONALEP system provide vocational education (see box 5.1). Over time, private providers of training are becoming more important, especially as the importance of in-service training has grown.

A System in Trouble?

During the half century of its existence, the Latin American model has also not spread outside the region; only the Democratic Republic of Congo and Morocco have adopted similar systems. This is in sharp contrast to the Latin American model of old-age income security, for example, which has spread to every corner of the world. While extraregional disinterest in the model is scarcely definitive proof of its failure, it should lead us to question the optimality of the approach even for Latin America.

As the economies in the region have become more and more complex, and as the pace of technological change has picked up, the demand for workers who are trainable (that is, those who can adapt and retool quickly and cost-effectively) appears to have increased relative to those who have been trained—that is, who have job- or technology-specific skills. This has put systems following the Latin American approach to vocational education and training under strain for the following reasons:

- The systems were designed to channel a large fraction of students at an early stage in the schooling cycle into vocational training institutes, which emphasized job-specific skills rather than developing strong learning faculties. As the economy demanded workers with learning skills, the training and education system could respond in two ways: either by increasing the fraction of students going into the general secondary stream after completing basic education, or by increasing the education levels of students going into vocational training institutes. Both solutions require close coordination between the ministries of education that run the education system and the ministries of labor or industry that run the vocational training system. In Latin America, this coordination is rarely present.[1]
- The changes in the nature of work and the pace of technical change required a shift in focus from "the

---

BOX 5.1

Mexico's CONALEP: How to Make a Vocational Education Institution Work

The Mexican government introduced CONALEP as an alternative technical education system to traditional upper-secondary education. CONALEP has undergone significant structural changes in the past decade. A major transformation took place in 1991, when the system reduced the number of specializations offered from 146 to 29 and introduced modular courses, the forerunner of the competency-based education and training model (CBET) now adopted in Mexico.

Examining CONALEP's performance compared to that of a well-designed control group, a recent evaluation sponsored by the World Bank found the following:

- CONALEP graduates search longer for a job, but they are more likely to find jobs that they were trained for. As in previous studies, this evaluation found that CONALEP increases graduates' earnings. However, the order of magnitude of earnings increase differs greatly from those in previous studies: on average, CONALEP increases graduates' earnings by 22 percent—not the 30 to 40 percent found in previous studies—compared to a control group.
- The second part of the evaluation examined the benefits of the 1991–92 CONALEP reforms. Results indicate that graduates from the pre-reformed program (1994 Survey) search longer for a job compared to those of the post-reformed program (1998 Survey).

Moreover, graduates from the post-reformed program have a 45 percent greater probability of finding a job than those from the pre-reformed program. Furthermore, the 1994 Survey cohorts earned higher hourly earnings than the 1998 Survey cohorts. A plausible explanation is that since 1994, real wages have decreased in Mexico by almost 40 percent.

- The third part of the evaluation examines CONALEP's cost-effectiveness. The results indicate that CONALEP is a cost-effective program. In addition, CONALEP has had spillover effects on the rest of the technical education system by stimulating other educational institutions to be more efficient and to adapt to the changing economic and social situation.

It is difficult to discern the relative contribution of the different factors responsible for the good overall performance of CONALEP, but it is safe to conclude that the special features of CONALEP as a whole have made this possible. These are autonomous organizational structure, decentralized operation, strong links to industry, industry-experienced instructors, and modular courses. However, further challenges remain, notably more rapid curriculum adjustment to changing market circumstances and the improvement of external and internal efficiency.

Source: Lopez-Acevedo (2002).

---

individual trainee to firms, a broadening of activities to include other productivity-related services and an increasing recognition of the importance of small firms" (ILO, 1999, p. 72). It is far from clear that governments in the region have recognized this, and attempts to systematically restructure training institutions and incentives to conform to these principles have usually been slow or half-hearted.

- The decline of employment in public enterprises relative to private sector firms and self-employment required a commensurate shift in emphasis from public to private training institutions and, even more importantly, from state-led to enterprise-based, market-oriented training. While some countries such as

Chile have made the shift from cooperative to state-led but demand-driven training systems, even such transformations of approach to training are rare in the region.

The shift from cooperative to more market-oriented approaches to training is under way in many Latin American countries; the question is whether these reforms are quick enough and go far enough.

It is important here to briefly address a concern that is occupying the attention of policymakers in the region: the need for development of systems for *lifelong learning*. Box 5.2 provides a brief summary of the evidence in favor of these arguments and their implications for training policy design.

BOX 5.2
Lifelong Learning: Concept, Evidence for LAC, and Implications

What Is Lifelong Learning?

Lifelong learning (LLL) has become a buzzword among educators and increasingly enters the agenda of policymakers. Lifelong learning preaches that human beings should learn "from cradle to grave" or "from womb to tomb." The centerpiece of the concept is the idea of a self-motivated and self-reliant person who learns based on his or her interests and needs. It is believed to constitute a paradigm shift from a traditional supply-driven method with a centrally decided curriculum and class teaching of children toward a demand-driven process taking place in all aspects and ages of life with the individual learner in the driver's seat. Table 5.2 provides a summary of the differences between lifelong learning and traditional education systems.

TABLE 5.2
Differences between Lifelong Learning and Traditional Education

ASPECTS	TRADITIONAL EDUCATION SYSTEM	LIFELONG LEARNING SYSTEM
What	Facts	Learning to learn
Who	Child and youth	All age groups
How	Class teaching	Individual learning
Where	Schools and colleges	Formal: School and colleges
		Nonformal: Private courses and self-study
		Informal: Workplace and friends
Delivery	Supply	Demand

While LLL is not a well-defined concept, we attempt here to make a distinction between the need for LLL from the need for retraining workers. *One interpretation could be that while retraining is necessitated by the obsolescence of skills acquired on the job (informally through learning by doing or formally through training), LLL is made necessary by the obsolescence of skills acquired during formal schooling.* This interpretation squares well with the observed increase in interest in LLL as the pace of technical change has accelerated during the last few decades.

What Is the Evidence?

There is considerable evidence for the United States that the increase in the wage gap between education groups expanded faster among younger workers than among older

workers during the 1980s and 1990s, suggesting that there were differential shifts in the experience profiles of different age groups (Card and Lemieux, 2001; Card and DiNardo, 2002; and Heckman and others, 2001). These changes have sometimes been interpreted as evidence that, in times of rapid technological change, skills are more likely to depreciate, or even become obsolete faster. In other words, when technology is changing rapidly only young workers may be able to offer the kind of skills that employers demand, and thus they may be the ones who reap most of the benefits from skill-biased technological change. If this is so, we would expect to see a steepening of the experience profile, as most of the returns to education are collected early on in one's career.

Unlike the United States, Latin America shows little evidence of such patterns. Figure 5.2 presents experience-earnings profiles for relatively educated workers in Brazil, Colombia, and Mexico in the first and second half of the 1990s. If skills were rapidly depreciating for older workers, we would expect the 1996–99 profiles to be steeper for low levels of experience and flatter for high levels of experience than those for the early 1990s. As it turns out, both profiles are almost identical for the two periods, and this pattern is found to hold for all three countries. While this implies that the need for LLL has not increased in these countries during the last decade, it does not rule out the possibility that there has always been an unmet need for LLL opportunities.

What Are the Implications?

In any case, the main implications of LLL appear to be for education, not training systems.

- The shift in emphasis from knowing vocation-specific skills to having better-developed faculties for learning new skills implies that *vocational education should be increasingly postponed* to higher levels of education, for example, from secondary to postsecondary levels in countries where secondary education enrollments are high.

(continues on next page)

115

BOX 5.2
Continued

FIGURE 5.2

Wage Profiles in Brazil, Colombia, and Mexico—Early and Late 1990s

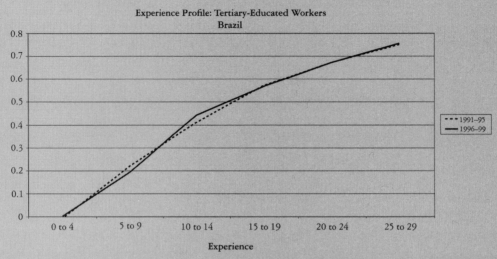

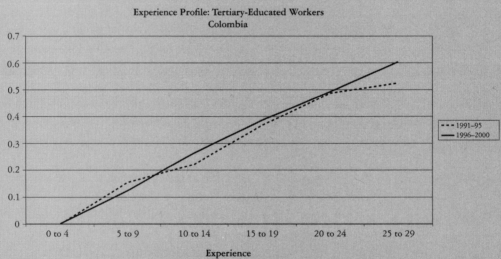

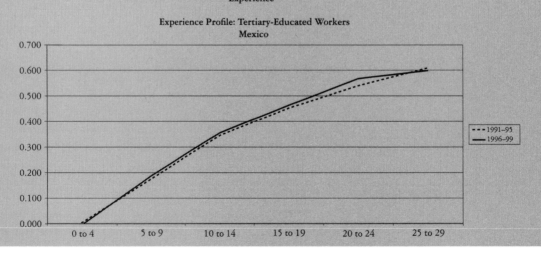

- There are implications for *curriculum* in schools, with an increased need for higher-order cognitive skills that aid learning, problem-solving, and analysis, rather than rote-memorization, simple literacy or numeracy, and knowledge of facts.
- Perhaps the most important training-related implication is the heightened need for sensible *certification mechanisms*, so that passage between the formal education system and the workplace is smooth and in *both* directions—from school to work and from work to school.

Source: Andreas Blom and Norbert Schady (World Bank staff).

How Employers View Training

Since training is an important instrument for firms in making the skills available in the workforce better complement the technologies they employ, we examine how employers in Latin America and the Caribbean regard training. This section is based on a note commissioned for this report by Batra (2002), which analyzes the skill- and technology-related findings of enterprise surveys in 16 Latin American countries conducted by the World Bank to assess the business environment. The results of these surveys are comparable across both countries and regions (see box 5.3 for details).

Using these data, we provide tentative answers to the following questions: Do employers in the region regard the shortage of skilled workers a serious constraint for productivity increases? What do employers do to address this shortage of skills, that is, when and whom do they train? Where do employers that train workers obtain training services?

Briefly, the results of these surveys indicate the following: First, employers in Latin America (and East Asia) rely overwhelmingly on private suppliers of training, even though policymakers have generally been fixated on public training institutions. Second, "skill shortages" appear to be less serious in Latin America than in East Asia, which seems somewhat surprising until one considers the possibility that the demand for more skilled workers is greater the more rapid the rate of adoption of new technologies by firms, and the higher the education levels of workers. As seen in the earlier chapters of this report, Latin America lags behind East Asia in both education levels and the pace of technical change. Finally, these findings suggest that while training policy reform has been seen in the region largely as synonymous with the reform of public training institutions, it would be more appropriate to see it as a package consisting of efforts to improve education and adopt new technologies,

BOX 5.3
World Business Environment Surveys

The World Business Environment Surveys (WBES) include information on firms' size (employees, sales, and assets); years in operation; sales, debt, and growth performance; sources of finance; and a mix of qualitative and quantitative evaluations of the business environment, including governance, predictability of economic policy, the judicial systems, financing, and general constraints to business operations. For Latin America, East Asia, and the OECD, WBES included a module on competitiveness with detailed information on enterprise training, technology, and productivity.

The WBES sample aimed to accurately represent the relative importance of manufacturing, service and commercial firms in each economy. To ensure comparability across countries, a sampling frame was developed using the distribution of private firms in each country, by sector, size, numbers of employees, and location. Because the surveys oversampled larger firms relative to their weights, and because the results presented are not weighted, aggregate training estimates should be viewed only as illustrative of broad patterns of training in sample countries.

Source: Batra (2002).

and training incentives that recognize that much of training provision in the region is private, not public.

Are Skills a Serious Constraint?

The supply of skilled labor—both professionals and production workers—is cited as a constraint to productivity in Latin America and the Caribbean (see figure 5.3). Almost

FIGURE 5.3

The Supply of Skilled Labor Is a Leading Constraint to Productivity in Latin America and the Caribbean

(Percentage of firms citing factor as a constraint to productivity 2000)

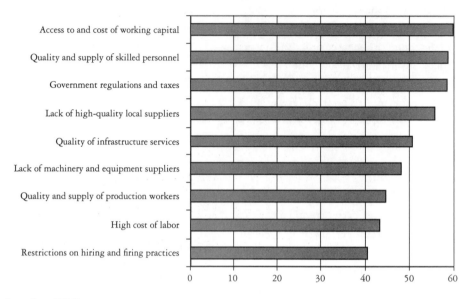

Source: Batra (2002).

60 percent of firms in the region cite quality and quantity of skilled personnel as a constraint, and about 45 percent cite the quality and quantity of production workers as a barrier to higher firm productivity.

The main finding is that quality and supply of skilled personnel was ranked as a major obstacle to firm productivity and competitiveness by almost 60 percent of firms in Latin America.

What Are the Firm-Level Correlates of Training?

Virtually all employers report providing some form of informal on-the-job training to their employees, especially new hires, so informal training is not a useful discriminator for our purposes—identifying efforts by firms to improve the match between skills and technology—and about 60 percent of surveyed firms provide some formal training. Considering the productivity gains from training, why do almost half of firms in Latin America not train?

The explanation could be related to technology, education, labor market functioning, or training supply: (a) The use of mature technologies obviates the need to train formally; (b) the lack of adequately educated workers makes it costly to train them; (c) high labor turnover makes it unprofitable to do so; or (d) there are weaknesses in the supply of training, or employers have poor information about

training providers. Responses to questions in the WBES provide some clues. The reasons are somewhat different in the two regions (see figure 5.4):

- The use of mature technologies is easily the most important reason for not training in both regions, indicating strong complementarities between training and technology. This is supported by the responses of firms suggesting that informal training is adequate in many cases.
- A related finding: Latin American and Caribbean firms that do not train state that they are likely to find adequate skills in workers, indicating either that the education system is supplying workers with appropriate skills, or that the demand for skilled workers is relatively low in LAC, or some combination of the two.
- In general, information asymmetries or financing constraints appear to be a less serious problem in Latin America than in East Asia.

The rationale for public subsidies for training appears to be weaker in Latin America and the Caribbean than in East Asia: labor turnover and resource constraints are less likely to be impediments to training in LAC than in East Asia.

These rankings are consistent by firm size as well. However, small firms are more constrained by resources, lack of

FIGURE 5.4

Use of Mature Technologies and Availability of Skilled Workers Are the Main Reasons Why Firms in Latin America Do Not Invest in Formal Training

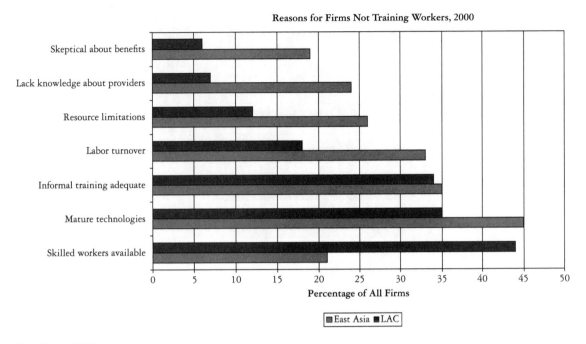

Source: Batra (2002).

knowledge about training benefits, and labor turnover than are large firms. The WBES fielded in Guatemala in 2000 provides some evidence of this (figure 5.5).

Failures in the market for training—too low private demand because of labor turnover, or too low supply, or poor information about demand or supply—pose more difficult questions. If market failures are responsible, what kinds of training policies are effective in addressing these failures? Do the low incidence of formal training and the striking differences in training by firm size reflect the weak training and technological capabilities of enterprises or market failures? Are firms constrained by poor access to financing for training or do they lack the interest, know-how, or capability to design and implement training programs? How important a constraint is "labor poaching," the hiring away of employees trained at another employer's expense, which prevents firms from recouping the returns to their sunk investments in training? Answers to these questions are crucial when designing public policy. Insights into some of the questions are provided by firm respondents in the competitiveness module; policymakers need to know **why** firms train and why they do not. But they require country-specific analysis in order to arrive at sound training policy design.

What does appear to be a general finding is that small and medium-size firms should be the primary targets for incentives to encourage training. What also seems to be true is that training incentives are often ineffective in reaching precisely these firms (see box 5.6, however, for a more effective training incentive scheme in Malaysia).

Where Do Firms Get Training Services?
The survey distinguished between formal training provided in-house by the employer and formal training provided by external training institutions, both public and private. Reliance on internal training is strong across all East Asian countries, accounting for about 40 percent of all training; private providers account for more external training than do public providers. In Latin America, 50 percent of enterprises provide in-house training (see figure 5.6). Of the external providers, public training institutions are not a popular choice—only 16 percent of enterprises use public institutes. These ratios may come as a surprise to many engaged in training policy reform in the region, which is regarded as synonymous with the reform of public training provision.

Employers rely most on private external training sources in Chile and Uruguay, both countries that do not follow the

FIGURE 5.5

Knowledge of Training Providers and Resource Considerations Are More Important Constraints for Micro-Enterprises, Guatemala 2000

Source: Batra (2002).

FIGURE 5.6

Almost 50 Percent of Training in Latin America Is Internal to Enterprises, and Another 40 Percent is Privately Supplied

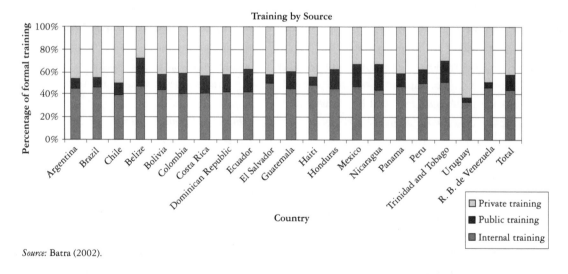

Source: Batra (2002).

Latin American mode of training. Public training suppliers play a relatively large role in Mexico, Ecuador, Belize, Trinidad and Tobago, and Nicaragua. Nevertheless, given the importance of internal training by enterprises, it would not be far from the truth to assert that even in these countries, about three-fourths of training provision is private.[2]

Correlates of In-Service Training: Evidence from Mexico

Recent research indicates that training significantly increases firm-level productivity. For example, in Malaysia and Colombia, firms that train are more than 25 percent more productive than firms that do not. Training effects of this

BOX 5.4

Enterprise Training and Productivity in Developing Countries

Using a simple production function approach, the productivity effects of formal training can be estimated. These estimates, shown in table 5.3, indicate that enterprise training is associated with much higher levels of worker productivity in private firms.

TABLE 5.3

Estimated Productivity Effects of Formal Training

COUNTRY	YEAR	PRODUCTIVITY EFFECT (PERCENT)
Nicaragua	2000	56.4
Guatemala	1999	49.0
Mexico	1992	44.4
Colombia	1992	26.6
Indonesia	1992	71.1
Malaysia	1994	28.2

In contrast, no significant productivity effects were found for in-service training provided by public institutions. Most of the productivity gains from training in private firms came from private training institutions and in-firm training programs. Finally, productivity effects of in-service training seem to be larger the poorer the country, possibly reflecting the scarcity of skills in lower-income countries.

Sources: Tan and Batra (1995); Batra (1999, 2000).

BOX 5.5

Firm-Level Cross-Section and Panel Data for Mexico

In a paper prepared for this report, Tan and Lopez-Acevedo (2002) use the 1992, 1995, and 1999 ENESTyC surveys; Ciecon (2001) uses the 1995 and 199 surveys to examine pre- and post-NAFTA incidence of training. The survey was also fielded in 2001, but data were not available at the time this paper was commissioned. The ENESTyC surveys a large, stratified random sample of manufacturing establishments and contains questions on employment, wages, worker characteristics, technology adoption and use, and formal and informal training. The ENESTyC also allows a cross-sectional analysis of the impact of training on wages.

Tan and Lopez-Acevedo also link firm panel data from the annual survey of manufacturing (EIA) to the ENESTyC to more rigorously estimate the impact of training on wages and productivity over time. The EIA, available annually from 1993 to 1999, contains detailed and comparable information on the productivity and wage outcomes of interest, but not in-firm training. So training information from the ENESTyC surveys is brought to bear on a subsample of EIA firms at three points in time. The firms in the subsample differ from the population in two important respects—they tend to be larger and, as survivors over a turbulent period between 1993 and 1996, are probably more productive on average than the typical firm.

Source: Tan and Lopez-Acevedo (2002); Ciecon (2001).

magnitude are not unusual for developing countries—some are even higher; in Guatemala and Nicaragua, the training premium is estimated to be twice as much (see box 5.4).

Given these estimates, training is (legitimately) seen as a potent instrument for raising productivity, and governments intervene pervasively to increase in-service training. But to design effective interventions, one has to understand why so many firms pass up opportunities for increasing productivity, and not train their workers. This section examines the experience of Mexico, for which available data allowed relatively rigorous analysis of the determinants of training.

Complementarities Confirmed: Evidence from Firm-Level Cross-Sectional Data

Ciecon (2001) estimates the correlates of in-service training in Mexico during the second half of the 1990s, using dis-

aggregated sectoral data. Box 5.5 presents the characteristics of the data used, and the main findings are presented in figures 5.7 through 5.10. The findings confirm the results found in the WBES for Latin America and the Caribbean at a more aggregate level, and using a smaller sample size per country.

- First, regression estimates using probit techniques point to education levels of workers as the most important correlate of training incidence, and this finding is robust for all subsectors of the Mexican economy—from agriculture to manufacturing to services (see figure 5.7).

FIGURE 5.7

In Mexico, Educated Workers Get Trained More Often ...

Marginal effect in the probability of taking a training course, computed at the mean values of the variables

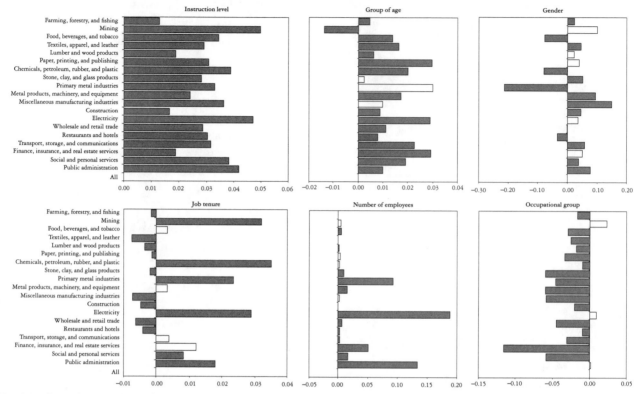

Note: White bars indicate that the estimate is not significantly different from zero.

Source: Ciecon (2001).

- Second, for a subsample of manufacturing firms for which measures of innovativeness were available, R&D spending is the second most important correlate of training (see figure 5.8).
- Third, for the full sample of all sectors, about two-thirds of training is in the workplace (see figure 5.9). About half of external training is from private providers (see figure 5.10). These numbers are very similar to those found for Latin America as a whole in figure 5.6.

Particularly noteworthy in Mexico is the high frequency with which respondents—both small and large—identified private companies, industry associations, and to a lesser degree public centers for worker training as the principal providers of external training. Also noteworthy is the growing role, between 1992 and 1999, of private training consultants and equipment suppliers. In both years, public and private universities and technology centers only played a

small role as providers of external training for firms (Tan and Lopez-Acevedo 2002).

What was driving the rise in training in the 1990s? Two hypotheses have been advanced in the literature as possible explanations for the growing demand for training: first, the effect of globalization and, in particular, the post-1994 growing integration of Mexico into the North American market under NAFTA; and second, the effect of technological change and adoption of new information and communication technologies (ICT), both of which are believed to be relatively skill-intensive (or skill-biased). Tan and Lopez-Acevedo (2002) provide causal evidence that both forces may have contributed to the rising trend in training incidence. Over time, training incidence trends upwards irrespective of technology or trade status, but these trends are especially pronounced for firms conducting R&D or exporting.

Simulations suggest that the observed rising training trend over the 1990s is attributable principally to the changing relationships between training and its covariates, rather

FIGURE 5.8

... and More Innovative Firms Train Their Workers More

Marginal effect in the probability that an establishment provides training to its workers, computed at the mean values of the variables

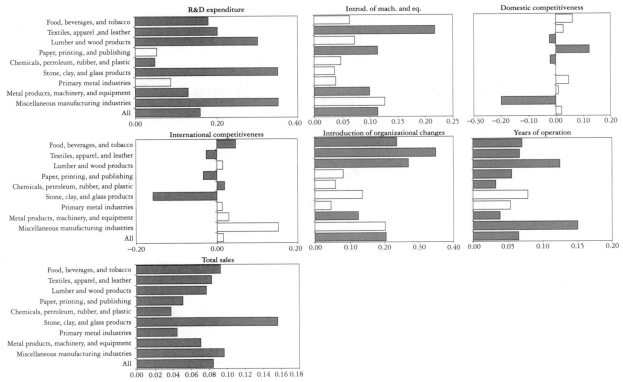

Note: White bars indicate that the estimate is not significantly different from zero.

Source: Ciecon (2001).

FIGURE 5.9

In Mexico, Two-Thirds of Training Is Internal ...

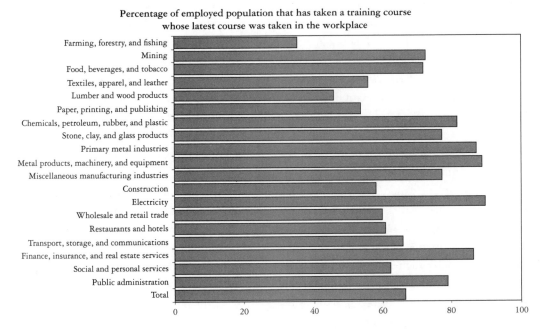

Percentage of employed population that has taken a training course whose latest course was taken in the workplace

Source: Ciecon (2001).

FIGURE 5.10

... and About Half of the Rest Is by Private Providers

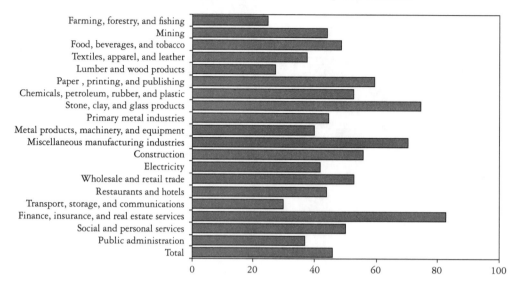

Percentage of employed population that took their latest course
outside their workplace who did it in a private institution

Source: Ciecon (2001).

than the covariates themselves. Changes over time in the means of these covariates—for example, changing industrial structure, size distribution of firms and geographic location, R&D, and exports—are less important.

Productivity Effects of Education, Training, and R&D: Evidence from Panel Data

Using regression techniques and firm panel data, in a paper commissioned for this report, Tan and Lopez-Acevedo (2002) analyze the interaction among skills, technology, and productivity during a period of increasing openness in Mexico between 1992 and 1999. Their main findings are as follows:

- An increase in average years of schooling raises the likelihood of training, a relationship that persists and becomes quantitatively more important over the 1990s. This provides more evidence in favor of the growing complementarity between education and training.
- The educational distribution of the workforce plays a key role in *both* technology and training decisions. The share of the workforce with a college education appears to drive training by employers; here, the results suggest that a highly educated workforce also indepen-

dently increases the likelihood of employer investments in new technology through R&D.
- R&D has a much greater impact on the likelihood of external training than on in-house training programs. The marginal effects of R&D on training more than doubled during this period of growing trade contacts with the rest of the world. For in-house training, the impact of R&D rose from 1.6 to 3.7 percent, and for external training it rose from 3.1 to 7.8 percent.
- Consistent with findings that export-oriented firms are more likely to train their workers, greater openness is associated with a higher incidence of training. But the results also show that training incidence has increased only in firms that do some R&D (figure 5.11).
- While a substantial number of (especially large) firms train but report no R&D, the likelihood that firms do R&D without training is extremely low. In 1999, no more than 7 percent of firms in any given size category reported doing R&D without training. In short, while firms may train for a variety of reasons, they seldom engage in R&D without complementary investments in worker skills.
- Training—especially if it is continuous—increases total factor productivity growth. Similar results hold for technology transfers and R&D conducted by the firm

(see figure 5.12). R&D, and technology transfer through licensing and patents, are statistically significant only for the firms that reported investing in these innovative activities for at least half of the intervening seven years.

These results confirm, using panel firm-level data for one country, what the WBES suggest at a region-wide level. Box 5.6 presents evidence from Malaysia presented in Tan (2002), which reinforces these findings. Box 5.6 also ana-

lyzes the effects of a training intervention—the Human Resource Development Fund (HRDF) scheme—in a framework that recognizes the importance of technology adoption in training decisions of enterprises.

Policies to Promote Training

The evidence on the correlates of training indicates that two of the three components of an effective training policy package are measures to increase *education* levels of workers—since training and education appear to be strong complements—and to increase the rate of adoption of new *technology*. An earlier chapter dealt with education policy; here it should suffice to point out that this may involve changes in the education and training systems so as to shift the balance between general and vocation-specific skills acquired in the formal education system. Two later chapters discuss policies to promote technology adoption in Latin America and the Caribbean. This chapter concludes with a discussion of the third component—incentives for firms to train their workers.

Rationale for Public Intervention

The policy intervention that is appropriate depends on the nature of the market failure. Table 5.4 provides an application of this approach for training markets. When poor information is the constraint, for example, the appropriate policy response is to disseminate best practices in training

FIGURE 5.11

In Mexico, Training Increases with Greater Openness, but Only if Firms Conduct R&D

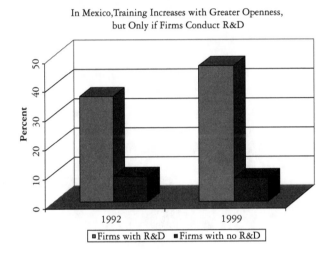

In Mexico, Training Increases with Greater Openness, but Only if Firms Conduct R&D

FIGURE 5.12

Training, Especially if It Is More Continuous, Facilitates TFP Increases

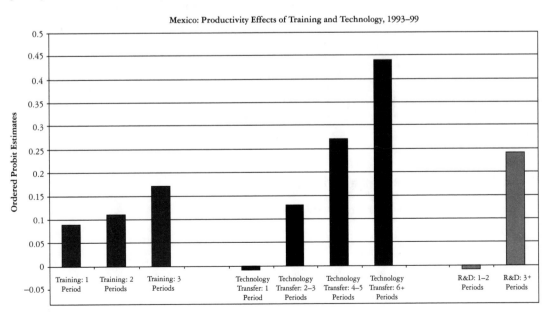

Mexico: Productivity Effects of Training and Technology, 1993–99

BOX 5.6

Complementarities between Skills and Technology: Training Interventions to Boost Firm Productivity in Malaysia

In 1993, Malaysia replaced its scheme for promoting training (double deduction for approved training-related expenses in calculating taxable income), which had been in operation since 1987 but found to be largely ineffective, with a training levy administered by a council of representatives of the private sector and selected government agencies. To start the scheme, the government provided a sizable grant that matched company levies.

Was the HRDF scheme effective in raising training and firm productivity? To answer this question, Tan (2002) uses firm-level panel data from 1988, 1994, and 1997, namely, comparing the training decisions and productivity outcomes before and after the intervention. However, this was a period of considerable dynamism for Malaysia, and other things that would affect training and firm productivity changed as well. In particular, the percentage of firms introducing new technology in the panel rose from 53 to 75 percent during the decade, and those using advanced process IT rose from 48 to 83 percent. The education level of the workforce also rose rapidly. The analysis considers these changes in assessing the effectiveness of the intervention.

By reimbursing some of the approved training expenses of participating firms and hence lowering the cost of training, the HRDF creates incentives to train on the cost side. In contrast, technological change creates incentives to train and to hire educated workers on the revenue side. The analysis yields the following findings:

- First, probit estimates show that training is significantly higher in firms that introduced new technology and that employed a higher proportion of skilled workers. The estimates also show that large

and medium-size firms train more frequently, and that participation in the HRDF scheme is associated with more frequent training.

- Second, simulations indicate that training increased more owing to the enactment of HRDF as compared with the effect of introducing new technology. The exception is for small firms, for which these two effects are roughly similar. The impact of HRDF is most pronounced for medium-size firms, while the impact of technical change is greatest among small firms.

- Third, the productivity impacts of training are sizable; even more important, there is evidence of strong complementarity between training and technology. The productivity impacts—of 50 and 23 percent, respectively—are twice as high in firms with new technology as compared with firms without new technology, providing "dramatic confirmation of the key intermediating role that training plays in realizing the productivity potential of new technology."

- Finally, productivity impacts of training are about half as large in small firms as in medium-size and large firms, suggesting an explanation for the frequent observation that training is less common in small firms. Training may simply be less productive in small firms because they do not make complementary investments in new and potentially more productive technologies. To address this, the HRDF has introduced group training schemes for small firms, and the national SME agency has stepped up its efforts to provide integrated business, training, and technology development services.

Source: Tan (2002).

TABLE 5.4

Rationale and Policy Options for Public Intervention in Training

	KIND OF INTERVENTION		
REASON FOR INTERVENTION	FINANCE TRAINING	PROVIDE TRAINING	COMPLEMENTARY POLICIES
External benefits	Preferred	Not justified	None
Market imperfections	Second-best	Not justified	Preferred: deal with source of market imperfection
Weak private training capacity	Not justified	Second-best or preferred	Preferred: build firm training capacity
Equity	Second-best	Not justified	Preferred: selective scholarships

Source: Middleton, Ziderman, and Adams (1993, p. 116).

know-how and information about the availability and cost of services. High rates of labor turnover may suggest that there are externalities in training: to the extent that firms are unable to internalize the benefits of training because skilled workers can be hired by other firms, there will be underinvestment in training. Mandates, collective action, or incentives can help to internalize some of these externalities. This section focuses on some of these public policy instruments employed in various countries and provides some examples of good practice.

Many countries, both advanced and developing, have put into place different policies designed to foster increased in-service training among their enterprises, including payroll-levy training funds and tax incentives for employer-sponsored training. These employer-targeted training policies take many forms: (i) levy-grant schemes, in which fund administrators use earmarked levies to make grants to employers for approved training, as in Singapore and previously in the United Kingdom; (ii) training levy rebate schemes, in which employers are partially reimbursed for approved training out of their payroll levies, as in Malaysia, Nigeria, and the Netherlands; (iv) levy exemption schemes, in which employers are exempt from levy payments provided they spend a given percentage of their payroll on training, as in France, Korea, and Morocco; and (iv) tax incentives for approved training paid out of general revenues, as in Chile and previously in Malaysia.

The Payroll Levy Grant System

The payroll levy is a common instrument in Latin America for overcoming the underprovision of training. Argentina, Barbados, Brazil, Chile, Colombia, Costa Rica, Ecuador, Honduras, Jamaica, Paraguay, Peru, and Venezuela have implemented levies, with mixed success. Brazil's levy, one of the oldest, suggests that factors influencing success include administrative independence of the levy fund, a combination of private ownership and public mission, and a management structure that includes industry and government. In Chile small and medium-size enterprises have overcome the tendency for levy funds to subsidize only large firms, by grouping together on a sectoral basis. Sectoral centers have also been established in Argentina, and small and medium-size enterprises have negotiated a sectoral rate with the national supervisory agency.

Levies can also be set and controlled through industry sector bodies (as in Mexico and South Africa); industry

collective agreements (Belgium, Denmark, France, Greece, the Netherlands, Sweden); or national insurance levies for displaced workers (France, Sweden). Levy exemption schemes have also been used as a means of subsidizing smaller firms and adult training providers (Austria and Germany); similar levy schemes have been implemented in Morocco and Turkey. Levy-rebate schemes have been used in Jordan, Korea, Malaysia, Mauritius, Singapore, and Taiwan (China). Some countries have modified payroll levies. Peru, for example, has lowered the levy and diversified the sources of finance. Argentina, Brazil, and Colombia have cofinancing arrangements with enterprises, communities, and vocational schools. Singapore and Taiwan (China) have used matching grants.

Experience with levies yields the following lessons (see also box 5.7):

- *Keep employers in charge*. Industries need to own the levy. Argentina, Brazil, and Chile have vested supervision of levies in industrial bodies; Malaysia's experience provides the clearest lesson in this matter.
- *Increase competition in provision*. Levy funds are not cost-effective when they support only government training providers.
- *Earmark funding strictly*. Funding levels are better maintained with levies than with government grants, which tend to decline with shrinking budgets. But levy funds should not be used for other government expenses, as has happened in the past in Costa Rica.
- *Provide support for smaller enterprises*. These schemes have typically been used by large firms and enterprises that already have a high skills base—support mechanisms are needed for small and medium-size firms and farms to participate. Mexico's CIMO program has been assessed as effective in supporting small and micro-enterprises (see box 5.8).

National Training Councils

Many countries have established national training councils (Argentina, Australia, Brazil, Chile, Côte d'Ivoire, Malawi, Mauritius, South Africa, and the United Kingdom). Their experience suggests that locating country management of training with the social partners (business, unions, and government) can improve the quality, relevance, and flexibility of training. Training funds managed by training partners have tended to become more diversified in how the money is collected and spent, including their use in the informal sector.

BOX 5.7
Well-Designed Levy-Grant Schemes Can Motivate Firms to Train

Several East Asian economies have used direct reimbursement of approved training expenses, funded through payroll levies, to encourage firms to train their employees. Successful schemes are flexible, demand-driven, and often accompanied by an information campaign and technical assistance to smaller firms.

The introduction of such a scheme in Taiwan (China) led to dramatic increases in training, which continued after the program ended in the 1970s. Singapore uses a levy on the wages of unskilled workers to upgrade worker skills through the Skills Development Fund. The fund's aggressive efforts to raise awareness of training among firms, to support development of company training plans, and to provide assistance through industry associations have led to a steady rise in training, especially among smaller firms. However, such schemes can also create disincentives to train when rigidly administered. In Korea, which required that training last a minimum of six months or that firms pay a fine, many firms paid the penalty rather than train to this standard. In addition, the fund provides grants for

developing training plans, organizes regional courses on training need assessments, and administers a variety of subsidized programs targeting small enterprises. A recent analysis indicates that the scheme has significantly increased the incidence of training.

In Malaysia, the HRDF was established in 1993 with a matching grant from the government. The act created a council (HRDC), with representatives from the private sector and from responsible government agencies, and a secretariat to administer the HRDF schemes. Eligible employers with 50 employees and above are required to contribute 1 percent of payroll to the HRDF. Those who have contributed a minimum of six months are then eligible to claim a portion of allowable training expenditures up to the limit of their total levy payments for any given year. The HRDC set rates of reimbursement, varying by type of training and generally lower for larger firms. Box 5.5 provides evidence of the impact of this intervention on firm productivity.

Source: Batra (2002).

In Argentina, Brazil, Chile, Mauritius, and Peru, industry associations have assumed responsibility for administering the levy. It has been important for these industry bodies to have responsibility for the bulk of the funds and to work with both training providers and enterprises. The Japan Industrial and Vocational Training Association is an association of employers that provides training programs for industry trainers. The association receives no funding but charges membership and course fees. The semi-autonomous Vocational Training Corporation in Jordan is an industry body that works closely with government and industry in providing in-house and external training.

In the United Kingdom, industry-administered training funds at the regional level, through Training and Enterprise Councils, are being replaced by regional Learning and Skills Councils that will combine a broader range of education and training functions.

There are many mechanisms for distributing training funds. Financing can go to state-run training institutions, it can be directed selectively to enterprises on the basis of training plans (Germany, Korea, Singapore), or it can be dis-

tributed through open tender, with the state as purchaser rather than supplier of training (Australia, Chile). A more radical measure has distributed funds to the user or trainee through voucher schemes, such as the United Kingdom Training Credits scheme.

Because different types of firms and workers require different types of training, it is important that the training market not be too inhibited through institutional constraints. In Colombia, despite an extensive and well-funded training system, many skilled workers have not used the formal training system.

Matching Grants Schemes

Some countries use matching grants schemes to increase training. The most successful schemes are demand-driven, with private sector implementation, and aim to facilitate the creation of sustained markets for service provision (Crisafulli 1998). Programs in Chile and Mauritius use private sector agents to administer the matching grants schemes. Both have reported positive results—and so has Mexico's program.

BOX 5.8

Mexico's Proactive Approach to Small and Medium-Size Enterprise Support

The Integral Quality and Modernization Program (CIMO), established in 1988 by the Mexican Secretariat of Labor, has proven effective in reaching small and medium-size enterprises and assisting them to upgrade worker skills, improve quality, and raise productivity. Set up initially as a pilot project to provide subsidized training to small and medium-size enterprises, CIMO quickly evolved when it became apparent that lack of training was only one of many factors contributing to low productivity. By 2000 CIMO had provided an integrated package of training and industrial extension services to over 80,000 small and medium-size enterprises each year and training to 200,000 employees. Private sector interest has grown, and more than 300 business associations now participate in CIMO, up from 72 in 1988.

All states and the Federal District of Mexico have at least one CIMO unit, each staffed by three or four promoters, and most units are housed in business associations, which contribute office and support infrastructure. These promoters organize workshops on training and technical assistance services, identify potential local and regional training suppliers and consulting agents, and actively seek out small and medium-size enterprises to deliver assistance on a cost-sharing basis. They work with interested small and medium-size enterprises to conduct an initial diagnostic evaluation of the firm, as the basis for training

programs and other consulting assistance. CIMO is expanding its support in two directions: assisting groups of small and medium-size enterprises along specific sectoral needs, and providing an integrated package of services, including information on technology, new production processes, quality control techniques, and marketing as well as subsidized training.

Evaluation studies in 1995 and 1997 found CIMO to be a cost-effective way of assisting small and medium-size enterprises. The study tracked two groups of small and medium-size enterprises over three years, one with firms that participated in CIMO in 1991 or 1992, and another with a broadly comparable control group of enterprises that had not participated in the CIMO program. CIMO firms tended to have lower performance indicators than the control group prior to participation in the program, but by 1993 labor productivity had either caught up or exceeded that of the control group. Other performance indicators showed similar improvements: increased profitability, sales, capacity utilization rates, and wage and employment growth—and reduced labor turnover, absenteeism, and rejection rates for products. The most dramatic impacts of CIMO interventions were among micro-size and small firms.

Source: STPS (1999); Tan (2000).

An increased investment in training has been matched by a reduction in enterprise failure. A side benefit has been the development of a network of industry management training consultants that are available to enterprises that want to invest in enterprise-based training. Singapore has undertaken a program to build up its stock of industry trainers, and Japan's Industrial and Vocational Training Association has trained over 30,000 industry trainers in the past 30 years.

Matching grant schemes can support the development of a training culture by providing both an incentive and a means of investing in training. It is important to build a training culture with a high level of training capacity in enterprises and a high propensity for workers to undertake training, so that enterprises continue to invest in training. In Japan most managers have a training function, and

regularly engage workers in informal training. The Basic Law for Vocational Training in Korea is designed to encourage in-company training. Strong training cultures have been established in some Asian countries (Japan, Korea, Singapore), some northern European countries (Germany, Netherlands, Scandinavia), and, judging on the basis of levels of in-company training, some Latin American countries (Brazil and Chile).

Matching grants schemes can also link educational and human resource development policies. The Singapore Skills Development Fund was designed and successively modified to provide an incentive for enterprises to increase the skill and pay level of their workers. But a matching grants scheme, by itself, will not lead to an expansion of the training market. And grants should not be restricted to state-run training institutions. Funds should support strengthening and diversifying the supply of training and stimulating demand. Mexico's Integral Quality and Modernization Program concentrates on the productivity of small enterprises, using both private training consultants and government and private training institutions (see box 5.8).

Training for the informal sector is typically provided as informal apprenticeships, often through nongovernmental organizations, which help to diversify the funding for training programs for the poorer sections of the economy. Argentina, Costa Rica, and Peru have successful programs of this type.

Summary

Productivity analyses in developing countries find that investments in firm-sponsored training—especially in-house training—have large payoffs. Yet a sizable fraction of manufacturing and services firms do not provide any formal training for their employees. This is especially pronounced for small and micro-size firms—over half of them provide no structured formal training. A significant number of large firms also report no training in Latin America and the Caribbean.

What accounts for this lack of interest in an activity that appears to have high payoffs in terms of productivity? The evidence indicates that firms are more likely to train when they employ an educated and skilled workforce, invest in R&D and technology, are relatively large, emphasize quality control methods, or have foreign capital participation or export to foreign markets. Thus there are strong complementarities between training and schooling and critical links among firms' training, technology, and competition in product markets. Firms that train use a variety of in-house and external providers. Private sector providers are as important as—if not more important than—government-run training institutions. These findings have implications for education, technology and training policy, and policies to promote small and medium-size enterprise development.

Since firms view training as an instrument to increase the complementarity between education and technology, government policies to encourage in-service training must consist of a package of actions and incentives to increase education levels, adoption of new technologies, and incentives to firms—especially small and medium-size enterprises—to train workers. Important recommendations include the following:

- *Increase general education levels.* Employers' decisions to train and the productivity outcomes of training depend on the stock of education and technical skills that individuals bring to the labor market. The maintained hypothesis is that it is more cost-effective to impart training to workers who are adept at learning. Even the effectiveness of public vocational training increases as education levels increase: as education has improved, vocational training institutes in many Latin American countries have reverted to their original mission of training for productive employment instead of implementing remedial adult education programs.

- *Postpone vocational education.* More rapid technical change necessitates a stronger education base: the main implication for vocational education and training systems is that vocational education should be pushed to post-secondary levels in countries that have attained universal primary education.

- *Promote adoption of new technologies.* Technology policy to improve access to new technologies and stronger incentives to adopt them is also an important component of an effective approach to training. The most innovative experiences in Latin America in training "conceive the latter as part of a set of technology transfer actions" (CINTERFOR/ILO, 2001, p. 29).

- *Adopt more effective training policies.* Training policies need to be well designed and implemented, and targeted firms need to be made aware of the policies. Several constraints on training—poor information about benefits, high training costs from the inability to exploit scale economies in training, weak managerial capabilities, absence of competitive pressures, or market imperfections—may be operative and policy initiatives to address these constraints should be explored.

- *Establish coordinated and proactive small and medium-size enterprise policies.* A high percentage of small and medium-size enterprises do not train. Such firms face a variety of training constraints, from high labor turnover to poor information and finance. Proactive measures are needed to seek out and deliver a package of integrated services to small and medium-size enterprises—including consultancies, training, and technology information and incentives.

There is reason to be optimistic in Latin America and the Caribbean. Education levels have been increasing, firms have

BOX 5.9

Recent Changes in Training Systems in Latin America and the Caribbean

Countries in the Latin America and Caribbean region have changed their approach to vocational training during the last few decades. In general, the changes have been in the right direction. A recent assessment summarizes these changes as follows:

- *Stronger links with technology*. Diverging from the "notion of training as a supplementary field of activity, divorced from technological innovation and development," many countries are now integrating the two sets of activities.

- *Stronger links with education*. Setting aside the notion of vocational training as separate—though theoretically complementary—from education systems, coordination efforts are being increased to build national education and training systems, capable of meeting a growing and diverse demand.

- *More firm- than institution-centered*. The notion of a school- or institution-based activity, concentrated in an early part of life to prepare individuals for specific occupations or jobs, is increasingly being replaced by the view that training is workplace- or firm-centered, and is a series of competencies.

- *More private than public*. Private training and vocational education provision, which used to be small relative to public providers, has grown enormously both because of economic changes and because of encouragement by government policy.

- *More diversification in finance*. Starting with a reliance largely on training levies and appropriations from the general budget, the financing of vocational training has evolved to also rely on incentives, rebates, and other government support.

- *More variation in approach*. In place of a relatively uniform approach in different countries that featured national institutions that monopolized vocational training activities, the region now has widely divergent organizational structures.

Source: CINTERFOR/OIT (2001).

increasingly more reasons and ability to institute new technologies, and recent diagnoses of training systems in the region point to noticeable improvements in their design and functioning (see box 5.9). These changes in training systems can be seen as evidence of a growing recognition of training as a link between education and technology, and of firms as the principal agent for strengthening this link in the most productivity-enhancing manner.

In conclusion, exploiting the complementarities among training, education, and technology implies that these systems have to be better integrated with one another. For training and technology, this integration is most naturally done at the enterprise level. The very nature of production implies that employers must assess their skill and technology needs simultaneously. Thus "enterprise-based" training systems may be best suited for countries that have reasonably well-developed education systems, and where economic pressures and incentives to acquire new technologies are present. Even developed countries such as Germany that have cooperative training systems—variants of those that proliferated in Latin America—have introduced elements that resemble those of

enterprise-based training systems like those of the United States. Such a move may require a transitional phase of state-led but demand-driven systems such as those of East Asian countries. Chile's training reforms provide perhaps the most important clues on how this can be done in Latin America, but policy reforms in other countries also provide the rationale and guidance for continued efforts to make training systems respond better to the needs of private enterprises.

Endnotes

1. CINTERFOR/ILO (2001) proposes that "vocational training grew in the region as a separate system from regular education schemes. Although theoretically complementary to each other, they showed in reality a disparity of objectives, little coordination between themselves."

2. A related and relevant question is whether firms that are better linked to world markets, through either product or factor markets, train their workers more. In particular, are foreign-owned firms, which ostensibly bring new technologies from abroad, more or less likely to train workers? Again, are enterprises that export goods more pressured to stay competitive and hence invest in new technology and skills? WBES from around the world indicate that the answer to both these questions appears to be yes.

CHAPTER 6

Technological Transitions and Elements of Technology Policy

ECHNOLOGICAL INNOVATION IS A KEY SOURCE OF ECONOMIC, INCOME, AND employment growth. This premise has been validated by theory and empiricism and by now has been accepted by most countries. As a consequence, countries are trying to secure technological and knowledge capabilities so as to reap their associated benefits. For the LAC countries, this is a matter of utmost urgency since, as we showed in chapter 3, the technology gap—however it is measured—between them and the East Asian countries, or between them and the natural resource–abundant countries, is quite significant, and has been widening through the 1990s. The issue for the LAC countries is how, given where they are now, they can best develop the capability to generate and manage technological change and innovation. That development is a process that does require the involvement of literally all actors in the economic environment, the public and the private sectors; and, in order for that development to be effective, it has to be coherent, coordinated, and tailored to country endowments and characteristics—as it was done in most of the successful East Asian and natural resource–abundant countries.

While the government cannot mandate innovation, it can and should provide the leadership, coordination, commitment, and incentives to induce the desired response from the drivers of the process—the firms

and individuals. Individuals make educational and skill acquisition choices and firms contract skills and make innovation, technology, and production choices; and those selections are not independent of each other. These choices and decisions respond to expected returns and competitive pressures and are shaped by country conditions and by the incentive structure provided by the umbrella of the legal, institutional, and fiscal framework provided by the government. And, as that environment evolves, so do the firms' choices. A key premise of this report is that the availability and quality of skills constrain the firms' choices and possible innovations.

Knowledge is the composite of technology and skills. The supply and quality of skills available influence the search for new technology, the monitoring of information about scientific discoveries around the world; and the assimilation of relevant local technology, whether from the spillover effects

of foreign direct investment (FDI), from supplying original equipment manufacturers, from imports of capital equipment, or from licensing. The key to absorbing technology, a task that generally rests on a country's indigenous R&D effort, is the availability of human capital and the readiness to fully master new products and means of production (Forbes and Wield 2000). Without the human capacity to act on new technologies, any leaps made in the supply of, and access to, new technologies are unlikely to translate into significant productivity gains. Yet, accepting that, we have to recognize, as the evidence here presented shows, that without a proper incentive and institutional framework the expected private-led response to develop technological capabilities generated by large investments in R&D—the key driver of technological advancement—will not happen. Many LAC countries by the mid-1990s had reached structural conditions—GDP/capita, years of education of labor force, educational attainment, access to foreign technology, open trade regime and foreign investment laws, and buoyancy of the private sector—that were very similar, if not better than, those that today's technologically successful countries had in the late 1970s when they took off. Yet, practically all of the LAC countries, as of 2002, have still to take off on the path of technological advancements.

The purpose of this chapter is to understand the process of developing technological capabilities, the patterns of successful transitions, to identify the main drivers and policy levers, and to consider which ones are the most appropriate for specific country conditions, to advance in this process. The chapter also evaluates the progress of the LAC countries, provides evidence of the determinants of technological efforts and of the impact on the productivity of the respective drivers, and provides policy recommendations. In the course of this exposition, the links between developing technological capabilities and skills are highlighted; however, a detailed discussion of these linkages is left for Chapters 5 (training) and 7 (networks).

Rationale for Government Action: Market and Coordination Failures

The pursuit and management of knowledge is distinguished by a number of market and coordination failures that inhibit the optimal level of private effort and investment and argues for government intervention to address those failures. Relying on the market alone will not induce appropriate levels of investment for innovation or optimal development of technological capabilities. Thus, government should play a broader role in correcting those market failures and shaping the incentives so that firms and individuals will make the "efficient" decisions. The main market failures here are induced as a result of the following:

- *Knowledge is not appropriable, it is a quasi-public good.* Firms making the investment are not always able to keep the resulting rents to themselves—unlike physical property, knowledge cannot be "owned" exclusively—and when agents are not compensated for the effect of their actions, they do not invest optimal amounts.
- *Knowledge and innovation generate significant positive externalities and spillovers.* The social rate of return on R&D expenditures is often three times as large as the private rate of return (Griliches 1992).

- *Investments in R&D are long-term and risky.* Financial markets in LAC seldom provide the right instruments and term structure for financing R&D expenditures.
- *There are indivisibilities in innovation expenditure.* Innovation is lumpy, requires critical mass of investments, and in a broader sense is subject to economies of scale.
- *The process of innovation involves bringing diverse agents together and that process is costly—it is subject to coordination failures and free-riding behavior.* The cost of bringing and coordinating the various agents and institutions involved in the production of knowledge or concerted actions is costly and not a single agent has incentives to bear those costs, since the benefits of such coordination are often not exclusive and thus it leads to free rider–type problems and results in coordination failures.
- *Diffusion is not appropriable.* No individual agent has any incentives to widely and quickly diffuse knowledge and innovation, since knowledge is not appropriable and it is costly, and once diffused it can be accessed by anyone.

Recognition that the process of knowledge acquisition and diffusion is plagued by market and coordination failures has led to an emphasis on the public interventions necessary to ensure the socially optimal level of innovation. Governments throughout the world have developed a long tradition for intervening in the science and technology (S&T) system in various ways. Practically all countries that have successfully managed to advance on innovation have addressed those market failures and taken the leadership of the process. First of all, governments have taken on the role as overall coordinator of S&T activities. This entails governments leading the effort, setting up institutions (public or private), and implementing and coordinating policy programs to maximize net social returns. Moreover, governments intervene to correct market failures by supplying funds, directly and indirectly, to public and private agents alike; subsidizing R&D expenditures; providing intellectual property rights (IPR) protection to innovation; and facilitating access to foreign technology. Finally, governments have also undertaken in recent years to correct so-called systemic failures (economies of scale, public goods, externalities, and coordination issues) by setting up training programs and specialized research centers (cooperation schemes designed to promote joint public-private R&D efforts and improve the dissemination of information in society), and facilitating the development of networks for effective and fast diffusion of knowledge. These latter types of interventions are dealt with at length in chapter 7.

The timing and extent of these interventions matter. Countries differ in terms of initial conditions of technological capabilities, educational attainment, institutions, and endowments. As a result, and to increase effectiveness—since those interventions are costly—the policies and types of intervention have to fit each country's initial conditions, institutions, endowments, and characteristics. For example, it might not make sense for a government to offer extensive benefits to stimulate R&D investments if the country has a very poorly trained labor force. As conditions evolve, so should the types and extent of government interventions. Failure to address this issue in a coherent way—as has been the case for most LAC countries, as we will argue—condemns countries to a slow and inefficient path of technological advancement.

Developing Technological Capabilities

The key drivers for firms to develop technological improvements and capabilities are competitive pressures and expected returns. These pressures force firms to constantly reevaluate and improve their production and organizational techniques in search of efficiency gains and new processes and products. Firms secure those improvements by adopting and adapting existing, usually foreign, technologies, to fit their needs; bringing in minor product and process innovations; and developing new ideas and creating new technologies. The traditional industrial organization theory used those modes to classify countries into stages of technological development.

Today, however, these stages are not as sharply delineated as they might have been in the past, particularly because of the information revolution and globalization effects, and—for any country—considerable overlaps exist. In each country, at any given time there are firms adopting, firms adapting, and firms creating. Further, the categories themselves are not exclusive. Most purchases of foreign technology involve some adaptation to local conditions and hence the number of cases of pure adoption may be few. Finally, countries never stop adopting and adapting technologies (OECD 2002). Eaton and Kortum (2000), for example, argue that 86 percent of France's technological progress is purchased from abroad, the remainder being generated locally. Jovanovic (1997) argues that resources dedicated to "adoption" in the United States,

widely recognized as the world leader in innovation, exceed those dedicated to innovation at the frontier by a factor of roughly 30 to 1. So, in some sense most of the world's firms are fundamentally adopting/adapting with a few doing little and a few doing cutting-edge innovation.

Furthermore, such typologies are rendered less useful by the fact that they are difficult to measure. Unlike the case for education—for which it is easy to tabulate progress in terms of enrollments and attainments of primary, secondary, and tertiary education—there are not natural or easy measures to classify firms into adoption, adaptation, and creation modes. We are left with imperfect aggregate measures of technological development. We can use proxies, albeit imperfect—such as patents, R&D investments, ICT technology index, or even GDP per capita or educational levels, all of them highly correlated—to classify countries into stages of technological development.

Figures 6.1 and 6.2 provide the estimated "standard" trajectories of countries—on measures of technological development—across the process of development. In all cases, we plot a standardized measure of an index of the variable in question against the log of per capita GDP. The x-axis is logged to "spread out" and cover the poorer countries in the sample (Latin America spans Haiti, with a value of 6, and Argentina, with a value of 8). The y-axis is not, since logging effectively minuscule numbers still carries the appearance of a significant quantity, even when it is not. This scaling does, however, overstate the degree of "takeoff" apparent, for instance, in R&D—which is partly, although not exclusively, an artifact of logging income. These trajectories are as is, not necessarily at all optimal. In fact, all of the successful—in terms of technological advancement—countries have significantly departed from those trajectories as we show later on in this chapter.

Several factors merit mention. First, purchases of foreign technologies, as measured by royalties payments, continue across the development process and are a complement to R&D expenditures. Similar arguments can be made—albeit less strongly—for FDI. That is, as mentioned before, countries never stop adopting/adapting foreign technologies. In fact, as recent surveys in OECD countries show (OECD 2002), many more firms do adoption than creation. Among the richer countries, however, the relative effort in innovation does steeply rise. Second, these "innovation inputs" are largely reflected as intermediate "output" measures as well. Patenting is low for the poorer of the LAC countries, but

FIGURE 6.1

R&D Effort, Licensing, and Development: Predictions from Median Regressions

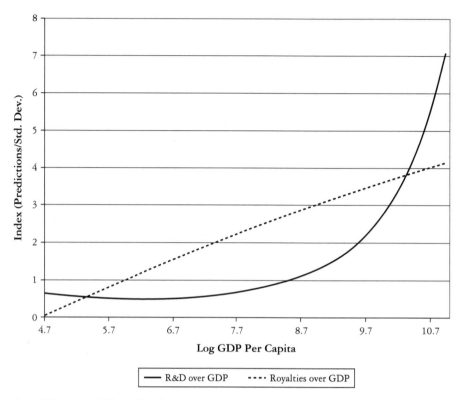

Source: Lederman and Maloney (2002d).

FIGURE 6.2

Innovation and Development

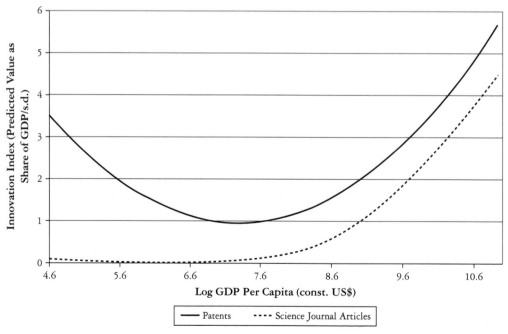

Source: Lederman and Maloney (2002d).

rises across time. It is important to remember that patenting in general is not "blue sky" innovation but often represents process modifications associated with the adaptation of existing technologies. In fact, we can think of the purchase of foreign technologies, the application of R&D to adapt to local conditions, and patenting as complementary activities that, over the course of development, move toward innovating at the frontier of a discipline and introducing entirely new products.

Finally, these stages may carry a normative implication that somehow a firm or country should be adopting or adapting at a given level of development. However, what is clear from the Asian experiences (see chapter 7) is that governments sought to leapfrog stages of product development in trying to move to the frontier of innovation as soon as possible. Ideally a poor country would get the highest return to innovating at the frontier. In fact, last year's study de Ferranti and others (2001) argued that to maintain the dynamism of its natural resource industries at the turn of the 20th century, LAC needed to innovate at the frontier—in mining, in forestry—despite being far poorer in per capita terms than many LDCs today.

What we find more useful in this report is classifying countries by the obstacles to their being an innovating country—and hence, by what policy packages make the most sense. We propose the following phases:

Phase I: Plugging in to the Global Knowledge Stock—Efficiency and Reconnaissance

Countries (and firms) in this phase concentrate their efforts in seeking access to foreign knowledge and technologies—through trade, FDI, and licensing—rather than developing their own. The argument is that substantial private sector R&D efforts, or efficiently used public efforts, will be foiled if the basic conditions for efficient functioning of the economy are not in place—which at this stage seldom are. Trade barriers and other market distortions impede not only competitive forces that prompt firms to improve but also prevent knowledge of what knowledge could be brought to bear. An absence of basic human capital means not only that spillovers from trade or FDI will be unrealized and, in fact, FDI is less likely to come. Poor communication and ICT infrastructure also impedes knowledge of the outside world and the ability to take advantage of even basic fragments of the global production chain (see Lederman and Xu 2002). (In fact, econometric evidence discussed in this chapter and

in chapter 7 shows that the effectiveness and efficiency of R&D depend on both the education of the populace and trade openness.)

The initial dependence on FDI or trade should not be seen as passive. The overall goal is for firms to learn to innovate over time and this implies active approaches toward ensuring spillovers and learning. This, however, will be limited to the degree of human capital, the coherence of the overall incentives to learn, and the overall functioning of the economy. The process usually begins with firms beginning to get exposed to newer products and process through trade and FDI, which become vehicles for the diffusion and adoption of technology. This exposure leads to imitation, and the process of technological mimicry—the first step toward any catch-up—begins.

Formal methods of technology transfer involving licensing and royalty payments may be, on average, less common at these early stages. Little formal R&D on the part of firms is expected at this stage, although universities and public research institutions and some firms may be engaged in conducting research in selected areas, such as in agriculture and natural resources. Yet even at that stage some R&D is necessary for its learning effects. Having access to a labor force that possesses general education and basic technical skills is a critical determinant of absorptive capacity. While some specialized skills may be called for, selective on-the-job training for secondary-educated workers can adequately fill the gap and remove some of the obstacles to the adoption of technology. Evidence from firms in Taiwan (China), Korea, Colombia, Mexico, and Malaysia, among others, supports the view that firm-led training and adoption of technology go hand in hand and that firms that do both reap the biggest productivity gains (see chapter 6).

Phase II: Catch-up and Consolidation of Innovative Infrastructure

Countries at this stage have reached a minimum adequate level of education of their labor force, with well-functioning universities. As firms begin to face increased competition, either domestically or by imports penetration, or when they try to move from domestic to export markets, the response is to improve quality, primarily involving new technology for agriculture and other primary sector goods and/or producing relatively standard products, but at reduced cost. This is driven by low wages as well as the lowered cost of technology through modifications. All this should be facilitated by beginning to develop innovation-related institutions and by increasing linkages with the private sector. R&D begins to play a significant role here and thus skill needs become more specialized at this stage. However, it is unlikely that a large pool of scientists and engineers can be fully utilized by firms. Most tertiary-educated workers at this stage of the economy find suitable employment in research institutions or universities, and firms call upon them from time to time to assist in making some of these adaptations to existing technology. Links between firms and some institutions begin to form, albeit in an unpredictable and spotty manner because of the information and cultural gaps that exist between these entities. The government here is beginning to play a major role leading the process, establishing the main components of a National Innovation System (NIS) and addressing market and coordination failures by providing fiscal and economic incentives for private R&D, and incentives for the collaboration of public and private institutions—such as setting up specialized sectoral scientific institutions or laboratories. In this phase, well-targeted public support for specific sectors—shown to be both important for the country and exhibiting signs of potential excellence—is warranted, as can be seen from the experience of successful (transition) countries. Increasing the financing of R&D and setting intellectual property rights, albeit at relatively lower levels of protection, are essential at this stage.

Phase III: Technological Leaders

At this stage, firms already involved in global markets—adapting existing technologies and selling the resulting products at lower cost than their competitors—find margins eroding as new low-wage entrants take away market share. Sustaining a position in global markets then necessitates a leap forward into creating new products and processes. This requires firms to make large investments in in-house R&D activity consisting of expensive plant and equipment for advanced laboratories and testing facilities. Given the externalities in knowledge creation arising from the less-than-full appropriability of the returns to such investments, this R&D push is likely to be compromised unless mechanisms that correct for this market failure—such as strong intellectual property rights (IPRs) or significant fiscal and economic incentives and a coherent incentive and institutional framework—are in place.

The role of the government here is crucial in creating strong incentives and an institutional framework, and in consolidating a highly effective NIS. The quantity and quality

of highly skilled labor both become crucial. Whereas the nature of innovations at earlier stages is essentially "coded" or embodied in products (hence making its transfer easier), it tends to become more "tacit" and disembodied during this phase. When new knowledge is not completely embodied in a product, spillovers from the sale and use of a product leading to imitation through reverse engineering also become restricted. Human capital takes center stage; more than the mere existence of skilled workers, their proximity to one another and their mobility become the medium of technology transfer and the fuel for innovation. This proximity and mobility are critical to connecting workers between firms as well as with researchers in university research institutions, and is often found to characterize places such as Silicon Valley, which have become synonymous with cutting-edge innovation. While R&D is the main element for the creation of knowledge, large amounts of private R&D is now the key factor and driver.

Policies for the First Stage of Transition: Spillovers, Diffusion Mechanisms, and Incipient and Selective R&D

Governments and firms have choices on the policies and instruments—and extent of use—to build their domestic technological stock and capabilities. These choices depend on a number of factors, and a critical one is the skill level of the labor force. Predictably, the availability of technical and managerial skills becomes the natural limit and often the most pressing constraint facing firms in advancing in the development of technological capabilities. Without an adequate skilled labor force, the impact of a full-fledged R&D program is bound to be ineffective and wasted. Then technology policy should aim to facilitate profitable exposure to foreign technology and on the leveraging via impact on facilitating diffusion and spillovers, and in incentivating incipient and selective R&D programs.

Foreign technology can be accessed through trade, FDI, and licensing. The rationale for trade, FDI, and licensing as instruments for the transfer of technology comes from endogenous growth theory (Romer 1986, 1990; Lucas 1988). That theory posits that the returns to the accumulation of knowledge capital and human capital do not diminish at the aggregate level because of positive spillover effects, and that policies can have a permanent impact on the rate of economic growth. Grossman and Helpman (1991) extend the analysis by exploring endogenous growth theory in an open economy setting.

The basic idea is that goods embody technological know-how and therefore countries can acquire foreign knowledge through imports. There are two principal mechanisms for technology diffusion through trade: One is through direct learning about foreign technological knowledge from the imports, and the second is through employing specialized and advanced imported intermediate products, which involves the implicit usage of the knowledge that was created with the foreign investors' R&D investment.

Thus, not surprisingly, more than any other imports, imports of capital goods are especially important for technology transfer, owing to their rich knowledge and potential productive applications. (Eaton and others 2000). The best-known example of a country following a deliberate strategy of acquiring technology through trade, and doing so successfully, is Korea. The government encouraged imports of capital goods and at the same time encouraged mastering of the technologies embodied in these imports through various incentives, including R&D for its learning effect.

In addition, FDI can provide technology transfer if local firms can copy or imitate technology used by affiliates of foreign firms operating in the local market, or if backward and forward linkages with the foreign firm lead to inter-industry technology upgrading (vertical spillovers), or by labor turnover from the multinational firms to local firms, bringing acquired technological know-how (horizontal spillovers). Foreign direct investment can also lead to technology upgrading by introducing competitive pressures. While in principle FDI could have a more direct impact on technology transfer, because of its in situ production, usually the FDI volumes relative to the trade volumes are much smaller (with rare exceptions), limiting their impact. The best examples of a country acquiring technological capabilities through FDI have been Singapore and Ireland.

The institutional and policy framework for FDI is usually embodied in specific legislation crafted for that purpose, and obviously in the effectiveness of its implementation. The more open, transparent, and fiscally favorable and the less administratively cumbersome economic conditions, the larger the flows of FDI. A complementary jump-starting instrument that has been reasonably effective in Latin America and the Caribbean in attracting FDI is the export-processing zones (EPZs) or free trade zones (FTZ), which function as an institutional shortcut to address broader problems in countries with institutions that impede FDI (de Ferranti and others 2001). The most common obstacles have been

limits to the share of foreign investment and restrictions on investing in certain sectors. A more complicated factor is the extent of fiscal benefits, such as preferential tax treatment. Two other key factors that impact FDI flows—market economic opportunities and the intellectual property rights framework—are discussed separately below.

Finally licensing involves the contractual transfer of knowledge between firms. Given that licensing provides knowledge in a more accessible manner than FDI, many countries such as Brazil, India, Mexico, and Japan have in the past actively discriminated against direct investment by firms and favored technology licensing. Multinational firms, on the other hand, have an incentive to prevent a reduction in the value of their knowledge-based assets. This can arise because the licensed firm becomes a competitor or because the licensed firm allows knowledge to leak. This seems to have led multinational firms to use licensing or joint ventures to transfer older technologies and use FDI for the latest technology (Mansfield and Romeo 1980).

Direct purchases of technology from abroad have been at the center of the make-versus-buy debate in the 1970s and 1980s. The evidence is that, for countries far from the technology frontier, and with low skill levels, the "buy" option translates into bigger productivity gains for firms. India, for example, tried to force an R&D push at early stages of development when adoption would have been more appropriate; Brazil may have a similar story. In the case of India, the rate of return to technology purchase is about 44 percent higher than the rate of return to domestic R&D. When the sectors are divided into two categories as scientific and nonscientific, even more interesting results emerge. In the scientific sectors, the rate of return to technology purchase is 166 percent, whereas the rate of return to R&D is merely 1 percent; in nonscientific sectors, the rate of return to technology purchase is 95 percent, as opposed to 64 percent for domestic R&D (Basant and Fikkert 1996).

These findings support the premise that the more uniform or standardized (what we call "embodied" and "codified") knowledge is, the greater its transferability, and hence the greater possible returns from its transfer through purchasing. The phenomenal differences in the rate of return to these two modes of upgrading discussed above clearly imply that restrictions on technology purchases come at great cost in terms of reduced productivity to firms.

While the role of trade, FDI, and licensing in pulling domestic firms closer to the frontier is acknowledged, it must also be noted that this process is far from automatic. And that is reflected by the empirical evidence. A plethora of results on the subject shows mixed results (Saggi 2002). Three things make technology diffusion non-automatic. First are the requirements of a threshold level of absorptive capacity, often captured in the quantity and quality of skills available, as we show below. Second is the need for complementary R&D expenditures at the firm level for at least their learning effects for adopting and adapting (box 6.1). Third are the information asymmetries and strategic interests and the extent of networks in the economy that impact the degree and speed of diffusion. Potential users face uncertainty, information and learning costs, and other externalities that may result in underinvestment in available technologies. Similarly, potential suppliers of information and assistance also face learning costs, may lack expertise, or face other structural barriers in promoting the diffusion of rewarding technologies. System-level factors such as the lack of standardization, regulatory impediments, weakness in financial mechanisms, and poorly organized interfirm relationships may also constrain the pace of technology diffusion. These constraining or facilitating factors in technology adoption can be placed in four categories:

- *Firm level.* At the firm level, managers face problems of time, cost, absorptive capacity, and technical expertise in accessing information on available technologies and available solutions.
- *Institutional infrastructure.* The degree and effectiveness of innovation-related institutions and their linkages to the private sector and the degree of networks play significant roles in aiding technology diffusion.
- *Business infrastructure.* The organization of industry and intensity of competition; the strength and nature of interfirm relationships, such as closeness to customers, suppliers, vendors, and subcontractors; and the associations within firms via trade, industry, or regional associations also play a role in aiding or impeding technology diffusion.
- *Social infrastructure.* Education, skill level, and training systems can again play a critical role in either enhancing or severely limiting a firm's capability to upgrade technology. Most firms devote too few resources to work force training, and educational institutions may not always be responsive to their training needs.

BOX 6.1

The Dual Role of R&D: Innovation and Learning

The endogenous growth literature casts industrial innovation as a key driver of growth (see Romer 1990; Aghion and Howitt 1992). In the literature, R&D, along with human capital, plays an important role in the creation of new technologies and innovations. However, if R&D were only a source of new innovations, its relevance to developing countries would be much smaller. Case studies show that much indigenous effort is required for technological change even in industrializing economies (see Pack and Westphal 1986). Thus, R&D has a second role—in developing a "firm's ability to identify, assimilate, and exploit knowledge from the environment—what we call a firm's "learning" or "absorptive" capacity" (Cohen and Levinthal 1989).

Empirical studies have typically tried to measure the impact of R&D on economic growth, without distinguishing between the two roles of R&D. These studies have seldom focused on Latin America because of a lack of information. Overall, these studies show a significant contribution of R&D to productivity growth, with social returns to R&D exceeding private returns. Private returns have been estimated in the range of 10–20 percent by OECD, and Griliches (1992) estimated social returns ranging from 20 to 60 percent (Yusuf and Evenett 2001). A few empirical studies have tried to distinguish between innovation and learning, the two roles of R&D. (Examples are Griffith, Redding, and Van Reenen 2001, for a panel of industries across 13 OECD countries; Parisi, Schiantarelli, and Sembenelli 2002, for a sample of Italian firms; and Ray and Bhaduri 2001, for Indian electronics and pharmaceutical firms.) While these studies use different methodologies, by and large they show that R&D has an important role to play in the learning and absorption of new technologies, in addition to its more traditional role of innovation.

A variety of policy measures have been pursued to address these constraints. A convenient way to organize thinking about them is as supply-side and demand-side measures (box 6.2).

Finally, to facilitate access to the global storehouse of knowledge, and to disseminate knowledge effectively, the development of the ICT sector is most warranted at this stage. The quicker the access to information and diffusion

BOX 6.2

Supply-Side and Demand-Side Measures to Improve Technology Diffusion

Supply-side tools: augment sources of information and assistance available to firms. Examples of supply-side instruments are information search and referral services, such as those offered by Valencia Institute of Spain, and the Awareness building technology demonstrations offered by Center for Manufacturing Information Technologies at the Georgia Institute of Technology in the United States. Information search services aim to reduce the information search costs associated with technology diffusion. Such services add further value by often qualifying information requests and matching user needs with appropriate resources. Technology demonstrations seek to make potential users more knowledgeable about available technologies, their possible applications, and their benefits and costs. Such demonstration services are offered by the Georgia Institute of Technology for potential users to see and try. Similarly, Japan's municipal technology center (Kohsetsushi) demonstrates new technologies to firms, often extending the assistance to hands-on training and pilot production. Similarly, Baden-Württemburg's model for technology transfer is carried out through the work of the Steinbeis Foundation in Germany. The main aim of the foundation is to help local firms keep up with the advent of new technologies via by identifying potential partners and assisting them in their negotiations; and offering expertise in special technologies, management, and marketing of the acquired technology.

Demand-side tools: increase willingness and absorptive power of firms to adopt technologies. Examples of measures that attempt to increase the absorptive power of firms to adopt new technologies are programs that offer training assistance or personnel exchanges. Because the effective deployment of technology and improved operational techniques involve changes in human capital requirements, training in the form of classroom training, management seminars, team-building workshops, and distance learning serves as a useful tool. These measures address the tendency of users to underinvest in human capital development, which not only hinders the initial decision to deploy a technology but can also lead to subsequent inefficiencies once in use. Two programs that serve as best practice are the Australian cooperative research centers that offer focused training on specific industry needs in specific technological areas, and the Local Enterprise Councils in Scotland, which identify industry training needs and support training initiatives with private and public resources. When firms lack the resources to apply (or train) their existing personnel to new research and technology projects, measures intended to support the secondment of personnel to technical centers or other firms where such technologies are developed or in use come in very handy. For example, in Japan, public technology centers accept staff from firms to receive training in new technologies.

of existing knowledge across the country, the larger the impact on the development of technological capabilities and the faster the transition. The starting point is an efficient and as competitive as possible telecommunications sector, followed by the implementation of the legal and regulatory framework for ICT as described below. But as mentioned earlier, the labor force's skill level is most important to securing the greatest benefits.

Trade as a Channel for Knowledge Transfer

Economic evaluation studies consistently confirm trade as a significant channel for technology transfer. Yet for any amount of trade, the impact of productivity is not fixed; it depends on a number of factors. The education and skill level of the labor force is a main factor and so is the degree of

integration within the supply chain, so spillover effects are maximized. (This latter factor is developed in the next chapter on networks.)

Coe and Helpman (1995) provide an empirical implementation of the open economy endogenous growth model. They construct an index of foreign R&D as the trade-weighted sum of trading partners' stocks of R&D. They find that for a sample of developed countries, both domestic and "foreign" R&D have a significant impact on total factor productivity (TFP), and that the latter increases with the general degree of openness of the economy and with openness toward the larger R&D-producing countries.

Coe, Helpman, and Hoffmeister (1997) examine the same issue for developing countries. They find that developing countries benefit more from foreign R&D spillovers, the more open they are and the more skilled their labor force is. These findings provide support for the hypothesis that trade is an important mechanism through which knowledge and technological progress are transmitted across countries. The idea is that importing countries (firms) learn from the knowledge embedded in the inputs that they import. Cross-country studies that have attempted to measure technology transmission through trade from developed to developing countries have found the elasticity of total factor productivity to some measure of foreign R&D capital stock[1] to vary between 0.02 to 0.10. In other words, a 100 percent increase in the R&D capital stock of developed countries raises TFP in developing countries by an average of 2 to 10 percent. Coe, Helpman, and Hoffmeister (1997) estimate that in 1990 the total spillover effects from R&D in the industrial countries may have increased output in the developed countries by about $US22 billion.

A background study for this report examines the impact of trade with OECD countries in raising the productivity of 9 LAC and 16 other developing countries through spillover of knowledge created by R&D (Schiff and Wang 2002). The study covers the period 1976–98. The variable "foreign R&D" is a weighted average of R&D in the OECD countries by industry, where the weights are a measure of bilateral openness with the respective country by industry. The measure of the stock of foreign R&D obtained by an importing country at the industry level explicitly incorporates the production structure of the economy as reflected in the input-output relationships. The study specifically examines the impact on TFP of international technology diffusion, education, and governance for the LAC region. It thus captures both the stock of knowledge available in the OECD

countries and the openness of the countries in the study that provided this stock of knowledge.

The study shows that, for the LAC countries, "foreign R&D" has a positive impact on R&D-intensive industries, but this impact is dependent on the level of education in the country. In other words, the greater the educational attainment of the country, the greater the impact of foreign R&D on TFP through trade. Educational attainment is measured as the share of the population aged 25 years and above that completed secondary education. *The study thus shows that education (skills) and foreign knowledge (R&D) are mutually reinforcing in their effect on TFP in R&D-intensive industries.* Second, from the construction of foreign R&D, the results for LAC imply that education and openness are also mutually reinforcing in their impact on TFP in R&D-intensive industries. Education reflects the capacity of the LAC countries to absorb knowledge from the North and transform it into higher productivity. And absorptive capacity is clearly more important in high R&D-intensive industries than in low R&D-intensity industries.

Tables 6.1 and 6.2 show that education helps in the absorption of foreign technologies—the complementarity

TABLE 6.1

Impact of Trade on LAC Countries and Education Effect

A 1 PERCENT INCREASE IN EDUCATION* IN LAC

Increases TFP by	5.78%	in	Low-Intensity R&D Sector
Increases TFP by	10.93%	in	High-Intensity R&D Sector

* This refers to an increase in the share of the population aged 25 and above that completed secondary education.
Note: Interaction effect between foreign R&D—trade related—and LAC education is positive and strongly significant.
Source: Schiff and Wang (2002).

TABLE 6.2

Impact through Trade of a 10 Percent Increase in Education on TFP Growth Rate (%), 1998

COUNTRY	IMPACT			SECONDARY SCHOOL COMPLETION RATIO	
	DIRECT	THROUGH ABSORPTION OF FOREIGN R&D	TOTAL	1998	WITH 10 PERCENT INCREASE OVER 1998
Bolivia	0.036	0.034	0.07	6.2%	6.8%
Chile	0.087	0.075	0.17	15.0%	16.5%
Colombia	0.049	0.041	0.09	8.4%	9.3%
Ecuador	0.046	0.041	0.09	8.0%	8.8%
Guatemala	0.015	0.013	0.03	2.5%	2.8%
Mexico	0.075	0.065	0.14	12.9%	14.2%
Panama	0.094	0.086	0.18	16.2%	17.8%
Trinidad and Tobago	0.071	0.065	0.14	12.3%	13.6%
Venezuela	0.025	0.021	0.05	4.3%	4.8%

Note: The R&D-intensive industries in the study are (1) 382—Non-Electrical Machinery, Office and Computing Machinery; (2) 383—Electrical Machinery and Communication Equipment; (3) 384—Transportation Equipment; (4) 385—Professional Goods; (5) 351/2—Chemicals, Drugs, and Medicines; and (6) 353/4—Petroleum Refineries and Products.
Source: Schiff and Wang (2002).

effect—and that this effect, shown in the second column of table 6.2, is almost as big as the direct impact of education on productivity. For example, raising the stock of adults with secondary school education by 10 percent raises the TFP growth rate from a low of 0.015 percent for Guatemala to a high of 0.094 percent for Panama. In addition, this increase in education also raises TFP growth rates by aiding the absorption of foreign technologies by 0.013 percent and 0.086 percent, respectively.

Impact and Determinants of Foreign Direct Investment

Most studies that deal with the impact of FDI on the domestic economy agree that *recipient* firms benefit from foreign investment. The few studies that deal with *inter*-industry spillovers usually find these to be positive. However, results on *intra*-industry spillovers are more ambiguous owing to a variety of factors (Schiff 2002). These studies typically estimate, at the firm or plant level, the statistical impact of some measure of FDI on a measure of productivity, most often total factor productivity (TFP).[2] A study commissioned for this report (Park 2002) shows very clearly the impact of the institutional regime on FDI flows as reported in table 6.3.

However, whether spillovers to domestic firms increase with stronger intellectual property rights (IPRs) is unclear because, even though technology transfers to licensed firms or recipients of foreign investment increase, the amount of leakage per unit of technology transfer is likely to fall because of the stronger IPRs (such as the ability to go to court to prevent leakage or get compensation). While there has been a strengthening of intellectual property regimes in most LAC countries over the last decade, they are still weaker than those

TABLE 6.3

Effects on Foreign Direct Investment

IMPACT ON FOREIGN DIRECT INVESTMENT (FDI) INFLOWS (AS A PERCENT OF GDP) OF A 1 PERCENT INCREASE IN	
ONE PERCENT INCREASE IN	PERCENT IMPACT ON FDI INFLOWS AS PERCENT OF GDP
Private R&D per worker	0.492*
Public R&D per worker	0.553*
Patent rights strength	1.578***
Enrollment in tertiary education	−0.030
Scientists and engineers	0.884***
Adjusted R^2	0.28
Number of observers	155

Note: Estimation is by fixed effects regression for 58 countries, including 19 LAC countries. ***, **, and * denote significance levels of 1 percent, 5 percent, and 15 percent, respectively. Since all variables except the constant (not shown above) were in log, the above numbers are just the coefficients from the regression equation.
Source: Park (2002).

of developed countries, but not weaker than those of many Asian countries. One reason is that not all types of FDI necessarily involve significant amounts of knowledge transfer. Balasubramanyam and others (1996) find that the growth effect of FDI is weaker in countries that pursue policies of import substitution rather than export promotion. This could be because export-oriented FDI is more likely to be internationally competitive. Another reason is that, even if the technology component of the FDI is important, foreign firms may take actions to limit spillovers to the host country's domestic firms. Furthermore, even though technology spillovers may be significant, there may be other negative effects of FDI that counteract the positive impact of the spillovers. For instance, FDI may reduce the share of the market left for domestic firms, and under economies of scale, a smaller output implies a higher average cost. Also, the composition of FDI matters. In a number of countries, a large component of FDI has been in the service sector and retail distribution, both low R&D intensive (for example, Brazil and Mexico). There the level of technology and knowledge transfer is reasonably small. Finally, while FDI can provide access to technology, the domestic firms' ability to effectively absorb knowledge spillovers can limit the usefulness of FDI. This last point resonates strongly with the main theme of this report.

Minimum Threshold of Human Capital Required to Reap FDI Benefits

As we have shown for trade, the skill level of the labor force plays a major role in determining the extent of benefits to be captured through FDI. Borensztein, De Gregorio, and Lee (1998) study the effect of FDI flows from industrial countries on economic growth from a sample of 69 developing countries over the 1980s and 1990s. They find that FDI has a positive overall effect on per capita GDP growth, and that the effect increases with the level of human capital in the host country, but it is subject to the existence of a minimum threshold level of human capital in the host country. They estimate this threshold level to lie between 0.52 and 1.13 years of average secondary school education in the male population aged 25 years or older (table 6.4).

In an attempt to identify the technology diffusion effect of multinational corporations (MNCs) among all their productivity-enhancing effects, Xu (2000) considers the impact of technology transfer spending of U.S. MNCs on productivity growth in 40 developed and developing countries from 1966 to 1994. The results from this study

TABLE 6.4

Human Capital Threshold Required for Positive Impact of FDI

STUDY	WHAT THE STUDY MEASURES	HUMAN CAPITAL THRESHOLD (MINIMUM AVERAGE YEARS OF SECONDARY SCHOOL EDUCATION IN MALE POPULATION >25 YEARS)
Borensztein, De Gregorio, and Lee (1998)	Impact of FDI flows from industrial countries on per capita GDP growth of 69 developing countries	0.52–1.13 years
Xu (2000)	Impact of technology transfer spending of U.S. MNCs on TFP growth of 40 countries	1.4–2.4 years

FIGURE 6.3

Mean Tariff Barriers (percent), 1990 and 1999

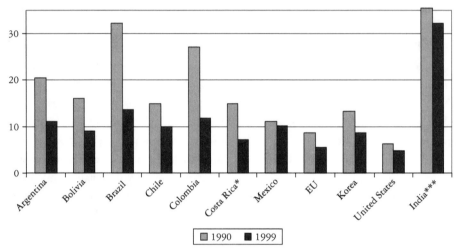

* 1992 & 1999. ** 1993 & 1997. ***

Note: External tariffs for the European Union have been used.

Source: World Bank (2001c).

support the previous one (table 6.4). The *presence* of MNCs has a positive and statistically significant effect on TFP growth for countries with average male secondary school attainment of at least 0.52 years in the population above 25 years of age. In addition, by distinguishing the technology diffusion effect of MNCs from other productivity-enhancing effects, the study shows that a much higher human capital threshold is required to benefit from technology transfer. They estimate this threshold to lie between 1.4 and 2.4 years. In other words, technology transfer from MNCs does not have a significant impact on the productivity of countries with male secondary school attainments below 1.4 to 2.4 years.

LAC's Performance

Trade Regime

LAC countries have made significant progress since the 1980s, when most countries were practically closed with

high levels of protection. The 1990s have seen significant lowering in the barriers to trade in most LAC countries, with mean tariff rates coming down dramatically (figure 6.3). Brazil has the highest rate (13.6 percent) among the LAC countries while Costa Rica has the lowest at 7.2 percent. These numbers compare favorably with those for Korea at 8.7 percent. The European Union (EU) and the United States had slightly lower rates, at 5.6 percent and 4.8 percent, respectively, in 1999. Since openness is a critical instrument for developing technological capabilities at all stages, LAC countries have done well at least with regard to tariff levels.

This opening up of the trade and investment regimes through tariff reductions and deregulation has caused a significant rise in the amount of goods, services, and investments flowing into the LAC region as was shown in chapter 3. However, Brazil and Argentina remain fairly closed economies compared to some other LAC countries such as Costa Rica, and countries such as Korea, Spain, and especially Ireland. Also, there has been a decrease in non-tariff barriers in most LAC countries. Yet in some countries—Brazil, Mexico, and Venezuela—they still remain high (table 6.5). Continued efforts there are needed to fully secure the benefits of increased trade, mostly through reductions in non-tariff barriers, particularly for the aforementioned countries.

Imports of capital goods are another measure of openness to foreign technologies and perhaps also a measure of the readiness and capacity of domestic firms to absorb foreign technology. The numbers for LAC countries remain low as shown in chapter 3. Among East Asian economies, China, Korea, Malaysia, and Thailand have all increased capital goods imports (Indonesia being the exception). Among LAC economies, only Argentina and Venezuela have increased capital goods imports, the others staying nearly the same over two decades (Brazil, Uruguay) or even falling (Chile, Columbia, Mexico, Peru).

The broad institutional and policy regime defining the trade regime rests on a country's external tariff regime, non-tariff barriers, safeguards, countervailing duties, and antidumping framework. While all are important, the main one clearly is the external tariff regime. The lower those barriers and tariffs, the larger the trade imports. Fiscal reasons and claims for the protection of domestic industries are usually the countervailing factors for not lowering tariffs.

There is little more that most LAC countries can do in the trade area to facilitate technological transfer or the transition to increased technological capabilities. While there are always improvements that can be made they are marginal and unlikely to provide a major boost to technology transfer. There are some exceptions such as Brazil and Argentina. Of course the benefits of trade can and will increase as the other pieces of a coherent science and technology system—improved skills of the labor force, stronger network linkages, selected increases of R&D efforts, and so on—fall into place, and that is where the efforts on LAC should be placed. In summary, trade policies in LAC are not any longer a lever to increase technological capabilities, however. While avoiding reversal on trade policies should be a given, the efforts should be placed elsewhere—that is, on capturing an increased share of the benefits of the trade volume, through expanding education, and facilitating spillovers by strengthening network development and linkages.

TABLE 6.5

Non-Tariff Barrier Levels for LAC and East Asian Countries

LAC COUNTRY	CORE NTMs	
	1989–94	1995–98
Argentina	3.1	2.1
Bolivia	0.0	—
Brazil	16.5	21.6
Chile	5.2	5.2
Colombia	55.2	10.3
Costa Rica	—	6.2
Dominican Republic	—	6.2
El Salvador	—	5.2
Mexico	—	13.4
Paraguay	27.8	0.0
Peru	—	—
Uruguay	6.3	0.0
Venezuela	32.3	17.7
	—	

ASIAN COUNTRY	CORE NTMs	
	1989–94	1995–98
Fiji	—	5.2
Hong Kong (China)	2.1	2.1
Indonesia	53.6	31.3
Korea	1.0	25.0
Malaysia	.1	19.6
Philippines	.2	—
Singapore	2.0	2.1
Thailand	36.5	17.5

Note: Non-tariff measures (NTMs) are calculated as frequency ratio in percent of all HS 2-digit product categories. Core NTMs include licensing, prohibitions, quotas, and administered pricing.

Foreign Direct Investment

Countries in Latin America and the Caribbean compare very favorably to newly industrialized countries (NICs) in securing FDI. In Latin America and the Caribbean, FDI flows increased from 0.5 percent of purchasing power parity (PPP) GDP in 1989 to 3.2 percent of PPP GDP in 1999 on average. Brazil is the most significant host of FDI in the region in absolute terms (US$34 billion in 1999), while in relative terms, Chile receives the largest fraction of FDI in the region (10.3 percent of PPP GDP in 1999). The overall increase in FDI largely reflects the liberalization of investment regimes throughout the region and fiscal incentives designed explicitly to attract foreign investors. The index of foreign investment barriers for LAC compares well with that for high-income countries, and is the lowest among all regions (table 6.6). Mexico's position as the second largest reservoir of FDI in the region is largely a result of NAFTA, which boosted U.S. investments into Mexico. Costa Rica is a case in point with regard to the effects of fiscal incentives on the flow of FDI. Also, a number of countries in LAC have used quite effectively the EPZ concept to attract FDI (de Ferranti and others 2001). However, despite liberalizing their FDI regimes, a number of LAC countries retain barriers to FDI. These relate more to the cost of doing business and apply to both domestic and foreign investors.

TABLE 6.6

Index of Foreign Investment Barriers, 2000

	SCORE
High-income countries	2.1
Developing countries	3.0
Europe and Central Asia	2.9
South Asia	3.0
East Asia and the Pacific	3.1
Sub-Saharan Africa	3.2
Latin America:	2.2
Argentina	2.0
Bolivia	2.0
Brazil	3.0
Chile	2.0
Colombia	2.0
Costa Rica	2.0
Ecuador	2.0
El Salvador	1.0
Guatemala	3.0
Guyana	3.0
Honduras	3.0
Mexico	2.0
Nicaragua	2.0
Panama	2.0
Paraguay	1.0
Peru	2.0
Uruguay	2.0
Venezuela	3.0

Source: Interregional Cooperation in Trade and Investment in Latin America (ST/ESCAP/2069).

The index of foreign investment barriers ranges from 1 to 5. The exact assessment of values is based on the following criteria: (1) having very low barriers to foreign investment means that there is open treatment of foreign investment and an accessible foreign investment code; (2) having low barriers means that there exist certain restrictions on sectors such as utilities and natural resources, but that there is a limited, efficient approval process for new projects; (3) having moderate barriers means that there are restrictions on many investments and a bureaucratic approval process, but at least there is an official policy that conforms to an established foreign investment code; (4) having high barriers means that foreign investment is permitted on a case-by-case basis with a bureaucratic approval process that may be marked by some corruption; (5) having very high barriers means that the government actively tries to prevent foreign investment and there is rampant corruption in the process.

Ireland is an extreme case with regard to FDI. Based on the evidence presented in figure 6.4, FDI represented approximately 25 percent of the country's GDP (PPP) in 1999 (with a large share originating in the United States), compared to 0.2 percent only 10 years earlier. This remarkable increase is partly a result of fiscal incentives, the presence of a skilled work force proficient in English, and a location within the Common European Market providing access to that market. Spain has also seen a notable increase over the past 10 years, but to a much

FIGURE 6.4

Foreign Direct Investment, 1989 and 1999

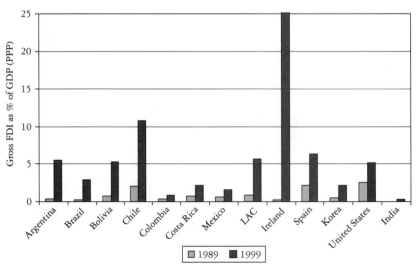

Source: World Bank (2001a).

smaller extent. In the case of Korea, FDI takes up a fairly low share of GDP (PPP). This, in turn, is partly testimony to government policies, which consistently have preferred import of capital goods to FDI (see Viotti 2001). Last, while FDI has negligible importance in India, it was a key instrument for Singapore (box 6.3, and see Pack 2000, p. 74).

A final point on the interaction between FDI and trade policy is worth bearing in mind. Much of the FDI flowing

---

BOX 6.3

Singapore's Reliance on FDI

Singapore's technological development can be attributed to reliance on international markets and FDI, with active and successful government intervention during the last 40 years. Historical circumstances forced Singapore to rely on export orientation rather than on import substitution, and on FDI rather than on indigenous companies. The lack of a sizable domestic market after the separation with Malaysia necessitated the export orientation, and the political turbulence made the government mistrust the domestic business community. Given these circumstances and policy choices, the government acted with pragmatism and efficiency to maximize the economic benefits of the nation. The ability to act on opportunity has been a characteristic of the Singaporean government, as witnessed by the initial efforts to attract foreign electronics companies when they became interested in outsourcing labor-intensive production, or the formation of an international currency trading market when international actors were looking for the opportunity of 24-hour-a-day trading.

There are reasons why the Singaporean government has been able to make politically difficult policy choices and why it has been development oriented. The government's autonomy from important interest groups has been crucial for its ability to shape the economic policies without much domestic interference. When the domestic business community and the labor movement became marginalized because of political conflicts, it made the government autonomous from the strongest interest groups in the society. Still, there is nothing that guarantees that an autonomous government will always act in a growth-enhancing way rather than enriching itself through various rent-seeking activities. The reason why the Singaporean government became development oriented is twofold. First, its public legitimacy has largely rested on the provision of increased living standards—most Singaporeans seem to have accepted restrictions on personal freedom as long as there is a steady increase in incomes. Second, given the

choice of becoming outward oriented and to rely on FDI, there is much less room for policy mistakes.

There are some lessons from Singapore's policies toward FDI:

- Singapore managed to get access to foreign knowledge and technology through a *laissez-faire* policy toward multinational corporations (MNCs) rather than by various requirements focusing on their operations.
- Since foreign MNCs started to locate in Singapore, the government has constantly been encouraging them to upgrade their activities.
- The government has repeatedly used strong economic incentives rather than legislation or requirements to achieve this upgrading. The economic incentives have ranged from tax exemptions to the training of workers and local suppliers, and the local MNCs have responded positively.

Recently, Singapore has tried to make the second transition to an economy that builds upon its own innovations and technology rather than importing ready-made technologies through MNCs. The policies have, once again, been based on financial incentives, including tax exemptions for the training of workers and local suppliers, to increase local knowledge, create a domestic business community in technology-intensive sectors, and make the MNCs locate R&D in Singapore. Whereas the domestic business community is still rather weak, the amount of R&D conducted in Singapore increased substantially during the 1990s. Much of this R&D took place within the MNCs. Most R&D that takes place in Singapore is advanced development rather than basic or even applied research.

Source: Blomström and others (2002).

to inward-oriented developing countries is undertaken to substitute for imports from richer countries, which often consist of relatively advanced products. The production technologies used by MNCs in import substituting economies are therefore often relatively capital- and skill-intensive compared to those employed by local firms. MNCs investing in outward-oriented economies, by contrast, can be expected to employ technologies that are more in line with the host country's factor endowments because these MNCs are exposed to tough competition from the world market (whether or not they are export-oriented) and tend to use production technologies that fit the host country's comparative advantage. To the extent that the trade regime then has implications for the technological composition of FDI, it also has very important implications for the amount of spillovers that can be expected.

Licensing

Korea ranks at the top in license payments, taking up approximately US$55 per resident in 1999, which in turn represents a doubling from the 1990 level. Similar developments have taken place in Spain and the United States. However, nowhere is the flow of licensed technologies greater than in Ireland, which paid close to US$2,000 per resident at the end of the 1990s, approximately 40 times as much as Korea. That complemented Ireland's FDI strategy nicely. During the period 1985–98, license payments per capital from East Asia went up from 2.7 to 26.6 (not including China). These economies clearly outstrip the LAC region, where the average license payments only took up US$5 per resident by the end of the 1990s, doubling from slightly above $2 in 1990. India's royalty payments remained negligible over the decade.

It should be noted that trade, FDI, and licensing ought to be evaluated as a package since there is a fair amount of substitutability, particularly between the latter two. The same foreign company is unlikely to both set up a subsidiary in a host country and provide a license to another host company. The choices by the firms often depend on the favorable treatment of foreign investment laws, distribution costs and strength of patent protection, and overall long-term firm strategy (Harvard University study 2002). Also, Blonigen (1999) has analyzed the relationship between trade and FDI and showed convincingly that imports of intermediate goods and sales of affiliates—are complements while imports and sales of final goods are complements. Overall LAC countries,

on average, have done reasonably well on access to foreign technologies, accomplishing most of what is required. While some specific countries should improve their regimes (such as Argentina and Brazil), most of them ought to focus on increasing the benefits of that exposure to foreign technology, by fostering education, network development, and selected R&D efforts. Without adequate human capital or investments in R&D, and integrated networks, spillovers from those vehicles are likely to be limited, as has consistently been shown (Saggi 2002).

The Telecommunications/ICT Sector: A Critical Instrument for Diffusion and Advancing the Development of Technological Capabilities

The telecommunications/ICT sector today more than ever underpins the process of technological development. Most of the countries that managed successful and rapid transitions make a special effort to enhance the ICT sector. It can be a powerful instrument for access to the global storehouse of technological information and for diffusion of knowledge, as well as for facilitating competition through fast and cheap access to information. While ICT in itself will not generate or increase global knowledge, it does increase *local* knowledge and is the key instrument for a broad and speedy diffusion of information and knowledge. ICT makes it possible to share knowledge in real time over great distances. Using it, researchers in Chile's wine industry can continuously learn from and coordinate their activities with the University of California, Davis. And ICT is the key element that accelerates the transition of knowledge. For example, computer usage is linked to technology adoption potential, and the number of Internet hosts to adaptation potential. Thus ICT is an essential component of a country's technology and at the core of the innovation system.

ICT is also increasingly becoming a dominant factor in the acquisition and transfer (through distance learning) of skills. It can impact firm productivity in various ways. These include increasing competitiveness and market discipline through better and faster information on prices and markets, reducing transactions costs, and providing better monitoring of the production process. ICT also enables the creation of more complex analytical tools that support decision-making, provides firms with valuable knowledge about customer demand, serves as a medium for technology transfer and communication of best practices, improves and increases information and communication, and diffuses existing knowledge. Practically all countries that have been successful in technological transitions placed a strong effort in modernizing and developing, through competition and special interventions, their telecommunications and ICT sectors.

The most immediate impact on LAC and other developing countries has often been through alleviating information-related constraints such as finding cheaper sources of required inputs, linking producers to nearby markets, uncovering and opening new markets, acquiring information about new forms of production, and so on. The pure information impact of ICT seems to be larger and more pervasive in developing countries mainly because their information deficiencies are larger and more pervasive.

An effective ICT framework consists of five well-developed components: (i) connectivity: the physical wiring, bandwidth, spectrum allocation, and associated technology needs to be in place and extensive; (ii) content: the available information online has to be significant, access-friendly, and preferably largely in the local language; (iii) transparency and security: the legal and regulatory framework for transacting online should be secure; (iv) a competitive telecommunications sector, so as to induce extensive coverage and low prices: the online prices should be as low as possible so as to facilitate use by a large share of the population; and (v) physical distribution network: the country should have an effective physical distribution network with low logistics costs to

deliver the goods transacted on the Internet. These components should also be complemented by a labor force that has the proper skills to use the technology effectively (see Guasch and Subramanian 2002).

Latin America and the Caribbean lags behind East Asia and OECD in the development and usage of ICT, as was shown in chapter 3. Yet there is a large variance among LAC countries' performance as shown in figures 6.5 and 6.6, where the countries have been classified as high and low performers on ICT on account of levels and improvements through the 1990s. Chile, Uruguay, Mexico, Colombia, and El Salvador have shown the highest improvements, while Panama, Honduras, and Nicaragua have barely advanced (Guasch and Brehon 2002).

The government has a key role to play in facilitating the development of ICT, particularly in the legal and regulatory arena. The ICT legal framework encompasses laws on electronic data interchange, consumer privacy, protection of intellectual property rights, and online security. Most countries have been quite late in introducing a law on electronic data interchange. That law is based on a model proposed by the United Nations Conference on International Trade Law (UNCITRAL). It (i) gives digital signatures the same legal status as handwritten ones; (ii) recognizes electronic documents and contracts as having the same legal value as contracts executed on paper; and (iii) defines the obligations of

FIGURE 6.5

High-Achieving LAC Countries

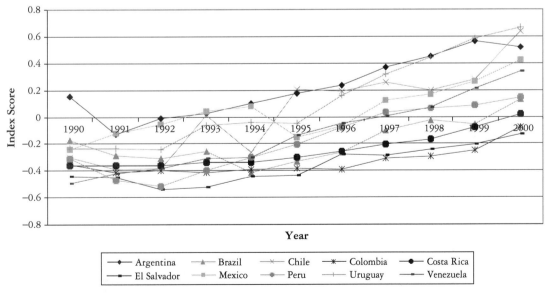

Source: Guasch and Brehon (2002).

FIGURE 6.6

Low-Achieving LAC Countries

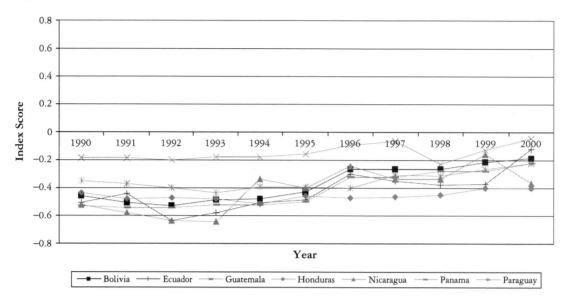

Source: Guasch and Brehon (2002).

institutions providing electronic certification. Although lack of interest and initiative from businesses in the e-commerce field has likely been the main reason for the slow takeoff of online sales in LAC, the slow approval process of the electronic data interchange law may have also played a role.

Although a law governing electronic contracts is necessary, there is more that a country can and must do to facilitate e-commerce. Electronic contracts can be effective only if they are complemented by protections for privacy (of consumers), property rights (of suppliers), and system security. Chile has been ahead of other Latin American countries in enhancing online privacy protection, through a data protection law enacted in 1999. The act includes rules governing the processing and use of personal data, the rights of individuals, the use of information by government agencies, and the use of financial, commercial, or banking data. A recent plan would also amend the law to include a bill containing a special section relating to e-commerce.

Most LAC countries are lagging in approving a law that addresses protection of intellectual property rights on the Internet. (This is proving a difficult issue for all countries—see the White House 1997 and CEPAL 2001.) At present, trademarks are covered by the same laws and international agreements on the Internet as they are in traditional media. Offline protection of intellectual property tends to be better enforced in Chile than elsewhere in the region but still falls

below developed-country expectations. On the other hand, on the issue of software piracy Chile is significantly below the rest of the region in this area.

Security is a complex topic that encompasses several areas, including the following: authenticity (evidence that a communication actually comes from the purported sender); integrity (proof that the content of a communication has not been altered during transmission); non-repudiation (prevention of later denial of the transmission of the message); and confidentiality (evidence that the contents of a transmission have not been disclosed to third parties) (Van Dam 1999; Feldman and Meranus 2000). For example, ad hoc certification technologies are typically used to ensure the confidentiality of transmissions to and from a Web site. This is an issue in practically all LAC countries. Only 17 percent of Chilean e-commerce sites were "secure" in 2002, versus 20 percent in Brazil and 25 percent in Argentina, according to a recent survey by the Santiago Chamber of Commerce. Although Brazil was only slightly ahead of Chile in terms of secure Web sites, it is much more advanced in terms of e-commerce in general. Another legal requirement that is critical for promoting use of ICT among businesses (and government) is approval of electronic invoicing, which most LAC countries do not have. Electronic invoicing will give businesses the opportunity to keep their invoices in electronic format and send them electronically to the government authorities. This would facilitate exchanges between government and business, reduce businesses' and government's inventory costs (SII estimates that thanks to electronic invoicing, a government's costs would decrease from $1.2 to $0.4 per invoice, generating total savings of about $300 million per year—SII 2002), and support online invoicing. Finally, LAC also lags behind in credit card penetration rate, the essential form of payment for electronic transactions, and its use of Internet-based payment systems is still behind the best-practice income comparator country. Supporting development of *medios de micropagos* (prepaid cards, debit cards, payment systems with direct charges to fixed or mobile phones) would increase e-commerce penetration, especially by giving lower-income populations the opportunity to buy online, provided they have access to computers.

Overall, it is important to underline that while governments should take certain regulatory steps to improve the policy environment for improving competition in the sector and doing business online, the focus must ultimately be on implementation. Governments should improve the protection of property rights on the Internet, ensure that the privacy law is amended to include a special section on e-commerce, support the development of a secure infrastructure when needed (promote an electronic invoice law, and intervene to increase access in selective areas such as in education and rural areas). Beyond that, however, the initiative must be taken by the private sector—the government's role should be to encourage and enable the private sector to take this initiative.

Advanced Technological Transition: R&D as the Key Driver

To reach advanced stages of technological capabilities the key instrument is significant R&D expenditures, particularly private. No country has ever secured advanced technological capabilities without significant private R&D expenditures. Thus the key policy issue is how to induce significant amounts of private R&D. To address this issue we first present the instruments governments have and then proceed to impute the determinants of private R&D from theory and empirical analysis.

Formal technological effort is captured by R&D expenditures on plant, equipment, and personnel. R&D is both capital- and skill-intensive and hence not typically conducted in any significant amount in economies at the very early stages of technological catch-up. Research and development

expenditures enable domestic firms to generate new technologies and innovation for local needs and to better absorb and adapt existing advanced technologies from abroad. It is the key instrument for creation and adapting. However, the strong public good characteristic of knowledge and the spillovers it generates demand particular government intervention. First, there is the issue of the *degree of spillovers, and hence appropriability, varying by the type of research,* and that matters because the degree of intervention has to match the extent of those spillovers. Basic research consists of experimental or theoretical work conducted to obtain new knowledge about the origin of fundamental phenomena and observable facts, without a specific application in mind. Given the fundamental nature of this research, spillovers are high and long-lasting.

Appropriability of benefits in a free market, correspondingly, is lower. Applied research, which consists of original work undertaken in order to acquire new knowledge with a specific goal in mind, is narrower in scope and hence has less spillover than basic research. Finally experimental development, which consists of systematic work based on existing knowledge and is directed toward the production of new materials or products, or toward improving products that already exist, has the least spillover. While R&D is mostly associated with the creation of knowledge, it also has an important role to play in facilitating the adaptation of existing technologies, as was shown in box 6.1 In addition to continued education expansion—now with particular emphasis on the completion of secondary education and increasing tertiary enrollments—and openness to FDI and licensing, to reach the advance stage of technological capabilities requires efforts to cultivate creativity through strengthening patent protection regimes; increase public funding (through tax incentives and subsidies) to secure significant private R&D investments; continue, perhaps even expand, public provision R&D aimed at basic research; facilitate and target R&D in special areas relevant to the country and showing signs or potential of excellence; and continue the advancement and deepening of ICT. But the key focus at this stage should be securing private investment in R&D.

A casual glance at trajectories of productive sector R&D, shown in figure 6.1 and confirmed in table 6.7, suggests that numerous countries, such as Korea, Israel, and Finland, have had "takeoffs" in productive sector R&D at roughly the same level of income as Mexico, Argentina, and Chile, which have made far fewer efforts (figure 6.7). Thus the central issue of

TABLE 6.7

Evolution of Total R&D Expenditures as a Percentage of GDP, 1960–99

	1960–64	1965–69	1970–74	1975–79	1980–84	1985–89	1990–94	1995–99
Australia			1.117	0.862	1.027	1.181	1.450	1.578
Spain	0.179	0.193	0.259	0.330	0.454	0.624	0.841	0.821
Finland		0.713	0.849	0.978	1.321	1.737	2.136	3.102
Ireland	0.420	0.591	0.706	0.683	0.699	0.824	1.062	1.342
Korea	0.240	0.366	0.357	0.529	0.833	1.692	2.098	2.565
New Zealand			0.779	0.814		0.883	1.007	1.051
Singapore		0.060		0.214	0.408	0.871	1.069	1.553
Sweden	1.180	1.270	1.463	1.735	2.361	2.835	2.965	3.663
Taiwan (China)				0.829	0.879	1.168	1.739	1.896
Group average				**0.764**		**1.329**	**1.615**	**1.957**
Argentina	0.595	0.560	0.704	0.936	0.392	0.382	0.315	0.413
Brazil			0.344	0.608	0.481	0.380	0.828	0.844
Chile				0.319	0.430	0.428	0.574	0.564
Colombia			0.014	0.081	0.110			0.270
Costa Rica			0.300	0.222	0.261	0.261	0.160	0.273
Mexico		0.168	0.194		0.543	0.285	0.255	0.354
Peru			0.177	0.270	0.261	0.102	0.025	0.058
Venezuela	0.094		0.257	0.478	0.318	0.308	0.422	0.358
LAC Average				**0.350**				**0.392**

Source: Guasch (2002) with data from Lederman (2002).

FIGURE 6.7

Evolution of R&D/GDP Expenditures on GDP Per Capita 1980–1995

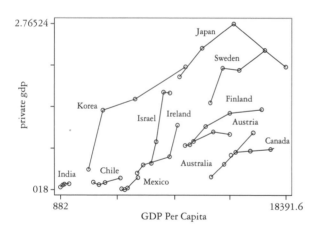 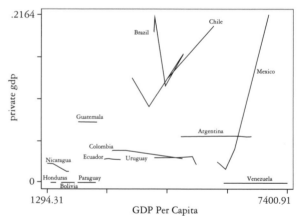

Source: Bosch and Maloney (2002).

this and the next chapter is how LAC can increase its participation in this area. Below, we discuss several policies employed to accomplish this.

Government Policies for R&D

The most widely used policies for correcting for market failures are (i) intellectual property rights; (ii) fiscal incentives and public funding of research and development; and (iii) public execution of R&D. Having in place intellectual property rights increases the appropriability of benefits to innovation. Fiscal incentives, such as tax credits, work by reducing the cost of R&D to the performing firm, thus better aligning them with the private benefits of R&D. Public funding works by either entirely or partially (as in the case of matching grants) providing public funds to compensate for the shortfall in private funding for R&D.

Intellectual property rights

Intellectual property rights work by giving the innovating firm the right to temporarily exclude others from using the new idea commercially so that it can appropriate some of the benefits of its R&D effort—particularly those related to patent protection, which are also a key determinant in technology transfer, trade, and FDI (box 6.4). Thus, copyrights protect the rights of authors (books, music, software); trademark registration protects trade logos and symbols; and patents protect inventions with industrial applicability (products as well as processes). For technology development, patents are most relevant; hence, this section focuses on the unique issues surrounding this instrument.

Patents are intended to spur innovation in a number of ways. First, they award exclusivity of use, sale, and manufacture, for a limited period of time, to the owners of the intellectual property, thus compensating them for undertaking expensive and risky innovative activities. In exchange for this benefit the owner must disclose the invention on the patent document for anyone "skilled in the art" to be able to replicate. Thus, patents are a tradeoff: A market distortion in the form of a temporary monopoly is created in exchange for disclosure of the information relating to the technology. Disclosure is intended to benefit society by disseminating new technologies and indeed encouraging competitors to invent around the new technology in a second round of innovation.

The link between IPRs, innovation, and productivity has stirred some controversy. Intellectual property rights have two opposing effects on R&D. On the one hand, they increase the degree of appropriability of the returns to R&D, thus providing incentives for R&D expenditures; on the other hand, that protection prevents the use and diffusion by others and increases the cost of R&D for rivals and/or follow-on inventors, which can impact R&D and productivity adversely.

In setting up an IPR framework, which is essential to fostering private R&D, the issue is how strong the framework should be and how it should evolve. Strong IPRs come at a cost to society and the argument can be framed in terms of a bargain between static and dynamic concerns. Advocating stronger intellectual property rights therefore must presume that the combined positive impact of the appropriability incentive for the innovator and the disclosure element for peers (resulting in greater innovation) outweighs the negative impact of the temporary market distortion (resulting in higher prices for consumers and slower technology

BOX 6.4

The Role of Intellectual Property Rights (IPRs) in Technology Transfer

Intellectual property rights have traditionally been regarded as a means to encourage research and development. There is, however, another role that IPRs may play: that of encouraging technology transfer. Since proprietary knowledge is valuable to foreign firms, they are likely to try to minimize its leakage to domestic firms. Although relatively new to the research, some studies show that weak intellectual property protection may deter investors in high R&D sectors. Similarly, some studies argue that IPRs in the host country may affect the amount of licensing. It is possible that the strengthening of IPRs in LAC may have had a role in the increase in FDI and licensing in the region. Smith (2001) finds that strong IPRs are positively correlated with U.S. affiliate sales and licenses, especially when host countries posses strong imitative capacity. Since evidence of large sales implies a relatively large-scale operation, the scope for spillover is higher than with smaller MNE presence. Similarly, with strong IPRs, licensing cost is much lower, facilitating more licensing from the United States to host countries. See also Glass and Saggi (2000) for a theoretical treatment of the IPR and FDI relationship with a product cycle model. For relationship between IPR and licensing, see Yang and Maskus (2001). Smarqynska (2002) finds that the composition of FDI depends crucially on the strength of IPR in transition economies. She finds that weak intellectual property protection deters FDI in high technology sectors. Furthermore, the type of FDI is also affected. She finds that weak IPR leads to more FDI in distribution rather than local production of goods for fear of imitation. But presumably, spillovers from FDI would be quite limited in the case of distribution compared to local production. In a study of 58 countries, Park (2002) shows that patent rights do indeed positively impact the amount of FDI coming into the region.

diffusion for producers). This is nearly impossible to test empirically and remains a highly debated subject to date.

The above discussion points toward the importance of the timing of strong IPR protection. Protecting IPRs very early

TABLE 6.8

Transitions of Strength of Patent Protection—IPR—for Selected Countries, 1960–2000

ECONOMY	1960	1965	1970	1975	1980	1985	1990	2000
Argentina	—	—	—	—	2.26	2.26	2.26	3.19
Brazil	—	—	—	—	1.85	1.85	1.85	3.05
Chile	—	—	—	—	2.41	2.41	2.41	3.07
Mexico	—	—	—	—	1.40	1.40	1.63	2.86
Sweden	2.04	2.04	2.04	2.04	4.33	4.33	4.33	4.75
India	1.85	1.85	1.42	1.42	1.62	1.62	1.48	—
Finland	1.90	2.04	2.04	2.04	3.95	3.95	3.95	4.35
Japan	2.85	3.18	3.32	3.61	3.94	3.94	3.94	3.94
Korea	2.8	2.8	2.94	2.94	3.28	3.61	3.94	4.20
Malaysia	2.37	2.37	2.37	2.37	2.57	2.9	2.37	2.85
Singapore	2.37	2.37	2.37	2.37	2.57	2.57	2.57	3.90
United States	3.86	3.86	3.86	3.86	4.19	4.52	4.52	4.86

— Data not available.

Note: The patent protection index ranges from 0 to 5, with 5 being the strongest protection of patent.

Source: Guasch (2002) with data from Park (2002).

in the technological catch-up process can choke off an important channel for technological learning. Failing to protect IPRs when private firms are launching R&D programs is likely to weaken incentives to conduct R&D. Table 6.8 shows the evolution of IPR strength for selected countries. Noteworthy is the case for Korea and Singapore, where we see the gradual strengthening of IPR, fitting country technological conditions as they evolve.

Also, IPRs can improve the effectiveness of public R&D. Much of the criticism of government R&D has been that it is disconnected from the needs of the private sector, and that the private sector has difficulty in using innovation produced by public R&D. That has been the case for LAC countries. In the United States the Bayh-Dole Act allowed universities and government institutes to patent their inventions, thus increasing their collaborative efforts with the private sector—although some would argue that this comes at the cost of compromising basic research. And if IPRs are clearly defined and portable (that is, if a worker can take all or part of the rights to the invention with him or her when he or she switches employers), firms are likely to fiercely compete for skilled labor and workers are likely to move in favor of more competitive terms. The mobility of labor is a key driver of innovation at the advanced stages and is discussed in more detail in the chapter on networks.

Potentially, learning at the early stages of technological catch-up through trade and FDI could also be influenced by IPRs. The effect of strong IPRs on trade is unclear—while it could increase imports as foreign intellectual property owners face increasing net demand for their products owing to displacement of "pirates," a title holder may choose to reduce sales in a foreign market because of greater market power in an imitation-safe environment. Whether market expansion or market power effects will be stronger is not known and empirical estimates have gone both ways. Survey data have shown that FDI is not especially sensitive to the IPR regime. This is because the importance of IPRs varies greatly by industry and because relatively little FDI is in R&D-intensive activities (particularly for nations at the earlier stages of technological catch-up). The data show that most R&D is done at the parent firm, with production or sales facilities being set up in major markets.

The case might be clearer for copyrights, trademarks, and geographical indications where no real market distortion is created because the underlying idea behind copyrighted materials can still be adopted. For trademarks and geographic indicators as well, an infinite supply potentially exists; hence the distortion is minimal. In fact, for countries at the early stages of adaptation, firms may be in dire need of mechanisms to signal quality or otherwise differentiate their products to build consumer loyalty. For instance, Chinese producers have reported difficulties in promoting their own brands of soft drinks, processed foods, and clothing. Having established some brand recognition through costly investments, enterprises find their trademarks applied to counterfeit products quickly, which damages the reputation of high quality producers and sometimes forces them to abandon their trademarks or even close down altogether (OECD 2001). In consequence, trademark and copyright protection appears more relevant at the adoption stage. The evidence on their impact on TFP shows that it is little in contrast to the impact of patents (Park 2002).

A question raised by critics of IPRs is this: Given the small domestic R&D sector, will not the strengthening of IPRs shift economic rent to foreign multinationals, which own most of the technologies? Also, since the LAC region is predominantly an imitator of Northern technologies, will not technology diffusion, and hence overall welfare in the region, suffer as a consequence of improved property rights? Though valid, these questions ignore the feedback between R&D activities and policies: that is, R&D sectors may be small in part precisely because the incentives to do R&D are weak, and the "switch from imitation to innovation" may be hampered by the lack of institutions supporting it. Another practical issue is that if individuals or firms in a developing nation have the capacity to infringe, they typically have the capacity to innovate. Thus, nations such as Brazil or India that succeed in producing and distributing patent-infringing goods usually reveal a capacity to innovate but also reveal an environment where the relative economic rewards of infringement are greater than those from innovation. Thus it is most important to have the right incentive structure, and part of that is to strategically manage IPR (see box 6.5).

Theoretically, there is also another reason to worry about IPRs at the earlier stages of the transition. Given that these countries are essentially technology importers from the North, the development of appropriate technologies in the North for use in the South can only be facilitated when technology creators see the South as markets where their investments can be recouped. While isolated and individual markets may not constitute a sufficient incentive, collectively their market influence on changing the focus of technology efforts in the North could be sizable. However, since the payoff to any single country from "free riding" is potentially quite high, a uniform upgrading of patent regimes is mandated and perhaps most effective when enforced through an international institution such as the World Trade Organization (WTO). The Trade Related Intellectual Property Rights (TRIPS) agreement, which has been signed and is in different stages of implementation in different countries, claims to deliver this benefit to developing countries in the long run (see box 6.6 for details).

In the short run, however, there are costs for developing nations in the form of higher prices and slower access to patented technologies borne by domestic producers, and higher-priced goods borne by consumers. What might governments do to mitigate these costs in the short term?

- *Two legal attributes of the patent processes could be tweaked.* First, public disclosure of the patent application early on disseminates the invention (unlike in the United States, where it is disclosed very late in the process) to competitors so that they can begin the "invent around." Second, narrowing the scope of the patent (one claim, one patent) also reduces the extent of the monopoly awarded to a single owner. Japan is an excellent example of a country that followed such an IPR regime during its technology-importing days, and revised it recently to suit its role of technology creator.

- *Two leeways in TRIPS could be exploited.* First, countries are allowed to determine their own criteria for compulsory licensing of patented technologies so long as the "national treatment" clause (in other words, treating foreigners and nationals equally) is not violated. Second, the decision to allow parallel imports is also within national boundaries because individual countries can determine when the "exhaustion" of patent rights has occurred.

- *Two extra-TRIPS instruments could be instituted.* First, these countries are strongly encouraged to institute utility models. Utility models are in principle like patents, but they differ in several important ways: they have much lower standards of novelty in order to protect minor innovations; they are not subject to the rigor of patent examinations (where absolute novelty is stressed); they are not nearly as expensive to file for; and they are valid for three to five years only. Thus, utility models are particularly suitable for boosting the domestic adaptation effort. Second, improving the general business environment to reduce costs through competition policy, improving logistics, and supply chain management become imperative for countries that are faced with enduring higher prices for patented goods in the short run.

Tax incentives and subsidies

As mentioned, the public good nature of knowledge and associated positive spillovers make knowledge's social benefits far larger than its private benefits, leading to underinvestment and argues for government intervention.[3] Further and more complicated are the imperfections of capital markets. Credit constraints and mismatch of terms of lending reduce the demand for R&D by firms. Credit

BOX 6.5

Managing Intellectual Property Rights (IPRs)

Intellectual property is increasingly recognized as a global asset that needs to be strategically managed. Many OECD countries have recently broadened and strengthened the laws and regulations covering intellectual property protection in order to increase incentives for innovation and improve returns on these investments. The changes in intellectual property regimes have influenced the behavior of firms and research organizations. Throughout the 1990s, the number of patent applications and patents issued in Europe, the United States, and Japan grew substantially. These increases may reflect a real rise in innovative activity, but they are also linked to the explosive growth of patent-intensive fields, such as biotechnology and ICT, and increased recognition of the strategic role of IPRs as a currency that allows firms to compete and cooperate.

Industries vary tremendously in the type of intellectual property protection that is relevant to their activities. Patent protection is considered essential for pharmaceuticals, medical technologies, and biotechnology. Software developers use a mix of patents and copyrights to protect code, but open source software is gaining in popularity. Such new technologies continuously challenge governments to search for the correct balance between the commercial need for incentives to innovation and the public need for disclosure and access to innovations. Governments should attempt to maintain stability in intellectual property regulations, but must determine whether a new balance needs to be struck between public and private imperatives for research and innovation as new technologies emerge and eventually mature.

To improve the diffusion and commercial impact of publicly funded research results, many OECD countries have experimented with novel approaches to the regulation and institutional management of intellectual property resulting from publicly funded research. Policy measures aim to accomplish the following:

- *Increase predictability and reduce transaction costs.* Regulations governing the ownership of intellectual property often vary within a country according to researcher status, the type of performing institution, or the source of the funding. Governments have tried to make patent and licensing procedures more uniform in order to simplify the transfer of research results to the private sector by standardizing ownership rules for publicly funded and publicly performed research.

- *Increase incentives to commercialize.* Exploiting intellectual property is a time-consuming and costly business. Public research organizations (PROs) cannot afford investments in the needed infrastructure and skills if they cannot be assured of sufficient remuneration (for example, through licensing or other fees). Some countries provide subsidies for local or institution-based technology transfer and licensing offices. Other countries let PROs elect title to their innovations in exchange for the promise to seek protection and eventually exploit the invention, thus letting the PRO profit from its research results.

- *Decrease costs of protection and exploitation.* For universities, public laboratories and small and medium-sized enterprises (SMEs), the cost of applying for, maintaining, and defending patents represents a burden that governments are seeking to reduce. Application and maintenance costs can be reduced or waived for these institutions, and mediation rather than litigation is encouraged.

- *Limit restrictions on publication and scientific enquiry.* Licensing agreements and research contracts can contain clauses that hamper the ability of scientists to continue their exploration in a field or slow the diffusion or access to fundamental research results by other researchers. To minimize clashes between the research and teaching mission of PROs and their commercial activities, governments can play a role in limiting the contractual demands placed on PROs.

Source: OECD (2001).

BOX 6.6

TRIPS: Developing Countries' Concerns Regarding the Universalization of IPRs

As part of the trade deal hammered out in 1994, countries joining the WTO also signed on to TRIPS, an international agreement that sets out minimum standards for the legal protection of intellectual property. These include extending intellectual property rights to include computer programs, integrated circuits, plant varieties, and pharmaceuticals, which were unprotected in most developing countries until the agreement came along. According to the terms of the agreement, most of the poor world had until the beginning of 2000 to bring their legal protections up to scratch. Developing countries were given an extension until the end of 2005.

TRIPS was pushed onto the trade agenda by the United States, Europe, and Japan, which together hold the lion's share of the world's patents and whose companies wanted more protection abroad. Meanwhile the poor countries still have misgivings about the agreement as they await the promised benefits of patent protection. Much of the poor world's anxiety about TRIPS is focused on two issues: access to medicines and protection of traditional resources. Many developing countries, including India and some sub-Saharan states, would like clarification on the agreement's provisions and exceptions to protect public health and the environment, and amendment of its articles on the patenting of life-forms.

From "The Right to Good Ideas," *The Economist*, June 23, 2001.

or R&D tax credit is based on a percentage of R&D expenditures. Under a *volume-based* system, the credit applies all of the R&D expenditures incurred during the period. Under an *increment-based* system, the credit applies to incremental R&D over a particular period. In the event that the total credit exceeds taxable income, there may in some jurisdictions be provisions for carrying forward (or carrying backwards) the excess (unused) credit. The kinds of firms that would benefit from *carry-forward provisions* would be start-ups or firms that suffer temporary losses.

- *Matching grants.* Another type of government intervention to stimulate R&D is matching grants, a cost-sharing instrument that potentially avoids the moral hazard problem that plagues outright subsidies. Recipients put up a certain percentage of research costs, thus signaling a precommitment to do a research project. Few countries have provided such programs and the understanding of these programs is still incomplete.

Various design issues need to be considered when coming up with incentives. In the context of LAC, revenue considerations and sustainability issues are important, given LAC's experiences with budgetary debt and deficits. The overall tax system may also significantly impact the effectiveness of fiscal incentives. When the prevailing tax system is distorted, the marginal effects of new fiscal measures are likely to be weak or offset. Furthermore, in LAC, where the R&D sector is small, some of the new R&D investments may come from the ranks of start-up firms, whose initial startup costs are high but whose revenues are low. They are thus not likely to have sufficient taxable income early on to take advantage of R&D tax incentives, such as an R&D tax credit. Allowing for "carry-forwards" will help them use the credits later on but, owing to the time value of money and inflation, these credits will be worth less. Defining R&D will be important in light of the practice of relabeling expenditures as R&D, as has been witnessed in OECD countries. A major design issue is whether a volume-based system or an incremental one is preferred. One needs to distinguish between *inframarginal* (what would have been done anyway) and *supramarginal* (what would not have been done without the tax incentive) R&D. However, with an incremental tax credit system, the marginal effective credit rate may be "negative," thus discouraging R&D investment.

While matching grants can be a useful way to link public and private R&D, governments need to be careful not to

constraints for R&D activity are exacerbated by the fact that R&D is risky and requires long-term financing. The most common type of intervention to counter these negatives is through fiscal incentives and subsidies. Governments provide a number of these to stimulate firms' R&D investments:

- *Depreciation rates.* By providing high and accelerated depreciation rates for current and capital expenditures on R&D, governments can favor R&D by allowing firms to avoid tax burdens on "assets" whose revenue-generating capability is active.
- *Tax credits.* A second type of fiscal incentive is the *R&D tax credit,* which enables firms to obtain deductions from income taxes. The precise amount of deduction

"crowd out" private funding. In order for public subsidies or grants to stimulate private R&D effort, the subsidies or grants must prompt firms to undertake projects they would not have otherwise found profitable (but which are socially valuable). To the extent that the government funds inframarginal R&D (which would have been undertaken anyway), there is little additional stimulus to overall R&D. However, politically, there can be great temptation for bureaucrats to support commercially attractive projects in order to demonstrate "success." These commercially attractive projects are also the ones that are more likely to have been undertaken privately. Thus funds spent may actually be a *rent* to private firms. Best practices here are based on "competitive" grants and a transparent process that involves the participation of experts and the private sector in the allocation. Finally, the organization structure to allocate and oversee competitive allocation of funds—subsidies—is far different, and probably less costly, than the one to provide for tax incentives.

Table 6.9 summarizes some pros and cons of tax credits versus matching grants.

Public Provision of R&D

Governments also provide direct—and often full—funding to a number of R&D activities, in principle as a measure to correct for market failures. In particular the public sector is supposed to finance "basic" R&D, which has more properties of a public good than does applied R&D, and which is unlikely to be financed by the private sector since it does not usually have direct commercialization use yet, recognizing that basic R&D generates significant positive externalities and spillovers. Moreover, at the earlier stages of technological development, as a way to jump-start the process, governments tend to finance specific programs and sectors, for potential economic impact and strategic reasons.

R&D is conducted by both private firms and public institutions, and the distribution between the two has received great attention. The public sector role in the provision and execution of R&D evolves as countries advance in acquiring technological capabilities and in increasing the skills of the labor force. The share of public R&D in total R&D expenditures declines as countries technologically advance, and that is another indicator of successful transitions. While all countries start with a high share of public R&D, the successful ones have managed to elicit increasingly higher levels of private R&D, so as countries evolve, the share of public R&D keeps decreasing (see table 6.10). Thus, eliciting high

levels of private R&D can be seen as a measure of the effectiveness of public R&D.

While the capability of firms or governments to engage in R&D at the early stages of technological catch-up is bound to be constrained by the limited learning that has been accumulated as well as the lack of highly skilled workers, some pockets of highly successful R&D activity are likely to occur in some enclaves, and the record from East Asia shows a high level of direct public involvement, as well as the record of Brazil with EMBRAER and Chile with CODELCO (de Ferranti and others 2001). It is generally accepted now that in the early stages of technological catch-up governments or universities should pursue selective research activity on their own and with selected firms—or sectors—in shop-floor tinkering, facilitated by contractual relationships with public research institutions. As the technological gap narrows, the importance of indigenous research grows and firms are best placed to conduct R&D in an effective manner—public R&D is largely focused on basic research, and growing private R&D takes the lead, becoming the key determinant of successful technological transitions, as we have seen it in NIC and natural resource–abundant countries. Hence, rather than the R&D to GDP ratio, the percentage of R&D financed by the private sector becomes central in explaining the transition into the creation stage as shown in table 6.10.

How Do These Factors Affect R&D Expenditures?

Based on a review of both the theory and the evidence, it seems accessing increased technological capabilities and successful transitions will only come through increased private R&D. While spending on research and development does not, in itself, ensure innovation or rapid growth rates, such spending is a necessary condition at all stages of development. The magnitude and the focus depend on the stage of a country's development. Without an adequate volume of R&D expenditures a country will most likely not ascend the technology ladder. *No country has managed successful technological transitions without significant private R&D expenditures.* Thus being able to guide any policy for LAC countries to stimulate private R&D is essential for understanding the determinants of private R&D investments. Those investments are done by firms, and their level depends on their expected returns, which in turn depend on (i) the costs of R&D, which are affected by fiscal policies and subsidies to R&D; (ii) the probability of success, which is affected by the skill of the labor force; (iii) the degree of appropriability of

TABLE 6.9

Tax Credits versus Matching Grants

	TAX CREDITS	MATCHING GRANTS
Advantages	• Less government interference • No need for governments to choose technologies • Tend to be open-ended	• Coordinates public and private R&D spending • In principle, could target areas with large gap between social and private rate of return
Disadvantages	• Start-up firms may be too small to qualify • Firms may relabel expenditures as R&D • Tax structure may be complex • Projects that generate greater short-run profits are likely to be favored • High intramarginal costs, small marginal effect ("crowding out" may be larger than in grants)	• Government may need to choose technologies • Pressures to show visible success may lead to financing of projects with high private rates of return, thus "crowding out" private investment. • Need to account for governance issues—transparency, incentive, and competitive granting
Preconditions	• Well-functioning tax system	None

TABLE 6.10

Evolution of the Ratio of Private to Public R&D Expenditures, 1980–95

	1980	1985	1990	1995
Argentina	0.1765	0.1765	0.1765	0.1806
Brazil	0.4749	0.4749	0.4749	0.4749
Chile	0.4493	0.4493	0.4205	0.4598
Cost Rica	0.0893	0.0891	0.0894	0.0892
Mexico	0.3850	0.1765	0.1111	1.3042
Finland	2.1738	2.1854	2.3337	2.4819
Ireland	0.8019	1.0618	1.2675	2.5971
Israel	0.5674	0.5674	1.6596	1.6954
Korea	1.6225	4.0136	4.4336	4.7961

Source: Guasch (2002) with data from Park (2002).

successful innovation, which is affected by IPRs; (iv) the extent of and access to supportive knowledge available, which is affected by public R&D and the quality and extent of research institutions; and (v) the degree of competition faced by the firms (Tirole 1996; Guasch 1985).

There has been a fair amount of research testing those theory implications. Earlier research (conducted in the 1980s) tends to find that fiscal incentives have a weak effect on R&D. Later research, conducted during the 1990s, tends to find more favorable evidence of the impact of R&D tax credits. Hall (2000) attributes the difference in results to the fact that the earlier elasticity estimates were based on a time period when firms were uncertain as to whether the R&D tax credits were permanent or temporary. Given the costs of adjusting R&D capital, firms appeared to choose to wait.

A problem with these studies is that they compare the tax credits to the amount of R&D generated rather than to the amount of benefits from the R&D generated. David, Hall, and Toole (1999) review evidence from micro- and macro-level studies, mostly for the United States, to conclude

(although their results are mixed), in favor of findings of complementarity between public and private R&D investments. The evidence from five programs in the United States and Israel reviewed in Park (2002) provides mixed results—some studies showing the positive impact of these programs on stimulating private R&D, with others highlighting some shortcomings in actual practice.

The experience in Korea, Chile, and Colombia, however, seems to show that competitive allocation of funds—subsidies such as matching grants—has a higher impact to stimulate private R&D than tax incentives. In a background paper for this report, Park (2002), using recent data, shows that fiscal incentives have a positive effect on private R&D even when patent rights and public R&D funding are controlled for. However, while public R&D is a strong determinant of private R&D for non-LAC countries, it does not have an impact for LAC countries. That result hints at the inefficiencies in LAC of public R&D and is corroborated by Lederman and Maloney (2002), who show that indexes for quality of public research institutions and extent of private-public collaboration are very low in LAC. They show that the effectiveness of public R&D as a determinant of private R&D—and patents—is strongly affected by those two indexes, a fact that explains the ineffectiveness of public R&D in LAC. The study also shows that for both LAC and non-LAC countries, private R&D is a function of an economy's level of intellectual property rights, and patent protection is the most important area of rights protection. Copyrights and trademark rights positively explain R&D, but not when patent rights are controlled for, which indicates that these variables likely picked up the effect of the omitted variable (patent rights). Thus, despite the fact that IPR violations have occurred in LAC, patent protection has been important to private research in

Latin America. But even more important in LAC, is the emergence as a determinant of R&D the education or skill level of the labor force. This is emphasized by the high elasticity as seen in table 6.11, where a summary of the results is provided, as well as in box 6.7.

The positive correlation between IPRs and private R&D can be seen in figure 6.8.

In summary, a coherent R&D framework is essential to successfully reaching advanced technological capabilities. Overall, we find that patent protection, public funding, and human capital are important to private R&D, and ultimately,

TABLE 6.11

Determinants of Private R&D Per Worker in LAC and Other Countries: Elasticities

	ALL COUNTRIES	LAC
Elasticity private R&D/patent rights	1.77	1
Elasticity private R&D/public R&D	*0.58*	*n.s.*
Weak positive effect of copyrights protection	Weak +	Weak +
Weak negative effect of trademark rights	n.s.	Weak −
Elasticity private R&D/fiscal incentive	−2.60	−1.1
Elasticity private R&D/education	0.33	1.32
Elasticity private R&D/competition	1.1	0.9

n.s.: not significant.
Note: All figures are significant at the 1 percent level.
Source: Park (2002) and Guasch (2002).

BOX 6.7

Human Capital, IPRs, and R&D Policies as Determinants of Private R&D and Their Impact on TFP—Methodology and Results

Based on an R&D supply and demand model, Park (2002) derives the steady-state stock of private R&D capital per worker (R_p/L) as a function of public R&D capital (R_g/L), physical capital per worker (K/L), human capital per worker measured by the scientists and engineers per 10,000 workers (SE) and tertiary enrollment rates (E), and the policy environment (for example, level of intellectual property protection and fiscal incentives) (IPR).

$$R_p/L = f(R_g/L, K/L, SE, E, IPR)$$

The technology stock is measured by the stock of domestic patent capital per 1,000 domestic workers (A_d) and is a function of public and private R&D capital, and human capital.

$$A_d = f(R_p/L, R_g/L, SE, E, IPR)$$

Finally, total factor productivity (TFP) is a function of the domestic and foreign (A_f) stocks of patent capital and human capital.

$$TFP = f(A_d, A_f, SE, E)$$

The stocks of public and private R&D capital, and domestic and foreign patent capital, are determined by the perpetual inventory method (assuming a 10 percent rate of depreciation).

Empirical analysis for the pooled sample of 20 developed, 19 LAC, 7 East Asian, and 12 other countries shows that patent rights and the human capital variables are a significant determinant of private R&D. Fiscal incentives (as measured by the B-index) are also weak determinants of private R&D. Human capital also directly increases TFP whereas fiscal incentives, public funding, and patent protection stimulate TFP indirectly by stimulating the determinants of TFP—for instance, domestic patent capital through private R&D spending.

Regressions performed for LAC countries alone are much less robust owing to lack of adequate data. However, one result that the data do seem to confirm is that public R&D spillovers to private R&D are negligible in LAC, which is confirmed by case studies.

The following table provides results of some simulation analyses for LAC countries based on the regression results. We use the estimated equations to predict the effects of changes in the independent variables on R&D and TFP. These results should be interpreted as a steady-state comparison (since the model was solved for in steady state). Since we are not able to estimate a complete set of R&D and TFP equations with all the R&D policy variables included, primarily because the number of observations for the fiscal incentive variable was small, we mix coefficients from different regressions.

	PERCENT CHANGE IN PRIVATE R&D SPENDING PER WORKER	PERCENT CHANGE IN TFP
10 percent increase in patent right strength (Index)*	4.00	0.08
10 percent increase in public R&D funding per worker	6.60	0.22
10 percent increase in scientists and engineers per 10,000 workers	2.03	0.95
10 percent increase in tax incentives (decrease in B-index)*	11.6	0.20

*These estimates hold for Brazil and Mexico only, since those were the only two LAC countries with B-index data.

FIGURE 6.8

Patent Rights and Privately Financed R&D
(1980–95 average for 58 countries)

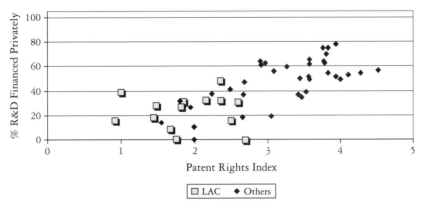

Note: The Patent Rights Index varies between 0 and 5. It is obtained by aggregating five subindices –
extent of coverage, membership in international treaties, duration of protection, absence of
restrictions, and enforcement. See Park (2002) for details.
Source: Park (2002).

as we show below, to total factor productivity. We find that the key determinants with the stronger impact on stimulating R&D, as measured by elasticities, are education—tertiary, in particular science and engineering disciplines—financial assistance, and patent protection strength. The causal mechanisms are as follows: patent rights, public funding, and human capital stimulate private R&D. Private R&D and public R&D in turn stimulate domestic and foreign patenting, which in turn contribute to the stocks of domestic and foreign-generated knowledge capital, which in turn are important determinants of total factor productivity—as we see below.

The Structure of R&D in LAC

Given the identified determinants of private R&D, the limited development of technological capabilities in LAC countries is not surprising, since most of them lack or are deficient in the provision and levels of those determinants, as we show below.

Weak Intellectual Property Rights

LAC countries typically have had weak IPR regimes, although there has been some strengthening in recent years, prodded by the developed countries. Nevertheless, IPRs are weaker in LAC than in most OECD and some East Asian countries, with Chile, Argentina, Panama, and Brazil in the lead; Mexico might be the outlier, with relatively weak IPRs. Indexes for three basic IPR instruments—namely, patents, copyrights, and trademarks—for selected LAC and non-LAC

countries are shown in table 6.12. Among the few LAC countries that had IPRs in 1995, there was stronger copyright and trademark protection than patent protection. This is an important issue, since the evidence shows stronger TFP effects from patent protection.

High Cost of R&D Financing

Not only are venture capital markets underdeveloped in LAC, so are regular capital markets. Thus, unless a firm is big enough to finance its research and development expenditures through internal funds, it is likely to find financing very costly. R&D is a long-term endeavor and thus requires long-term financing. The current paradigm in the LAC financial sector of very high interest rates and practically no long-term financing is clearly a factor in the limited private investment in R&D. Also, macroeconomic instability hampers incentives for long term investments. Moreover, R&D investments are lumpy, a reasonably large amount of R&D is needed just to start, and the relatively small size of firms in LAC makes securing or committing that critical mass not feasible. Venture capital is usually, then, the alternative to secure funding for existing or new, innovative firms. However, venture capital markets are extremely underdeveloped in LAC, in contrast to OECD and NIC countries. In any event, as Hall (2002) argues, venture capital may be a limited solution to financing innovation. Given the information and administrative requirements placed on venture capital, it tends to focus on a few sectors and to make investments with a minimum size that may be too large for start-ups in some

TABLE 6.12

Intellectual Property Rights Index, 1995

	PATENT RIGHTS INDEX	COPYRIGHT INDEX	TRADEMARK INDEX
Nicaragua	0.92		
Costa Rica	1.80		
Guatemala	1.80		
Turkey	1.80	2.42	2.75
Honduras	2.10		
Thailand	2.24	2.85	3.42
Bolivia	2.31		
Dominican Republic	2.41		
Colombia	2.57	3.42	3.17
Hong Kong (China)	2.57		
Uruguay	2.60	2.88	3.00
Philippines	2.67	2.68	2.50
Ecuador	2.71		
Peru	2.71	3.30	2.83
Paraguay	2.80		
Malaysia	2.85		
El Salvador	2.86		
Mexico	2.86	2.99	2.33
Venezuela	2.90	3.12	2.92
Portugal	2.98	3.83	4.00
Argentina	3.19		
Haiti	3.19		
Ireland	3.32	2.88	2.70
Brazil	3.50	3.59	3.80
Panama	3.52		
Canada	3.57	3.63	3.75
Israel	3.57	3.12	3.78
United Kingdom	3.57	3.80	4.33
Chile	3.70	2.83	2.50
Australia	3.86	3.87	4.80
Germany	3.86	4.54	4.17
New Zealand	3.86	3.48	3.12
Belgium	3.90	4.50	4.67
Norway	3.90	3.66	4.80
Singapore	3.90	2.60	3.17
Switzerland	3.91	3.70	4.67
Japan	3.94	4.10	3.50
Finland	4.19	4.28	4.67
Italy	4.19	4.42	4.42
Korea	4.20	3.80	3.25
Sweden	4.24	4.67	4.67
Netherlands	4.38	4.10	4.67
Denmark	4.50	4.33	4.33
France	4.50	5.00	5.00
Spain	4.50	4.65	4.75
Austria	4.57	4.33	4.42
U.S.A.	4.86	4.35	4.17

Source: Park (2002).

fields. Furthermore, in order for venture capital investors to have an exit strategy that allows them to move on to financing new start-ups, an active stock market in new and young stocks is critical. Hall thus concludes that the effectiveness of government incubators, seed funding, loan guarantees, and other such policies for funding R&D deserves further study.

Weak Skill Supply of Labor Force: Not "Enough" High-Quality Research Personnel

Human capital is an important determinant of research and development activities in a country. The level of education in LAC countries as shown in chapter 4 (as well as the level and quality of research workers) is a cause for concern in LAC. The supply of researchers is highly concentrated in a few "high-quality" institutions. For instance, in Mexico, the National University of Mexico (UNAM), the *Instituto Politecnico Nacional* (IPN), and the private *Instituto Tecnologico de Monterrey* (ITM) produce most of the graduate-level scientists and engineers in the country. The University of Chile and the Catholic University of Chile produced almost 90 percent of all Chilean scientific publications at the end of the 1990s (Wolff and Albrecht 1992). Argentina's major universities—especially the University of Buenos Aires—receive the bulk of research funding going to higher education. These universities turn out relatively few research-trained scientists and engineers because of relatively small graduate programs in these areas. In addition, high-quality graduate programs may have trouble expanding because of the limited number of high-quality trained undergraduates (those that graduate from the few "high-quality" institutions). Moreover as we show in the next chapter the linkages between research centers and the private sector are extremely weak.

In 1997, 140,500 researchers were engaged in R&D in the LAC countries, a number that corresponds to only 7 researchers per 10,000 in the labor force. The difference between LAC and countries such as Spain and the United States is tremendous—the relative number of researchers in the latter examples is about 10 times as high as the LAC average (figure 6.9). Even Chile, which is usually a star among LAC countries, shows significant deficiencies there. The country's stock of human capital for the knowledge economy is still thin and uneven. Chile had only 369 scientists and engineers per one million inhabitants in 1999, compared with 2,132 in Ireland (World Bank, SIMA database, 2002). The recent figure for Chile is roughly the same as that in the early 1990s. But having said that, the comparison of LAC numbers—at least for the most advanced countries—in 2000 with those of the successful technological transition countries in the late 1970s, when they took off, is rather favorable. Few scientists and engineers are employed in productive activities. Two out of three S&T researchers are located in universities, with weak links to business, and only 6 percent operate in private companies. This compares to more

FIGURE 6.9

Researchers, 1999*

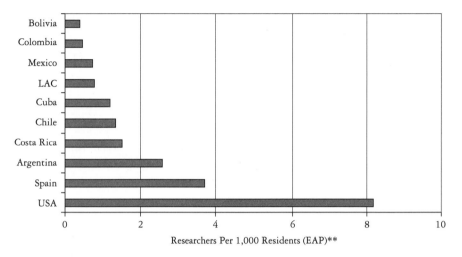

Researchers Per 1,000 Residents (EAP)**

* Or latest year available.
** Economically active population.
Source: RICyT (2001).

than a third in leading OECD countries with a tradition of close firm–university collaboration in research. Only Argentina, which features high gross tertiary enrollment ratios and high levels of enrollment in science-related fields, has fairly high concentrations of researchers compared to the average LAC level.

Yet, there may be some circularity in this argument. It may be counterproductive to turn out a lot of research-trained scientists and engineers if there are no jobs for them in the economy. Unless private and public industries expand their research activities, research-trained scientists and engineers will be limited to working in the education sector or in jobs that do not require their research skills. Changing industrial culture requires public policies (for example, incentives, as in Korea or the United States) that are outside the education sector.

Lack of Market Discipline

Firms in LAC traditionally—up until the 1990s—have not faced competitive pressures for technology upgrading. A critical element of the incentive regime and a key determinant of technological advancement is the extent of competitive pressure that firms face in their domestic markets (foreign markets for the export-oriented firms). As firms face increased competition, their response is to fold over or seek productivity gains, usually through technological upgrading. In the absence of competition, firms can continue to reap quasi-

monopoly rents unchallenged. Thus firms have less incentive to pursue technological innovation in order to ward off or stay ahead of competitors. The historic protectionist practices in LAC countries and the levels of concentration and relationship among domestic producers in the same sector have not favored or induced the desired market discipline that forces firms to seek technological upgrading. As trade barriers have fallen in LAC during the 1990s, we have seen episodic and sectoral responses but, with some notable exceptions, these have been slow—perhaps owing to a lack of credibility in the reform program—and not as extensive as elsewhere. As of today, according to the standard, albeit imperfect competitive indicators, most LAC countries score below the average.

Brazil's attempt to develop its information technology industry provides an illustration. Brazil tried its hand at protecting and developing its domestic personal computer industry through the *Informatics Law* (in the 1980s). It provided various fiscal incentives to firms in the IT sector to undertake R&D. Personal computers and peripherals were reserved exclusively for national firms, and foreign participation was prohibited. However, by October 1992 it was clear that this policy had not created a vibrant, innovative domestic computer industry in Brazil, and the domestic market protection on informatics officially ended. A major problem with the policy was that local firms had little incentive to engage in technological innovation in the absence of foreign competition. In an environment of protected markets, public R&D funding may be used to further the market power of incumbent firms. Furthermore, by disallowing imports and foreign participation, the government discouraged technology transfer in an industry that is characterized by a high rate of technological innovation, and the users had to work with costlier and lower-quality computers (Mani 2002).

Limited Fiscal Incentives and Subsidies

Most countries in Latin America and the Caribbean do not offer any fiscal incentives. Table 6.13 presents a brief comparison of R&D fiscal incentives across countries. Brazil and Mexico are the only two countries that provide some fiscal incentives for R&D among the LAC countries, and even this support has been marginal and volatile. One way to see that is the B-index, which is an index of fiscal generosity toward R&D. It tells us what benefit, B, is needed to cover the cost of an initial outlay of R&D of $1. The smaller the B-index, the more generous the R&D tax support system.[4] As pointed out earlier, LAC countries have rarely used matching grants to stimulate private R&D (there is some limited experience through *Fundacion Chile* and *Colciencias* in Colombia). Overall, LAC countries have not made a great effort to provide fiscal incentives for R&D to firms. The reasons are varied, and include fiscal austerity and shortage of public funds; limited demand from the private sector, induced by macroeconomic stability issues; shortage of skills and own funding; lack of credibility for sustained assistance,

and so on. For most of the LAC countries, which are farther away from the technology frontier and have distorted tax systems, it probably was the right decision.

LAC governments have, however, mounted significant R&D efforts in universities and think tanks. This, along with the relatively low private sector effort, has led to a situation in which, by global standards, the region has a relatively high public/productive R&D ratio (see figures 6.10 and 6.11) in both the financing and the execution of R&D.

This is not intrinsically bad. It has generally been the case that countries jump-start the innovation process with public efforts.

The low private participation in R&D is reflected in low experimental development

The path to industrialization Korea followed—importing capital, learning how to use it, making further expansions, and then exporting it to others—provides a stark example of the importance of experimental development in firms to building technological capability. Experimental development is defined as systematic work based on existing knowledge and is directed toward the production of new materials and products or toward improving products that already exist—a key component to the adapting stage and for the transition to the creation stage. By 1995 more than 65 percent of all Korean R&D was undertaken by the private sector. More than

TABLE 6.13

Fiscal Incentives Regimes for R&D as of 2000

	CURRENT R&D DEPRECIATION METHOD	CAPITAL R&D DEPRECIATION METHOD	CARRY-FORWARD PROVISION	TAX CREDIT RATE	BASE FOR TAX CREDIT	B-INDEX 1995
Australia	150%	3 years	3–10 years	None	—	0.893
India	100%	100%	?	None	—	N/A
Ireland	100%	100%	?	>100%	?	1.000
Korea	100%	20%	?	10–25%	Incremental	0.893
Spain	Capitalize	100%	3–5 years	15–30%	Incremental	0.658
Sweden	100%	30%	?	None	—	1.015
Taiwan (China)	100%	Like invest.	4 years	15–20%	Volume	N/A
USA	100%	3 years	3–15 years	20%	Incremental	0.893
Brazil	100%	Like invest.	4 years	None	—	1.030*
Mexico	100%	3 years	?	None	—	1.015
Peru	—	—	—	None	—	N/A
Argentina	—	—	—	None	—	N/A
Chile	—	—	—	None	—	N/A
Colombia	—	—	—	None	—	N/A
Costa Rica	—	—	—	None	—	N/A

*1980.

"?" refers to unclear information; N/A and − refer to nonexisting.

Note: Depreciation methods of 100 percent (or more) indicate that R&D is fully expensed. Under "Capital R&D," the number of years refers to the duration of the straight-line depreciation method. Under "Base for tax credit," "Volume" refers to the fact that the tax credit applies to total R&D, while "Incremental" refers to the fact that the tax credit applies to the excess of R&D over some base (usually past R&D or a moving average of past R&D).

Source: Hall and Van Reenen (2001); OECD (1996) in Park (2002).

FIGURE 6.10

Financing of R&D Expenditures, 1999

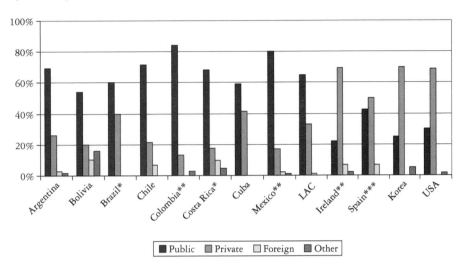

*1996, ** 1997, ***1998.

Note: For purposes of international comparison, public general university funds (GUF) are included under "public." These are funds that higher education establishments allocate to R&D from the general grant they receive from the Ministry of Education or from the corresponding provincial or local authorities in support of their overall research/teaching activities. "Other" includes funds from the private nonprofit sector (PNP).

Source: RICyT (2001); OECD (2002).

FIGURE 6.11

Gross R&D Expenses by Executing Sector, 1994–98

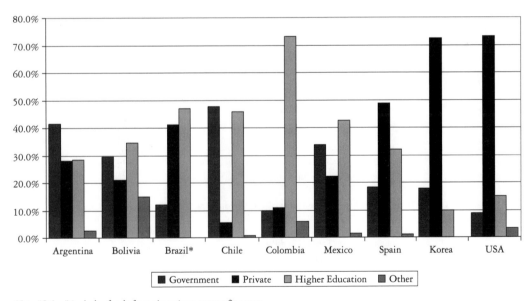

Note: "Other" includes funds from the private nonprofit sector.

Source: RICyT (2001); OECD (2001); MOST, Korea, http://www.most.go.kr/index-e.html.

60 percent of all R&D expenditure in 1999 was in experimental development (table 6.14). The United States similarly directed more than 60 percent of its research and development effort toward experimental development in 1999.

The Latin America and the Caribbean region, by contrast, puts much less effort into development research, as a result of the low share of private R&D, since that type of R&D is generally done by the private sector (figure 6.12). In 1999,

TABLE 6.14

R&D Expenditure by Activity (in percentages)

COUNTRY	BASIC RESEARCH		APPLIED RESEARCH		EXPERIMENTAL DEVELOPMENT	
	1995	2000	1995	2000	1995	2000
Argentina	28.6	28.0	48.1	44.8	23.3	27.2
Bolivia		49.0		39.0		12.0
Chile	58.6	55.3	36.5	31.6	6.7	13.1
Colombia	39.7	22.3	21.5	49.7	38.8	28.0
Ecuador*		30.1		64.0		6.0
El Salvador*		58.8		31.8		9.4
Mexico	35.9	23.3**	33.1	47.7**	31.1	29.1**
Panama	51.6	47.6*	24.2	45.9*	24.1	6.5*
Peru		38.3ᵃ		48.3ᵃ		13.4ᵃ
Korea	12.5	12.6	25.7	24.3	62.5	63.1
Portugal	24.9	26.2ᵃ	45.0	42.6ᵃ	30.1	31.2ᵃ
Spain	25.3	22.0ᵃ	37.0	36.9ᵃ	37.7	41.1ᵃ
USA	15.8	18.3	20.8	22.9	61.8	61.1

ᵃData for 1999.
*Data for 1998.
**Data for 1997.
Note: "Basic research" consists of experimental or theoretical work in order to obtain new knowledge about the origin of fundamental phenomena and observable facts, without any specific application. "Applied research" consists of original and new works undertaken in order to acquire new knowledge with a practical and specific goal in mind. "Experimental development" consists of systematic work based on existing knowledge that came from research or practical experience. This is directed toward the production of new materials and products or toward improving products that already exist. Note that the Korean dataset calls the category of experimental development "development research."
Source: Red Iberamericana de Indicadores en Ciencia y Tecnologia (RICyT) *Principales indicadores de ciencia y tecnologia,* http://www.ricyt.edu.ar/; Korean Ministry of Science and Technology (MOST), http://www.most.go.kr/index-e.html.

FIGURE 6.12

Private R&D Performance and Experimental Development

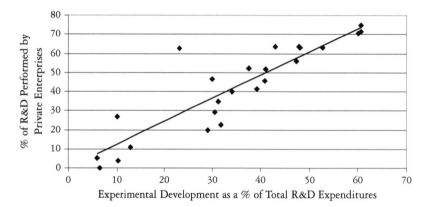

Note: Data are for 1999 or the latest prior year available including and after 1995. Data are for 13 OECD and 8 LAC countries for which data were available. For Argentina, Ecuador, and Peru, data are for science and technology. The Latin American countries included are Argentina, Bolivia, Chile, Ecuador, Colombia, Mexico, Panama, and Peru.
Source: OECD Basic Science and Technology Statistics (2001); RICyT (2002), available at http://www.ricyt.edu.ar/.

Argentina and Mexico were among the largest spenders on development research, with approximately 29 percent of R&D expenditures. Uruguay and Brazil, not shown in table 6.14, also appear to do well. The rest of the LAC countries lagged far behind, with Ecuador and Panama devoting only around 6 percent of their research and development expenditures to experimental development.

The low involvement of the private sector in LAC in research and development reflects this deficiency in experimental development activities (see figure 6.12).

Box 6.8 presents the contrasting approaches to R&D in Korea (private and performance-based R&D focus) and Mexico (public and non-competitive R&D focus). In summary, table 6.15 presents the R&D predicament in LAC

BOX 6.8

The Contrasting Approaches to R&D by Korea and Mexico

Two opposite poles of R&D systems are represented by the Korean and Mexican systems in terms of spread of R&D capabilities. Acquisition and development of technology in Korea results mainly from R&D undertaken in firms. By 1999, more than 70 percent of R&D was funded and undertaken by the private sector. Research institutes still did about one-fourth of the R&D in the late 1980s. The institutes are specifically organized to support industry and received the bulk of public monies for research. By 2001, there were 27 government research institutes (GRIs) supporting research capabilities in various strategic areas. The government also financially encouraged, and still does, private firms to establish research centers and research unions with other firms. By 1995 there were 2,210 research institutes and 63 research unions in the Korean private sector.[5] Within the university sector, there are various universities with well-developed research capabilities. To provide an illustration, the AsiaWeek ranking of Asia-Oceania universities by research had 13 Korean universities in the top 50 as compared to 8 for Japan and 10 for Australia.[6] Starting in 1989, the government introduced Centers of Excellence (COE) in Korea, namely Science Research Centers (SRCs), Engineering Research Centers (ERCs), and Regional Research Centers (RRCs), to encourage basic research in major universities. These centers were selected on the basis of creativity and research capability, and in the case of RRCs, also based on their contribution to the regional economy and community. Once the centers are selected, they receive government funding for nine years, provided that the interim evaluation done

every three years shows good progress. By 2000, 36 SRCs, 47 ERCs, and 37 RRCs had been selected and funded.

The structure of R&D in Mexico is quite different. Except for state-owned companies, such as Pemex and the electrical utility company, the government does not provide research and development funds or incentives for R&D in firms. The research and development effort is centered in federal and state research projects (primarily in agricultural and medical research), and in the public universities. About 40 percent of all public university R&D is at the National University of Mexico (UNAM). One-third of all the researchers registered in the late 1980s by the national system of researchers (SNI) worked at UNAM.

Thus, outside of agricultural, petrochemical, and medical research carried out in specialized public institutions, publicly financed R&D is highly concentrated in public universities, and much of that research in one university. Indeed, UNAM is not only the main institution for scientific research in Mexico, but perhaps in Latin America as a whole (Guevara Niebla 1990, pp. 445–52). According to the President of Mexico's 1990 state of the union message, from 1976 to 1990, UNAM carried out almost 37,000 research projects and 1,500 technology development projects—16,000 were in exact and natural sciences, 10,000 in social sciences and humanities, 3,500 in engineering, and more than 6,000 in medicine (Martinez and Ordorica 1991, p. 91). The research is done in 24 institutes and 13 research centers. Clearly, UNAM represents one of the single largest research systems in the developing world.

TABLE 6.15

Patterns of R&D Expenditures: LAC versus OECD and East Asian Tigers, Averages for 2000

R&D EXPENDITURES		LAC	OECD AND EAST ASIA
Total expenditure (as percentage of GDP)		0.5%	2.1%
Financing	Public sector	75%	23%
	Private sector	20%	66%
Executing	Public sector	45%	12%
	Private sector	14%	70%
Theme of R&D	Basic	53%	18%
	Applied and experimental	17%	63%

Source: Guasch (2002).

countries and contrasts it with OECD and newly industrialized countries, illustrating the key differences and the weak position of LAC countries in terms of their transition to advanced stages of technological development.

Conclusion

In sum, much of Latin America has gotten through the "plug in" phase of opening to foreign technology through trade and FDI and getting the basic institutions of property rights and infrastructure in the form of ITC in place. However, few have experienced a takeoff in productive sector R&D that appears to be the requisite for being an innovative and high growth economy. Part of the reason is that some of the basic tools that countries have used to boost R&D—such as fiscal incentives offered to the private sector—have not been used in the region. Governments have not addressed the pervasive market and coordination failures.

But the problem in fact lies deeper. LAC has made large investments in higher education, and in research in universities and government research centers, yet these have not had the effect of either stimulating investments in innovation by the private sector, or moving the region to the innovation frontier. As of 2000, a number of LAC countries have equal, if not better, educational numbers than the countries that today are technologically successful had in the late 1970s, when they took off (table 6.16). So there is no reason why those countries could not take off in the successful path of technological advancement.

The next chapter argues that the failure of the LAC countries to take off on the technology path is because the institutions, when created, charged with resolving the market failures inherent to innovation are both internally dysfunctional and uncoordinated among themselves. Addressing this issue is the challenge faced by the more advanced countries of the region.

TABLE 6.16

Similarity of Education Patterns in LAC (1990s) versus Technology-Successful Economies (1980)

	YEARS OF EDUCATION OF LABOR FORCE	% OF POST-SECONDARY EDUCATION
Non-LAC (1980)		
Finland	8.33	11.9
Hong Kong (China)	6.73	7.1
Ireland	7.60	7.9
Korea	6.81	8.9
Singapore	3.65	3.4
Spain	5.15	7.1
Taiwan (China)	6.37	9.3
LAC (2000)		
Argentina	8.49	19.7
Brazil	4.56	8.4
Chile	7.89	15.8
Colombia	5.01	9.9
Costa Rica	6.01	18.6
Mexico	6.73	11.3
Peru	7.33	22.4
Uruguay	7.25	12.5
Venezuela	5.61	18.0

Source: Barro and Lee (2000).

Endnotes

1. For example, Coe, Helpman, and Hoffmeister (1997) construct a foreign R&D capital stock variable for every developing country in their sample as a weighted average of the domestic R&D capital stocks of the country's 22 industrial country trading partners, with bilateral machinery and equipment import shares of each developing country in relation to the respective industrial country serving as weights.

2. See Aitken and Harrison (1999) for Venezuela; Aitken, Hanson, and Harrison (1998) for Mexico; Girma and Wakelin (1998) for the United Kingdom; Hoekman and Djankov (2000) for the Czech Republic; and Kugler (2000) for Colombia.

3. Rates of return inclusive of such inter-industry spillover effects—that is, social rates of return (SRR)—have been estimated by a few investigators. In agricultural R&D projects, the SRR was 150 to 300 percent greater than the private rate of return (PRR). Studies for industrial countries have also estimated that a 1 percent increase in spillover caused average costs of other firms to fall by 0.2 percent. Across the major industries that were studied, non-electrical machinery, chemical, rubber and plastics, and petroleum were found to be major spillover sources. Their SRRs ranged from four times the PRR in non-electrical machinery, to three times the PRR in chemical products, and to twice the PRR in the other two industries (Bernstein 1989).

4. The B-index makes a number of simplifying assumptions. It assumes equal interest rates across countries (that is, the cost of finance is the same for all countries). It also assumes away international differences in the definition of R&D for tax purposes. Other taxes that may indirectly affect the motivation to do R&D are ignored (for example, commodity taxes, property taxes, capital gains taxes). This omission would be rather serious in jurisdictions without corporate income taxation but which rely on a host of other types of taxes. Another drawback is that countries with high corporate tax rates and high R&D fiscal incentives will score high on the B-index, as opposed to countries with low levels of both. Finally, another simplifying assumption is that the firms are large corporations, rather than small businesses. The methodology assumes that firms have sufficient taxable income and thus does not incorporate explicitly any carry-forward or carry-back provisions.

5. Ministry of Science and Technology, Republic of Korea, http://park.org/Korea/Pavilions/PublicPavilions/Government/most/policye3.html.

6. http://www.asiaweek.com/asiaweek/features/universities2000/schools/multi.research.html.

CHAPTER 7

Networks and National Innovation Systems

THE PREVIOUS CHAPTERS OF THIS BOOK DEALT WITH THE STOCKS OF FACTORS that are essential to the innovation process and policies to increase them. This chapter focuses on how these factors interact—in other words, on the networks of public, private, and international actors and institutions that form the "National Innovation System." As chapter 6 detailed, knowledge is especially susceptible to market failures and these have given rise to a variety of nonmarket institutions and legal protections:

Appropriability problems impede innovation and diffusion. Given the difficulty of excluding others from ideas, innovators will not appropriate the full social benefits of their work. This has given rise to intellectual property rights (IPRs) protections, such as patenting that creates a market for new ideas. However, the social value of the innovation is itself a function of the degree and speed of diffusion, which in some dimensions is impeded by the IPR system—the cost of using the innovation is higher than the marginal cost of its diffusion.[1] This contradiction can be resolved to a degree by public universities or think tanks explicitly set up to provide the public good, or by research consortia in which numerous firms together bear the cost and reap the benefits of research. The same market failure that impedes investment in innovation slows

its transmission as well. A firm that incurs the costs of tapping into the global stock of knowledge by, for instance, a study tour or making contact with foreign universities will soon find its discoveries adopted by other firms that free-ride on the investment. This basic failure extends from the simplest problem of identifying market niches to, as Hausman and Rodrik (2002) argue, a country discovering its comparative advantage. Historically, this has given rise to institutions ranging from agricultural extension services to public research institutions designed to act as "antennae" for new ideas at the sectoral and national levels.

Lumpiness and scale economies dictate specialization. R&D and innovation are characterized by economies of scale and lumpiness. To be effective, resources need to be concentrated in a manner beyond the capacity of the individual firm. This, combined with the fact that even patents are not effective

at resolving the non-appropriability problem in "pure science," provides a rationale for institutions dedicated to R&D and innovation efforts, such as research centers and universities. Innovation and knowledge developed by those institutions tend to be nonexclusive and are made available to all and any interested parties, guided by an appropriate allocation of property rights. The issues that emerge then are how those institutions are developed and how they are financed. Even more relevant, because the knowledge is produced by some who are nonusers and used by others, is ensuring that what the institutions produce is in tune with what the users want and need—in other words, an incentive issue.

Innovation, diffusion, and application require collaboration among many institutions and firms. Although innovation is sometimes the product of one firm alone, the more common pattern is one of joint efforts, among various firms, among firms and R&D-related institutions, or among various R&D-related institutions. Furthermore, progress does not proceed linearly from pure science to applied technologies, but moves in both directions (Nelson and Rosenberg 1993); and feedback from frontline users of technology to researchers is essential for the refinement of products and production processes (Rosenberg 2001). Finally, as a result of specialization, the full supply chain of knowledge is not fully integrated, either vertically or horizontally. Technological advance is therefore not necessarily evenly diffused throughout the supply chains. In each example, success requires coordination and cooperation across all necessary actors—a process that is subject to coordination failures and transaction costs. In many industrial countries, these issues have given rise to national institutions devoted to fomenting or eliminating impediments to technological collaboration among different institutions.

Information asymmetries: The very long-run and risky nature of R&D further compounds standard problems of information asymmetries. A firm may have a hard time knowing whether a researcher conducting basic research is incompetent or whether the problem is simply extremely difficult. This again argues for specialization of functions—universities have systems for evaluating the quality of their members,

which may be too cumbersome for an individual firm to attempt.

Much knowledge is difficult to codify. Often, knowledge is tacit—not easily codified in blueprints or documents—and hence can only be communicated through the interaction of individuals. This slows the diffusion process and provides a rationale for initiatives facilitating the interaction of these individuals, ranging from conferences, study-abroad programs, and faculty exchanges to the promotion of geographic agglomerations of firms using similar technologies.

National Innovations Systems: Coherence and Incentives

The development and necessary interaction and coordination of these market and nonmarket institutions has led to the concept of National Innovation Systems (NIS) and an extensive literature that we can only touch on here. (See Nelson 1993; OECD 1998, 2001; Lundvall and others 2002.) Figure 7.1 sketches a simple NIS capturing the ideal interaction of these various institutions and, where applicable, the human capital employed in them. In theory, the networks of public institutions and private firms interacting in a concerted way to generate and adopt technologies form the mechanisms through which nations learn. This "national

FIGURE 7.1
A Simple NIS

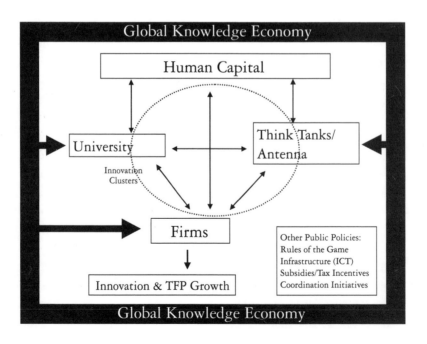

learning capacity," as numerous observers have called it, is what permits economies to adopt and innovate in their initial areas of comparative advantage and helps create new ones. (See Furman, Porter, and Stern 2002; Romer 1990; Nelson 1993; Wright 1999.)

Examples of the importance of such a learning capacity abound in both manufacturing and in natural resource sectors. In Taiwan (China), for example, a network of firms reverse-engineered an IBM AT personal computer and produced a successful clone, in the process learning enough to move to the frontier of notebook computer production (Mathews 2001). As discussed in *From Natural Resources to the Knowledge Economy* (de Ferranti and others 2002), the Finnish firm Nokia began as a highly innovative forestry firm embedded in a network of institutions that continually introduced new productivity-enhancing techniques and continues to make the sector very dynamic. But what was striking was that the same capacity to learn was transferable to the telecommunications sector as Nokia diversified into information technologies. This suggests that a key characteristic of the NIS is its flexibility in the face of new innovation possibilities. The nature of the next innovation is unpredictable, but, as Pasteur noted, "Chance favors only the prepared mind" or, by analogy, a country with a well-functioning NIS.[2]

Working the in tradition of endogenous growth, Peter Howitt and David Mayer of Mexico's CIDE (2002) offer a formalization of Pasteur's insight in their notion of countries falling into distinct "convergence clubs" based on their level of innovative capacity. When faced with the arguably near-random advent of a new technology, countries with a high level of capacity will be able to use it and then innovate upon it. Countries with lower levels of capacity will be able only to use it, but their inability to take it further will limit their ultimate level of development—they will never converge with innovators. Finally, those with truly deficient capacity will not be able to absorb new technologies, and stagnate. The absence of this complementary capacity embodied in a well-functioning NIS partly explains why LAC has had lower TFP growth in both agriculture and manufacturing than those at the frontier, despite the existence of technologies for the taking, and why it became dependent on foreign technologies over the course of the last century.[3] This logic also implies that the greater exposure to ideas—whether embodied in FDI, imported intermediate goods, or otherwise—through trade agreements such as NAFTA may not be enough to drive convergence with the richer partners.

A complementary effort to improve the depth and functioning of the NIS is also essential.

In fact, the term NIS must be treated with some caution. First, many critical interactions may, in fact, not be national but rather of a primarily regional character: many of the key innovation institutions in Chile's southern forestry industry may have little interaction with those of the northern mining sector. Such subsystems are often termed knowledge or innovation "clusters." Far more critical, however, is that these "national" systems—and even regional clusters—are and must be fundamentally international. The critical element of successful growth for developing countries is the ability to take advantage of the stock of knowledge abroad and apply it domestically and then work toward becoming contributors to the international flow of new innovation. This implies that national learning capacity is fundamentally a function of how plugged-in the economy is to the global centers of innovation.

A second caveat is that the innovation system depends heavily on factors that may or may not be strictly innovation related. Since the center of the innovation process must necessarily be the firm, all factors that impinge on its perception of gains from R&D and the barriers to innovating must be considered part of the "extended" NIS.

- In trade policy, access to technologies embodied in imported intermediate or capital goods and cooperative R&D projects with foreign investors are proven channels for transferring technology. Competitive pressures also appear to be critical factors encouraging innovation. Japan and the Republic of Korea saw the temporary granting of excess profits through trade protection of fledgling industries to be an incentive to innovate. However, prolonged protection and entry restriction to "targeted" industries led to the late entry of Korean firms into international R&D competition and slow growth (Cho and Sakakibara 2002). An open trade policy can be a useful disciplining device in the product market to complement efforts to get firms to collaborate in innovation. Kim (1993) argues that the market power of the Chaebols in Korea reduced the overall dynamism of the NIS.
- Since R&D is fundamentally a risky and longer-term project, well-functioning capital markets are essential. In fact, Trajtenberg argues (2002) that in Israel technology policy was, to a large degree, credit policy.

BOX 7.1

Venture Human Capital in the United States and Israel

Innovation is fundamentally a long-term and risky prospect and hence, particularly for start-ups, venture capital funds are necessary complements to other elements of the NIS. In the United States Microsoft, Cisco, Compaq, Federal Express, Apple Computers, Genentech, and Amazon.com all counted on venture capitalist participation and 30 percent of companies going public relied on it. These markets are distinctly absent in LAC.

However, venture capital is about more than capital. In fact, as de Carvalho, Gledson, and Amaro de Matos (2002) argue in "Venture Capital as Human Resource Management," the volume of financing in the United States is relatively small, averaging roughly $US 7 billion per year of $US 1 trillion in fixed investment. But as important as the provision of credit is the access to a network of management expertise that venture capitalists offer. When asked which of the functions of venture capitalists—providing financing, benchmarking performance, providing industry knowledge, developing a business strategy, recruiting managers, and two blank

options—were most important, 17 percent of receiving firms reported recruiting managers as the most important activity and 54 percent listed it in the top three.

This was recognized by Israel in its design of the Yozma program to jump-start the country's venture capital markets (Trajtenberg 2002). In 1992, Yozma set up a number of venture capital funds with a total of $US 200 million—initially funded by the government as well as domestic and foreign entrepreneurs from the United States, France, Germany, and Taiwan (China). Foreign investors were especially valued precisely for their management expertise and, as an incentive, were given the option in five years time to buy Yozma's shares at a fixed price.

Yozma was expected to be phased out after seven years but was fully privatized within five. The venture capital market now has 80 funds in operation and has raised $5 billion. The self-sustaining ability of the venture capital funds means the government can now focus its subsidies on aligning social and private benefits and leave financing per se to the private sector.

- Entrepreurial and managerial capital is cited by numerous authors as critical to converting ideas into value added (see, for example, Nelson and Pack 1999). De Carvalho and De Matos (see box 7.1) argue that venture capital markets are as much about management networks—linking firms developing new technologies with experienced managers—as the finance function.

- Labor market regulations may impede the adoption of new technologies (see Hirschman 1958; Parente and Prescott 2000) or the flow of workers from universities to firms and back again, and hence restrict the communication of tacit knowledge. The OECD (2001) finds that the tax wedge, unemployment benefits, and employment protection legislation were all negatively correlated with specialization in R&D-intensive industries.

- All the usual factors cited as important to firm growth—stable macro-economies, access to intermediate inputs—all appear again as *sine qua non* for encouraging firm innovation, regardless of explicit

technological policies. Leipziger and Thomas (2000) and Noland and Pack (2002) stress this as central to the "Asian Miracle."

In sum, a heightened focus on the NIS does not imply that the first- and second-generation reforms to date are in any way less important.

The final caveat, and the central focus of this chapter, is that the idea of a "system" connotes a deliberateness of design and coherent functioning that is often not the case. In fact, a critical feature of the NIS is that there are few market forces that guarantee that the various components in themselves will remedy the market failures they were inspired by, or engage the actors they were designed to serve. By their very nature, many of the institutions developed to remedy market failures are not market based, and as a result they do not respond to price signals that would ensure that they function well. Hence, it is necessary to think "systematically" about the incentive structures that govern the interactions within the NIS to ensure that they are internally coherent and generate the desired results. These include those embodied in national laws or administrative codes that act directly on private firms, or indirectly through their interactions with universities, think tanks, and other institutions.

Ensuring the effective interaction of the available innovation-related factors poses Latin America's second great challenge after remedying the gaps in its stock of innovation-related factors. In fact, the LAC region has evolved many of the "boxes" found in the more sophisticated versions of figure 7.1; however, case study evaluations of its functioning are fairly consistently depressing.[4] The families of institutions are often dysfunctional: not only is the available human capital not organized in a fashion most conducive to innovation, but balkanized institutions inhibit the desired interactions. In sum, the region needs to work toward establishing a coherent set of institutions and incentives that encourage firms to grow, innovate, and look outward.

Benchmarking the LAC NIS

Quantitative benchmarking of the functioning of the NIS, and hence of the region's performance, is difficult. The measures of stocks of innovation-related factors presented in earlier chapters are relatively easily available but standardized measures of the productivity of interactions among the various actors in the system are not.[5] Table 7.1 offers a tentative list of indicators that might be employed in the region and also helps structure much of the rest of the chapter. The first section of the table measures the stocks of innovation-related factors, especially human capital, and section III of the table, the supporting elements of the "greater" innovation system discussed above such as credit markets, labor markets, and the like.

Section II of table 7.1 corresponds to the core of this chapter and deals particularly with measures of innovative activity per se and the functioning of the NIS proper. The quantitative indicators suggested are available for the OECD or elsewhere and hence are comparable. Unfortunately, at this point most measures are not available on a consistent basis for the region and in the following sections we are forced to rely on fragmentary or merely related indicators to get a rough picture. A central element of the diagnosis of a NIS must, therefore, also include the quality information available on the system.

Indicators of Innovation Outcomes

As a measure of the overall functioning of the system, Total Factor Productivity (TFP), the share of growth not accounted for by the growth of physical factors of production, is perhaps most relevant here and, as discussed in earlier chapters, has been low in Latin America. As chapter 2 notes, LAC's performance in the 1990s has been subpar for most countries with the exception of perhaps Chile. Other "macro" performance variables such as growth more generally or unemployment are probably not related specifically enough to the innovation process to be useful. More relevant although still highly imperfect are measures of intermediate outputs, such as patents, or academic articles per GDP. Figures 7.2a–f suggest that while comparator economies— Korea, Israel, Finland, Sweden, Canada, India, and Taiwan (China)—have performed above predicted levels, and often dramatically so, Brazil, Mexico, and Argentina have fallen progressively behind while Chile and Venezuela have performed at an "average" level.[6]

Levels of R&D and Licensing

The measure most cited as an indicator of the functioning of the NIS is the level of *productive* sector financing of innovation since the firm, as figure 7.3 stresses, is the vehicle through which knowledge is converted into productivity— and growth in particular. Two of the high performers, Israel and Finland, viewed targeted R&D as the critical benchmarking measure and the means to improve the quality of the NIS. Arguably the analogous level of licensing payments, often although not always associated with foreign investment, is also a measure of the firm's awareness of technological possibilities and willingness to adopt them. Cohen and Levinthal (1989) among others stress the importance of technological absorptive capacity in firms and how this is highly related to their investment in R&D. R&D functions as the firm's learning unit, helping to benchmark the firm; it sets the "technological tone" and eventually builds an independent design and, more generally, innovative capacity (Forbes and Wield 2000). However, much of the literature suggests that firms fundamentally need to learn how to learn and that this does not happen naturally. At any moment in time firms of differing levels of technological awareness or capacity coexist.

Ideally comparable firm-level surveys of absorptive capacity would permit cross-country comparisons, but they are not available. At the aggregate level, figure 7.4 presents a striking pattern of R&D expenditures versus the fitted value for the sample as a whole. What is clear is that Korea, Israel, and Finland have experienced dramatic takeoffs.

TABLE 7.1

Potential Benchmarks for the LAC NIS: A Wish List

	MEASURE	SOURCE OF COMPARATOR DATA
I. Stocks of Innovation-Related Inputs		
Basic Competencies	Avg. Education, Secondary, Tertiary Enrollment	UNESCO_#
Science Personnel	# # Scientists, engineers	UNESCO_#
Education Quality	Standardized test scores	TIMSS_#
Training relevant to private sector	Share of students interning in industry	OECD02a_Q
Incidence of Training	Share of firms that train	OECD02a_#
II. Functioning of NIS		
Output		
Overall Productivity Growth	TFP Growth	LFC_#
Intermediate Outputs	Patents, Articles per GDP	LS_#
Input Levels	R&D (Private, Public), Royalties	LS_#
Private Sector Absorptive Capacity	Measures of awareness, effectiveness	_Q
Efficiency of Resource Use		
Patenting	Patents/$R&D or # Researchers, adjusted	LS#, L & M#
Articles	Academic articles in journals/Researcher	LS
Collaboration		
Contract and collaborative research	R&D financing by industry of HE and PL	OECD02a_#
Faculty consulting with industry	R&D consulting with firms by HE, PL	OECD02a_Q
Cooperation in innovation projects	Innovative firms cooperating with HE, PL	OECD02a_#/ GCR_Q
HE, PT as science information source	Innovative firms that use HE, PL	OECD02a_#
Quality of collaboration partner	Perceived quality of R&D institutions	GCR_Q
Degree of collaboration	Perceived level of interaction	GCR_Q
Incentives to bring ideas to market	Royalties sharing guidelines	OECD02a_#
Gov't incentives to collaborate	Promotion programs/gov't R&D financing	OECD02a_#
Incentives to interact with private sector	Presence of tech transfer offices	Q
Administrative burden	Degree of centralization, accounting	Q
Mission of universities/PL	Stated mission/organization	Q
Cluster innovative capacity	Revealed innovative comparative advantage	LM_#
Profitability of collaboration initiative	DNPV of intervention	
Mobility of researchers	Researchers at HE, PL moving to industry per year	OECD02a_#,Q
Antennas		
Brain circulation	Number of tertiary-ed. workers abroad	CD_#
Student studying abroad	Share of tertiary student with U.S. F-1 visas	IEE_#
Interactions with foreign universities	Agreements	
Interactions with foreign innovators	Percentage of scientific publications/patents with foreign co-author	OECD02b_#
Joint ventures		Q
Technology outposts		Q
III. Extended NIS		
ICT		
Connectivity	# Internet hosts/1000	ITU_#,
Participation	# PCs/capita, computer imports	ITU_#, CC_#
Potential	Telecom regulations	ITU_#
Investment	ICT investments as % GDP	OECD02b_#
Credit Markets		
Credit availability	Private sector credit/GDP	IBRD_#
Venture capital availability	Venture capital financing/GDP	OECD02b_#
Regulatory environment	Taxation, minority shareholder rights	Q
Intellectual Property Rights	Index	

174

TABLE 7.1

Continued

	MEASURE	SOURCE OF COMPARATOR DATA
Labor Markets		
Mobility among firms	Researchers in HE, PL moving to industry	OECD02b
Framework	Pension portability, hiring/firing costs, and so on	ILO, HP_#
IV. Data	Coverage of above	

Key:
# = Quantitative measures available.
Q = Qualitative measures available.
HE = Higher education.
PL = Public laboratories.
Sources: CC = Caselli and Coleman (2001). CD = Carrington and Detragiche (1999). GCR = Global Competitiveness Report. HP = Heckman and Pages-Serra (2000). IBRD = World Bank. ILO = International Labor Organization. ITU = International Telecommunication Union. LFC = Loayza, Fajnzylber, and Calderon (2002). LM = Lederman and Maloney (2003, 2003b). LS = Lederman and Saenz (2003). OECD = Organisation for Economic Co-operation and Development. OECD02a (2002a) = Benchmarking Industry-Science Relationships. OECD02b (2002b) = Science and Technology Outlook. TIMSS = Third International Mathematics and Science Study. UNESCO = United Nations Educational, Scientific and Cultural Organization.

For four countries about which we are confident in the disaggregation, figure 7.3 suggests that this was largely driven by the "productive" sector's (in other words, firms') R&D. Similar efforts are found in the much poorer China and India, so this is not purely a function of income. Figures 7.2a–f show the results of a more careful benchmarking and confirm the takeoff in total R&D expenditures of many of the comparator countries and that LAC has consistently underperformed. This is less severe in licensing, where, again, many of the comparator countries have maintained above-median licensing expenditures, thus complementing their R&D takeoffs. LAC's licensing has been below median and declining over time.

It is reasonable to ask whether the over-performance of some countries is not, in fact, due to well-functioning NIS that encourage the development of innovative firms, but rather indulgence in high-tech white elephants not justified by expected returns. The equation of returns to investments in innovation to the cost of investment should be the true benchmark. The existing evidence suggests that these investments are justified. Most of the estimates to date of the impact of R&D spending on TFP in selected U.S. firms and industries are astronomical—ranging from 30 to 120 percent—which, compared to a return on capital of 7 percent, implies that the United States should invest more by a multiple of around at least 4 (see Jones and Williams 1998 and the annex).

On the other hand, developing countries may invest less in R&D precisely because returns are lower. However, Lederman and Maloney (2003b) find rates of return that are higher for developing countries—principally in LAC and Asia—than those for the advanced countries (see figure 7.5

and the annex). Calculated at the estimated rate of return on physical capital, developing countries should be investing over twice what they presently do. At global interest rates of 7 percent, the number is closer to 10 times. Though estimates for licensing are slightly lower, the orders of magnitude are similar, suggesting that for a while increases in both R&D and licensing as shares of GDP should be seen as moves toward the optimum level, even for countries that have diverged so dramatically from the norm.

There are a range of explanations for why LAC underperforms, ranging from a short planning horizon brought on by persistent macro volatility, to defective credit markets, to a *rentier* mentality due to a long history of passive natural resource exploitation, to the intrinsic conservatism of the Catholic religion (although Ireland is apparently an exception). There has, however, been little systematic study of firm behavior to date. An aspect that probably merits more emphasis is simply that when Scandinavian, Israeli, and newly industrializing countries' (NIC) firms were being encouraged to compete and to learn how to innovate (see box 7.2), LAC compounded its weak educational and technical background by walling itself off from outside influence. Yet, as Chudnovsky (1999) notes, even for countries such as Argentina where education levels are quite high, opening to trade and competition has not been enough. Technological progress in the 1990s was largely due to ease of access to imported inputs and massive FDI, but innovative activity by nationals as measured by patents stagnated across the period while that by nonresidents doubled. It is likely that the weak supporting elements of the NIS did not provide fertile ground for innovative private firms to evolve.[7]

175

FIGURES 7.2A–F

Patenting, Licenses, and Royalties and R&D Benchmarking

Figure 7.2a: Patenting in Beta Countries

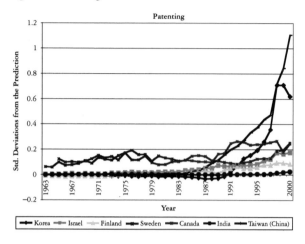

Figure 7.2b: Patenting in LAC

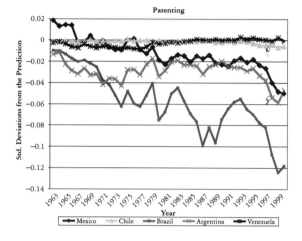

Figure 7.2c: Licenses and Royalties in Beta Countries

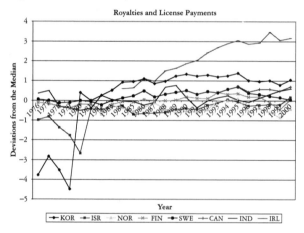

Figure 7.2d: Licences and Royalties in LAC

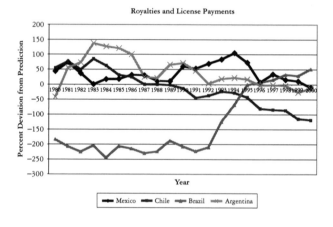

Figure 7.2e: R&D Expenditures in Beta Countries

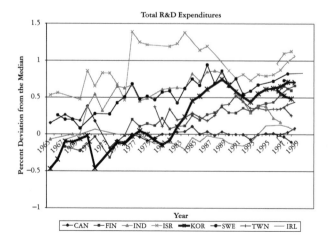

Figure 7.2f: R&D Expenditure in LAC

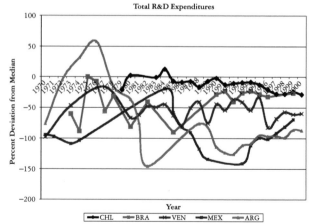

Source: Lederman and Maloney (2002b).

FIGURE 7.3

R&D Expenditure and R&D Financed by the Productive Sector: Taiwan (China), Korea, Finland, and Israel

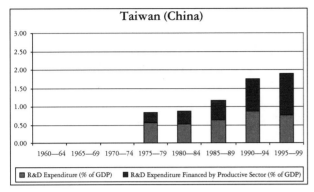

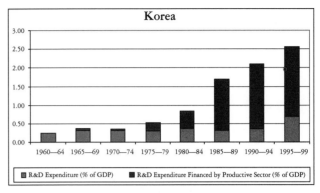

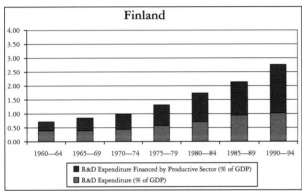

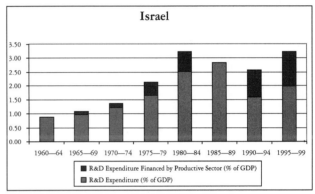

FIGURE 7.4

Predicted and Observed R&D/GDP

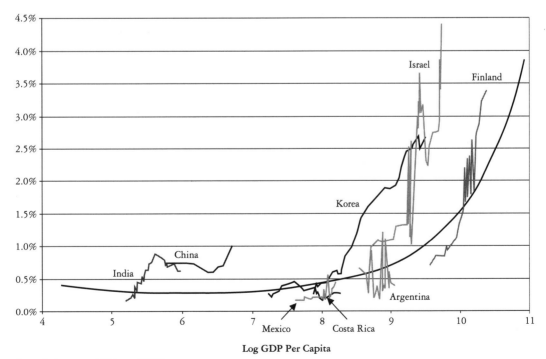

Source: Lederman and Maloney (2002).

FIGURE 7.5

Returns to R&D and Physical Capital

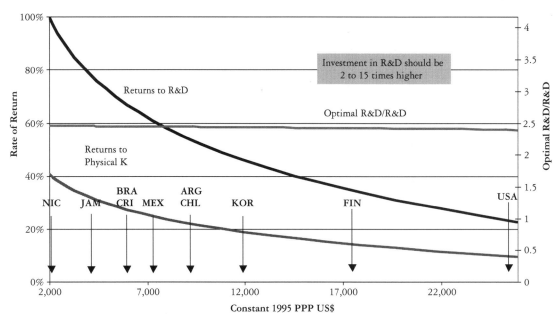

Source: Lederman and Maloney (2000b).

Before looking at this aspect in more detail, it is worth mentioning two variables not included as benchmarking the successful functioning of the NIS.

First, there is a temptation to use the share of "high tech" exports, defined by the Standard Industrial Trade Classification (SITC) categorization, as a proxy for entry into the high innovation leagues. As argued in *From Natural Resources to the Knowledge Economy*, the literature to date is not supportive of this view. Agricultural products show higher rates of TFP growth than manufacturing (Martin and Mitra 2001) globally, and recent econometric research suggests that countries with high natural resource exports grow *faster* partly because of higher TFP growth (Lederman and Maloney 2003c).[8] Hunt and Tybout (1998) argue that TFP growth in "lower tech" industries grew at roughly the same rates. More generally, any product can be produced either with a highly innovative process or not. Intuitively, maquila assembly of computers will require a far less sophisticated NIS than advances in forestry in Scandinavia or mining in Australia have, or, for that matter, advances in wine production, salmon harvesting, or genetic engineering (see boxes 7.3 and 7.11) would. What is a disincentive to growth is excessive specialization in any one product, and this partly explains Finland's desire to move into the telecommunications sector

and its present preoccupation with being excessively dependent on it. But an export structure that consists entirely of assembled microchips cannot be considered intrinsically preferable to a diversified basket of dynamic natural resource–based industries.

Second, information and communication technologies (ICT) comprise a particularly important element of infrastructure that is revolutionizing information flows and accelerating the dissemination of ideas with vast consequences for the organization of the economy. Furthermore, the sectors themselves—computer and peripherals, for example—have shown tremendous productivity growth. That said, ICT is to the NIS as nerves are to the brain—while vital, they are not to be confused with the cognitive organ itself and the mere fact that an economy has numerous Internet nodes does not in itself signify capacity for innovation. For the purpose of benchmarking, we include them as a vital input in the extended NIS.

Efficiency of Use of Resources and Collaboration

How a country uses its resources dedicated to R&D, whether public or private, offers additional insight into the functioning of the NIS. Simple indicators such as patents or articles per researcher or per R&D offer a good first cut and,

Jump-starting a National Innovation Effort: The NIS in Israel and Finland

Both Israel and Finland had per capita incomes similar to those of Mexico, Costa Rica, or Chile and below that of Argentina when they began their spectacular takeoff in R&D. In both countries, governments targeted a level of R&D and recognized that the entire NIS had to be examined to achieve this goal.

Israel established the Office of the Chief Scientist (OCS) in 1968 with the mandate to subsidize commercial R&D projects. Previously, government support had been restricted to national R&D labs, especially those dedicated to defense and agricultural sectors. Industrial R&D expenditure grew 14 percent a year for the next 20 years. The next key innovation was the Law for the Encouragement of Industrial R&D in 1985. The goal was to develop science-based, export-oriented industries. The centerpiece of the program was a system of financial incentives, particularly matching funds of up to 50 percent of R&D expenses in established companies and 66 percent for startups. These subsidies are thought to have "crowded in" an additional 41 cents of R&D spending for every dollar. Successful firms are required to repay royalties of 3 percent of annual sales up to the dollar-indexed amount of the grant. Paybacks now account for 32 percent of the OCS budget. R&D must be executed by the applicant firm itself, products developed must be manufactured in Israel, and the know-how acquired may not be transferred to third parties.

The magnate program, discussed in box 7.8, sought to integrate the fragmented industrial landscape and encourage cooperation among firms and between firms and Israel's world-class universities. The Incubators program sought to provide support for fledgling entrepreneurs and provide a variety of services not available from the market—startup capital, managerial skills, and so on. The government also signed a variety of bilateral agreements with foreign governments designed to encourage cooperation with foreign firms and cofinance R&D projects with foreign governments to foment research in both countries. Both the R&D subsidies and the Yozma venture capital start-up funds (see box 7.1) were designed to remedy failures in the capital markets.

Finland targeted a rise in R&D spending from 1.5 percent of GDP in 1983 to 2.7 by 2000. From the beginning, the government took a "systems" approach, viewing all elements of the NIS as essential to the R&D goal. A National Technology Agency, *Tekes*, was established in 1983 to finance applied and industrial R&D, especially through clusters. In 1987 the Science and Technology Policy Council (STPC) was expanded to include representatives from industry and the research community, its status raised within the government, and its mandate set to include ensuring collaborating across ministries. STPC reviews science and technology policy every three years, identifies main policy challenges facing the country, and makes recommendations for all actors. The deficient venture capital market was addressed partly by financial liberalization, and partly by *Tekes* policy of financing 30–40 percent of total R&D costs in product development projects it runs. These programs require cooperation and networking between business enterprises and research institutes and promote technology transfer and internationalization. Universities were allowed to collaborate with industry in a reversal of previous policy. See box 7.7 for discussion of consortia policy in East Asia.

to a great degree can be standardized across countries. However, more careful work requires controlling for a variety of factors affecting a country's propensity to structure. For example, the individual components of the manufacturing processes are much more heavily patented than those of other industries. Furthermore, countries that trade with the United States are more likely to patent there (see, for example, Trajtenberg 2001).

Table 7.2 reports estimates of the determinants of patenting activity in the United States (Bosch-Mossi, Lederman, and Maloney 2003). As expected, the greater the R&D effort, the higher the trade volume with the United States; and the lower the natural resource component of exports, the higher the level of patenting. Interacting the R&D variable with a LAC dummy yields a strong negative coefficient suggesting that LAC underperforms in converting innovative resources

BOX 7.3

Build a Better Mouse and the World Will Beat a Path to Your Door (or Is Playing God a Low-Tech Activity?)

In 1988, Scientists at Harvard's medical school patented a mouse genetically altered to develop cancer. The "Onconomouse" is now used throughout the world for cancer research and enjoys patent protection in the United States, Japan, and several European countries. The patents give Harvard University exclusive rights to create the mice and charge licensing fees.

In December 2002, the Canadian supreme court ruled that higher life forms cannot be patented and rejected Harvard's application, although it would permit patenting the process by which the mouse is altered. Canadian law does permit the patenting of bacteria, single-celled organisms, plants, and agricultural crops. The issue is hotly debated, with religious groups praising the decision on ethical grounds and others agreeing with the court that Harvard was not really inventing the mouse, only tinkering with it. Nonetheless, industry observers argue that the inability to receive life-form patents could create a chilling effect on scientists doing research in Canada, especially since for many emerging companies, patent royalties are their only source of income. There are 403 registered biotechnology companies in Canada with a total of 58,000 employees and $US 3.21 billion in annual revenue (*Wall Street Journal*, December 6, 2002, p. B6).

All biotech products, including the Onconomouse, are classified under agriculture in the SITC categories and hence would not count as "high-tech" exports.

into actual innovation. Figure 7.6 presents graphically the estimates of the interactive parameter for a variety of countries of the region. What is immediately apparent is that LAC, with the exception of Costa Rica and Venezuela, is among the worst performers, with its coefficient roughly 5 percent below that of the OECD and far below that for Korea, Finland, or Israel. That is, *not only does LAC underinvest in R&D, but it uses it inefficiently*.

The next rows of table 7.2 pursue the possible causes of this underperformance. Sachs' measure of openness and general market functioning does show up as a significant determinant of efficiency in many specifications as does years of

education. But neither these variables nor ICT infrastructure knocks out the LAC dummy. What does is either a measure of the quality of research institutions or a measure of collaboration between the private sector and universities taken from the Global Competitiveness Report. In the complete specification, it is the quality of research institutions that drives the LAC dummy. These factors are the focus of the next sections.

University/Research Center/Firm Linkages: The Core of the NIS

Critical to the development and continuation of the R&D capacity of firms in the high-performance countries has been the close interaction of government agencies and universities. As chapter 6 showed, LAC has a very large presence of both, executing the bulk of the R&D budget. A partial explanation for this pattern is found in low private sector investment and in the existence of state-owned public agencies in the postwar period that developed R&D capacity in order to better exploit the available natural resources and to jumpstart industries to supply local demand. For less clear reasons, universities play the dominant role in the region in both government funding for innovation and attracting most of the skilled researchers.

There may be nothing intrinsically wrong with a high share of the public sector or university sector in the execution of R&D. The previous section stressed the importance of the productive sector making an increasing effort over time. But given the extraordinarily high rates of return to R&D, it would seem perverse to view a strong complementary public sector effort, particularly in the area of basic science, as somehow bad.[9] However, consistent with the regression results above, the literature on Brazil, Mexico, Chile, and Argentina referred to below stresses lack of coordination among public sector institutions and the private sector as one of the major obstacles to improving their science and technology capacities.

LAC has few measures with which to benchmark coordination. One is simply to "follow the money." In Mexico, for example, there is virtually no cross-financing: Only 20 percent of the private sector's R&D expenses are financed outside, and mostly by foreigners. One hundred percent of the governments' spending is self-financed. And in the higher education sector only 7.8 percent is financed by the private sector. From this Bazdresch (2002) concludes that the three sectors function more or less autarkically. In effect, Mexico,

TABLE 7.2

Determinants of Patenting in the United States

Observations	512	512	512	512	419	419
Countries	53	53	53	53	50	50
ln (Average Patents 1963–64)	0.37 ***	0.25 ***	0.32 ***	0.27 ***	0.37 ***	0.29 ***
ln (R&D Expenditure)	0.50 ***	0.24 ***	0.36 ***	0.33 ***	0.49 ***	0.24 ***
ln (Ustrade)	0.32 ***	0.31 ***	0.29 ***	0.36 ***	0.17 ***	0.22 ***
Natural Resources	−0.03 **	−0.07 ***	−0.08 ***	−0.10 ***	−0.05 ***	−0.10 ***
LAC*ln (R&D)	−0.05 ***	0.00	−0.01	−0.02 ***	−0.02 ***	0.00
Openness*ln (R&D)	0.02 **	0.02 *	0.01	0.00	0.01	0.00
ln (Quality)*ln (R&D)		0.17 ***				0.10 ***
ln (Collaboration)*ln (R&D)			0.11 ***			−0.03
ln (years of Education)*ln (R&D)				0.10 ***		0.08 ***
ICT × ln (R&D)					0.01 ***	0.00
Time Trend	0.03 ***	0.03 **	0.03	−0.01	−0.07 ***	−0.03 *
Pseudo R-squared	0.19	0.20	0.20	0.21	0.23	0.26

× implies an interactive term between two variables.
* indicates significance at the 10 percent level.
** indicates significance at the 5 percent level.
*** indicates significance at the 1 percent level.
Negative binomial estimates, presample mean period for fixed effects; control 1963–64; see annex for details.
Source: Bosch, Lederman, and Maloney (2002).

FIGURE 7.6

Inefficiency of LAC Countries in Patenting in the United States

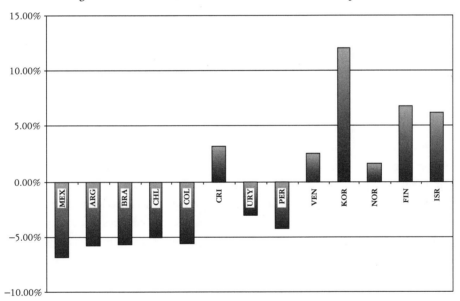

Interactive Effects of LAC Countries with R&D Expenditures and People in a
Negative Binomial Estimation of Patents on R&D Variables Compared to the OECD

Source: Bosch, Lederman, and Maloney (2000).

like Latin America more generally, systematically set up the institutions for innovation without institutionalizing an innovation system. Ensuring the effective interaction of the available innovation-related factors poses LAC's second great challenge after remedying the gaps in its stock of innovation-related factors.

Government-Financed Research Institutes

As chapter 6 suggests, these institutes enjoy a disproportionate share of the national research budgets. The logic has tended to be that fledgling industries often lack the in-house capability to undertake the necessary research. Alternatively, the same problems of appropriability and lumpiness suggest that industry-level institutions can address an important market failure. However, as Rosenberg (2000) argues, in practice, government institutions established for these purposes may have limited impact for two reasons. First, in general, government researchers have relatively little understanding of the specific needs of industry and hence the necessary feedback is absent. Second, it is difficult to provide researchers as public institutes with strong incentives to be responsive to industrial needs. In the LAC region, the latter factor emerges as especially critical, compounded by the competition of other non-innovation-related agendas.

The development of think tanks during the import substitution period, in which competition was stymied and outward orientation discouraged, led to inward looking and bureaucratized institutions with little connection with the private sector. In Mexico (Bazdresch 2002), the roughly 150 Public Centers of Investigation are dependent on the secretariat to which they belong and frequently oppose any efforts of the secretariat to contract firms or outside universities that might be more qualified than they are to investigate a particular question. They thus often monopolize the possible incentive that government procurement can have. Further, the lack of competition has had the usual depressing effects on quality and created obvious disincentives to work with other institutions that might be potential rivals. Proposed reform laws foresee greater autonomy for the centers and further offer the possibility that research funds will be allocated by competition and not automatically to the particular center of investigation. For unclear reasons, the incentives in the Caribbean have led to vital regional agencies, such as the Caribbean Tourism Organization, to be relatively slow in monitoring basic trends, compiling and disseminating data for reference and analysis, or collaborating with other agencies working in what remains a critical sector in the region.

But the existence of national agendas competing with that of jump-starting a dynamic private sector has also taken a toll. In Brazil, Dahlman and Fischtak (1993) attribute the low interaction with the private sector to a preoccupation with foreign exchange generation in the 1980s, combined with weak incentives to adapt to the changing needs of the private sector over time. With the exception of the *Instituto de Pesquisas Tecnologicas* (IPT) in São Paolo, the *Centro Tecno-*

logico da Aeronautica, and the *Empresa Brasileira de Pesquisa Agropecuaria* (EMBRAPA), they conclude that most of the 18 primary public research institutes have had limited impact, precisely because of their limited contact with industry. A survey of sources of technology found that less that 2.5, 5.1, and 3.9 percent of product designs, tool designs, and manufacturing processes, respectively, originated in research institutes (Braga and Matesco 1989). Again, benchmarking with comparable numbers is difficult. OECD numbers on "Innovative Manufacturing Enterprises That Use Public Laboratories as an Information Source in Innovation" are also somewhat low, with the maximum in Ireland at 7.4 percent. Such comparisons are rendered dubious by critical definitional issues—such as what is considered an "innovative firm." Further, though the data are not available, in Korea, Japan, or Taiwan (China), where public laboratories are credited with providing the big push toward the knowledge frontier, the number would presumably be much higher.

Chudnovsky (1999) finds a similar distortion of mission in Argentina, where the National Atomic Energy Commission absorbs substantial government R&D resources while the National Institute of Industrial Technology (INTI) receives less than 5 percent of the budget despite the manufacturing sector generating 25 percent of GDP. Lack of coordination among the programs of different organizations, lack of precise objectives and evaluation objectives, and lack of long-run projects prevent effective technological transfer and innovation to critical productive sectors.

Universities

The university as a collection of scientists, interacting with the private sector, emerges as a critical element in stories of the relative success or failure of the industrial countries (see box 7.4). This is also true historically in Latin America, and universities claim a large share of the region's overall research budgets (see figure 7.7) [10]

There are several channels through which universities enrich the innovation network. First, the production of tertiary-educated workers is the lifeblood of the NIS and perhaps its most important function. Interviews with high-tech companies in Costa Rica highlight the issue of generation of quality human capital in a country as an order of magnitude more important than other measures discussed in

BOX 7.4

What Is a College Education For?

The integration of universities with industry emerges as a central explanation of the disparate performance of U.S. and U.K. economies. To quote Nelson and Wright (1996):

> As with education more generally, what is important is not the sheer number of students or the quantity of their training, but the effectiveness with which that training is integrated into the process of improving the technology of operating firms. In interwar America that coordination was advanced to a high state of refinement, as the curricula of educational institutions came to be closely adapted to the requirements of the "positions" that graduates would be taking; and vice versa ... in 1919, for example MIT launched its Cooperative Course in electrical engineering, a program that divided the students' time between courses at the Institute and at General Electric, which hired half of the students after graduation. The program was later joined by ATT & Bell Labs, Western Electric, and other firms. Whatever the merits of ... reservations about the close links between universities and private firms, what [emerged] is an effective network of training

and utilization operating efficiently at a national level because it was self-contained, internalizing the resource base and market demands of the national economy. (p. 147)

This can be compared to Lazonik's (1994) diagnosis of the very different role of U.K. universities, a central factor in explaining the failure of British enterprises to take advantage of the technological and market opportunities of the second industrial revolution:

> Lacking industrial roots, the aristocracy who controlled these elite institutions during the era of the second industrial revolution had no need for an educational system that developed technologists. They valued the study of science as a branch of sophisticated knowledge but had no interest in its application to industry. Indeed, the British elite positively resisted the notion that a concern with technology had any place in an aristocratic education. They wanted education to set them apart from the lower classes. (p. 170)

FIGURE 7.7

Allocation of R&D Resources

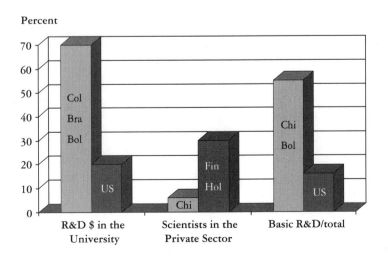

Source: Hansen, Agapitova, Holm-Nielsen, Vukmirovic (2002).

chapter 6—IPRs, R&D incentives, and so forth. Second, as discussed earlier, universities are better suited to carrying out larger, long-term, less immediately applicable research. Third, they are often more likely to maintain contacts with research centers in industrial countries and hence perform the search for new technologies. In all cases, the degree to which they remedy the underlying market failures is dependent on the tightness of the links to the private sector—that is, the degree to which they help solve problems, train students, or identify foreign knowledge that is relevant to the production process in some way.

Today, the higher education sector plays the dominant role in the region in both government funding for innovation and providing the most skilled researchers. As the previous chapter suggests, at least 50 percent of total R&D expenditures in Brazil, Bolivia, Chile, and Colombia is through the universities. Further, generally, most researchers are found in the universities. In Chile, for example, two of every three R&D professionals are found in academia, and only 6 percent are in private enterprises. By contrast, in more industrial countries such as Finland and the Netherlands, a third or more of scientists and engineers are found in firms (Brunner 2001).

The high concentration of R&D in the universities has an impact on the nature of the research done. Hansen and others

(2002) argue that this high fraction of universities in total R&D effort translates into a heavy emphasis on basic research, which accounts for approximately 60 percent of total R&D spending in Chile and 50 percent in Bolivia. In the United States, where higher education amounts to only 15 percent of total R&D expenditure, basic research accounts for approximately 16 percent of total R&D spending (figure 7.7). The appropriateness of this mix remains debated. Pavitt (2001), for instance, argues that if, in fact, small countries could simply take the basic research of the advanced countries, the extraordinary efforts in basic research in Scandinavia, or even Korea and Taiwan (China) would appear irrational. Not so, however, when the importance of basic research in training human capital and in identifying and facilitating the absorption of foreign technologies is acknowledged. In general, basic research is not as easily communicated across countries as often assumed and developing countries cannot confine themselves to simply adapting shelf technologies.

Nonetheless, a measure of the value of this nonapplied research to the economy can be captured by the degree of interaction with firms. Figure 7.8 suggests that the perception of entrepreneurs of the degree of collaboration is far below that in other parts of the region and this is borne out by country and industry studies as well. For example,

FIGURE 7.8

Quality of Scientific Research Institutions and University Industry Research Collaboration

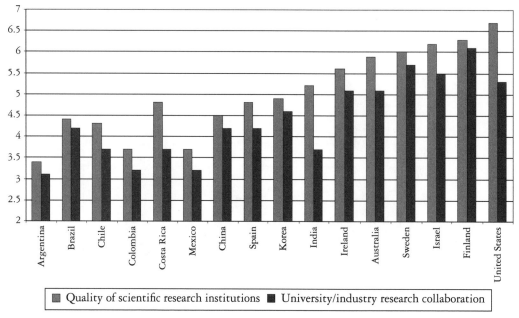

Legend: ■ Quality of scientific research institutions   ■ University/industry research collaboration

Source: Based on World Economic Forum (2001/02).

TABLE 7.3

Tentative Benchmarks of Interaction of Higher Education (HE) and Public Laboratories (PL) with Firms

	FINLAND	GERMANY	IRELAND	SWEDEN	UK
Innovative manufacturing firms that cooperate with HE	47.3	10.4	13.8	26.1	—
Innovative manufacturing firms that cooperate with PL	38.0	13.6	6.3	16.3	—
Innovative manufacturing firms that use HE as information source	6.9	6.7	5.0	4.5	3.9
Innovative manufacturing firms that use PL as information source	5.3	2.9	7.4	—	1.9

—. Not available.
Source: OECD (2002a).

in Finland, at least 40 percent of firms have collaborative arrangements with universities (Brunner 2001 and table 7.3), and as Blomström, Kokko, and Sjöholm (2002) document, these interactions have been vital to the continued dynamism of both the high-tech and more traditional forest industries. Brunner notes that in Chile, 32 percent of firms acknowledge benefiting from innovations from universities and 25 percent actually have signed contracts. Nonetheless, surveyed firms did not report that external interactions were crucial to the firm and most new ideas came from within. In a similar vein, in his study of Avimex, a veterinary pharmaceutical company in Mexico, Mayer (2002) notes that despite a high 10–15 percent of sales spent on R&D and world-class innovations in joint projects with U.S. research institutes, the major disadvantage Avimex and Mexican firms in general face is the lack of research institutions available for joint research projects.

There are success stories of university–private sector collaboration. Rodriguez-Clare (2003) argues that the most critical element in the development of the software industry in Costa Rica was the strength and dynamism of the *Universidad de Costa Rica* and the *Instituto Tecnológico de Costa Rica*, which have pushed the country to the top of Latin America in the perceived quality of scientific research institutions and an "impact index" of its publications. This has translated, for instance, into the setting up of a center for software development and semiconductor design by Intel. The Chilean fruit sector provides another example of the importance of universities to the diffusion of technology and the development of innovations appropriate to local conditions. However, a generalized picture is one of monasteries, where the most talented of the scientific brotherhood are cloistered away from the applied innovation needs of the economy.

There are a number of factors—along the themes of poor design and faulty incentives—responsible for the dearth of effective linkages and collaboration between scientific insti-

tutions and the private sector in LAC. These are summarized below.

- *Real or perceived low quality of scientific institutions.* Surveys suggest that, in the LAC Region, the private sector's opinion of the quality of scientific institutions is not very high, with the exception of Costa Rica—and this seems highly correlated with the level of interaction (figure 7.6) and explains why collaboration disappears as a critical variable in the patent regressions above when quality is included. More concretely, common measures such as academic publications, or patents per university researcher, can offer an indication of the quality of the university.

- *Lack of incentives for universities to link and address private sector knowledge needs.* The incentives within the universities are generally biased away from collaboration with business.

- *University culture.* Arguably in universities there is a more "liberal arts" as opposed to a "technical" culture, with deep historical roots that resonate with Lazonik's analysis about the inappropriateness of the U.K. system (see also Maloney 2002). Agapitova and Holm-Nielsen (2002) argue that, overall, the university mentality in Chile is not geared to solving problems on a business time scale, and Mullin (2001) argues that overall academic interests tend to be narrow and unapplied. The experience of Mexico suggests that the inward orientation of academia to a large extent follows from the rules guiding promotion, which put extensive stress on academic performance that is of little relevance to society at large. As the exception that appears to prove the rule, observers of Costa Rica's two excellent technical schools stress not so much incentives but the "foundational impulse"—a desire to be patterned more on the Massachusetts Institute of Technology (MIT) or other technical schools of excellence than on those with a liberal arts bias.

- *Intellectual property rights.* Beyond this bias, a rich literature discusses how the incentives in academia—intrinsic, reputation, and financial—are distinct from those in industry, and hence there is no guarantee that the two sets of organizations will interact productively. Globally, the incentive to innovate and then contribute to bringing products to market has been a source of debate (see box 7.5). The overall allocation of rights to the benefits of innovation, the faulty incentive regime to appropriate the benefits of public-financed R&D that exists in LAC countries, does not favor cooperation. (A U.S. survey finds that at least 71 percent of the inventions require further involvement by the academic researcher if they are to be successfully commercialized. Forty-eight percent of the ideas are in proof-of-concept stage, 29 percent have a prototype available on a lab scale, and manufacturing feasibility is known for only 8 percent.) (See Goldfarb, Henrekson, and Rosenberg 2001.) Although the numbers for Latin America are likely to be different, there is no reason to believe that commercialization of inventions will require less involvement of the researchers, and the incentives for that are lacking in LAC. Because researchers cannot appropriate the benefits of innovation, they have little incentive to undertake innovations and link with the private sector. Various developed countries allow ownership rights to government-funded R&D and in some instances, such as in the United States and Japan, explicitly in the national patent laws (see box 7.5 and table 7.4). The allocation of property can also influence whether the researcher stays affiliated with a university or must leave to pursue the commercialization of the product.

Arocena and Sutz (2001) argue that these reforms may be less germane to the Latin American case. High costs of patenting abroad, and low enforcement of patenting domestically, means a focus on fostering university-firm relations less intermediated by patents. In fact, this implies that direct collaboration between the two sectors must be even better than in the industrialized countries.

- *Bureaucratic disincentives.* In the United States universities and government think tanks have established technology transfer offices (TTOs) that appear to have

BOX 7.5

Did the Bayh-Dole Act Increase the Commercialization of Publicly Funded Research?

From 1980 to 1984, a series of laws, the most famous being the Bayh-Dole act, allowed universities to patent the results of federally funded research. The main argument for the act is that intellectual property rights would help accelerate the commercial exploitation of labs and universities' discoveries because of the additional investments needed to turn university and laboratory R&D into commercially viable products for the marketplace.

Mowery (1999) and Mowery and Ziedonis (2002) argue that the Bayh-Dole Act did not stimulate university patenting and licensing—the trend had already begun before the act. Other factors, such as the increase in the number of Technology Transfer Offices, stimulated universities to patent more—as did the emergence of the biotech and software fields. Henderson, Jaffe, and Trajtenberg (1998) found that the explosive growth of patents was probably supported by the legal changes but that after the mid-1980s there was a decline in the quality of the patents as measured by citations.

Jaffe and Lerner (2001) examined the behavior and quality of patenting by U.S. Department of Energy laboratories in reaction to both Bayh-Dole and the earlier Stevenson-Wydler Act (1980), which specifically encouraged the commercialization of their research. They found that, until 1980, national labs had lagged behind universities in terms of patents per R&D dollar. But post-1980, national labs reached parity with universities in patenting activity. The citation rates for national laboratories either rose or remained constant.

had important impacts on stimulating collaboration. Universities also often have liberal policies on faculty leaves of absence and consulting privileges that allow faculty members to pursue commercial opportunities while keeping their position at the university intact. The roots of Sweden's lower rate of university spillovers are found in the absence of such policies (Goldfarb, Henrekson, and Rosenberg 2001).

In Latin America, the barriers are much more mundane. Mayer (2002) and Brunner (2001) argue that, in Mexico and Chile, bureaucratic rigidities make it

TABLE 7.4

Guidelines for Sharing Royalties from IPRs

SHARE OF ROYALTIES

	APPLY TO	INVENTOR	LABORATORY/ DEPARTMENT	INSTITUTION	NO SHARING
Australia	Universities	33%	33%	33%	
Austria	General Practice				100% to owner
Belgium	Flemish Universities	10 to 30%	50%	20 to 30%	
Canada	Federal Research	35% by law	variable	variable	
France	Public Labs	25%	25%	50%	
Germany	Max Planck and HGF Centres	33%	33%	33%	
Hungary		0%	undetermined	up to 100%	
Israel	Hebrew University	33%	33%	33%	
	Weizmann Institute	40%	0%	60%	
Japan	Universities				100% to owner
Korea	KIST Institute	up to 60%	0%	40%	
Netherlands	Public Labs				100% to owner
Poland			no general rule		
United Kingdom	BBRCs [CK]		Sharing encouraged by institute guidelines		
United States	Universities		Sharing required by law		
	Stanford	33%	33%	33%	
LAC					
Chile	General Practice	No general rule, researcher <30%			
Mexico	Public Labs				100% to owner

Source: Table from OECD (2002a) updated by authors.

TABLE 7.5

Policies for Improving Academic/Private Sector Collaboration

INTERACTION MODES	CONSTRAINTS FACED	POLICY INSTRUMENTS	EFFECTIVENESS OF INSTRUMENTS/CAVEATS
Licensing	Universities not allowed to "own" research	Modify IPR law	May reduce incentives for basic research?
Consulting	Culture gap between universities and firms Bureaucratic barriers Weak infrastructure	Improve contractual certainty (IPRs) Reduce public funding to encourage private contracts Decentralize systems and offer greater autonomy Improve accounting systems to allow for contracts	May reduce incentives for basic research? May "corporatize" academic collegiality? May mistakenly patent basic research?
Collaborative	Information asymmetries Coordination failures Agglomeration externalities	Incubators Technoparks Science parks Consortia Cluster policy	May turn into subsidized real estate ventures May lapse into old Industrial Policy Distract from necessary horizontal measures

difficult to write contracts and get access to the use of laboratories and equipment from the university. Arocena and Sutz (2001) cite the inadequacy of the university accounting systems as slow, heavy, and unsuitable for handling resources and contracts with the private sector rapidly. Numerous universities have generated pseudo-TTOs although these tend to be passive, waiting for the private sector to discover relevant university research rather than "selling" it.

Policies to Improve Collaboration

Aside from the necessary horizontal policies related to education, IPRs, and internal incentives within government agencies, and those that are essential elements of the extended NIS-ICT-well-functioning credit markets, and outward trade and investment orientation, governments have experimented with a variety of policy measures to actively improve the interactions among elements of the NIS (table 7.5).

187

Industry Clusters: Subsystems of the NIS

The best-known network concept is that of clusters that, in the present context, can be seen as subsystems of the NIS. Well-known examples in the United States are Silicon Valley and Boston's Route 128 (IT and biotechnology), greater Seattle (software and aircraft), and North Carolina's Research Triangle (electronics, pharmaceuticals, biotechnology). Similar examples can be found in Sweden and Finland (forestry), and Australia (mining). Recent studies of the LAC Region have identified emerging innovation clusters of differing varieties and size in Argentina, Brazil, Costa Rica, Cuba, Peru, and Mexico—although none that could be considered "mature" (Bortagaray and Tiffin 2000). As in innovation more generally, the high potential sectors may be in high technology—related activities, but may as well be in fruits, vegetables, tourism, wine, and so forth as well as manufacturing.

The rationales for cluster formation are the same market failures discussed in chapter 6.

- Clustering may further ensure that technological spillovers are, in fact, reaped by other related firms through greater flows of relevant information. Clustering encourages nonmarket transactions, which reduce transaction costs and permit a greater level of transparency and trust, which is important in managing the appropriability problems of knowledge. The punitive consequences of free riding are immediate, and this lowers the transaction costs of interaction, which translates into efficiency gains for all.
- Tacit knowledge is more easily diffused through offering the possibility to be able to observe firsthand and share its application and the learning-by-doing process. Access to skilled labor, the principal vector of tacit knowledge, is automatically made easier for firms because labor itself chooses to locate in areas where several employment options exist, lowering job search costs arising from acquiring, processing, and acting on information about relevant jobs. Labor mobility then becomes the key to building the dynamism of technology clusters.
- Indivisibililities of all kinds justify coordination among firms. Clearly, technology's lumpiness and riskiness dictates cooperation as discussed earlier, but

the issue is broader. New technology generation is highly capital intensive, and having producers of machinery intensively interface with users increases the chances of a "better fit." Similarly, owners of specialized equipment may want to spread out the costs of new investments by renting it out to other firms. The same applies to labor, which also becomes highly specialized. In fact, co-specialization of labor via joint training programs is a common feature of clusters attempting the transition into the innovative stages. Another example is information and communication technologies, where innovative clusters rely on timely market intelligence and efficient logistics management to ensure on-time delivery and tracking to far-flung markets through high-quality facilities. When the provision of infrastructure entails high fixed costs, significant savings per user can be obtained when consumption of these infrastructure services is spread out over many firms in one place. Furthermore, financing of R&D by suppliers of risk capital is extremely risky, and traditional banking instruments are unable to bear this risk because they are ill equipped to value the collateral at the early stages—often an idea in the heads of researchers. Venture capitalists specialize in this and concentrate near high-tech businesses because proximity to these intangible assets is the best way to evaluate quality.

The discussion has thus far focused largely on innovation clusters as opposed to the more traditional notion of backward and forward linkages often stressed. As *From Natural Resources to the Knowledge Economy* stressed, in an age of rapidly decreased transport costs and the fragmentation of global production, the latter focus is perhaps less central than previously and, to the degree that it creates industrial policy working against a country's comparative advantage, counterproductive.

That said, a concern with improving conventional interactions among firms and sectors can be seen as a common strategy of promoting industry dynamism. Guasch (2002) identifies several stages of cluster evolution:

- *Diagnosis phase.* Identification and elimination of problems and bottlenecks.

- *Economies-of-scale phase.* Facilitating coordination to capture economies of scale, transportation, marketing, licensing, commercialization, purchasing, and accessing markets.
- *Spillover phase.* Capturing knowledge spillover effects and disseminating current knowledge within the supply chain—forward, backward, and lateral linkages.
- *Knowledge creation phase.* Joint learning and innovation.

The relatively quick and easy-to-secure benefits of the diagnosis and economies-of-scale phases are persuading some LAC governments to promote cluster development focusing primarily on three broad policy areas: export promotion and attraction of inward investment, value chain integration, and networking/SME policy. However, few clusters reach or are intended to reach the knowledge creation phase (Bortagaray and Tiffin 2000). This raises the concern that a lack of attention to the innovation dimension will lead to an inability brought on by the initial stages. As an example, Lee and Lim (2001), among others, argue that countries may initially compete in derivative industries on the basis of low cost, but

over the long run they will need to develop an innovative capacity that will allow further product differentiation, along with quality and productivity increases. Korea, they argue, lost its original edge in computers precisely because it rested too long on the cost advantage and simple turnkey plants. Taiwan (China), on the other hand, reverse-engineered the IBM AT, assigned the component parts to individual firms for local production, and not only had a functioning clone within one year but had "learned" enough as a country to innovate at the frontier of laptops within five years (Mathews 2001). The lesson is that neither trade opening nor a focus on the first two phases of cluster formation unaccompanied by an aggressive technology program will lead to sustainable growth.

One way to benchmark the success of a clustering effort is to measure the development of "innovation revealed comparative advantage" (IRCA), calculated as the flow of patents in industry k in country j over total new patents in country j relative to the same ratio for the world as a whole. A value over 1 suggests that a country has a comparative advantage in innovation in that industry. Figure 7.9 looks at two prominent experiences in the region. The first is the aircraft and parts industry dominated by Embraer in Brazil. Though a

FIGURE 7.9

Brazil and Mexico: IRCA in Aircraft and Computing Equipment

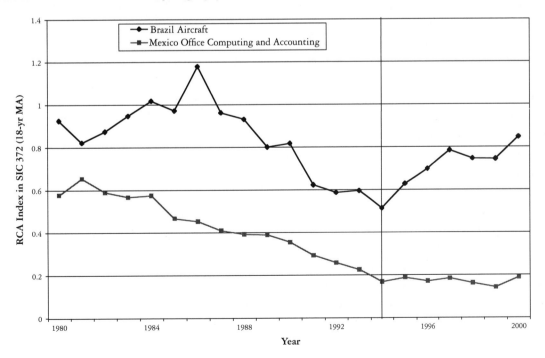

strong competitor in the global market, the high import content of the aircraft raises some concern about whether, in fact, the industry has the innovative potential to continue as a dynamic player. The IRCA since privatization in 1994 suggests a slow and steady trend toward 1, which suggests that it does have the potential to remain a dynamic sector over time. Somewhat more worrisome is the computing sector in Mexico, which, despite the presence of IBM and HP for over 20 years, does not and will not have IRCA in the near future. This raises the question about whether Mexico really has the capacity to be a participant in the sector over the long run.

Policies to Foment Interfirm Collaboration in Innovation

Approaches to encouraging interfirm collaboration in innovation range from the surgical to the promethean. Feser (2002) argues for an approach that seeks to "leverage" innovative synergies among existing or emerging businesses rather than seeking to initiate particular clusters. Leveraging implies using the most important insights of the cluster literature—the notions of cooperative competition and collective efficiency, supported by standard policy analytical tools (public goods and market failure) to strengthen innovative synergies. This appears to have been a large part of Finland's (box 7.6) approach—ensuring that all related firms took advantage of possible spillovers. This may or may not imply a regional dimension, but it allows key formal and informal linkages to occur at all spatial scales and between different kinds of firms.

Encouraging firms to collaborate in innovation has also characterized the Finnish and Asian approaches—and for reasons that are perhaps even more appropriate in the developing-country context. Resolving one market's failures can often exacerbate another. Strengthening intellectual property rights reduces the non-appropriability problem but can lead to sub-optimal diffusion of new innovations since the owner of a patent charges more than the almost-zero diffusion cost. Socially optimal innovation is thus at odds with socially optimal diffusion. Research consortia, in theory, internalize the externalities and solve both problems. They may also help alleviate the problem of costly patenting and weak enforcement in developing countries discussed earlier, which make market intermediation of ideas so expensive. In theory, consortia share risks, the fixed costs, benefit from scale

BOX 7.6

The Cluster Approach of Finnish R&D Policy

With limited domestic resources for R&D in Finland, it was imperative that the available public funds were used efficiently—so the government sought to ensure that all possible spillovers would occur. The degree to which potential spillovers are realized depends on the intensity of contacts between innovators and related firms, as well as the ability of related firms to absorb the potential knowledge externalities—factors that led to a "cluster" focus in Finnish R&D policy. By subsidizing R&D in industries and companies that belong to major clusters—where input and output linkages are strong—it was possible to concentrate resources in sectors where the likelihood of spillovers is relatively high while at the same time addressing the non-appropriability issue in both invention and diffusion. Furthermore, by explicitly including small and medium-size firms in publicly funded R&D projects, which are often dominated by large MNCs such as Nokia, it was also possible to strengthen the absorptive capacity of these firms and achieve a faster rate of technology diffusion. Thus, the basic idea was to support the development of the cluster as a whole rather than supporting individual companies and "improving integration, collaboration, and division of labor within the whole research system." This last emphasis is important since the intense focus of the Finnish government on improving the functioning of the NIS, especially through eliminating bottlenecks caused by shortages of skilled workers and venture capital, suggests that necessary horizontal policies were not sidelined by the cluster approach.

In this sense, Finnish cluster policy, as with Israeli policy, attempted a kind of "informed neutrality." The long-run goal is to ensure a well-functioning NIS that will allow the emergence of new sectors while at the same time boosting those sectors in which the country clearly has comparative advantage.

Source: Blomström, Kokko, and Sjöholm (2002).

economies, and avoid duplication. But where firms differ in abilities or capacity, they have also importantly served as vehicles for one partner to upgrade by internalizing others' learning (see box 7.7).

BOX 7.7
Research Consortia in Japan: Did They Work?

Japan's experience with cooperative R&D gained attention among close follower countries, such as Korea and Taiwan (China), and more recently among academics seeking to evaluate their impact. The most celebrated example was the VLSI (Very Large-Scale Integrated Circuit) project that involved all of the major Japanese semiconductor manufacturers, led to a worldwide leadership in the field afterwards, and arguably spurred the U.S. formation of the analogous SEMATECH and the European EURECA and ESPRIT projects.

The logic varied among different types of consortia. "Technological Research Consortia," introduced in Japan in 1961 and broadly patterned on British research associations, were a reaction to the postwar trade liberalization and were intended to promote R&D as a means of increasing the productivity of Japanese industries. Others have included petroleum-alternative energy development projects (the Sunshine Project), energy conservation initiatives (the Moonlight project), and large-scale projects that the private sector could not have initiated.

Government subsidies depended on the mission of each consortium. The original TRCs benefited from tax benefits, accelerated or instant depreciation of fixed R&D assets, and discounts of R&D-related property. VLSI was subsidized 20 percent, the Sunshine and Moonlight projects 100 percent, and the Key Technology Development project 70 percent. The most active companies in various consortia between 1959 and 1992 have been household names such as Hitachi, Toshiba, and Mitsubishi. Overall, Japanese government spending has been low by U.S. standards. In a study of the impact of consortia on patenting, Branstetter

and Sakakibara (2002) found that what appeared more important than the level of financing by the government was the organization of the consortium and, in particular, whether it was more oriented to basic research.

Surveys of participants found the most important benefit to be gaining access to complementary knowledge, a finding similar to those from Germany, and one of the least important to be the sharing of fixed costs often emphasized in the literature. Firms also benefited moderately from researcher training, a quicker pace of R&D development, and an increased awareness of R&D in general. In a global market where product cycles grow shorter over time, this is potentially important.

Although studies of the U.S. semiconductor consortium have yielded mixed results, Branstetter and Sakakibara (1998) and Sakakibara (2001) suggest that the legendary Japanese consortia at least partly deserve their fame: participation in a consortium led to a 2–9 percent increase in R&D, and patenting per R&D dollar of between 4 and 8 percent, amounts which, in the aggregate, can be substantial. In addition Sakakibara (2001) finds that a greater diversity of knowledge in the consortium leads to higher R&D spending, a conclusion also found for the United States.

Somewhat counterintuitively overall, however Sakakibara (1997) finds that firms did not find the consortia critical to their competitive position. It is doubtful that this finding would hold up in Taiwan (China), or even Korea, where the consortia appear to have served a nurturing role in creating a taste for research and defining a mission for sectors that have since become dominant.

The literature is ambiguous on what the actual impact of research consortia on R&D should be. If the consortium members compete in the same output market, increased variety or quality of competition may actually lead to lower returns and R&D, a problem presumably ameliorated by an aggressive export strategy. On the other hand, as Cohen and Levinthal (1989) argued, if the firm's ability to appropriate spillovers is a function of the amount of R&D, then participation in consortia may lead to higher total R&D.

Evaluations of consortia have been few and preliminary (see box 7.7).

Despite the obvious benefits of collaboration, numerous authors note the apparent difficulty of initiating it, perhaps because, in practice, some firm or agent needs to bear the coordination costs and this provides a role for government intervention. Intel in Costa Rica was able to work with local universities to bring the curriculum in line with their needs, but it is not clear that a group of loosely linked industries could organize itself to do the same. Partially for these reasons, in Japan—and in Korea and Taiwan (China), close imitators—government agencies were charged with coordinating industries (particularly in the highly diffuse Taiwanese industrial structure), serving as a gateway for the diffusion of external research and interaction with foreign firms. Not only did government laboratories identify and provide original research to nourish an emerging research consortium, they set target technologies to catch up to and, most important, sought to upgrade firms, creating within them "a taste for research" (Cho 2001; Sakakibara and Cho 2002; Mathews 2001).[11] In fact, they can be seen as encouraging and enabling firms and consortia of firms to move up the technological ladder, not only by providing the basic ingredients but also providing a focus and mission for emerging firms. Returning to the earlier discussion of the role of public think tanks, Taiwan's Industrial Technology Research Institute (ITRI) was founded in 1973 and its laboratories served a similar role to those in the United States, Europe, and Japan as a core vehicle for R&D collaboration, but also more specifically focused on rapid adoption of new standards, products, and processes and rapid diffusion to as many firms as possible, rather than extending the envelope of R&D. The initiative for the formation of early alliances came exclusively from public agencies, with the private sector taking an increasingly active role.

Such consortia are also found in Europe and the United States. One of the most famous is SEMATECH, a research consortium of semiconductor manufacturers set up in 1987 by 14 U.S. semiconductor firms with the financial assistance of the U.S. government, which has been given credit for reviving the industry in the face of Japanese competition (Irwin and Klenow 1995). But similar success stories are found in the *Instituto de Capacitación e Investigación del Plastico y del Caucho* in Colombia, which provided the focal point for technology transfer and development in the revived Colombian plastics industry. Similarly, the Mexican *Unión Nacional Avicola* partly concerns itself with raising the quality of technological inputs into the production process—again, with important interest in importing foreign technologies (Mayer 2002). In all three cases, the dominant private sector presence ensures relevance.

Clearly, the Asian experience in fomenting coordination involved targeting industries, which to some degree makes sense—given scarce innovation resources and vast unrealized returns to innovation, governments probably should back their winning horses. There are the usual attendant risks and concerns about government administrative capacity or simply foresight. As Noland and Pack (2002) argue for Chile, "It is unlikely that government officials considering export promotion measures would have had agriculture, no less peaches, grapes, apricots, and plums grown in November through March, on the list of potentially profitable export sectors" (p. 52). The case of Curitiba, Brazil, illustrates the particularly troublesome political economy issues. Not only was the government unable to persuade members of the city's advanced IT cluster to cooperate in an effort to work on a software project with Japan, but by playing favorites and fomenting rivalries among supporting institutions, it actually discouraged collaboration.[12]

Further, Feser notes that even where governments are very capable, highly specialized cluster-building initiatives can unintentionally help lock a region into an industrial specialization or innovation competency that will eventually face decline. An economic policy regime with a narrow set of competencies targeted to a particular cluster is less nimble when economic and technological conditions change, as they must. Furthermore, targeting—and in fact applied cluster analysis more generally—are heavily data intensive on real innovative or entrepreneurial strengths and may be unrealistic in many contexts (Feser and Luger 2002). Hence, in both the Finnish and Israeli cases, the focus is on ensuring that the NIS in general functions well so that potential industries that are not on the government's radar will find the conditions to grow. In short, cluster-type policies cannot be a substitute for a well-functioning NIS over the long run.

Science Parks and Incubators in LAC

The literature is skeptical about the public sector's capacity to build innovation clusters from scratch even in advanced countries (Feser 2002). Again, the canonical example of Brazil's failed informatics industry provides a dramatic example. On the other hand, reforming the NIS so that it provides a fertile and level field for cultivating new ideas is a long-run process. Science parks and incubators have been employed to help firms and universities overcome informational and technical barriers to collaborative R&D efforts, and, to some degree, to act as microcosms of a well-functioning NIS. They are managed spaces, typically on the campus of a university or technology institution, where firms of varying size and age can operate in proximity to scientific personnel, although increasingly they are virtual.

Science parks establish formal cooperation links among universities, research institutions, and high-tech enterprises. Silicon Valley, for example, is an offspring of the Stanford Technological Park. Such institutions can be useful in the early stages of development, when firms do not conduct large amounts of in-house R&D but draw upon a common pool of scientific personnel for "hand-holding."

Technological incubators provide a supportive environment that offers fledgling entrepreneurs an opportunity to develop innovative new ideas and commercialize them. Israel introduced this program in the early 1990s to help Soviet immigrants who had valuable human capital and ideas but lacked basically all necessary skills, ranging from basic Hebrew to managerial training (Trajtenberg 2002 and box 7.8). The incubator seeks to increase the entrepreneurs' prospects of raising capital, finding strategic partners, and developing a self-sustaining business on their own. Incubators represent the first vital stage for starting a business, after all the initial planning has been done. They may provide a physical infrastructure for entrepreneurs to set up their first office; they may also help with marketing and searching for funding (Agapitova and Holm-Nielsen 2002).

The literature is moderately positive about the impact of incubators. Colombo and Delmastro (2002) find in a survey of new technology-based firms that on-incubator firms showed higher growth rates, higher levels of human capital, and higher rates of adoption of advanced technologies and participation in international technology programs, higher levels of collaboration with universities, and easier access to financing. They argue that the science parks are especially useful in countries such as Italy where the NIS is weak. Mian (1996) finds substantial value added in a study of six University Technology Business Incubators, specifically in terms of university image, laboratories and equipment, and student employees. Less conclusively, looking at 273 firms on and off science parks in Sweden, Lindelöf and Löfsten (2002) find higher rates of job creation and sales growth, although not profitability—and higher links with universities, although not higher patent rates.

Cluster innovations, science parks, and incubators all share the same caveat: shell institutions cannot substitute for poor university or research institution quality, institutions that are coherent and consistent with the goal of innovation, and a well-functioning NIS more generally. Silicon Valley, for example, was not created through top-down planning, but rather emerged spontaneously in the context of an open

BOX 7.8
The Israel Magnet Program

Notwithstanding the rapid growth of the high-tech sector in Israel since the late 1960s, it became clear by the early 1990s that the country's industrial landscape was fragmented and, with few notable exceptions, Israeli industrial companies were too small to be able to meet the escalating costs of developing new technologies in cutting-edge fields. Moreover, Israel boasted world-class research universities, but they operated largely in isolation from surrounding industrial developments and needs, and hence the vast economic potential embedded in both the highly qualified academic manpower and in university research remained largely untapped.

Against this background, in 1993, the Office of the Chief Scientist established the Magnet Program to support the formation of consortia of industrial firms and academic institutions and develop generic, precompetitive technologies. These consortia are entitled to multiyear R&D support (usually three to five years) consisting of grants of 66 percent of the total approved R&D budget, with no recoupment requirements. The consortia must comprise the widest possible group of industrial members operating in the field, together with Israeli academic institutions doing research in scientific areas relevant to the technological goals of the consortia.

Mindful of possible conflict with antitrust provisions, consortium members must pledge to make the products or services resulting from the joint project available to any interested local party, at prices that do not reflect the exercise of monopoly power.

Source: Trajtenberg (2002).

economy, an entrepreneurial business culture, a consolidated legal framework, and a highly developed financial system.

As a final caveat, the difficulty of measuring the spillovers associated with innovation clusters should not lead to completely abandoning the basic net present value calculations applied to any project or justifying any level of financing. Despite Embraer's successes, Fajnzylber (2001) was unable to find any evaluations of the total costs of the project, inclusive of government subsidies. Though it is not clear what the math was, in general, the governments of Japanese and Korea funded only about 20–30 percent of the costs of research consortia. In Taiwan (China), the government contributed roughly 30 percent of the costs of the 20 consortia involving hundreds of firms over two decades (Mathews 2001). Benchmarking cluster performance must necessarily include such calculations.

International Networks

The final theme of this chapter is the international dimension of the NIS. Because the vast stock of knowledge is largely found in the advanced countries, closing the technology gap requires going beyond the technological transfers through trade and investment, as discussed in chapter 6, moving to substantial augmentation of international networks among researchers, entrepreneurs, business service providers, and firms, as well as institutions such as think tanks and universities. It should be pointed out, however, that given the tacit nature of much knowledge and the importance of personal contact, the actual movement of people through either short- or long-term migration assumes an importance that is higher than is often acknowledged. In fact, these various types of linkages are extremely complementary and need to be discussed together.

Migration and Study Abroad

Moving individuals among countries has traditionally been one of the most effective means of transferring knowledge among them. As box 7.9 shows, the impulse for manufacturing sectors in Chile and Mexico came primarily from foreigners immigrating to those countries. Arguably, the lower rates of in-migration to Latin America, compared with the United States or Canada, explain to some degree the slower diffusion of new European technologies.

Graduate study in the centers of innovation is effectively temporary migration for the same purpose of communicating tacit knowledge. Finland relied on this to the exclusion of FDI as a means of transferring know-how (Myllyntaus 1990)—and in Taiwan (China) by the mid 1980s more than 20 percent of executives had studied either in Japan or the United States and all employees with graduate degrees in manufacturing had studied abroad (Pack 2000). Comparative data on LAC are ambiguous. Figure 7.10 suggests that

---

BOX 7.9

Migration as a Vector of Innovation

History is clear on the extraordinary dependence on immigrants as innovators and entrepreneurs in Latin America. Industrialization in Mexico in the late 19th century was almost entirely undertaken by the resident foreigners (Hansen 1971). Using machinery from their homeland, the French started the textile industries in Veracruz and Puebla (Buffington and French 1999), and foreigners also started Mexico's first iron and steel plant in 1903, the *Fundidora de Fierro y Acero de Monterrey*, which would build on the region's ore deposits and anchor its industrial development. Hansen argues that there were entrepreneurial spillover effects that drew many Mexicans into the capitalist ranks, but the initial impulse came from foreigners.

Collier and Sater (1996) also note the influence of immigrants in introducing new industry and technologies in Chile. Immigrants set up many of the industrial enterprises of the 1860s and 1870s: 36 of the 46 dressmakers counted in 1854 were French; Americans installed the flour mills; Americans and British built the railroads. Loveman (1979, p. 193) notes that the list of officers and members of the executive committee of SOFOFA, the principal organization of industrialists, showed the disproportionate influence of immigrants: "Only three Spanish surnames accompanied those of the other members of the directorate: Edwards, Subercasseaux, Hillman, Tupper, Tiffou, Mitchell, Gabler, Lanz, Klein, Muzard, Lyon, Bernstein, Crichton, Osthous, Stuven" (Maloney 2002).

---

the region has more students as a fraction of tertiary enrollees in the United States than any other region in 1998. Asia has far more tertiary-educated workers; however, the logic for study in the United States for LAC is much greater than for any other region, and before its crisis, Asia actually had more students studying.

The move toward establishing local graduate programs is a double-edged sword. On the one hand, costs of domestically trained students are perhaps 20 percent of external training, and returning academics have a ready supply of

FIGURE 7.10

Student Migration Rate: 1993–98

Students Abroad/Tertiary Enrollment

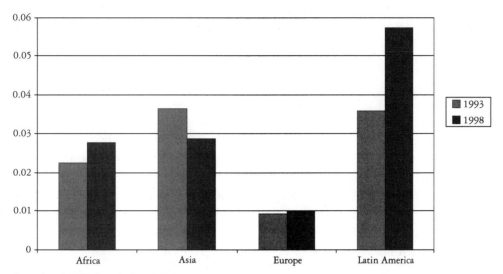

Source: Angel-Urdinola and others (2002).

graduate students for research assistants who can help start a local research program. On the other hand, what is lost is the contact with the most recent generation of thinking at the frontier, and a certain amount of intellectual inbreeding is possible without very stringent standards at international levels.

Local doctoral programs are also seen as a way of averting "brain drain," which implies a deadweight loss to the developing country after years of public spending on the education of these individuals. But what has been less well considered is the importance of emigrants to establishing contacts and serving as the advance guard of the NIS.

The last decades of the 20th century have provided some dramatic examples of the importance of return migration as a stimulus to innovation, as box 7.10 notes. Arguably, the software industries in Ireland and India and the technology sector more generally in Israel would have been far less dynamic or even nonexistent were it not for return migrants. But as important may be keeping individuals abroad. In fact, both Korea and Taiwan (China) leveraged their scientists and engineers abroad very well to bridge the knowledge gaps that existed between their countries and the United States. U.S.-based Korean engineers were designated "R&D outposts" who advised the Korean government on

technical and business trends and helped design policies to take advantage of them. Similarly, the Chinese Institute of Engineers, founded in 1979 by a small group of Taiwanese engineers working in Silicon Valley, organizes an annual seminar in collaboration with their counterpart organization in Taiwan (China), and provides consultative services to the Taiwanese government. Private firms have established research centers abroad precisely with the goal of industrial reconnaissance.

Diasporic networks of emigrants also stimulate capital flows and business opportunities more generally because emigrants are better placed to evaluate investment opportunities and retain contacts in their home countries, helping foreign direct investment sources find trustworthy and competent partners. As Saxenian (1999) observes, "The scarce resource in this business environment is the ability to locate foreign partners quickly and manage complex business relationships across cultural and linguistic boundaries. This is particularly a challenge in high tech industries in which products, markets and technologies are continually being redefined—and where product cycles are routinely shorter than nine months." Saxenian's view corresponds very much with the Indian IT success story, in which immigrants have not returned to India as much as facilitated outsourcing of

Return Migration in Israel and Ireland

In both Israel and Ireland, the impact of recently returned migrants on innovation has been dramatic.

Carmel and de Fontenay (2001) note that from 1989 to 1991, Israel experienced a return migration of perhaps the quintessential diaspora, on the order of a million immigrants from the former Soviet Union. The Soviet Union's emphasis on theoretical sciences made Israel a mathematical superpower by the end of 1991: 5,300 newly arrived scientists registered with the government. These immigrants are now heavily represented in most technical and engineering groups. Trajtenberg (2001) argues that this inflow is largely responsible for the sharp jump in patenting after 1994.

Irish software industries benefited from returning expatriates who went abroad during the 1980s and 1990s to meet a chronic U.S. shortfall in IT workers. Along with the United Kingdom, Ireland constituted the largest European Union (EU) source of emigration to the United States, with California as a principal destination. In the 1990s, however, net immigration has been positive and more than half are returning emigrants. Twenty-five percent of male emigrants with completed tertiary education returned during the 1990s. More than 40 percent of Irish graduates under the age of 40 have worked abroad for at least one year.

service development to their homeland. Return migrants have been a source of knowledge for their home countries, a source of contacts within their countries for U.S. firms, and links to foreign capital markets, filling in gaps in domestic credit markets. (Arora, Gambardella, and Torrissi 2001).

Figure 7.11 suggests that no LAC country, with the exception of the islands, has had as much tertiary-educated migration as Korea and Taiwan (China).[13] Box 7.11 presents the view of a prominent Brazilian commentator, who cites the deficient brain drain as a major failing of his country's NIS. Brazil, perhaps more than most Latin American countries, has invested massively in sending students to study abroad. Yet measures to attract expatriates of the kind that Korea and Taiwan (China) employed yielded few returnees—most were already back. Surveys of Colombians abroad found that 75 percent saw their foreign work as only a phase in

their career but planned eventually to return to Colombia (Angel-Urdinola, Takeno, and Wodon 2002). The Millennium Science Initiative in Chile proved successful in attracting back Chilean world-class researchers and establishing science nuclei—the core of an incipient knowledge cluster—in several promising fields (box 7.12).

The critical problem seems to be using diasporas most efficiently. The Colombian Network of Scientist and Engineers Abroad (Red Caldas, named after one of Colombia's first notable scientists) was established in 1991 when COLCIENCIAS, the government agency in charge of national research, sought to complement the commercial opening with a higher profile for science and technology. COLCIENCIAS appointed a staff member to create the network, which began as an e-list of Web-linked professionals in 21 nodes around the world; a meeting with expatriates in Paris, Madrid, and Mexico; a study of the profile of the emigrant community; and an ongoing upscale electronic "chat room" accommodating scientific dialogue. Unfortunately, enthusiasm for the ultimate goal of Red Caldas—the realization of joint projects—has waned as the limitations of this low-budget virtual approach became clear. The experience of the Bio-2000 project to launch a joint U.S.-Europe-Colombian effort in the biomedical applications of physics offered an example in this regard. Despite efforts on the part of the expatriate community to include exceptional foreign scientists and line up financing commitments with financing organizations, COLCIENCIAS' low rate of response and coordination ability led to a radical downscaling of goals over time to several joint studies linking universities in Spain, Italy, Brazil, and Peru—but, perversely, none from Colombia. The absence of strong accompanying institutional affiliations has also led to problems whereby individual expatriate scientists want to participate in the Colombian project but effectively have to do it pro bono since the home institution's agenda in, say, Sweden is unlikely to coincidentally overlap much with that of a researcher in Colombia.[14]

Institutional Linkages

More successful than networks of individual scientists have been international linkages among institutions and firms. Numerous modalities appear, but it is again the case that such linkages suffer from the usual market failures affecting diffusion, and hence may have a role for government intervention. Korea's Hyundai, Daewoo, and Samsung have established think tanks as outposts in the centers of their

FIGURE 7.11

Brain Circulation: Migration/Population with Tertiary Education

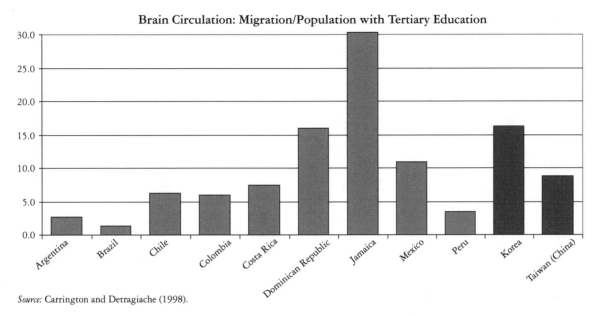

Brain Circulation: Migration/Population with Tertiary Education

Source: Carrington and Detragiache (1998).

respective industries[15] and Finland's Nokia has 55 research centers in 15 countries (Blomström, Kokko, and Sjöholm 2002). Other governments have explicitly financed the external antenna. In Taiwan (China), whose less concentrated industrial structure makes coordination more difficult, the government research agency actively searched for new technologies and served as a clearinghouse for interactions with large foreign firms. In Israel's bilateral agreement with the United States, both governments subsidized collaborative research among firms.

Several examples suggest the importance of connections to foreign universities and think tanks. Chile's legendary revolution in fruit production traces its roots to a 10-year agreement signed in 1965 between the University of California, Davis and the public University of Chile; the agreement is credited with helping to establish a first-rate department in fruit-related sciences, with spillovers to other agencies and universities (Jarvis 1992). This pairing highlights how foreign institutions may be more appropriate than other potential national or Latin American partners: the ecosystems of the central valleys in California and Chile share many similar characteristics. When Colombia's plastics industry sought to modernize, it sent graduate students to the "frontier" institutions in the field in Germany and its industry-wide think tank maintains active connections, largely funded by foreign aid. One of Red Caldas more successful projects occurred when

a university research center in Paris joined forces with another in Cali, jointly funded by COLCIENCIAS and the French government to gain know-how in the production of robotics. Even in economics the tremendous links developed over the last decades, involving both public and private universities and particularly with the United States, have almost certainly contributed to narrowing the parameters within which the debate over economic policy occurs and hence helping to avoid some of the more adventurous experiments of the past.

However structured, the clear lesson is that the best strategy to reach the knowledge frontier is to actively engage it rather than turn inward to learn by doing before opening to the world. One illustration is offered by the Costa Rican and Brazilian strategies in the "informatics" area (box 7.13).

As discussed above, in Asia public laboratories working within consortia of private firms served a critical role as antennas for foreign ideas in technology. In Latin America, one of the most successful parallels is *Fundación Chile*, originally a joint effort between the Chilean government and the U.S. firm ITT, but now largely autonomous. Fundación Chile uses four main techniques in its technology transfer and dissemination work: (1) It creates innovative enterprises, almost always in association with companies or individuals; (2) It develops, adapts, and sells technologies to clients in the productive and public sectors, both domestically and abroad; (3) It fosters institutional innovations and incorporates new transfer

BOX 7.11
Deficient Brain Drain in Brazil

A prominent Brazilian social scientist, Claudio De Moura Castro, argued in the weekly *Veja* that despite the evidence that the vast majority of Brazilians returned, Brazil could not be complacent:

"So then, does this mean that there is no problem of … brain drain? Unfortunately, this is not the case. We have a grave problem. Science is internationalized. Firms need to operate globally (at the very least to export). The best business is undertaken between actors who have a global view. We are at a double disadvantage. We still have ancient vices of self-sufficiency and isolation (which a visit to Disney World doesn't fix). The second defect is that we don't have a diaspora to function as Brazil's window on the world, like the thousands of Koreans who, from the outside, provide their country with the technologies they need.

"There are almost no Brazilians in the exterior in universities, international organizations or the business world. For Brazil, this diaspora would be of vital importance to generate collaboration in research, to get and give invitations for seminars, to receive the latest paper, to identify consulting work, and to vaccinate our science against intellectual isolation. Korea and Taiwan more or less are equal to Brazil in scientific production, but many of their authors are abroad, airing and internationalizing their research.

"For this reason, we have a problem of brain drain, but it's the opposite. Our drain is insufficient and negligible. We produce 5,000 doctors each year. We need to lose some of these so that, this way we can irrigate our science and technology with the knowledge of the great production centers abroad. We need to lose engineers and businessmen so that, later, they return with experience that you can't learn in school. The big drama of the Brazilian brain drain is its absence."

Source: De Moura Castro, Claudio. *Veja,* November 28, 2001. "O drama da evasão de cerebros."

mechanisms; and (4) It captures and disseminates technologies to multiple users (as a technological antenna) through seminars, specialized magazines, project assistance, and so on.

The creation of "demonstration" companies by Fundación Chile has undergone successes and failures, but overall has proved effective as a method for disseminating new technologies. The companies are transferred to the private sector once the technologies have been proven in practice and their economic profitability has been established. The organization has created more than 40 enterprises in numerous sectors, of which about 30 have been sold, with the cost of resources invested recovered and then reinvested in new projects. One of the most successful cases, which exhibits many elements of the successful development of a knowledge cluster, is that of the salmon industry, which in a period of 10 years grew to become a dynamic export sector.

Conclusion

One of the abiding mysteries in development economics has been why poor countries have not aggressively exploited the immense global stock of knowledge to accelerate growth. Increasingly the literature focuses on shortcomings in national innovative capacity, and the discussion here of the NIS draws together the various themes developed through the report. High levels of human capital and exposure to foreign technologies, for instance through trade or FDI, are critical not only in their own right, but also vitally in how they complement each other. As countries seek to accelerate the pace of technological progress, ensuring that the right human capital is available and used effectively becomes central.

The evidence is clear that the higher-performing countries that were able to make a transition to full partners in global innovation—Israel, Finland, and Korea, for example—have dramatically increased their level of human capital, their investments in innovation, and the quality of their policies in a concerted fashion. In addition to getting the basics right in terms of plugging into the global knowledge economy, gaining exposure to international competition and ideas, promoting openness to interactions with foreign capital, fomenting ICT, establishing property rights, and addressing credit market deficiencies, they also came to terms with two fundamental issues affecting every country following in their footsteps.

First, knowledge as a commodity is characterized by extraordinary market failures and hence the market will not generate the optimal level of innovation. To repeat, serious analysts argue that the United States should probably increase its R&D by a factor of 4 and we have offered evidence in this chapter that LAC's level is also far below optimal. Further,

BOX 7.12

Catalyzing an Innovation Cluster: The Millennium Science Initiative in Chile

The Millennium Institute for Applied and Fundamental Biology (*Instituto Milenio de Biología Fundamental y Aplicada*, MIFAB) was established in 2000 as one of three Millennium Science Institutes in Chile, and it has already made remarkable contributions in genome research and in research on infectious biological agents. During 2001 MIFAB analyzed and patented the DNA sequence of a bacteria (*Piscirickettsia salmonis*) that causes infections of the Chilean salmon. This is critical for identifying and diagnosing infectious diseases, but particularly for developing vaccines. Important advances have also been made on diagnostic tools and preventative measures against the bacterium *Alexandrium catenella* (red tide). MIFAB has also been studying a vineyard virus (*Vitis vinifera*), and progress has been made toward diagnosis and improvement of viral resistance in the gene pool of the grape.

The MIFAB has 11 senior scientists, 6 associate scientists, 12 post-docs, 39 Ph.D. students, 42 master's degree students, 10 technicians, and administrative personnel—a total of about 120 people. Its existence is due to the efforts of the Millennium Science Initiative (MSI), a joint initiative by the government and the World Bank. Under the oversight of a high-level consultative body with international participation, $US 15 million were partly allocated to funding three world-class research groups (Science Institutes) and 10 emerging groups of high quality (Science Nuclei). The idea was to provide adequate levels of medium-term funding to enable the best scientists to return to Chile in a situation in which they could compete with their international peers, perform pioneering scientific research, and provide training to graduate and postgraduate fellows. The selection of beneficiaries was placed entirely in the hands of a group of international academics headed by Dr. Phillip Griffiths of the Princeton Institute of Advanced Study to ensure quality and transparency.

Several factors merit note. First, the MSI catalyzed this emerging cluster from a primordial soup of world-class scientists already working in fields strongly relevant to Chile's comparative advantage. The necessary high quality is guaranteed by the competitive selection process. Second, the growing interest, and potential investment by the private sector—most obviously the critical Chilean wine and salmon sectors—in the output of the Millennium Science Institutes, attunes their research agenda to the needs of the Chilean economy over the long run. The MSI effort therefore played strongly to Chile's strengths. Third, the teams and their leadership are guaranteed autonomy to pursue science at global best-practice levels with minimal interference of other agendas.

Source: Holm-Nielsen and Norsworthy (2002).

the institutions evolved to resolve these market failures—universities, government laboratories, and intellectual property rights—lie, by definition, outside the market and hence are not coordinated by the price mechanism.

Second, a critical aspect of the process of development is that firms, and the country as a whole, "learn to learn." In particular, increasing the technological absorptive capacity of the firm has required a supportive set of policies and institutions ranging from well-designed fiscal incentives and subsidies to the active promotion of collaboration through incubators, technological parks, clusters, to the creation and coordination and direction of industrial consortia that share the costs and risks of R&D and serve as learning laboratories for less advanced firms, and to promoting antennas for identifying ideas from abroad.

Both considerations suggest an integrated approach and a coordinated, even leadership role for government. At a minimum the state needs to ensure a consistent and coherent set of incentives to ensure that the institutions created to address market failures collaborate fruitfully with firms. But, in the highly successful countries, governments have not been shy about stimulating private R&D and financing it where it has broad spillovers. The U.S. government remains the largest financer of research and development in the world (Jaffe and Lerner 2001). It is also the case that virtually no country has managed the big innovation push without government playing a leadership role.

Not all countries are at a stage where undertaking such policies is feasible. It probably does not make sense to contemplate broad government financing of R&D if the

The Perils of Intellectual Autarky, the Rewards of Trade

Costa Rica and Brazil offer two alternative paths to establishing high-tech industries. The success of Costa Rica's software industries rests on two first-class universities whose roots were firmly in the exterior. Two brothers, Alberto and Daniel Cañas, received their doctorates from the University of Waterloo and the University of Texas at Austin and returned to Costa Rica to set up the *Instituto Tecnológico de Costa Rica* (ITCR). Then they both went back to the United States, where they hold professorships at Wake Forest and Pensacola—now foreign outposts of Costa Rica's NIS. The desire to compete with the ITCR allegedly inspired the *Universidad de Costa Rica* to send a small team of mathematicians to study toward graduate degrees in the United States and Europe. One of the graduates of the ITCR's first class also studied for a doctorate abroad, then returned to head the Center for Computer Research at the ITCR and made breakthroughs in automating the process of migrating software from one language to another—an important and lucrative advance, given the stock of valuable code with applications in other languages. He and several students received seed money from Oracle of Central America to set up a firm, ArtinSoft, and within seven years developed "Freedom," which had almost complete code recovery rates compared with the next best program's rate of 70 percent. Venture capital from Intel aided further development, and Microsoft eventually signed an alliance with ArtinSoft to include Freedom as part of its software development package for e-business and the Internet (Rodriguez Clare 2003).

As the inevitable contrast, we can invoke the canonical case of Brazil's experience with the informatics industry, begun in 1976 and managed by the powerful Special Secretary for Informatics. As Dahlman and Frischtak (1993) note, the attempt to develop domestic firms' technological capabilities while *blocking* foreign investment and influence led to the development of an uncompetitive industry with adverse effects on downstream user industries forced to use second-class inputs. The attempt to achieve "autonomy" and displace multinational firms from key industrial segments deterred the attraction of best-practice technology. The combination of weak domestic technological efforts and restricted access to the best of foreign technologies impeded the modernization of Brazilian firms.

economy remains closed, if basic institutional integrity is in doubt, or as the report has stressed, if the required human capital is absent. That said, the successful countries have consistently taken an active approach to integration in the world economy by upgrading the learning capacity of firms, selectively financing R&D, encouraging the licensing of foreign technologies, and extending intellectual property rights and ICT infrastructure—in short, progressively deepening and tuning up their NIS rather than passively waiting for MNCs or imports to transfer technology. Thus engagement in the long process of undertaking the necessary institutional reforms needs to start early in the development process. Further, as chapter 6 showed, many of our countries show levels of income and education similar to those of the innovation superstars when they began their big innovation push. A concerted effort to raise the level of especially private R&D should start now using the instruments shown to have positive impacts in the industrialized world.

Though arguments for traditional mechanistic "industrial policy" have largely been discredited, an active and efficient "innovation policy" is called for to provide the necessary innovation and education-related complements to previous reforms. This poses a challenging policy agenda over the next decades. But as this report has shown, Latin America lags in almost every dimension of educational and technological achievement. As a region, to rephrase Pasteur's quote, our collective mind is not yet prepared to take advantage of the unpredictable technological opportunities that the new millennia will offer us.

Annex

How Much Should LAC Be Spending on R&D?
As table 7A.1 shows, it is common in the literature to find social rates of return to R&D of 30 to 100 percent. Lederman and Maloney (2003b) estimate comparable rates of return

TABLE 7A.1

Social Rates of Return to R&D

		RETURN (OWN)	SPILLOVERS	SOCIAL RETURN	OPTIMAL R&D/ACTUAL
Sveikauskas	1981	.17			2.4
Griliches	1994	.30			4.3
Griliches and Lichtenberg	1984	.34			4.9
Terleckyj	1980	.25	.82	1.07	11.7
Scherer	1982	.29	.74	1.03	10.6
Griliches and Lichtenberg	1984	.30	.41	.71	5.9
Jones and Williams	1998	.35			5.0
Lederman and Maloney	2003b			1.02	2–10

Source: Jones and Williams (1998); Authors.

for both R&D and licensing using a panel of emerging and industrialized countries.

They begin with a simple production function

$$Y = K^{\alpha} L^{1-\alpha} S^{\lambda}$$

where S is the stock of accumulated R&D. This can be rewritten as

$$\Delta \ln Y = r_k \left(\frac{I}{Y} \right) + r_s \left(\frac{\dot{S}}{Y} \right) + (1-\alpha) \Delta \ln L$$

using the fact that $\beta_x \Delta \ln(X) = r_x \left(\frac{\dot{X}}{Y} \right) = r_x(x)$

where r_x is the rate of return on factor X, dx is the share of investment in X over Y and β the output elasticity of X from a standard log production function. If we remove the influence of physical factors to get TFP, the social rate of return to R&D is

$$r_s = \Delta \ln TFP/s$$

where s is the share of R&D spending in income. Following Jones and Williams (1998), the optimal level of R&D expenditure occurs where $r_s = r$, the real interest rate. So, the ratio of the optimal level of R&D investment to actual R&D investment along a balanced growth path can be expressed as the ratio of the social rate of return to R&D over the real interest rate

$$\frac{s^*}{s} = \frac{r_s}{r}$$

A GMM system estimation has been employed using five-year averages of the variables from 1975 to 2000. Figure 7.5 has been constructed using column one where Growth of GDP is

regressed on initial income Investment/GDP and labor growth R&D/GDP. Additionally, R&D/GDP and Investment/GDP have been interacted with the initial level of GDP per capita in an attempt to study the way the returns to different input accumulation vary as the countries become richer. As pointed out in the text, the returns to R&D and licensing are high relative to the investment in physical capital. The negative signs on these interactive terms indicates the decreasing nature of the returns to R&D and physical capital. These results are robust to alternative specifications including additional regressors.

Endnotes

1. Consider, for example, the well-known case of medicine to fight AIDS. Patenting, by guaranteeing property rights, does encourage the development of the drugs and facilitates the diffusion of the architecture of the drugs themselves. But it does substantially raise the cost of the innovation to the user and thus restricts the benefits that could accrue.

2. Our thanks to Daniel Lederman for bringing this quote to our attention: http://www.lucidcafe.com/lucidcafe/library/95dec/pasteur.html.

3. Maloney (2002) argues that a decrease in the relative capacity of LAC over the last century left it dependent on the advanced countries for technology. The Chilean copper industry, for example, once dominated the copper market, yet by the beginning of the 20th century, it had virtually disappeared, largely because it had not made the incremental advances in technology that were required to stay at the frontier.

4. See Da Motta e Albuquerque (1999), Dahlman and Frischtak (1993) for Brazil; Bazdresch (2002) for Mexico; Chudnovsky (1999) for Argentina; and Mullin (2001) for Chile.

5. In fact, there is little literature on the subject—the OECD's (2002a) recent *Benchmarking Industry—Science Relationships* offers some pilot studies of benchmarking in France, the United Kingdom, and Japan. Given how recent this literature is in the OECD, it is not surprising that there would be no work on LAC. See also Niosi (2002).

6. Benchmarking from Lederman and Maloney (2003b). Conditioning variables for patents are GDP, number of workers and their squared terms, year dummies, exports to the United States, and natural resource endowments.

7. Patents by nonresidents doubled from 1,955 in 1990 to 4,012 in 1996. However, patents by local residents fell from 1,000 per year in the 1980s and 900 in the early 1990s to less than 700 in 1994 and 1995. Lederman and Maloney (2003a) similarly argue that NAFTA is not enough to put Mexico on a dynamic growth path.

8. Lederman and Maloney (2003c) find using the Systems GMM panel estimator that not only does Leamer's measure of net exports of natural resource–intensive products per worker correlate positively with growth, but Sachs and Warner's measure of NR exports/GDP does as well if Singapore and Trinidad and Tobago are not substituted with Net NR/GDP. Lederman and Xu (2001) also show that countries with

a high knowledge index were more likely to export forestry products than average.

9. Preliminary work with relatively sparse panel data suggests that within countries, the ratio of productive sector to non productive sector R&D first rises with development, but then the very rich countries see again a relative rise in the non-productive sector component. This would be consistent with the public sector trying to kick start the private sector by fostering public research institutes, the private sector coming in, but then at high levels of income near the innovation frontier, very basic science performed in universities or think tanks again increases.

10. In Latin America, universities have also historically anchored many of the growth miracles of the region. The *Antioquia Escuela de Minas* in Colombia was founded to serve the mining sector, but grew to provide talent for emerging industry in Colombia's most dynamic manufacturing regions (see, among others, Safford 1976). In Brazil, Baer (1969) sees the critical event for the development of the native steel industry as the foundation in 1879 of the *Escola de Minas at Ouro Preto, Minas Gerais,* which led to the establishment of the first new blast furnace since the failures of the beginning of the century. Graduates of the *Escola de Engenharia do Exercito*, established in 1930, would lead the steel industry as it developed through the 1960s. In Mexico, the precursor to the *Universidad Nacional,* the *Real Seminario de Mineria*, was founded in 1792 and taught higher mathematics, physics, chemistry, topography, dynamics, and hydraulics, which

helped make Mexico one of the primary exporters of technical knowledge on the continent and to occupy the vice presidency of the World Mining Association at the turn of the nineteenth century. (See Maloney 2002.)

11. See also Leipziger and Thomas (2000); Dahlman and Sananikone (2000); Kihman and Leipziger (2000); Kim (1993).

12. Quale (2001), cited in the World Economic Forum, Global Competitiveness Report (2002).

13. This is an extremely crude measure that is effectively the number of tertiary-educated individuals over 25 years of age registered in the U.S. census who report having been born in another country. Some adjustment is made for the possibility that these "immigrants" are in fact presently studying.

14. This section based on Angel-Urdinola, Takeno, and Wodon (2002).

15. Numerous successful innovating firms in emerging economies have physically located part of their research operations in the centers of knowledge generation. Korea's LG has laboratories in Tokyo, Sunnyvale, Chicago, Germany, and Ireland; Samsung in San Jose, Maryland, Boston, Tokyo, Osaka, Sendai, London, Frankfurt, and Moscow; Daewoo in France and Russia; Hyundai in Michigan, San Jose, Frankfurt, Singapore, and Taipei. Samsung, LG, and Hyundai have all bought firms in Silicon Valley to monitor advances there (Forbes and Wield 2000).

Bibliography

The word *processed* describes informally reproduced works that may not be commonly available through libraries.

Abelmann, Charles, Lee Kian Chang, and Pinchuda Tinakorn Na Aydhaya. 2001. "Thailand: Secondary Education for Employment." Report #22660-TH. World Bank, Washington, D.C.

Acemoglu, Daron. 2000. "Technical Change, Inequality, and the Labor Market." National Bureau of Economic Research Working Paper 7800, Cambridge, Mass.

———. 2001. "Directed Technical Change." National Bureau of Economic Research Working Paper 8287, Cambridge, Mass.

Acemoglu, Daron, and Joshua Angrist. 1999. "How Large Are the Social Returns to Education? Evidence from Compulsory Schooling Laws." Department of Economics Working Paper 99/30, Massachusetts Institute of Technology, Cambridge, Mass.

Acemoglu, Daron, and Fabrizio Zilbotti. 2001. "Productivity Differences." *Quarterly Journal of Economics* 116(2): 563–606.

Acemoglu, Daron, Philippe Aghion, and Fabrizio Zilibotti. 2002. "Distance to Frontier, Selection, and Economic Growth." National Bureau of Economic Research Working Paper 9066, Cambridge, Mass.

Adams, James. 2001. "Comparative Localization of Academic and Industrial Spillovers." National Bureau of Economic Research Working Paper 8292, Cambridge, Mass.

Agapitova, Natalia, and Lauritz Holm-Nielsen. 2002. "Chile—Science, e-Science, Technology and Innovation." World Bank, Washington, D.C. Processed.

Aghion, Philippe, and Peter Howitt. 1992. "A Model of Growth Through Creative Destruction." *Econometrica* (March): 323–51.

Aitken, Brian, Gordon Hanson, and Ann Harrison. 1997. "Spillovers, Foreign Investment, and Export Behavior." *Journal of International Economics* 43(1/2): 103–32.

Aitken, Brian, and Ann Harrison. 1999. "Do Domestic Firms Benefit from Direct Foreign Investment? Evidence from Venezuela." *American Economic Review* 89(3): 605–18.

Albrecht, Douglas, and Adrian Ziderman. 1993. "Student Loans: An Effective Instrument for Cost Recovery in Higher Education." *World Bank Research Observer* 8(1): 71–90.

Altbach, Philip G., Cheong Siew Yoong, Margaret S. Gremli, and Hui-Ling Pan. 1989. *Scientific Development and Higher Education: The Case of Newly Industrialized Nations.* New York: Praeger.

Andersen, Esben S., Bent Dalum, Bjorn Jonson, and Bengt-Ake Lundvall. 2002. "National Systems of Production, Innovations and Competence Building." *Research Policy* 31(2): 213–31.

Angel-Urdinola, Diego, Taizo Takeno, and Quentin Wodon. 2002. "Policy Interventions for Maximizing Brain Gain: Framework and Case Studies." Processed.

Angrist, Joshua David, Eric Bettinger, Erik Bloom, Elizabeth M. King, and Michael Kremer. 2002. "Vouchers for Private Schooling in Colombia: Evidence from a Randomized Natural Experiment." *American Economic Review* 92(5): 1535–58.

Arocena, Rodrigo, and Judith Sutz. 2001. "Changing Knowledge Production and Latin American Universities." *Research Policy* (30)8: 1221–34.

Arora, Ashish, Alfonso Ganbardella, and Salvatore Torrisi. 2001. "In the Footsteps of Silicon Valley? Indian and Iris Software in the International Division of Labour." Stanford Institute for Economic Policy Research, Stanford, Calif.

Attanasio, Orazio, Pinelopi K. Goldberg, and Nina Pavcnik. 2002. "Trade Reforms and Income Inequality in
Colombia." Paper prepared for the 2002 IMF Conference on Macroeconomic Policies and Poverty Reduction, March 14–15, Washington, D.C.

Autor, David H., Lawrence F. Katz, and Alan B. Krueger.
1998. "Computing Inequality: Have Computers
Changed the Labor Market?" *Quarterly Journal of Economics* 113(4): 1169–1213.

Baer, Werner. 1969. *The Development of the Brazilian Steel
Industry*. Nashville, Tenn.: Vanderbilt University Press.

Balasubramanyam, V. N., M. A. Salisu, and D. Sapsford.
1996. "Foreign Direct Investment and Growth in EP
and IS Countries." *Economic Journal* 106(434): 92–105.

Barro, Robert J., and Jong-Wha Lee. 1996. "International
Measures of Schooling Years and Schooling Quality."
*American Economic Association Papers and Proceedings:
Economic Reform and Growth* 86(2): 218–23.

———. 2001. "International Data on Educational Attainment: Updates and Implications." *Oxford Economic Papers*
3(2001): 541–63.

———. 2002. "International Measures of Schooling Years
and Schooling Quality" [data set]. Available at http://
www.worldbank.org/research/growth/ddbarle2.htm.

Basant, R., and B. Fikkert. 1996. "The Effects of R&D,
Foreign Technology Purchase, and International and
Domestic Spillovers on Productivity in Indian Firms."
The Review of Economics and Statistics 78(2): 187–99.

Batra, Geeta. 1999. "Skills Upgrading and Competitiveness in Guatemala." World Bank, Private Sector Advisory Services, Washington, D.C.

———. 2000. "Private Sector Training and Competitiveness in Nicaragua." World Bank, Private Sector Advisory Services, Washington, D.C.

———. 2001. "Skills Upgrading, Technology and Productivity: Evidence from the WBES." Working Paper, Private
Sector Advisory Services, World Bank, Washington, D.C.

———. 2002. "Training, Technology, and Firm-Level
Competitiveness—Evidence from the World Business
Environment Survey for Latin America and the
Caribbean." Background paper, World Bank, Washing-
ton, D.C. Processed.

Batra, Geeta, and Hong Tan. 2002. "Upgrading Workforce
Skills to Create High-Performing Firms." In Ijaz Nabi
and Manjula Luthria, eds. *Building Competitive Firms*

Incentives and Capabilities. Washington, D.C.: World
Bank.

Baumol, William J., and J. Gregory Sidak. 1994. *Toward
Competition in Local Telephony*. Cambridge, Mass.: MIT
Press.

Bazdresch, Carlos. 2002. "Consideraciones generales sobre
el sistema mexicano de ciencia y tecnologia." CONA-
CyT (National Council for Science and Technology of
Mexico), Mexico, D.F. Processed.

Behrman, Jere, Nancy Birdsall, and Miguel Székely. 2001.
"Economic Policy and Wage Differentials in Latin
America." Washington, D.C.: Inter-American Develop-
ment Bank. Processed.

Behrman, Jere, Piyali Sengupta, and Petra Todd. 2001.
"Progressing Through PROGRESA: An Impact Assessment of a School Subsidy Experiment." Processed.

Berman, Eli, and Stephen Machin. 2000. "Skill-Biased
Technology Transfer around the World." *Oxford Review
of Economic Policy* 16(3): 12–22.

Berman, Eli, John Bound, and Zvi Griliches. 1994.
"Changes in the Demand for Skilled Labor within U.S.
Manufacturing: Evidence from the Annual Survey of
Manufactures." *Quarterly Journal of Economics* 109(2):
367–97.

Berman, Eli, John Bound, and Stephen Machin. 1998.
"Implications of Skill-Biased Technological Change:
International Evidence." *Quarterly Journal of Economics*
113(4): 1245–79.

Bernstein, J. I. 1998. "Inter-Industry and U.S. R&D
Spillovers, Canadian Industrial Production and Productivity Growth." Carleton University and NBER. Working Paper 19. National Bureau of Economic Research,
Cambridge, Mass.

Bishop, John H., Ferran Mane, and Michael Bishop. Forth-
coming. "Secondary Education in the United States:
What Can Others Learn from Our Mistakes?"
Processed.

Black, Sandra E., and Lisa M. Lynch. 1996. "Human-
Capital Investments and Productivity." *American Economic
Association Papers and Proceedings: Technology, Human
Capital, and the Wage Structure* 86(2): 218–23.

Blom, Andreas, and Lauritz Holm-Nielsen. 2002. "The
World Bank in Tertiary Education in Latin America and
the Caribbean." Information Note, World Bank, Washington, D.C.

Blom, Andreas, and Vicente Paqueo. 2001. "Summary of Evaluation of the Impact of Student Aid in the State of Sonora, Mexico." World Bank, Washington, D.C. Processed.

————. Forthcoming. "Do Student Loans Increase Enrollment? Evidence from Sonora, Mexico." World Bank Working Paper, World Bank, Washington, D.C.

Blom, Andreas, and Wesley Yin. 2002. "Higher Education in Latin America: Unmet Demand in a Segmented Market." World Bank, Washington, D.C. Processed.

Blomström, Magnus, Ari Kokko, and Fredrik Sjöholm. 2002. "Growth and Innovation Policies for a Knowledge Economy: Experiences from Finland, Sweden, and Singapore." Background Paper for the LAC flagship report, World Bank, Washington, D.C.

Blonigen, B. A. 1999. "In Search of Substitution between Foreign Production and Exports." Working Paper W7154. National Bureau of Economic Research, Cambridge, Mass.

Blyde, Juan. 2001. "Trade and Technology Diffusion in Latin America." Washington, D.C.: Inter-American Development Bank.

Borensztein, E., J. De Gregorio, and J-W. Lee. 1998. "How Does Foreign Direct Investment Affect Economic Growth?" *Journal of International Economics* 45(1): 115–35.

Bortagaray, Isabel, and Scott Tiffin. 2000. "Innovation Clusters in Latin America." Fourth International Conference of Technology Policy and Innovation, Curitiba, Brazil.

Bosch Mossi, Mariano, Daniel Lederman, and William F. Maloney. 2003. "Patenting and R&D Efficiency." Office of the Chief Economist for Latin America and the Carribean, World Bank, Washington, D.C. Processed.

Braga. H., and Matesco, V. 1989. "Desempenho Technólogico da Industrial Brasileira: uma Análise Exploratoria." Textos Para Discussao Interna No. 162: Rio de Janeiro: INPES/IPEA.

Bresnahan, Timothy F., Erik Brynjolfsson, and Lorin M. Hitt. 2002. "Information Technology, Workplace Organization, and the Demand for Skilled Labor: Firm-Level Evidence." *Quarterly Journal of Economics* 117(1): 339–76.

Branstetter, Lee, and Mariko Sakakibara. 1998. "Japanese Research Consortia: A Microeconometric Analysis of Industrial Policy." *Journal of Industrial Economics* 0022-1821, No. 2.

————. 2002. "When Do Research Consortia Work Well and Why? Evidence from Japanese Panel Data." *The American Economic Review*, March 2002.

Bresnahan, Timothy, Alfonso Gambardella, AnnaLee Saxenian, and Scott Wallsten. 2001. "'Old Economy' Inputs for 'New Economy' Outcomes: Cluster Formation in the New Silicon Valleys." Working Paper, Stanford Institute for Economic Policy Research. Stanford, Calif.

Brunner, José Joaquín. 2001. "Chile: Informe e Índice Sobre Capacidad Tecnológica." Universidad Adolfo Ibáñez, Santiago de Chile. Processed.

Buffington, Robert M., and William French. 1999. "The Culture of Modernity." In Michael C. Meyer and William Beezley, eds., *The Oxford History of Mexico*. Oxford: Oxford University Press.

Calderón, César, Pablo Fajnzylber, and Norman Loayza. 2002. "Economic Growth in Latin America and the Caribbean: Stylized Facts, Explanations, and Forecasts." World Bank, Washington, D.C. Processed.

Callart, Maria Antonia. 2001. "Job Training in Latin America: Past, Present and Future." Paper presented at the UNESCO Seminar on Prospects for Education in Latin America and the Caribbean, Santiago, August 23–25.

Card, David, and John E. DiNardo. 2002. "Skill Biased Technological Change and Rising Wage Inequality: Some Problems and Puzzles." National Bureau of Economic Research Working Paper 8769, Cambridge, Mass.

Card, David, and Alan B. Krueger. 1996. "School Resources and Student Outcomes: An Overview of the Literature and New Evidence from North and South Carolina." *Journal of Economic Perspectives* 10(4): 31–50.

Card, David, and Thomas Lemieux. 2001. "Can Falling Supply Explain the Rising Return to College for Younger Men? A Cohort-Based Analysis." *Quarterly Journal of Economics* 116(2): 705–46.

Carmel, Erran, and Catherine de Fontenay. 2001. "Israel's Silicon Wadi: The Forces behind Cluster Formation." SIEPR Discussion Paper No. 00-40. Stanford Institute for Economic Policy Research, Stanford, Calif.

Carnoy, Martin. 2002. "Is Latin American Education Preparing Its Workforce for 21st Century Economies?"

Background paper for the LAC flagship report, World Bank. Washington, D.C.

Carrington, William, and Enrica Detgragiache. 1998. "How Big Is the Brain Drain?" International Monetary Fund Working Paper WP/98/102. Washington, D.C.

Caselli, Francesco, and Wilbur John Coleman II. 2000. "The World Technology Frontier." National Bureau of Economic Research Working Paper 7904, Cambridge, Mass.

———. 2001. "Cross-Country Technology Diffusion: The Case of Computers." *American Economic Association Papers and Proceeding: Technology, Education, and Economic Growth* 91(2): 328–35.

CEPAL (Economic Commission for Latin America and the Caribbean). 2001. *Informe Anual.* Santiago, Chile.

Cetto, Ana Maria, and H. Vessuri. 1998. "Latin America and the Caribbean." In *World Science Report.* UNESCO, Paris.

Cho, Dong-Sung, and Mariko Sakakibara. 2002. "Cooperative R&D in Japan and Korea: A Comparison of Industrial Policy." *Research Policy* 673–92.

Chudnovsky, Daniel. 1999. "Science and Technology Policy and the National Innovation System in Argentina." *CEPAL Review* 67: 157–76.

Ciecon (Centro de Investigación sobre Economía Laboral y Gestión del Conocimiento). 2001. "The Incidence of Training in Mexico." Background Paper for *Mexico: Training Mechanisms.* Washington, D.C.: World Bank.

CINTERFOR/OIT. 2001. "Modernization in Vocational Education and Training in the Latin America and the Caribbean Region." Paper presented at the Regional Workshop on the Modernization of VET in LAC, Rio de Janeiro, December 2000.

Coe, D. T., and E. Helpman. 1995. "International R&D Spillovers." *European Economic Review* (39) 859–87.

Coe, David, Elhanan Helpman, and Alexander Hoffmeister. 1997. "North-South R&D Spillovers." *Economic Journal* 107: 134–49.

Cohen, Wesley, and Daniel Levinthal. 1989. "Innovation and Learning: The Two Faces of R&D." *Economic Journal* 99: 569–96.

Collier, Paul, and William F. Sater. 1996. *A History of Chile 1808–1994.* Cambridge, U.K.: Cambridge University Press.

Colombo, Massimo G., and Marco Delmastro. 2002. "How Effective Are Technology Incubators? Evidence from Italy." *Research Policy* 31(7): 1103–22.

CONACyT (National Council for Science and Technology of Mexico). 2001. *Annual Report 2001.* Mexico, D.F. http://www.conacyt.mx/.

Contreras, Dante. 2001. "Evaluating a Voucher System in Chile: Individual, Family and School Characteristics." Universidad de Chile/Yale University. Processed.

Corbucci, Paulo Roberto. 2000. "As Universidades Federais: Gastos Desempenho, Eficiência e Produtividade." Texto para discussão No. 752, IPEA (Instituto de Pesquisa Econômica Aplicada). Brasilia, Brazil.

Corseuil, Carlos Henrique, and Marc-Andreas Muendler. 2002. "Skills, Innovations and Wages in Brazilian Manufacturing." Background paper for the LAC flagship report 2002, World Bank, Washington, D.C.

Cunningham, Wendy. 2001. "Gender in the Maquila Sector in Mexico and the Dominican Republic." Unpublished note, LCSPG/World Bank, Washington, D.C.

———. 2002. "The Well-Being of Latin America's Men and Women 1990–2000." World Bank, Washington, D.C. Processed.

Cunningham, Wendy, and William F. Maloney. 2000. "Child Labor, School Attendance, and Credit Constraints in Argentina and Mexico: A Dynamic Panel Approach." World Bank, Washington, D.C. Processed.

Dahlman, Carl J., and Jean Eric Aubert. 2001. *China and the Knowledge Economy: Seizing the 21st Century"* World Bank, Washington, D.C.

Dahlman, Carl J., and Claudio R. Frischtak. 1993. "National Systems Supporting Technical Advance in Industry: The Brazilian Experience." In R. R. Nelson, ed., *National Innovation Systems.* New York: Oxford University Press.

Dahlman, Carl J., and Ousa Sananikone. 1997. "Taiwan, China: Policies and Institutions for Rapid Growth." In Danny Leipzinger, ed., *Lessons from East Asia.* Ann Arbor, Mich.: University of Michigan Press.

Da Motta e Albuquerque, Eduardo. 1999. "Domestic Patents and Developing Countries: Arguments for their Study and Data from Brazil (1980–1995)." *Research Policy* 29: 1047–60.

David, Paul A., Bronwyn H. Hall, and Andrew A. Toole. 2000. "Is Public R&D a Complement or Substitute for

Private R&D? A Review of Economic Evidence." *Research Policy* 29: 497–529.

De Ferranti, David, Daniel Lederman, William F. Maloney, and Guillermo E. Perry. 2001. *From Natural Resources to the Knowledge Economy: Trade and Job Quality.* World Bank Latin American and Caribbean Studies, Washington, D.C.

De Ferranti, David, Guillermo Perry, Indermit Gill, Luis Serven, Francisco H.G. Ferreira, Nadeem Ilahi, William Maloney, and Martin Rama. 2000. *Securing Our Future in a Global Economy.* Washington, D.C.: World Bank.

Duflo, Esther. 2001. "Schooling and Labor Market Consequences of School Construction in Indonesia: Evidence from an Unusual Policy Experiment." *American Economic Review* 91(4): 795–813.

Easterly, William, and Ross Levine. 2001. "It's Not Factor Accumulation: Stylized Facts and Growth Models." *World Bank Economic Review* 15: 177–219.

Eaton, Jonathan, and Samuel Kortum. 1999. "International Technology Diffusion: Theory and Measurement." *International Economic Review* 40(3): 537–70.

———. 2000. "Technology, Geography and Trade." Boston University and NBER. Processed.

España, Sergio, Suhas D. Parandekar, and Maria Paula Savanti. 2002. "The Impact of the Crisis on the Argentine Educational Process." World Bank, Washington, D.C. Processed.

Fagerberg, Jan. 1994. "Technology and International Differences in Growth Rates." *Journal of Economic Literature* 32(3): 1147–75.

Fajnzylber, Pablo. 2001. "Aircraft Manufacturing in Latin America? Notes on Brazil's EMBRAER." World Bank, Washington, D.C. Processed.

Feenstra, Robert C., and Gordon H. Hanson. 1997. "Foreign Direct Investment and Relative Wages: Evidence from Mexico's Maquiladoras." *Journal of International Economics* 42(1997): 371–93.

Feldman, K., and J. Meranus. 2000. "Electronic Identity and Authentication in the 21st Century: The Role of Government as a Certificate Authority." STP 305 Final Paper. Processed.

Feldman, Maryann P., and Frank R. Lichtenberg. 1997. "The Impact and Organization of Publicly Funded Research and Development in the European Community." Working Paper 6040. National Bureau of Economic Research, Cambridge, Mass.

Fernandes, Ana M. 2002. "Trade Policy, Trade Volumes and Plant-Level Productivity in Colombian Manufacturing Industries." Yale University, New Haven, Conn. Processed.

Feser, Edward. 2002. "The Relevance of Clusters for Innovation Policy in Latin America and the Caribbean." Background paper for the LAC flagship report, World Bank, Washington, D.C.

Feser, Edward, and M. Luger. Forthcoming. "Cluster Analysis as a Mode of Inquiry: Its Use in Science and Technology Policymaking in North Carolina." *European Planning Studies.*

Filmer, Deon. 1999–2001 (continually updated). "Educational Attainment and Enrollment Profiles: A Resource 'Book' Based on an Analysis of Demographic and Health Surveys Data." Available at http://www.worldbank.org/research/projects/edattain/edbook.htm. Development Research Group, World Bank, Washington, D.C.: World Bank.

Forbes, Naushad, and David Wield. 2000. "Managing R&D in Technology-Followers." *Research Policy* 29(9): 1095–1109.

Foster, Andrew D., and Mark R. Rosenzweig. 1996. "Technical Change and Human-Capital Returns and Investments: Evidence from the Green Revolution." *American Economic Review* 86(4): 931–53.

Frydman, Carola. 2002. "Evolution of Public and Private Higher Education in Latin America: Cost Sharing and Financial Aid." Background paper for the LAC flagship report. World Bank, Washington, D.C. Processed.

Furman, Jeffrey L., Michael Porter, and Scott Stern. 2002. "The Determinants of National Innovative Capacity." *Research Policy* 31: 899–933.

Garnier, Leonardo. 2002. "Costa Rica within the 'New Economy': The Role of Education, Training and Innovation Systems." Background paper for the LAC flagship report, World Bank, Washington, D.C. Processed.

Gauri, Varun. 1998. *School Choice in Chile: Two Decades of Educational Reform.* Pittsburgh, Pa.: University of Pittsburgh Press.

Gerschenkron, Alexander. 1962. *Economic Backwardness in Historical Perspective, a Book of Essays.* Cambridge, Mass.: Harvard University Press.

Gill, Indermit. 2002. "An Economic Approach to the 'Knowledge Economy': Technology-Skill Complementarities and Their Implications for Productivity and

Policy." Background paper for this report, World Bank, Washington, D.C. Processed.

Gill, Indermit S., and Harry A. Patrinos. 2001. "Human Capital Policies for Growth in a Middle-Income Country." World Bank, Washington, D.C. Processed.

————. 2002. "Labor: Investments in Human Capital." World Bank, Brazil: Vol. 2 of "The New Growth Agenda" (World Bank Report 22950-BR). Processed.

Gill, Indermit, Fred Fluitman, and Amit Dar. 2000. *Vocational Education and Training Reform: Matching Skills to Markets and Budgets*. New York: Oxford.

Gill, Indermit S., Claudio E. Montenegro, and Dörte Dömeland. 2002. *Crafting Labor Policy.* Washington, D.C.: New York: Oxford.

Girma, Sourafel, and Katharine Wakelin. 2000. "Are There Regional Spillovers from FDI in the UK?" University of Nottingham, Centre for Research on Globalization and Labour Markets. Research Paper (UK); No. 2000/16: 1–19.

Glass, Amy Jocelyn, and Kamal Saggi. 2002. "Intellectual Property Rights and Foreign Direct Investment." *Journal of International Economics*, (56): 387–410.

Gledson de Carvalho, A., and Joao Amaro de Matos. 2002. "Venture Capital as Human Resources Management." Universidade de São Paulo/Universidade Nova de Lisboa. Processed.

Glewwe, Paul. 2002. "Schools and Skills in Developing Countries: Education Policies and Socioeconomic Outcomes." *Journal of Economic Literature* (U.S.) 40(2): 46–82.

Goldfarb, Brent, Magnus Henrekson, and Nathan Rosenberg. 2001. "Demand vs. Supply Driven Innovations: U.S. and Swedish Experiences in Academic Entrepreneurship." SIEPR Policy Paper 00-035, February. Stanford Institute for Economic Policy Research, Stanford, Calif.

Goldin, Claudia. 1999. "Egalitarianism and the Returns to Education during the Great Transformation of American Education." *Journal of Political Economy* 107(6): S65–S94.

————. 2001. "The Human-Capital Century and American Leadership: Virtues of the Past." *Journal of Economic History* 61(2): 263–92.

Goldin, Claudia, and Lawrence F. Katz. 1996. "Technology, Skill, and the Wage Structure: Insights from the Past." *American Economic Association Papers and Proceedings: Technology, Human Capital, and the Wage Structure* 86(2): 252–57.

————. 1998. "The Origins of Technology-Skill Complementarity." *Quarterly Journal of Economics,* August: 693–732.

————. 1999. "The Shaping of Higher Education: The Formative Years in the United States, 1890 to 1940." *Journal of Economic Perspectives* 13(1): 37–62.

Gordon, Robert. 2000. "Does the 'New Economy' Measure Up to the Great Inventions of the Past?" *Journal of Economic Perspectives* 14(4): 49–74.

Griffith, Rachel, Stephen Redding, and John Van Reenen. 2001. "R&D and Absorptive Capacity: Theory and Empirical Evidence." Institute for Fiscal Studies Working Paper, London, England.

Griliches, Zvi. 1990. "Patent Statistics as Economic Indicators: A Survey." *Journal of Economic Literature* 28(4): 1661–1707.

————. 1992. "The Search for R&D Spillovers." *Scandinavian Journal of Economics* 94: 29–47.

Grossman, Gene M., and Elhanan Helpman. 1991. *Innovation and Growth in the Global Economy.* Cambridge, Mass. and London: MIT Press.

Grossman, Gene, and Edwin Lai. 2002. "Intellectual Property Rights, the WTO, and Developing Countries." Presented at the Annual Bank Conference on Developing Economics, World Bank, Washington, D.C.

Guasch J. L. 1985. "A Primer on Innovation and Competition" Lecture notes, University of California at San Diego. La Jolla, Calif.

————. 2000. *Argentina: Labor Market in the New Millennium.* Washington, D.C.: World Bank.

————. 2002. "A Conceptual Framework for Cluster Development and Analysis." World Bank, Washington, D.C.

Guasch, Jose Luis., and D. Brehon. 2002. "The Technology Gap for LAC Countries: A Principle Component Analysis." The World Bank, Washington, D.C. Processed.

Guasch, Jose Luis, and Prita Subramanian. 2002. "Information and Communication Technology: A Key Instrument for Knowledge." Background paper for the LAC flagship report, World Bank, Washington, D.C.

Guerrero, Jaime Ramirez. 2002. "The Financing of Vocational Training in LAC," Paper presented at the Inter-American

Tripartite Seminar on Training, Productivity, and Decent Work, Rio de Janeiro, May 15–17, 2002.

Guevara Niebla, Gilberto. 1990. "La UNAM y la Nacion." In Jose Blanco and Gilberto Guevara Niebla, eds., *Universidad Nacional y Economia*. Miguel Angel Porrua, pp. 429–52.

Hall, Bronwyn. 2002. "The Financing of Research and Development." National Bureau of Economic Research Working Paper 8773, Cambridge, Mass.

Hall, Bronwyn H., and John Van Reenen. 2000. "How Effective Are Fiscal Incentives for R&D? A Review of the Evidence." *Research Policy* 29: 449–69.

Hall, Robert E., and Charles I. Jones. 1999. "Why Do Some Countries Produce So Much More Output Per Worker than Others?" *Quarterly Journal of Economics* 114(1): 83–116.

Hansen, Roger D. 1971. *The Politics of Mexican Development*. Baltimore: Johns Hopkins University Press.

Hansen, Thomas Nikolaj, Natalia Agapitova, Lauritz Holm-Nielsen, and Ognjenka Goga Vukomirovic. 2002. "The Evolution of Science and Technology: Latin America and the Caribbean in Comparative Perspective." Background paper for the LAC flagship report, World Bank, Washington, D.C.

Hanson, Gordon, and Ann Harrison. 1999. "Who Gains from Trade Reform? Some Remaining Puzzles." *Journal of Development Economics* 59(1999): 125–54.

Hanushek, Eric A. 1995. "Interpreting Recent Research on Schooling in Developing Countries." *World Bank Research Observer (International)* 10: 227–46.

————. 1996. "Measuring Investment in Education." *Journal of Economic Perspectives* 10(4): 9–30.

————. 2002. "The Failure of Input-Based Schooling Policies." National Bureau of Economic Research Working Paper 9040, Cambridge, Mass.

Hausmann, Ricardo, and Dani Rodrik. 2002. "Economic Development as Self-Discovery." National Bureau of Economic Research Working Paper 8952, Cambridge, Mass.

Heckman, James, and Carmen Pages-Serra. 2000. "The Cost of Job Security Regulation: Evidence from Latin American Labor Markets." *Economia: Journal of the Latin American and Caribbean Economic Association* 1(1): 109–44.

Heckman, James J., Lance J. Lochner, and Petra E. Todd. 2001. "Fifty Years of Mincer Earnings Regressions." Processed.

Henderson, Rebecca, Adam B. Jaffe, Manuel Trajtenberg. 1998 "Universities as a Source of Commercial Technology: A Detailed Analysis of University Patenting, 1965–1988." *Review of Economics and Statistics* 80(1): 119–27.

Hoekman, B., and Simeon Djankov. 2000. "Foreign Investment and Productivity Growth in Czech Enterprises." *World Bank Economic Review (International)* 14(1): 49–64. Available at http://www.worldbank.org/research/journals/wbermast.htm.

Hsieh, Chang-Tai, and Miguel Urquiola. 2002. "When Schools Compete, How Do They Compete? An Assessment of Chile's Nationwide School Voucher Program." Princeton, N.J., and Ithaca, N.Y.: Princeton University and Cornell University. Processed.

Hunt, Julie, and James Tybout. 1998. "Does Promoting High-Tech Products Spur Development?." Georgetown University. Processed.

ESCAP (United Nations Economic and Social Commission for Asia and the Pacific). 2000. *Interregional Cooperation in Trade and Investment: Asia–Latin America,* Trade and Investment Division, Studies in Trade and Investment 43 (ST/ESCAP/2069). Bangkok, Thailand.

ILO (International Labour Organization). 1999. *World Employment Report 1998–99: Employability in the Global Economy—How Training Matters.* Geneva, Switzerland.

Irwin, Douglas A. and Peter J. Klenow. 1995. "High-Tech R&D Subsidies Estimating the Effects of Sematech." *Journal of International Economics* 40: 323–44.

Jacoby, Hanan, and Emmanuel Skoufias. 2002. "Financial Constraints on Higher Education: Evidence from Mexico." World Bank and International Food Policy Research Institute, Washington, D.C. Processed.

Jaffe, Adam. 1989. "The Real Effects of Academic Research." *American Economic Review* 79(5): 957–70.

Jaffe, Adam B., and Josh Lerner. 2001. "Reinventing Public R&D: Patent Policy and the Commercialization of National Laboratory Technologies." *RAND Journal of Economics* 32(1): 167–98.

James, Vanus, Roland Craigwell, Rosalea Hamilton, and Winford James. 2002. "Knowledge in the English-Speaking Caribbean: Reconsidering Education, Training, and Technology Policies." Background paper for the LAC flagship report, World Bank, Washington, D.C. Processed.

Jimenez, Emmanuel, and Yasuyuki Sawada. 1999. "Do Community-Managed Schools Work ? An Evaluation of El Salvador's EDUCO Program." *World Bank Economic Review (International)* 13(3): 415–11.

Jimeno, Juan F. 2002. "Education, Innovation, and Complementarity between Skills and Technological Progress: The Spanish Case." Universidad de Alcalá and FEDEA, Spain. Processed.

Johnson, George E. 1997. "Changes in Earnings Inequality: The Role of Demand Shifts." *Journal of Economic Perspectives* 11(2): 41–54.

Jones, C. I., and John C. Williams. 1997. "Measuring the Social Return to R&D." Working Paper 97002, Stanford University, Department of Economics.

———. 1998. "Measuring the Social Return to R&D." *Quarterly Journal of Economics* 113: 1119–35.

Jovanovic, Boyan. 1997. *Advances in Economics and Econometrics: Theory and Applications: Seventh World Congress.* Volume 2. Cambridge: Cambridge University Press.

Kane, Thomas J., and Cecilia Elena Rouse. 1995. "Labor-Market Returns to Two- and Four-Year College." *American Economic Review* 85(3): 600–614.

———. Kane, Thomas J., and Cecilia Elena Rouse. 1999. "The Community College: Educating Students at the Margin between College and Work." *Journal of Economic Perspectives* 13(1): 63–84.

Katz, Jorge. 2001. "Structural Reforms and Technological Behavior: The Sources and Nature of Technological Change in Latin America in the 1990s." *Research Policy* (Netherlands) 30(1): 1–9.

Katz, Lawrence F., and David H. Autor. 1999. "Changes in the Wage Structure and Earnings Inequality." In Orley Ashenfelter and David Card, eds., *Handbook of Labor Economics.* New York: Elsevier Science, North-Holland.

Katz, Lawrence F., and Kevin M. Murphy. 1992. "Changes in Relative Wages, 1963–1987: Supply and Demand Factors." *Quarterly Journal of Economics* 107(1): 35–78.

Keller, Wolfgang. 2002. "Trade and the Transmission of Technology." *Journal of Economic Growth* 7: 5–24.

Kenny, Charles. 2002. "Information and Communication Technology—A Role in the Development of Argentina, Chile, and Uruguay?" World Bank, Washington, D.C. Processed.

Kenny C., and Marialisa Motta. 2002. "The ICT Framework in Chile." World Bank, Washington, D.C. Processed.

Kihman, Kim, and Danny S. Leipziger. 1997. "Korea: A Case of Government-Led Development." In Danny Leipzinger, ed., *Lessons from East Asia.* Ann Arbor, Mich.: University of Michigan Press.

Kim, Gwang-Jo. 2001. "The Expansion of the Education System in Korea." Processed.

Kim, Linsu. 1993. "National System of Industrial Innovation: Dynamics of Capability Building in Korea." *Systems of Innovation: Growth, Competitiveness and Employment* 1: 391–417.

———. 1997. *Imitation to Innovation: The Dynamics of Korea's Technological Learning.* Boston: Harvard Business School Press.

King, Elizabeth M., and Berk Ozler. 2001. "What's Decentralization Got to Do with Learning? Endogenous School Quality and Student Performance in Nicaragua." World Bank, Washington, D.C. Processed.

Kremer, Michael R. 1995. "Research on Schooling: What We Know and What We Don't—A Comment on Hanushek." *World Bank Research Observer (International)* 10: 247–54.

Krueger, Alan B. 1993. "How Computers Have Changed the Wage Structure: Evidence from Microdata, 1984–1989." *Quarterly Journal of Economics* 108(1): 33–60.

———. 2002. "Inequality, Too Much of a Good Thing." Princeton University and National Bureau of Economic Research. Processed.

Krueger, Alan B., and Mikael Lindahl. 2001. "Education for Growth: Why and for Whom." *Journal of Economic Literature* 39(4): 1101–36.

Kugler, Maurice. 2002. "Market Reform, Technology Adoption and Skill Formation: Evidence from Colombia." Background paper for the LAC flagship report 2002, World Bank, Washington, D.C. Processed.

Lam, David, and Robert F. Schoeni. 1993. "Effects of Family Background on Earnings and Returns to Schooling: Evidence from Brazil." *Journal of Political Economy* 101(4): 710–40.

Lederman, Daniel, and William F. Maloney. 2002. "Open Questions About the Link between Natural Resources and Economic Growth: Sachs and Warner Revisited." World Bank, Washington, D.C. Processed.

———. 2003a. "Innovation in Mexico: NAFTA Is Not Enough." Office of the Chief Economist for Latin America and the Caribbean, World Bank, Washington, D.C. Processed.

———. 2003b. "R&D and Development." Office of the Chief Economist for Latin America and the Caribbean, World Bank, Washington, D.C. Processed.

———. 2003c. "Trade Structure and Growth." Office of the Chief Economist, Latin America and the Caribbean Region, World Bank, Washington, D.C. Processed.

Lederman, Daniel, and Laura Saenz. 2002. "A Database of Innovation Indicators for the World, 1960–2000." Office of the Chief Economist, Latin America and the Caribbean Region, World Bank, Washington, D.C. Processed.

———. 2003. "Innovation around the World: A Cross-Country Data Base of Innovation Indicators." Office of the Chief Economist, Latin America and the Caribbean Region, World Bank, Washington, D.C. Processed.

Lederman, Daniel, and Lixin Colin Xu. 2001. "Comparative Advantage and Trade Intensity: Are Traditional Endowments Destiny?" World Bank, Washington, D.C. Processed.

Lee, Keun, and Chaisung Lim. 2001. "Technological Regimes, Catching-Up and Leapfrogging: Findings from the Korean Industries." *Research Policy* 30(2001): 459–83

Leipziger, Danny M., and Vinod Thomas. 2000. "An Overview of East Asian Experience." In Danny Leipziger, ed., *Lessons from East Asia, Studies in International Trade Policy.* Ann Arbor, Mich.: Michigan University Press.

Levy, Frank, and Richard J. Murnane. 1996. "With What Skills Are Computers a Complement?" *American Economic Review* 86(2): 258–62.

Lindbeck, Assar, and Dennis J. Snower. 2000. "Multitask Learning and the Reorganization of Work: From Tayloristic to Holistic Organization." *Journal of Labor Economics* 18(3): 353–76.

Lindelof, Peter, and Hans Lofsten. 2002. "Science Parks and the Growth of New Technology-Based Firms-Academic-Industry Links, Innovation and Markets." *Research Policy* 859–76.

Loayza, Norman, Pablo Fajnzylber, and César Calderón. 2002. "Economic Growth in Latin America and the Caribbean: Stylized Facts, Explanations, and Forecasts." World Bank, Washington, D.C. Processed.

Lopez-Acevedo, Gladys. 2002a. "Technology and Firm Performance in Mexico." World Bank, Washington, D.C. Processed.

———. 2002b. "Technology and Skill Demand in Mexico." World Bank, Washington, D.C. Processed.

———. 2002c. "Determinants of Technology Adoption in Mexico." World Bank, Washington, D.C. Processed.

Loveman, Brian. 1979. *Chile, the Legacy of Hispanic Capitalism.* New York: Oxford University Press.

Lucas, Robert E., Jr. 1988. "On the Mechanics of Economic Development." *Journal of Monetary Economics* 22: 3–42.

Lundvall, Bengt-Åke, Björn Johnson, Esben Sloth Andersen, and Bent Dalum. 2002. "National Systems of Production, Innovation and Competence Building." *Research Policy* 31(2002): 213–31.

Machin, Stephen, and John Van Reenen. 1998. "Technology and Changes in Skill Structure: Evidence from Seven OECD Countries." *Quarterly Journal of Economics* 113(4): 1215–44.

Maloney, William F. 2002. "Missed Opportunities: Innovation, Natural Resources and Growth in Latin America." *Economia* 3(1): 111–150.

Mani, Sunil. 2001. "Government, Innovation and Technology Policy, an Analysis of the Brazilian Experience during the 1990s." INTECH Discussion Paper Series #2001–11. Maastricht, the Netherlands.

Mansfield, E., and A. Romeo. 1980. "Technology Transfers to Overseas Subsidiaries by U.S.-Based Firms." *Quarterly Journal of Economics*, Vol. 95, pp. 737–50.

Mariscal, Elisa, and Kenneth L. Sokoloff. 2000. "Schooling, Suffrage, and the Persistence of Inequality in the Americas, 1800–1945." In Stephen Haber, ed., *Political Institutions and Economic Growth in Latin America. Essays in Policy, History, and Political Economy.* Stanford University, Stanford, Calif.: Hoover Institution Press.

Martin, William, and Devashish Mitra. 2001. "Productivity Growth and Convergence in Agriculture and Manufacturing." *Economic Development and Cultural Change* 49(2): 403–22.

Martinez, Salvador, and Imanol Ordorika. 1991. "UNAM: Espejo del Mejor Mexico Posible." Processed.

Mathews, John A. 2001. "The Origins and Dynamics of Taiwan's R&D Consortia." *Research Policy* 31: 633–51.

Mayer, David. 2002. "Liberalization, Knowledge, and Technology: Lessons from Veterinary Pharmaceutics and Poultry in Mexico." Background paper. Office of the Chief Economist, Latin America and the Caribbean Region, World Bank, Washington, D.C. Processed.

Mayer, David, and Andrew Foster. 2002. "Scale, Technological Change and Human Capital: Manufacturing and Development in Mexico." World Bank, Washington, D.C. Processed.

McEwan, Patrick J. 2000. "The Effectiveness of Public, Catholic, and Non-Religious Private Schools in Chile's Voucher System." *Education Economics* 9(2): 103–28.

Melitz, Marc. 2002. "Exports versus FDI." Working paper, Harvard University, Cambridge, Mass.

Meza González, Liliana, and Ana Belén Mora Yagüe. 2001. "Why Mexican Manufacturing Firms Invest in R&D?" Universidad Iberamericana and Georgetown University. Processed.

Mian, Sarfraz A. 1996. "Assessing Value-Added Contributions of University Technology Business Incubators to Tenant Firms." *Research Policy* 25(3) (May): 325–35.

MICIT (Ministerio de Ciencia y Tecnología). 1999. *Annual Report, 1999.* San José, Costa Rica.

Middleton, John, Adrian Ziderman, and Arvil van Adams. 1993. *Skills for Productivity.* New York: Oxford University Press.

Mincer, Jacob. 1974. *Schooling, Experience and Earnings.* New York: National Bureau of Economic Research Press.

Mizala, Alejandra, and Pilar Romaguera. 1999. "School Performance and Choice: The Chilean Experience." *Journal of Human Resources* XXXV(2): 392–417.

———. 2002. "Evalucion Del Desemperno E Incentivos En La Educación Chilena." *Caudermos de Economia*, ano 39, No. 118.

Moretti, Enrico. 2000. "Estimating the Social Return to Education: Evidence from Longitudinal and Repeated Cross-Sectional Data." Department of Economics, UCLA. Processed.

MOST (Ministry of Science and Technology, Republic of Korea). n.d. "Promotion of Basic Science and Development of High-Quality Manpower." Available at http://park.org/Korea/Pavilions/PublicPavilions/Government/most/policye3.html.

Mowery, David C. 1999. "The Effects of the Bayh-Dole Act on U.S. University Research and Technology Transfer." *Industrializing Knowledge: University-Industry Linkages in Japan and the United States:* 269–306. Cambridge, Mass.: MIT Press.

Mowery, David C., and Arvids A. Ziedonis. 2002. "Academic Patent Quality and Quantity Before and After the Bayh-Dole Act in the United States." *Research Policy* 31(31): 399–418.

Muendler, Marc-Andreas. 2002. "Trade, Technology, and Productivity: A Study of Brazilian Manufacturers, 1986–1998." University of California, Berkeley. Processed.

Mullin, James. 2001. "Science, Technology, and Innovation in Chile." International Development Research Centre, Ottawa.

Murphy, Kevin M., W. Craig Riddell, and Paul M. Romer. 1998. "Wages, Skills, and Technology in the United States and Canada." National Bureau of Economic Research Working Paper 6638, Cambridge, Mass.

Myllyntaus, Timo. 1990. "The Finnish Model of Technology Transfer." *Economic Development and Cultural Change* 38(3): 625–43.

National Center for Education Statistics. 1995. "Third International Mathematics and Science Study." Office of Educational Research & Improvement, U.S. Dept. of Education, Washington, D.C. Available at http://nces.ed.gov/timss/.

———. 1999. "Third International Mathematics and Science Study—Repeat." Office of Educational Research and Improvement, U.S. Dept. of Education, Washington, D.C. Available at http://nces.ed.gov/timss/.

Nelson, Richard R. 1993. *National Innovation Systems: A Comparative Analysis.* New York: Oxford University Press.

Nelson, Richard, and Howard Pack. 1999. "The Asian Miracle and Modern Growth Theory." *The Economic Journal* 109(457): 416–36.

Nelson, Richard R., and Edmund S. Phelps. 1966. "Investment in Humans, Technology Diffusion, and Economic Growth." *The American Economic Review* 56(1/2): 69–75.

Nelson, Richard, and Nathan Rosenberg. 1993. "Technical Innovation and National Systems." In *National Innovation Systems: A Comparative Analysis.* New York: Oxford University Press.

Nelson, Richard, and Gavin Wright. 1994. "The Erosion of U.S. Technological Leadership as a Factor in Postwar Economic Convergence." In William J. Baumol,

Richard R. Nelson, and Edward N. Wolff, eds., *Convergence of Productivity: Cross-National Studies and Historical Evidence*. New York: Oxford University Press.

Neri, Marcelo, and Mark Thomas. 2002. "Household Responses to Labor-Market Shocks in Brazil: 1982–1999." World Bank, Washington, D.C. Processed.

Niosi, Jorge. 2002. "National Systems of Innovations Are 'X-Efficient' (and X Effective): Why Some Are Slow Learners." *Research Policy* 31 (2002): 291–302.

Noland, Marcus, and Howard Pack. 2002. "Industrial Policies and Growth: Lessons from International Experience." Working Paper 169. Central Bank of Chile.

OECD (Organisation for Economic Co-operation and Development). 1998. *Technology, Productivity and Job Creation: Best Policy Practices*. Paris: OECD Publications.

———. 1999. *Managing National Innovation Systems*. Paris: OECD Publications.

———. 2000. *Literacy in the Information Age: Final Report of the International Adult Literacy Survey*. Paris: OECD Publications.

———. 2001a. *Basic Science and Technology Statistics*. Paris: OECD Publications.

———. 2001b. *Innovative Clusters: Drivers of National Innovation Systems*. Paris: OECD Publications.

———. 2001c. *Knowledge and Skills for Life*. Paris: OECD Publications.

———. 2001d. "The Cross-Market Effects of Product and Labour Market Policies." In *OECD Economic Outlook* No. 70, December 2001. Paris: OECD Publications.

———. 2002a. *Benchmarking Industry-Science Relationships*. Paris: OECD Publications.

———. 2002b. *Science, Technology and Industry Outlook*. Paris: OECD Publications.

Pack, Howard. 2000. *Technology, Learning, and Innovation: Experiences of Newly Industrializing Economies: The End of the Road? Commentary*. Cambridge (U.K.): Cambridge University Press.

———. 2001. "The Role of Acquisition of Foreign Technology in Taiwanese Growth." *Industrial and Corporate Change* (10)2.

Pack, Howard, and Larry Westphal. 1986. "Industrial Strategy and Technological Change: Theory versus Reality." *Journal of Development Economics* 22(1986): 87–128.

Parente, Stephen L., and Edward Prescott. 2000. *Barriers to Riches*. Cambridge, Mass.: MIT Press.

Parisi, Maria Laura, Fabio Schiantarelli, and Alessandro Sembenelli. 2002. "Productivity, Innovation Creation and Absorption, and R&D: Micro Evidence for Italy." Universita di Padova, Boston College, Universita di Torino, Working Paper.

Park, Walter G. 2002. "Institutions and Incentives for R&D: Implications for LAC Economies." Background paper for the LAC flagship report, World Bank, Washington, D.C.

Patrinos, Harry Anthony. 2001. "A Review of Demand-Side Financing Initiatives in Education." Background paper for the *World Development Report 2003,* World Bank, Washington, D.C. Processed.

Pavcnik, Nina. 2002a. "What Explains Skill Upgrading in Less Developed Countries?" Dartmouth College and National Bureau of Economic Research. Processed.

———. 2002b. "Trade Liberalization, Exit, and Productivity Improvement: Evidence from Chilean Plants." *Review of Economic Studies* 69(1): 245–76.

Pavcnik, Nina, Andreas Blom, Pinelopi Goldberg, and Norbert Schady. 2002. "Trade Liberalization and Labor Market Adjustment in Brazil." World Bank, Washington, D.C. Processed.

Pavitt, Keith. 2001. "Public Policies to Support Basic Research: What Can the Rest of the World Learn form U.S. Theory and Practice? (and what they should not learn)." *Industrial and Corporate Change* 10:3 pp. 761–779.

Paxson, Christina, and Norbert R. Schady. 2002. "The Allocation and Impact of Social Funds: Spending on School Infrastructure in Peru." *World Bank Economic Review* 16(2): 297–319.

PREAL (Partnership for Educational Revitalization in the Americas). 2001. *Lagging Behind: A Report Card on Education in Latin America*. The Inter-American Dialogue, Washington, D.C. and the Corporation for Development Research, Santiago, Chile.

Pritchett, Lant, and Deon Filmer. 1999. "What Education Production Functions Really Show: A Positive Theory of Education Expenditures." *Economics of Education Review* 18(2).

Quale, Addison. 2001. "The Culture of Competition and Cooperation in Curitiba, Brazil: A Barrier to Competitiveness." Harvard University, Cambridge, Mass. Processed.

Ray, Amit, and Saradindi Bhaduri. 2001. "R&D and Technological Learning in Indian Industry: Econometric

Estimation of the Research Production Function." *Oxford Development Studies* 29(2): 155–71.

———. 2001. "The Politics of Learning: The Struggle for Educational Opportunity in Latin America." Draft for Victor Bulmer-Thomas, John Coatsworth, and Roberto Cortes Conde, eds., *Cambridge Economic History of Latin America*.

Rodriguez-Clare, Andres. 2003. "Innovation and Technology Adoption in Central America." World Bank, Washington, D.C. Processed.

Romer, Paul M. 1986. "Increasing Returns and Long-Run Growth." *Journal of Political Economy*. 94: 1002–37. October.

———. 1990a. "Human Capital and Growth: Theory and Evidence." *Carnegie-Rochester Conference Series on Public Policy* 32(0): 251–86.

———. 1990b. "Endogenous Technological Change." *Journal of Political Economy* 98(5): 71–102.

———. 1993. "Endogenous Technological Change." In Edwin Mansfield and Elizabeth Mansfield, eds., *The Economics of Technical Change*. United Kingdom: Elgar.

Rosenberg, Nathan. 2000. "Why Do Firms Do Basic Research (With Their Own Money)?" *The Economics of Science and Innovation* 2: 197–206.

———. 2001. "The Role of the Private Sector in Facilitating the Acquisition of Technology in Developing Countries: A New look at Technology Transfer." Working paper, Stanford University. Processed.

Rosenzweig, Mark R. 1995. "Why Are There Returns to Schooling?" *AEA Papers and Proceedings*. 85(2): 153–58.

Safford, Frank. 1976. *The Ideal of the Practical: Colombia's Struggle to Form a Technical Elite*. Austin, Texas: University of Texas Press.

Saggi, Kamal. 2002. "Trade, Foreign Direct Investment and International Technology Transfer: A Survey." *World Bank Research Observer (International)* 17(2): 191–235. Fall.

Sakakibara, Mariko. 1997. "Evaluating Government-Sponsored R&D Consortia in Japan: Who Benefits and How?." *Research Policy* 26(4–5): 447–73.

———. 2001."The Diversity of R&D Consortia and Firm Behavior: Evidence from Japanese Data." *The Journal of Industrial Economics* 49(2): 181–96.

Sánchez-Páramo, Carolina, and Norbert R. Schady. 2002. "Off and Running? The Rising Demand for Skilled Workers in Latin America." World Bank, Washington, D.C. Processed.

Saxenian, AnnaLee. 1999. "Silicon Valley's New Immigrant Entrepreneurs." http://www.ppic.org/publications/PPIC120/ppic120.ch4.html#h3 (p. 1).

Schady, Norbert R. 2001. "Convexity and Sheepskin Effects in the Human Capital Earnings Function: Recent Evidence for Filipino Men." World Bank Policy Research Working Paper 2566. Washington, D.C. (Forthcoming in *Oxford Bulletin of Economics and Statistics*.)

———. 2002a. "Caselli and Coleman in Latin America: Computing Technology Diffusion, Human Capital, and Trade Openness." World Bank, Washington, D.C. Processed.

———. 2002b. "The (Positive) Effect of Macroeconomic Crises on the Schooling and Employment Decisions of Children in a Middle-Income Country." World Bank Policy Research Working Paper 2762. Washington, D.C.

Schiff, Maurice, and Yanling Wang. 2002. "Education, Governance and Trade-Related Knowledge Spillovers in Latin America." Background paper for the LAC flagship report, World Bank, Washington, D.C.

Schiff, Maurice, Yanling Wang, and Marcelo Olarreaga. 2002. "Trade Related Technology Diffusion and the Dynamics of North-South and South-South Integration." Policy Research Working Paper Series 281, World Bank, Washington, D.C.

Schultz, T. Paul. 2001. "What Are the Returns to Poverty Reduction: Evaluation of PROGRESA in Mexico." Processed.

Schwartzman, Simon. 2002. "Higher Education and the Demands of the New Economy in Latin America." Background paper for the LAC flagship report, World Bank, Washington, D.C.

SeCyT (Secretaría de Ciencia, Technología e Innovatíon Productiva). 2001. *Annual Report*, 2001. http://www.secyt.gov.ar/.

Shimer, Robert. 1999. "The Impact of Young Workers on the Aggregate Labor Market." National Bureau of Economic Research Working Paper 7306, Cambridge, Mass.

SII (Servicio de Impuestos Internos). 2002. *Annual Report, 2002*.